REDEFINING

EQUALITY

Edited by
Neal Devins
&
Davison M. Douglas

New York   Oxford
OXFORD UNIVERSITY PRESS
1998

Oxford University Press

Oxford   New York
Athens   Auckland   Bangkok   Bogota   Bombay   Buenos Aires
Calcutta   Cape Town   Dar es Salaam   Delhi   Florence   Hong Kong
Istanbul   Karachi   Kuala Lumpur   Madras   Madrid   Melbourne
Mexico City   Nairobi   Paris   Singapore   Taipei   Tokyo   Toronto   Warsaw

and associated companies in
Berlin   Ibadan

Copyright © 1998 by Oxford University Press, Inc.

Published by Oxford University Press, Inc.
198 Madison Avenue, New York, New York 10016

Library of Congress Cataloging-in-Publication Data
Redefining equality / edited by Neal Devins and Davison M. Douglas.
p.   cm.
Includes index.
ISBN 0-19-511664-X;   ISBN 0-19-511665-8 (pbk.)
1. Equality—United States.   2. Equality before the law—United
States.   I. Devins, Neal E.   II. Douglas, Davison M.
JC575.R43   1997
323.42'0973—dc21   97-1884

1 3 5 7 9 8 6 4 2

Printed in the United States of America
on acid-free paper

To Our Siblings

Alicia, Marc, and Joyce

N. D.

John M. Douglas, Jr., and James O. Douglas

D. D.

Acknowledgments

A great many people contributed to the completion of this book. First and foremost, we would like to thank the contributors, who worked with us as we tried to mold this group of essays into a book that will help shape the ongoing dialogue about equality. We would also like to thank our research assistants Allison Cox, Amy Laderberg, Ken Mahieu, Catherine Rogers, and Chris Wesser for their tireless work in tracking down elusive sources and proofreading the final text, and Adrienne Parker for preparing the index. Della Harris and Felicia Burton of the William and Mary Law School provided wonderful clerical support. The William and Mary Law School also provided financial assistance. Helen McInnis and Paula Wald of Oxford University Press offered important encouragement along the way. Finally, we would like to thank the editors of the *William and Mary Law Review* for hosting two symposia on equality. Not only did several of the contributors to this volume participate in these symposia, but the idea of assembling a multidisciplinary collection of essays on equality emerged from these symposia.

Williamsburg, Virginia   N. D.
August 1997   D. D.

Contents

Contributors

KATHRYN ABRAMS is a professor of law at Cornell Law School. She has written many works in the area of feminist jurisprudence, including articles in the *Yale Law Journal, Stanford Law Review, Michigan Law Review*, and *Columbia Law Review*.

ERWIN CHEMERINSKY is Legion Lex Professor of Law at the University of Southern California Law Center. He writes widely in the areas of constitutional law and civil rights law and is the author of *Constitutional Law: Principles and Policies* (1997); *Federal Jurisdiction* (1994); and *Interpreting the Constitution* (1987).

DREW S. DAYS III is Alfred M. Rankin Professor at Yale Law School. From 1993 to 1996, he was Solicitor General of the United States. He writes in the area of race relations law and has published articles in the *Yale Law Journal, Texas Law Review, Vanderbilt Law Review*, and *William and Mary Law Review*.

RICHARD DELGADO is Charles Inglis Thomson Professor of Law at the University of Colorado. He is the author of many books and articles on critical race theory, including *The Rodrigo Chronicles: Conversations about America and Race* (1995); *Critical Race Theory: The Cutting Edge* (1995); *The Price We Pay: The Case against Racist Speech, Hate Propaganda, and Pornography* (1995); and *Failed Revolutions: Social Reform and the Limits of Legal Imagination* (1994) (with Jean Stefancic).

NEAL DEVINS is a professor of law and a lecturer in government at William and Mary. He writes in the area of constitutional law and politics and is the author of *Shaping Constitutional Values: Elected Government, the Supreme Court, and the*

Abortion Dispute (1996); *Political Dynamics of Constitutional Law*, 2d ed. (1996) (with Louis Fisher); and *Public Values, Private Schools* (1989).

DAVISON M. DOUGLAS is a professor of law and Director of the Institute of Bill of Rights Law at William and Mary Law School. He writes in the area of race and American law and is the author of *Reading, Writing, and Race: The Desegregation of the Charlotte Schools* (1995) and *School Busing: Constitutional and Political Developments* (1994).

DAVID J. GARROW is a Presidential Distinguished Professor at Emory University. He has written several books on the modern civil rights movement, including the Pulitzer Prize–winning book *Bearing the Cross: Martin Luther King, Jr., and the Southern Christian Leadership Conference* (1986) and *Protest at Selma: Martin Luther King, Jr., and the Voting Rights Act of 1965* (1978). He is also the author of *Liberty and Sexuality: The Right to Privacy and Making of* Roe v. Wade (1994).

HUGH DAVIS GRAHAM is Holland N. McTyeire Professor of History at Vanderbilt University. He has written several books on modern American history, including *The Civil Rights Era: Origins and Development of National Policy, 1960–1972* (1990); *The Uncertain Triumph: Federal Education Policy in the Kennedy and Johnson Years* (1984); and *Southern Politics and the Second Reconstruction* (1975) (with Numan Bartley).

JENNIFER L. HOCHSCHILD is a professor of politics and public affairs at Princeton University. She is the author of several books on equality, including *Facing Up to the American Dream: Race, Class, and the Soul of the Nation* (1995); *The New American Dilemma: Liberal Democracy and School Desegregation* (1984); and *What's Fair: American Beliefs about Distributive Justice* (1981).

JEREMY RABKIN is an associate professor of government at Cornell University. He writes about American politics and is the author of *Judicial Compulsions: How Public Law Distorts Public Policy* (1989) and *The Fettered Presidency: Legal Constraints on the Executive Branch* (1989) (with Gordon Crovitz).

GERALD N. ROSENBERG is an associate professor of political science and a lecturer in law at the University of Chicago. He spent the 1995–96 academic year as a visiting fellow in the Law Program of the Research School of Social Sciences at the Australian National University. He writes widely in the area of courts and politics and is the author of *The Hollow Hope: Can Courts Bring about Social Change?* (1991, 1994).

CHRISTINE H. ROSSELL is a professor of political science at Boston University. She is the author of numerous publications dealing with school desegregation, including *The Carrot or the Stick for School Desegregation Policy* (1990) and *The Consequences of School Desegregation Policy* (1983) (with Willis Hawley).

REVA B. SIEGEL is a professor of law at Yale Law School. She is the author of numerous publications dealing with legal history and feminist jurisprudence, including articles in the *Yale Law Journal, Stanford Law Review*, and *Georgetown Law Journal*.

JEAN STEFANCIC is a research associate at the University of Colorado Law School. She writes on legal scholarship and law reform and is the author of *Failed Revolutions: Social Reform and the Limits of Legal Imagination* (1994) (with Richard Delgado).

DAVID A. STRAUSS is Harry N. Wyatt Professor of Law at the University of Chicago Law School. He is also coeditor of the *Supreme Court Review*. He writes widely in the area of constitutional law and jurisprudence and has published articles in the *Yale Law Journal, Columbia Law Review*, and *University of Chicago Law Review*.

REDEFINING

EQUALITY

1

Introduction

The Pursuit of Equality

DAVISON M. DOUGLAS
NEAL DEVINS

The notion of equality is central to American civic life. Enshrined in two of the nation's central documents—the Declaration of Independence (''We hold these truths to be self-evident, that all men are created equal'') and the U.S. Constitution (''No state shall . . . deny to any person within its jurisdiction the equal protection of the laws'')—equality is one of the basic foundations of our national life.

Yet in the most diverse nation on the planet, the notion of equality has proved elusive. A cursory survey of American history reveals the many ways in which Americans have not been treated equally under the law. We need think only of the treatment of African Americans in slavery and later in Jim Crow segregation, of women and their lack of full civil and political equality until the recent past, of the genocide and repression of this country's native population, of the variety of indignities suffered by gays and lesbians, and of the exclusionary treatment of a vast array of immigrant groups for us to realize that equality has been denied to many Americans.

In the 1990s, the issue of equality—for whites as well as for racial minorities, for men as well as for women—continues to bedevil our civic life. Cries of unequal treatment continue to be heard in both public discourse and the courts. America is far from having reached consensus over the meaning of equality and whether we have in fact achieved it. Competing views of what constitutes equality have erupted into a cultural conflict that looms large in contemporary American politics. As we move toward the twenty-first century, the debate over affirmative action, for example, promises to become an ever more explosive political issue that brings theoretical conversations about equality into the living rooms and polling places of America. Our ongoing struggle to define equality is far more than an exercise in legal definition. The conflict over the meaning of equality is in reality a battle for

3

the soul of America. How we as a nation ultimately choose to define equality will dramatically shape our social and political life.

This book contributes to this growing debate. By presenting an array of views about the meaning of equality and the ways in which we have sought to achieve it, this volume provides new perspectives for the ongoing debate over equality. In particular, by bringing together lawyers, historians, social scientists, and political theorists from across the ideological spectrum, this collection presents a range of opinions and insights that speak to America's ability to find a common language— let alone a common ground—in sorting out the equality riddle.

Defining Equality

Part of what is troubling about our national conversation about equality is that it is difficult to reach agreement about what equality actually means. Equality has often been characterized as the elimination of formal legal barriers of exclusion based on certain immutable characteristics such as race and gender. This view of equality, sometimes referred to as "the antidiscrimination principle," is reflected in contemporary calls for a "color-blind" society. According to this view, equality is measured in terms of equal opportunity, not equal results, and thus broad disparities in economic and political power do not necessarily reflect a failure of equality.

Yet this view of equality has been attacked for precisely this reason. Pointing, for example, to the roadblocks that stand in the way of a minority child raised in an urban ghetto with limited economic and educational opportunities, many civil rights leaders condemn this notion of equality for failing to take into account that many Americans do not possess equal opportunity to compete for economic and political power. Indeed, the failure of antidiscrimination prohibitions to address vast disparities in power and wealth helps explain the emergence of a broad array of social policies and legislative initiatives that use race and gender in a "benign" manner. Affirmative action programs in employment and education have given preference to women and members of certain racial minority groups. Race-conscious pupil assignments coupled with school busing have been used to achieve racially mixed urban schools. Racially gerrymandered electoral districts have sought to increase the number of black and Hispanic elected officials.

America, however, has never reached consensus about the desirability of such race-conscious programs. In part, these measures have been opposed as violative of the principle of "color-blindness"—that race (and gender) should be irrelevant in public and private decisionmaking. Opponents have also dubbed these initiatives counterproductive—doing little to narrow the income, education, and political gap between minorities and nonminorities and doing much to exacerbate racial tension. Thus, at the root of the current equality debate is a fundamental disagreement about how to achieve equality. This book seeks to illustrate the broad range of views about the meaning and pursuit of equality.

Kathyrn Abrams, in "Equality and Impasse: Mobilizing Group-Based Perspectives in an Era of Group-Blindness," argues that gender-and race-neutral policies often mask more subtle forms of exclusion. A staunch advocate of legal doctrines that allow the affirmative use of race, such as affirmative action and racially gerrymandered electoral districts, Abrams derides recent Supreme Court decisions for placing color-blindness ahead of the interests of the victim-outsider. Abrams blames courts—even the more liberal Warren Court—for failing to appreciate the experience of discrimination from the perspective of the outsider and argues that therefore judicial decisions that appear "neutral" are often not.

Building on this theme, Reva Siegel's "Civil Rights Reform in Historical Perspective: Regulating Marital Violence" offers a concrete example of the way in which neutral legal standards can mask inequality. Siegel traces both the demise of the doctrine of chastisement, which permitted a husband to "chastise" or beat his wife with impunity, and the concurrent emergence of the doctrine of marital privacy, which provided certain tort and criminal immunities within the context of marriage. Although seemingly neutral, the marital privacy doctrine in fact allowed the continuation of physical beating, and hence gender inequality, inside the marital unit.

David Strauss, in "The Illusory Distinction between Equality of Opportunity and Equality of Result," goes much further than do Abrams and Siegel in attacking the color-blind vision of equality. Whereas Abrams and Siegel implicitly embrace the notion that equality doctrine is properly concerned with the provision of equal opportunity for outsider groups—as defined in racial, ethnic, or gender terms— Strauss contends that equality doctrine should be concerned with eradicating inequality on a far broader scale.

Strauss invites us to consider a notion of equality of opportunity that takes into account barriers to opportunity over which a person has no control—in addition to race and gender—such as talents, abilities, and family wealth. If the foundation for antidiscrimination prohibitions is an abhorrence of exclusion due to factors outside our control, then, asks Strauss, should we not be equally disturbed over the disfavoring of individuals who have limited talents and abilities and family wealth to employ in their pursuit of material and political success? Strauss's argument is all the more provocative given that the effect of limited talents and abilities has become far more dramatic than ever before, as the gap between the "haves" and "have-nots" has progressively widened.[1] Abrams, Siegel, and Strauss—with different emphases—invite us to consider whether the elimination of formal barriers to full participation in America's social and economic life is in fact sufficient to create a society in which there is equal social and economic opportunity. Each suggests that formal equality does not translate into true equality.

Jeremy Rabkin offers a vastly different vision of equality in "Racial Divisions and Judicial Obstructions." Pointing to the role that affirmative action and other Great Society programs have had in exacerbating the divide between black and white America, Rabkin endorses the color-blind view of equality and argues that defining equality in any other way invites intrusive governmental regulation that in fact undermines minority interests. Hence, Rabkin implicitly questions the assumption of Abrams, Siegel, and Strauss that equality should be measured by equality of result.

Finally, Jennifer Hochschild, in "The Word 'American' Ends in 'I Can': The

Ambiguous Promise of the American Dream,'' explores the ideology of "the American dream''—the promise of unlimited opportunity for economic and social advancement for all Americans and its relationship to equality. Hochschild argues that although the possibility of such unlimited advancement holds a powerful allure, in fact the "dream" is not attainable by all Americans and the "losers" often suffer unwarranted and corrosive denigration at the hands of the "winners."

Minority Attitudes toward Equality

Part of the difficulty in defining equality is the widespread belief that the meaning and content of equality vary among racial groups. Several of the authors in this volume attempt to assay the attitudes of minority groups toward equality. Some observers have assumed that racial minorities have a monolithic view of what constitutes equality. Certainly, as Hugh Graham notes in "The Politics of Clientele Capture: Civil Rights Policy and the Reagan Administration," the civil rights establishment has sought to convey such a sense of unanimity in its political advocacy. Yet the minority community's views on affirmative action, school busing, and other equality issues are far more diverse and nuanced than the views often represented in the political process. For example, many African Americans have increasingly questioned the value of affirmative action or school busing.[2]

Two of the essayists in this volume address this topic by examining the issue of busing to desegregate urban schools. In "The Convergence of Black and White Attitudes on School Desegregation Issues," Christine Rossell challenges the assumption that African Americans generally support race-conscious pupil assignments coupled with school busing to overcome racially identifiable schools. Relying on extensive empirical surveys of the attitudes of African American parents, Rossell concludes that a majority of African American parents in fact favor neighborhood schools or voluntary magnet schools. Black support for these alternative arrangements has significantly increased since the mid-1980s, suggesting that for many in the African American community, equality is not contingent on racial mixing but on greater educational and economic opportunity.

Drew Days, in "*Brown* Blues: Rethinking the Integrative Ideal," argues that much of the decline in black support for racial mixing in the public schools is due not to an embrace of racial isolation but rather to the recognition that African Americans have borne so much of the cost of school desegregation in terms of both the loss of black values and institutions and the tangible burdens of blacks' being forced to assimilate into white environments. Hence, Days explains the decline in black support for school integration not in terms of a rejection of racial mixing and embrace of neighborhood schools, as Rossell might suggest, but rather in terms of minority support for policies that minimize the burdens African Americans have been obliged to assume in the wake of desegregation initiatives.

The divergence between Days and Rossell reveals the different perspectives that Americans bring to the concept of equality and suggests the difficulty in assessing racial attitudes concerning both the meaning of equality and the desirability of race-conscious remedies. Needless to say, if it is this difficult to assess attitudes toward equality, there is little hope of reaching consensus in America about the meaning of equality.

Do Courts Matter?

Consensus over the mechanisms by which government can secure equality also seems impossible, as suggested by the ever-increasing divide over the propriety of court-ordered social change. Many observers have heralded the courts for playing *the* central role in the quest for equality during certain periods of American history. In particular, during the 1950s and 1960s, the Supreme Court issued a broad range of decisions that struck down various governmental and private arrangements that excluded certain minority groups from economic and political benefits. The most celebrated of these decisions—the Supreme Court's 1954 decision in *Brown v. Board of Education*—is testament to a Supreme Court willing to challenge a long-standing governmental practice that enjoyed broad and intense political support.

But in recent years, fundamental questions have been raised about the extent to which the courts have actually delivered equality.[3] Concluding that those interested in gaining racial and gender equality should pursue their goals in the political process, many liberal scholars now argue that the main gains of racial equality in this country's history have come not through the courts but through the political process: the abolition of slavery by statute, the Reconstruction amendments to the U.S. Constitution, and the civil rights legislation of the Reconstruction era and the 1960s. Conservatives also advocate a diminished judicial role but for quite different reasons. Claiming that court-ordered reform is little more than the exercise of raw power by judges and civil rights leaders, conservatives decry judicial activism for standing in the way of innovative democratic solutions to equality.

Several of the essayists in this volume address the vital issue of the role of the courts in the quest for equality. Siegel offers the view that equality gains secured by courts often mask the retention of inequality under new legal standards. She examines the way in which legal elites have preserved their status privileges in the face of "pro-equality" court decisions. As Siegel concludes, civil rights reform can alter legal rules, but the new legal doctrines often leave in place the original inequalities as legal elites subvert the new changes in their own favor.

Critical race theorists Richard Delgado and Jean Stefancic, in "The Social Construction of *Brown v. Board of Education*: Law Reform and the Reconstructive Paradox," also express skepticism about the ability of courts to engage in meaningful reform in the face of political and cultural opposition. Specifically, Delgado and Stefancic conclude that decisions of courts—including the Supreme Court's *Brown* decision—have had far less impact in securing equality than we have previously suspected because courts are inherently constrained by broader political and cultural factors.

This "limited" view of courts—and particularly of the *Brown* Court—has much to recommend it. The *Brown* decision in fact did not lead to widespread southern school desegregation. Most southern schools remained segregated for the next decade. Not until Congress and the president sought to make *Brown* a reality by enacting the Civil Rights Act of 1964 did black children enter white southern schools in appreciable numbers.

Indeed, Gerald Rosenberg demonstrates that most Americans are unaware of the actions of the Court and that its decisions on equality have had limited effect on public opinion. For this reason, Rosenberg, in "The Irrelevant Court: The Supreme Court's Inability to Influence Popular Beliefs about Equality (or Anything Else)," concludes that courts are far less able than we have previously suspected to trigger widespread social reform. Public attitudes toward racial and gender equality have changed dramatically during the past forty years, but the Supreme Court's role in that change has been relatively minor.

Along the same lines, Neal Devins, in "The Judicial Role in Equality Decision-making," cautions that there are inherent limits on judicial authority and argues that the laments of judicial activists about the failure of the courts to extend the rights of women and minorities do not fully appreciate the institutional limits that courts face. To Devins, courts are confronted with a broad range of competing interests that require balancing, and as a result, courts are constrained by broader social and political concerns. Thus, courts cannot champion equality interests to the extent that judicial activists might hope for. In this sense, Devins agrees with Rosenberg, Delgado, and Stefancic in their view of the inherent limits on courts in securing racial change.

The Role of Courts

Increasing skepticism over the potency of judicial action, however, has hardly quieted liberal defenders and conservative critics of interventionist judicial review. Erwin Chemerinsky, in "Can Courts Make a Difference?" delivers an impassioned defense of judicial activism. While conceding that African Americans continue to lag behind other groups in their struggle for a greater share of the American dream, Chemerinsky claims that the failure of courts to achieve certain equality goals is not simply a function of the inherent limits of judicial power but rather is a function of judicial unwillingness, particularly with the Burger and Rehnquist Courts, to wield this power. Similarly, Abrams champions the role that courts can play in securing meaningful equality but concludes that courts have failed to exercise such power because of inattentiveness to victim-outsider concerns.

David Garrow, in "The Supreme Court's Pursuit of Equality and Liberty and the Burdens of History," agrees in part with Chemerinsky's and Abrams's view of the inherent power of courts to affect the struggle for equality. Garrow examines the Supreme Court's decisions affecting equality and liberty interests of the post-*Brown* era and concludes that the Court aggressively pursued equality and liberty interests not because the requisite constitutional doctrines required such decisions but because the Court wished to achieve policy goals it deemed morally compelling. In this way, the Court proved to be an important protector of equality interests and helped reshape attitudes in America about the rights of women and racial minorities. Garrow, for example, concludes that the Court's decision in *Brown* is not supported by history but that because of the compelling nature of the black litigants' claims in the case, the Court decided not to remain tethered to traditional understandings of the meaning of equal protection and hence proceeded to strike down segregated schools.

As both Chemerinsky and Garrow argue, certain court decisions have obviously had a profound impact on American life, even if those decisions failed, as Rosenberg suggests, to reshape public attitudes. The most obvious examples are those court decisions designed to desegregate schools in America's cities. Courts throughout the nation ordered urban school systems during the 1970s to adopt mandatory pupil reassignment plans coupled with extensive school busing notwithstanding vigorous opposition to such plans. Although these busing orders prompted strong reaction in both Congress and the executive branch and triggered a number of legislative efforts to restrict the use of busing to desegregate urban schools, such remedies would remain an important method of desegregating urban schools for the next two decades. Certainly the courts' busing decisions did not favorably influence public opinion—indeed, they inspired spirited opposition—but notwithstanding that failure, those decisions had a profound impact on both urban public school systems and the meaning of equality in America's cities.

Although most scholars, including several in this volume, celebrate the role of the courts, particularly the Supreme Court, in vindicating the equality concerns of minority groups in the face of majoritarian hostility, Rabkin argues that courts have undermined equality of opportunity for minority groups through a number of decisions that have misapplied constitutional doctrines. In Rabkin's view, the courts in many instances have been so unduly solicitous of perceived violations of individual rights that they have harmed the interest of the broader community. Rabkin contends that despite judicial and legislative activism during the past thirty years, the minority underclass suffers as much as ever and that such activism has had a negative effect on the struggle for equality of opportunity.

Although not as directly critical of modern judicial activism as is Rabkin, Hugh Graham also suggests that the courts have the ability to subvert the popular political process and have done so on certain equality issues, particularly school desegregation and affirmative action. In particular, Graham calls attention to the ways in which the courts have blocked elected governmental reforms by becoming the willing captive of civil rights interests.

Equality and Politics

Skepticism of the courts' role in the modern struggle for equality is well founded. Although the Supreme Court in the *Brown* case articulated a dramatic shift in equal protection constitutional doctrine, perhaps the central achievements in the struggle for racial and gender equality of the last half century have been two acts of Congress: the Civil Rights Act of 1964, directed at eliminating racial discrimination in employment, public accommodations, and education, and the Voting Rights Act of 1965, directed at enfranchising African American voters. Although the 1964 Act failed to eliminate much racial and gender discrimination, it did constitute a major affirmation of the principle of equality at a time when segregation and overt discrimination were widespread. Over the course of the next few years, as a result of the 1964 Act, initial steps were made toward eliminating discrimination in the workplace and dramatic gains were made in desegregating southern schools and public accommodations. During the same period, black voter registration significantly increased throughout the South in response to the Voting Rights Act and the number of black elected officials in the South substantially increased in the late 1960s and early 1970s.

In time, the antidiscrimination measures of the 1960s gave way to race-conscious initiatives. In 1969, the Nixon administration ordered racial preferences in hiring at federally assisted construction projects. Following this executive order, the use of affirmative action in education and employment in both the public and the private sector increased. Subsequently, in the early 1980s, Congress approved the use of racially gerrymandered electoral districts to assist the election of minority candidates.

These various legislative and executive initiatives occurred as a result of cultural and political support for improving the status of certain outsider groups—racial and ethnic minorities and women—that had traditionally been excluded from full participation in America's civic and economic life. At the same time, political and social divisiveness followed this shift away from strict equality of opportunity. The 1980 election of Ronald Reagan was testament to this emerging fault line in the equality debate. Reagan (and George Bush after him) vehemently opposed affirmative action, proclaiming: "We must not allow the noble concept of equal opportunity to be distorted into federal guidelines or quotas which require race, ethnicity, or sex—rather than ability and qualifications—to be the principal factor in hiring or education."[4] From 1980 to 1992, however, limited action was taken to reverse governmental affirmative action policies. Graham, in his essay on the Reagan administration, helps explain why. In doing so, Graham reveals much about the politics of equality in America.

According to Graham, the civil rights establishment wielded significant influence over federal agencies and departments charged with administering affirmative action programs. As a result, the heads of those agencies and departments successfully lobbied the president for the retention of their affirmative action programs. In effect, Graham blames the difficulties in altering civil rights policies on interest-group politics in which advocacy groups have become highly skilled at using the political process—and the courts—to prevent rollbacks in certain civil rights programs that might otherwise enjoy popular support.

Rabkin likewise holds the civil rights establishment responsible for the failure of elective politics in the quest for equality. To Rabkin, many policy initiatives might help the underclass—such as welfare reform, crime-fighting measures, and public support of private schools—but they have foundered because of aggressive opposition by civil rights groups and restrictive court decisions.

The politics of equality, however, have changed during the past decade. The minority community, as Rossell, Days, and others have suggested, is not monolithic in its support of race-conscious remedies. Moreover, with growing dissatisfaction among white voters with affirmative action, politicians are increasingly willing to risk the opprobrium of the civil rights establishment by opposing affirmative action.

As a result, the politics of equality has once again exploded with a new fury. Populist initiatives on affirmative action launched in California and elsewhere promise to accelerate the debate on the continued wisdom and viability of government-sponsored affirmative action programs. Attacks on race-conscious pupil assignments are ongoing, and proposals for voluntary methods of desegregating urban schools proliferate. And racially gerrymandered electoral districts are under increasing fire from both the courts and the politicians. The political debate over equality will certainly continue prominently into the next century, particularly as the economic gap between black and white in America remains broad.

Whence Equality?

The essays in this volume are intended to contribute to our national conversation about equality in America. But at the same time, the broad range of perspectives and basic disagreements about the core meaning of equality reflected in these essays reveals the profound difficulty in resolving one of this nation's central dilemmas. For proponents of the color-blind theory, we should establish neutral rules and let the resulting inequalities be addressed through individual and private initiative. But for others, neutrality imposed on a society with the history of this nation in its treatment of racial and ethnic minorities cannot be meaningful, and more aggressive measures are thus required.

The fight over equality is about much more than whether color-blindness or group consciousness should prevail. It is also about the capacity of courts to mandate change, the danger of elected officials' being captured by interest groups, and the difficulty of sorting out minority attitudes toward governmental action. Answers to these concerns are as much about values and life experiences as anything else. Complicating matters further, historians, social scientists, economists, lawyers, and political theorists see these questions through different lenses. Indeed, if the essays in this volume demonstrate anything, they demonstrate the broad range of perspectives about this most difficult issue.

Equality concerns, of course, will continue to play a major role in American politics and social debate. Although broad consensus about the meaning and content of equality will continue to be elusive, it is crucial that the conversation continue, that the assumptions of various perspectives on the issue be set forth with clarity. It is with this purpose that the editors have assembled this volume of essays, that it might contribute to our nation's ongoing debate over equality.

NOTES

1. See, e.g., Philip Cook and Robert Frank, *The Winner Take All Society* (New York: Free Press, 1995).

2. See, e.g., Thomas Sowell, *Civil Rights: Rhetoric or Reality* (New York: W. Morrow, 1984); Glenn C. Loury, *One by One from the Inside Out: Essays and Review on Race and Responsibility in America* (New York: Free Press, 1995).

3. Gerald N. Rosenberg, *The Hollow Hope: Can Courts Bring About Social Change?* (Chicago: University of Chicago Press, 1991); Michael J. Klarman, "*Brown*, Racial Change, and the Civil Rights Movement," *Virginia Law Review* 80 (1994): 7–150.

4. Quoted in Gary L. McDowell, "Affirmative Inaction: The Brock-Meese Standoff in Federal Racial Quotas," *Policy Review* 48 (Spring 1989): 32.

2

Equality and Impasse

Mobilizing Group-Based Perspectives in an Era of Group-Blindness

KATHRYN ABRAMS

For more than a decade, critical legal commentators have observed a tension between doctrinal understandings of equality and the perspectives of outsider, or victim, groups.[1] This tension has grown into frank divergence as "color-blindness" has become a constitutional sword, used to dismantle governmental programs from state and federal set-asides to "safe" minority electoral districts. Underlying this tension is a conflict not simply about the nature of discrimination but about a range of related concepts: namely, the meaning, dynamics, and consequences of group membership, in which "group" connotes those connected by race, sex, or other largely inalienable characteristic that has assumed social salience. This essay will trace the escalating tension between doctrinal understandings and outsiders' understandings of these concepts. It will then ask how the law might accommodate outsiders' understandings of "group-ness" and group-based discrimination, at a time when mainstream constitutional doctrine prevents institutional actors from considering the social consequences—indeed the very fact—of group membership.

Early Equal Opportunity: A Dominant View and an Alternative

Discrimination as Erroneous Ascription of Difference

A doctrine broad enough to include constitutional claims, as well as federal employment and electoral law, is inevitably complex. Yet it is possible to identify themes that unify federal equality doctrine, creating coherence in its approach to discrimination and the groups it affects. In the period between the judicial assault on school desegregation and the more recent retrenchment in areas such as affirmative action, a dominant strain in this doctrine has characterized discrimination as the erroneous ascription of difference. In this view, discrimination occurs when decisionmakers ascribe differences to socially marginalized groups, in which no such differences exist.[2] This flawed ascription of difference most often results from ignorance or prejudice, which leads decisionmakers to see traits such as race or gender as affecting a range of qualities and capabilities. These erroneous judgments operate to restrict the access of affected groups to public goods, such as political participation or employment. For example, decisionmakers might reason that women are not physically or emotionally capable of serving as firefighters or that blacks are of sufficiently distinct abilities or "social station" that it is not appropriate to grant them the franchise or educate them with whites. The misstep is to believe that outsider group membership entails differences that it does not entail and to allocate valuable opportunities on this basis.

This view of discrimination has often been described as part of a "perpetrator perspective."[3] This label seems appropriate for several reasons. First, the analysis posits particular agents—decisionmakers, "perpetrators"—as the determinative force behind discrimination. This focus on the decisions of individual agents arises partly from the premises of liberal theory—liberal assumptions about responsibility, agency, and causation have made it easier for us to think about social phenomena as arising from the acts of individuals. It arises partly from the solipsism of often-privileged legal thinkers who tend to identify more readily with those agents who might be held responsible for discriminatory decisions than with those who might suffer because of them. However, the premise that analysis of discrimination should begin with the agent, and the agent's process of judgment, rather than with the target and the effect of the agent's judgment on the target's life, means that many forms of group-based discrimination are largely excluded from analysis. For example, how discriminatory decisions or judgments set in motion patterns that continue to produce group disadvantage without renewed differentiating decision-making or how group-specific insensitivity that does not rise to the level of a differentiating judgment can produce disadvantage are matters that are rarely discussed within this conceptual paradigm.

A second reason that this view of discrimination might be labeled "perpetrator"-oriented is that it reflects a skeletal conception of what it means to be a member of a victim group, a conception more typically of perpetrators than of group members themselves. First, the wrong implicit in actionable "discrimination" is viewed from the perspective of the decisionmaker rather than from the perspective of the group subject to the negative characterization. For example, an employer's judgment that women should not hold particular jobs because they will inevitably abandon them to have children is described as wrong because it is incorrect as applied to many women. It is not relevant, from the standpoint of doctrine, that this judgment stigmatizes women workers or limits their professional opportunities.

Second, and more important, the dominant view embodies a simplified notion of how the characteristics associated with group identity operate in the lives of members. The characteristics that define group-ness, in the leading statutory and constitutional cases, are thought to be biologically transmitted and static rather than socially constructed, complex, or malleable. Although the cases acknowledge the fact that not all members of a group are identical or fungible—there are, for example, women of different races, as well as African Americans or Asians of both sexes—this fact has only limited salience for the operation of doctrine. The cases do not highlight hierarchies or antagonisms that arise within a group, making group-based identity more complex for its subjects. Nor, in their general focus on perpetrators' cognitive errors, do the cases describe the ways that discrimination may operate differently across different subsets of a group's members, reflecting diverse stereotypes and judgments. For example, the stereotypes and epithets through which women are harassed in the workplace may vary according to the race, age, and demeanor of the targeted woman. Even the comparatively flexible sexual harassment law that has emerged under the 1964 Civil Rights Act's Title VII prohibition of employment discrimination has had difficulty accommodating this fact.[4] This lack of descriptive nuance may arise from the fact that the leading cases regard group membership as incidental to the essential human nature of any legal subject. Group membership is not a sufficiently rich or variable influence to play a determinative role in shaping the consciousness of individuals, and it is likely to lead to erroneous categorization when decisionmakers take it into account. Guided by such assumptions, legal decisionmakers have often viewed group-based characteristics as qualities that are best overlooked.

Results Analysis as a Partial Alternative

Despite the prevalence of this early conceptualization, it was not the only available framework for understanding discrimination. A distinct understanding of discrimination, and how it operates in the lives of victim groups, emerged from those portions of antidiscrimination doctrine that found discrimination in disparate "effects" or "results." This alternate focus, which did not require a specific perpetrator, let alone a flawed ascription of difference, came about in a variety of ways. Scrutiny of actual results first began as a means of measuring remedial compliance with strong, if amorphous, equal protection mandates. Analyzing the extent of racial integration in a school operating under a desegregation decree, for example, helped to determine whether the district was acting appropriately to eliminate segregation "root and branch." *Washington v. Davis*,[5] a 1976 Supreme Court decision best known for its refusal to constitutionalize discriminatory effect as an independent index of discrimination, generated an instrumental use for "results" analysis: racially disparate effects could function as evidence of the pivotal, but often elusive, discriminatory intent.[6]

In still other cases, the practice of scrutinizing results operated less as a means of identifying or rectifying agent-based discrimination than as a distinct way of understanding discrimination. In federal employment discrimination law,[7] courts determined that equality for covered groups could be undermined by "built-in headwinds": tests, selection norms, or other institutional practices that operated to the disadvantage of race or gender groups, without being structured by a specific discriminatory mindset. In the frankest departure from the predominant approach, the amended section 2 of the Voting Rights Act required an analysis of "results" that cut the assessment of minority vote dilution loose from questions of agent-centered judgment or intent. Moreover, the early section 2 cases established the "opportunity to elect the candidates of [one's] choice" as the index of an undiluted vote—a standard that often required the construction of race-conscious (or "safe" minority) districts.[8]

Voting rights was not, of course, the only context in which an analytic framework that focused on results began to go hand-in-hand with explicit race-conscious remediation. In the school desegregation context, as noted above, results analysis became an instrument of race-conscious remediation. Moreover, in the workplace and in higher education, race-conscious programs gained prominence as a prophylactic measure, which seemed consistent with a result-centered analysis.

This alternate approach to identifying discrimination correlated more strongly with the way that outsider groups understood their own circumstances, leading some commentators to describe it as "victim-oriented."[9] It shifted the focus of judicial scrutiny, demonstrating that the salient thing about discrimination was not the flaws in decisionmakers' reasoning but the barriers that differential results created to the livelihood, education, or civic participation of politically marginalized groups.[10] In so doing, this approach characterized as discrimination those practical consequences that outsider groups were most likely to find burdensome or oppressive in their own lives. From this perspective, it was also possible to glimpse aspects of discrimination, often perceived by victim groups, that had been erased or obscured by the dominant view. Effects analysis made clear that discrimination could be associated with apparently benign, impersonal practices, as well as prejudiced human motives. And in its more various, nuanced portrait of the way in which outsider groups are disadvantaged, this approach encouraged legal actors to view discrimination as a variable, institution-specific phenomenon rather than a pattern of misapprehension that is repeated from context to context.

Some elements of this view of discrimination also pointed to a richer conception of group membership. The development of a view distinct from the agent-centered perspective—a vantage point informed by, or at least consistent with, the experience of suffering discrimination—highlighted the affirmative, constitutive role of group membership. Group membership was not simply an incidental characteristic, capable of misleading biased or ignorant decisionmakers. Whether through the shared experience of discrimination or through other elements of group culture, group membership shaped ways of seeing the world that had distinctive, affirmative value. The role of group membership in forming the individual consciousness of group members was also underscored by the arguments in favor of group-conscious remedies. The diversity that was invoked as a justification for affirmative action in the educational setting and the emphasis on the shared political perspectives of minority groups in the context of the Voting Rights Act made clear that group membership affected the political preferences and substantive contributions of those socialized in a particular group context.

In other respects, however, this body of doctrine disturbed few of the dominant understandings about group membership. Groups were still defined biologically, even if group membership was understood as reflecting a cultural or social overlay. And groups were most often characterized as unitary rather than marked by subgroup variations and tensions. It was during this period, for example, that several leading Title VII cases declined to recognize the distinctive injuries suffered by black women.[11] This reluctance among legal decisionmakers of the period to see group experience as embodying both similarities and differences among members— as in the sexual harassment example above—prevented them from seeing the full variability and contextualization of discrimination.

It is partly for this reason that the first two decades of antidiscrimination decisions reflected a subtle tension rather than a stark divergence between the agent, or ''perpetrator,'' focus prevailing in mainstream doctrine and the ''outsider,'' or ''victim,'' focus that surfaced intermittently in approaches such as disparate impact or results analysis. The two approaches shared several conclusions about the nature of group membership. Moreover, the punctuation of the dominant approach with ventures into results analysis suggested to outsiders that their perspectives were not wholly excluded from equality doctrine.[12] In the past fifteen years, however, two developments have rendered the tension between these analytic approaches both sharper and more visible.

The first is the steady erosion of the outsider focus in federal antidiscrimination doctrine. This focus has been curtailed in part by doctrinal changes in Title VII that have narrowed the scope of disparate impact analysis. But it has been most effectively undermined by a group-blind interpretation of equal protection, which has been applied to educational and employment settings as well as to the context of the Voting Rights Act. These changes have resulted not simply in the triumph of the ''perpetrator'' perspective as outlined above but in its metamorphosis toward a broad constitutional right to individualized (i.e., group-blind) treatment.

Paradoxically, however, this more decisive submergence of the victim perspective in antidiscrimination law has been coupled with a burgeoning of outsiders' perspectives on discrimination in feminist, critical race, and gay legal theory. This second development, with its emphasis on experiential epistemology, has generated fuller, more concrete, accounts of how discrimination operates in the lives of its victims. More important, perhaps it has generated more sophisticated understandings of how groups themselves are constituted. It has demonstrated how multiplicity within acknowledged groups not only creates hierarchies among group members but also alters and pluralizes the dynamics of discrimination itself.

Contemporary Equality Doctrine: A Tension Amplified

The rejection of victim-oriented analysis has come about in a variety of ways. One of the subtler, and perhaps less indelible, forces of erosion has been the judicial revision of burden of proof rules under Title VII. In some cases, defendants have been permitted considerable vagueness in their articulation of nondiscriminatory reasons, to the point at which they have sometimes prevailed on the basis of accounts that do not explain why another applicant was given a particular job rather than the plaintiff.[13] Plaintiffs, on the other hand, have increasingly been held to the specificity of a smoking gun in arguing that defendants' ostensibly legitimate reasons constituted a pretext for discrimination. For example, a recent holding that even a showing that the defendant lied about his nondiscriminatory reasons was insufficient to prove pretext set a high watermark in interpreting the plaintiff's burden of persuasion.[14]

By making it more difficult for plaintiffs to prevail under a disparate impact standard, these cases have reduced the extent to which this approach provides an independent basis of recovery. More important, they have threatened the conceptual distinctness of this claim by requiring something perilously close to a demonstration of discriminatory judgment in proving pretext. Yet they may in the long run do less damage than the second salient doctrinal development of this period: an effort to curtail group-conscious governmental programs with a group-blind interpretation of the equal protection clause.[15] The Title VII decisions, as judicial efforts at statutory interpretation, may still be subject to congressional revision, a power that has been used on several occasions to limit judicial interpretations of this statute. Moreover, while these cases limit the scope of one victim-oriented framework (the disparate impact approach), they neither directly delegitimate it nor undo gains achieved under it in earlier contexts. The constitutional attack on race-conscious remedies—or affirmative action—has achieved these more ambitious objectives as well. The challenge it poses to the assumptions of the victim-oriented model, and the ways in which it expands even the earlier "perpetrator" perspective, may be seen by examining three conceptual shifts that this line of cases has brought about.

The first has been the separation of the equal protection clause from its historic role as the instrument for protecting blacks and, by analogy, other oppressed groups. In a series of decisions, beginning with the landmark *Bakke* case of the late 1970s,[16] the equal protection clause has been interpreted to protect an individual's right to equal treatment rather than to secure particular, politically marginalized groups against unfair or oppressive governmental action. The justification has been partly historical—the nation has passed the point at which it can maintain a "two-class" structure of protection for blacks only[17]—but it has also been largely pragmatic. If the Court acknowledged a right to group-based protection in this context, some justices have argued, they would be deluged with a complex, shifting mass of claims that the Court, as a principle-bound, apolitical body, is not suited to distinguish.[18] This redefinition of the equal protection clause, as the "neutral" arbiter of individual rights, is underscored by the Court's decision, previewed in the early cases and consolidated by a majority in 1989,[19] to apply strict scrutiny to all race-based classifications, including "benign" plans that favor members of socially marginalized groups. The justices assert that it is virtually impossible to distinguish benign from discriminatory programs and that even the best-intended plans may have highly prejudicial consequences, both for the whites asked to bear the burden and for their intended beneficiaries.[20] The decoupling of the equal protection clause from the vindication of minority opportunity is also clear in a final feature of these cases: the increasing stringency with which the Court has viewed any state justifications for departing from group-blind treatment. In early cases, such as *Bakke*, the Court accepted justifications including compensation for past discrimination and cultivation of diversity in a university's student body and endorsed race-conscious programs such as Harvard University's admissions program as instruments for advancing these goals.[21] In subsequent cases, the Court became increasingly exacting in the showings of institutional discrimination that it judged sufficient to justify a race-conscious remedial plan.[22] In the most recent cases, epitomized by *Shaw v. Reno*, the Court has evinced skepticism about many apparently strong justifications for race-conscious state action, including compliance with the Justice Department's interpretation of the Voting Rights Act.[23]

These cases also reflect an increasing distance, on the part of the Court, from the perspectives and perceptions of victims of group-based discrimination. The justices' concern about the institutional difficulty of mediating among multiple group-based claims has often seemed to overshadow their concern about rectifying the injustices represented by those claims—a clear retreat from the viewpoint of the victim toward the mindset of the governmental decisionmaker. Moreover, the Court's insistence on the possibility—indeed, the justice—of considering individuals from all groups similarly situated disregards the concrete, experiential knowledge of outsider groups. These "individuals" do not perceive themselves to be similarly situated in their access to public benefits or their need for governmental protection; in their view, the distinctions among groups that the Court has despaired of making can be grounded in broad social, or more particularized local, patterns of interaction. The Court's insistence on abstracting from these life-defining circumstances reflects a frank rejection of outsider claimants' experientially based knowledge. In addition to its insistence on the similar situation, for constitutional purposes, of all racial groups, the Court has often provided its own "counternarratives" to contest outsiders' claims that their circumstances reflect remediable discrimination. In its 1989 repudiation of the minority business set-aside plan in Richmond, Virginia, for example, the Court hypothesized that the low numbers of minority business enterprises in local contractors' associations—a circumstance the state had offered as evidence of discrimination—might well be attributable to lack of interest by minority group members in the construction industry.[24] The Court also flouted the expressed perspectives of many minority voters in *Shaw v. Reno* by suggesting that the state's assumption that minority voters shared salient political interests was a stereotype-laden insult to those voters' independence and heterogeneity.[25]

The affirmative action cases, in the end, do more than dispute outsiders' knowledge: they also reflect a subtle change in the mainstream, perpetrator-oriented understanding of discrimination. Cases involving race-conscious remedies—unlike those involving straightforward discrimination—raise no inferences about the abilities of the excluded, or disadvantaged, contenders. Whether the justification is compensation for past discrimination or cultivation of diversity, these plans' preference for members of minority groups reflects no judgment that whites are incompetent or unable to compete.[26] Hence one might plausibly say that these cases are less about protection from erroneous differentiating judgments than about protection from judgments that reflect or produce any group-based differentiation at all. Equal protection seems to establish one's presumptive entitlement to be treated simply as an individual or as an exemplar of universal, rather than group-specific, human characteristics.[27]

The Development of Outsider Perspectives on Groups and Group-ness

Paradoxically, however, even as antidiscrimination doctrine was being purged of group-based claims and other conceptualizations reflecting outsider perspectives on discrimination, these perspectives were undergoing a renaissance in the domain of legal theory. The 1980s saw the dramatic growth and development of a critical jurisprudence aimed at elaborating the vantage point of politically oppressed or marginalized groups. This work was stimulated in part by a methodological shift in the social sciences: a critique of objectivity and objectivist epistemologies that gradually worked its way into law.[28] The critique challenged the traditional view of legal principles as natural, necessary, or inevitable means to govern social life. These principles, like any other ideas or "truths," were partial, contingent, and the product of situated perspectives. It was the authority—the privileged social and professional positions—of those who pronounced them, critics contended, that permitted legal decisionmakers to characterize these partial perspectives as natural or universal. One strategy that critics used to contest the universality of legal principles was to make visible the alternative understandings that had been excluded by legal decisionmakers. Often using the tool of experiential narrative—which supplied the stories that law had rendered marginal and emphasized the role of one's perspective in shaping one's view of the proper legal standard—outsider scholars reconceptualized discrimination in terms informed by their own experience. Thus, Catharine MacKinnon argued that gender discrimination is not the flawed estimation of the similarities and differences between men and women: women's stories suggest, instead, that discrimination consists in the inequalities men impose on women through sexualized dominance and other forms of power.[29] And Derrick Bell challenged the ostensible tension between affirmative action and academic merit in his "Chronicles"—quasi-fictional dialogues in which he and Geneva Crenshaw, an intrepid black female interlocutor, interrogate conventional antidiscrimination doctrine.[30]

These jurisprudential perspectives placed the phenomenon of discrimination in a new light. First, they set out in palpably concrete terms what it means to be a target of group-based discrimination, supplying, in some respects, an antidote to the perpetrator focus of mainstream doctrine. Intentional discrimination is described not as an inaccurate ascription of difference by decisionmakers but as a stigmatizing, devaluative characterization that erodes the self-conception and subtly constricts the life possibilities of the victim. When Patricia Williams describes her exclusion from Bennetton's by an impassive, gum-chewing, buzzer-wielding salesperson, she does not dwell on his error in assuming she had no resources for making a purchase; she focuses instead on her confusion, humiliation, and fury in being excluded.[31] Moreover, the emphasis, in this literature, on the practical and personal consequences of discriminatory treatment has also challenged mainstream doctrine's exclusive focus on intentional forms of discrimination, highlighting as well discrimination perpetuated by a range of "neutral" institutional practices and selective insensitivities. Patricia Williams's account of how an "aesthetic of uniformity" kept black women out of the Rockettes[32] or Charles Lawrence's description of how an interviewer's elaborate praise of a Latino candidate's English was perceived as a condescending and hurtful slight[33] vividly document these patterns and support the group-affirming corrective of race-conscious remedies.

While this literature has mounted an explicit challenge to elements of the "perpetrator" approach, it has also introduced perspectives not entirely comprehended by the kind of "victim" orientation reflected in results analysis. Feminist and critical race scholarship have characterized discrimination as a force that is not only institutionally particularized, as some disparate impact accounts suggest, but also capable of metamorphosing over time or in relation to altered circumstances. Accounts of how sexual harassment often follows the end of formal exclusion of women from professions and trades,[34] for example, demonstrate not just the multiplicity but also the durability and adaptability of discriminatory practices. Such accounts also suggest a sense of entitlement among perpetrators—a belief in the legitimacy of their privilege—that explains features of discrimination unelaborated by earlier accounts: how practices thought to be neutral might operate discriminatorily or how those in positions of power might respond with naked animus when their sense of control is called into question. Finally, while these outsider accounts of discrimination highlight the ways in which discrimination restricts public opportunities, such as in employment and political participation, they also underscore a number of other consequences that are less frequently remarked in antidiscrimination doctrine. The devaluation of sexual harassment, for example, might result in the denial or forfeiture of a job but might also make the conditions of the job more onerous or make it difficult to perform at the level expected.[35] The devaluative assumptions applied to single black motherhood, to take another example, might result in the denial of welfare or health care benefits but might also result in more intrusive governmental surveillance.[36] These insights create a more comprehensive, complex picture of how discrimination operates and what it means for the life circumstances of those who suffer it.

Yet even more dramatically revisionary than outsider jurisprudence's account of discrimination is its understanding of group-ness and group membership. In contrast to the proponents of the dominant doctrinal view, outsider scholars have not described group-ness as an incidental overlay on a shared, essential humanity. Wary of the marginalizing power of the ostensibly universal, and convinced that one's life narrative is given shape by one's particularity, these scholars have seen group membership as defining and constitutive for outsiders. Although this insight reflects some similarity with the premises of result-based doctrinal approaches, this scholarship in many respects offers a more sophisticated analysis of the dynamics of group membership than has yet been manifested in any facet of antidiscrimination doctrine.

First, group membership is rarely viewed as a function of simple biological transmission. The color of one's skin, for example, may begin as a function of heredity, but even the identity that would seem to be conferred by biology is less predictable and stable than one might suspect. Judy Scales-Trent, for example, writes about the experience of being a "black person who looks white in a world that doesn't tolerate ambiguity very well."[37] Her accounts of "passing" as white, "coming out" as black, and trying to carve out an identity amid the confusion of those around her suggest that even the categories we view as most polar and biologically ordained do not always declare themselves with unambivalent clarity.[38] The extent to which the perceptions of others in Scales-Trent's life render malleable and contingent an identity that is biologically consistent illustrates a second point: the role of social construction in shaping the boundaries of group membership. Patricia Williams writes tellingly of a debate among her colleagues over whether she was "really black."[39] Kimberle Crenshaw describes how Anita Hill was "deraced" by her defenders' resort to the conventional "rape trope" of sexual harassment and by Clarence Thomas's invocation of the "high-tech lynching" metaphor.[40] None of these interpretations prevailed because the woman in question was too light-skinned to be immediately identifiable as black. They transpired because, as both authors conclude, race is invested with a variety of sometimes-conflicting social meanings, and those more privileged than the bearer of the disputed characteristics often enjoy the power to decide how those meanings will be assigned and how a particular person will be placed within the operative categories.

The Anita Hill example points to a third insight communicated by these theorists: that group membership is not singular or monolithic but multiple and intersecting. Even a single group-based element of a person's identity may not have a predictable or consistent effect on his or her experience or political commitments. But more important, within each "group" are members with diverse, intersecting characteristics. This intersectionality means that there is not only variation but also hierarchy and exclusion within groups. Lesbian feminists and feminists of color, for example, have explained in compelling terms how feminist accounts have marginalized their subgroup members and posited a "universal woman" who is actually white and heterosexual.[41] Intersection of multiple group-based characteristics also means that particular individuals may integrate those characteristics differently from one context to another. A particular woman may identify primarily with her gender in one setting, with her race in another, or with her parental status or sexual orientation in a third. Influencing the way in which a given outsider integrates her multiple characteristics are the perceptions of a society that has difficulty comprehending complexity and that may understand certain group-based characteristics in ways that effectively erase intersections. One reason Anita Hill's supporters resorted to a "rape trope" patterned on the experiences of white women, Crenshaw explains, was because dominant society had such difficulty conceptualizing life at the intersection of race and gender discrimination.[42]

These observations, in turn, highlight dynamics of discrimination—sources of variability and complexity—that were not made visible even by "victim-oriented" doctrinal approaches, such as disparate impact. They reveal that intentional discrimination may take forms that are different for different subgroups of the targeted category, as in the sexual harassment example provided above. Yet this intragroup differentiation does not make the discrimination that occurs any less "gender" or "race" discrimination: it simply means that perpetrators take into account the fact that there are, for example, several racial variants of the gender female and that perpetrators can be insulated from legal reach if decisionmakers take one subgroup's experience of discrimination as a groupwide norm. These outsider insights also suggest that discrimination that operates through "neutral" practices or otherwise without intent may have differential impact across different subgroups of a protected category. For example, the practice of employing only those applicants known to an incumbent employee may favor men over women, but it may also favor white women over women of color. Finally, recent outsider scholarship makes clear that social and institutional decisions about who is considered to be a member of a particular group can themselves be a source of harm—in the way that Anita Hill was harmed by being de-raced—because they often operate on the basis of unjustified stereotypes and allocate important institutional and legal opportunities in disparate ways.

Mobilizing at the Impasse: Strategies for Instilling Group-Based Perspectives in Antidiscrimination Law

Antidiscrimination law has thus reached a peculiar impasse: outsider theorists have developed increasingly sophisticated understandings of group membership and group-based discrimination at the same time that antidiscrimination doctrine has required legal and other institutional actors to abstract from the very fact of group membership. One must next ask whether there are any potential legal vehicles through which outsider groups might resist the effort to drive group consciousness from equality doctrine and express their increasingly complex views of group identity and discrimination. What bodies of law might permit outsiders to describe discrimination as a variable phenomenon that encompasses intentional devaluation, selective insensitivity, neutral practices with disparate effects, and flawed ascription of difference; that erodes self-esteem or enhances institutional surveillance as well as diminishes public opportunities; that finds and exploits the distinctive characteristics of subgroups as well as impedes the group as a whole?

Some efforts might be made, in the first instance, to limit the move toward group-blindness in leading areas of antidiscrimination law. One can scarcely deny the fact that recent doctrinal changes have made many of these areas far less hospitable venues for the implementation of group-based perspectives. Yet it may be possible not only to strike group-preserving compromises but also to use the courts' suspicion of strict race-based programs, for example, to create classifications that highlight the complexity and contingency of race and other categories. Outsiders might support affirmative action programs that combine racial characteristics with indices of economic disadvantage, as is being contemplated in some government contractor programs.[43] This strategy reflects some acquiescence in the paradoxical development that characteristics not viewed as suspect may be less vulnerable to challenge than the long-protected characteristic of minority race. But it also continues to protect the professional opportunities of many minority contractors, while highlighting the extent to which race-based disadvantage has a palpable class-related component.

A second goal might be to identify claims that can serve as the successors to "results" analysis or affirmative action doctrine, in the sense that they incorporate in law a view of discrimination and group membership that corresponds more closely to outsider perspectives. One plausible candidate lies squarely within federal antidiscrimination doctrine: the Title VII claim for sexual or racial harassment. The nature of the harassment claim, and the ways in which it has been elaborated over the past fifteen years, underscore many of the points made by feminist and critical race scholars about group membership and discrimination. It reveals, first and fore-most, that discrimination arises not only from flawed perceptions of difference but also from the insensitivity born of privilege and from the willful imposition of unequal power. The harasser injects into a professional setting prejudiced responses to group membership that have no place there. He may do it willfully, to keep the target off balance in a professional context new to racial minorities or women. He may do it ignorantly, because he is unable to think of minority or female employees as anything but members of those groups and his privilege has protected him from having to think critically about this mental habit. Both dynamics convey crucial insights about discrimination that can be usefully highlighted by this claim.

Second, because harassment has the virtue, if one may call it that, of making the prejudiced conceptions of the perpetrator vividly clear, it can demonstrate dis-crimination's variable, contextualized character, particularly in relation to hetero-geneous groups. A perpetrator's language may show, for example, that he devalues only some subgroups; or devalues several subgroups but demeans them through distinctive subgroup-specific language; or targets only those whose biological sex or race coincides or conflicts with their social characteristics. Highlighting these variable patterns underscores the diversity within what we sometimes take to be monolithic groups and reveals that "race" or "gender" discrimination may com-prise a number of prejudiced attitudes toward subgroups, which have both common and disparate themes.

Finally, because harassment is on the boundary between discrimination that pro-duces denial of access to public opportunities and discrimination that produces other, less-familiar kinds of injuries, it may be used to highlight those categories of harm that need to be brought to public attention: harm to self-esteem, or im-pediments to the effective performance of one's job, or disproportionate official surveillance.

A third way in which outsiders might mobilize group-based perspectives is to employ disparate impact analysis as a political, rather than a legal, tool. Many forms of discrimination that subject their victims to increased governmental in-tervention or surveillance, rather than to more traditional denials of opportunity, operate by producing a disparate impact on outsider groups. Governmental inter-vention in the fertility or parenting of minority women is a prime example.[44] The prescription of Norplant as part of the resolution of child-neglect claims, or the pressure to undergo sterilization imposed by medical practitioners or welfare pol-icies, or the reporting of suspected substance abuse by pregnant women are all policies that embody no explicit group-based classifications. These policies impose an automatic disparate impact on women, given the biology of human reproduction. But they also produce a disparate impact on the basis of race, with nonwhite women being targeted for such intervention more frequently than white women and black women being targeted most frequently of all.[45] Increasingly, outsider scholars have decried this effect as an unattended form of discrimination in the operation of welfare and family programs.[46] This critique might serve as a model for other outsider scholars and advocates. Discussion of the sources of disparate impact illuminates the many forms of discrimination that fail to conform to the model of flawed ascription of difference. Moreover, the political pressure applied by such arguments may be sufficient to terminate newly commenced or particularly controversial programs; even in settings in which such claims lack the legal power or political influence necessary to end the challenged practices, they keep the necessity of considering group-based impact on the public agenda.

This last benefit points to a final, long-term strategy for proponents of outsider perspectives on discrimination. The very act of elaborating these perspectives is a critical resource in their translation or incorporation into law. Scholarship and political discourse embodying these views preserve and develop them for a time when courts may be more willing to incorporate group-based perspectives in antidiscrimination doctrine. They may, more important, play an indirect role in bringing that time about—a role that is not unprecedented in antidiscrimination law. One force that contributed to the revolution of *Brown* was the development of a body of views, drawing both on social science[47] and on individual narrative,[48] that made clear the effect of segregation as it was perceived and experienced by black children. In the face of this persistent, concrete testament, legal fictions of a separation that communicated no disrespect to either group ultimately had to give way. Proponents of group-based perspectives, confronting a legal world of presumptively equally situated individuals, could do no better than to heed this example.

NOTES

I would like to thank Henry Shue for numerous conversations on the subject of this chapter and Neal Devins and Davison Douglas for helpful comments on an earlier draft.

1. ''Outsider'' is a term that is frequently used in the critical jurisprudential literature to refer to socially and politically marginalized groups. See, e.g., Richard Delgado and Jean Stefancic, ''Images of the Outsider in American Law and Culture,'' in Richard Delgado, ed., *Critical Race Theory: The Cutting Edge* (Philadelphia: Temple University Press, 1995), 217. In this chapter, I use the term primarily to refer to people of color, particularly blacks, and women; but others have also used the term to refer to gays and lesbians, members of minority religious groups, and people with disabilities.

2. This understanding is reflected in the equal protection premise that like entities must be treated alike or in the requirement that differentiating legislative classifications must be justified by rationales that characterize groups as unlike or describe specific instances of dissimilar treatment as relating to an important public purpose. This assumption also informs Title VII disparate treatment doctrine, which permits differential treatment of statutorily covered groups only when authorized by a ''bona fide occupational qualification.''

3. The first person to use the term ''perpetrator perspective'' in the literature on race appears to have been Alan Freeman in his article ''Legitimizing Racial Discrimination Through Anti-Discrimination Law: A Critical Review of Supreme Court Doctrine,'' *Minnesota Law Review* 62 (1978): 1049. Catharine MacKinnon used a similar expression in her early articles on gender inequalities, when she wrote that rape law in this society embodies the view of the ''reasonable rapist.'' See Catharine MacKinnon, ''Feminism, Marxism, Method, and the State: Toward Feminist Jurisprudence,'' *Signs* 8 (1983): 635.

Implicit in the term ''perpetrator perspective'' is the assumption that what is to be known about discrimination is not a single truth, or a universal constant, but rather varies, depending on the perspective of the observer or knower. This epistemological assumption is sometimes at odds with the positions taken by the courts in discrimination cases, in which they assert or project the understanding that there is a single appropriate way of characterizing discrimination or an alleged discriminatory incident. The most notorious example of this judicial view is the Supreme Court's opinion in *Plessy v. Ferguson*, in which the majority stated that "separate but equal" is a badge of inferiority, "solely because the colored race chooses to put that construction upon it." 163 U.S. 537 (1896).

4. A fuller description of this difficulty is contained in Kathryn Abrams, "Title VII and the Complex Female Subject," *Michigan Law Review* 92 (August 1994): 2479.

5. 426 U.S. 288 (1976).

6. See *Village of Arlington Heights v. Metropolitan Housing Development Corp.*, 429 U.S. 252 (1977).

7. See *Griggs v. Duke Power Co.*, 401 U.S. 424 (1971).

8. See, e.g., *Thornburg v. Gingles*, 478 U.S. 30 (1986) (describing "opportunity to elect the candidates of [one's] choice" as the core value protected by section 2 of the Voting Rights Act); *Ketchum v. Byrne*, 740 F.2d 1398 (7th Cir. 1984), cert. denied sub nom *City Council of Chicago v. Ketchum*, 471 U.S. 1135 (1985) (affirming importance of supermajority or "safe" minority districts in remedying Voting Rights Act Violations).

9. See, e.g., Freeman, "Legitimizing Racial Discrimination"; D. Marvin Jones, "No Time for Trumpets: Title VII, Equality, and the Fin de Siecle," *Michigan Law Review* 92 (August 1994): 2311.

10. The imposition of race-or gender-conscious remedies, grounded sometimes on a generalized showing of societal discrimination, demonstrated that correcting entrenched and often complex patterns of injustice was as compelling a mandate as identifying the specific agent responsible for a particular practice.

11. For a compelling discussion of these cases, see Kimberle Crenshaw, "Demarginalizing the Intersection of Race and Sex: A Black Feminist Critique of Antidiscrimination Doctrine, Feminist Theory, and Antiracist Politics," *University of Chicago Legal Forum* (1989): 139.

12. In fact, the strong beachheads established by "results" analysis in statutory areas, such as Title VII and the Voting Rights Act, gave their proponents reason to hope that they might one day become predominants or at least be incorporated into constitutional doctrine— a hope that may have triggered the Court's constitutional rejoinder in *Washington v. Davis*, 426 U.S. 229 (1976), and its more recent effort to neutralize the power of the Voting Rights Act in *Shaw v. Reno*, 113 S. Ct. 2816 (1993).

13. *Texas Dep't of Community Affairs v. Burdine*, 450 U.S. 248 (1981).

14. *St. Mary's v. Hicks*, 113 S. Ct. 2742 (1993). The lower courts are divided on whether evidence of lying is sufficient to support a jury verdict; the Supreme Court held only that it is not sufficient to justify finding liability without the trial court's submitting the case to a jury.

15. The same may be said of a development on which I do not comment here: the Court's refusal to constitutionalize the "effects" approach in *Washington v. Davis*, 426 U.S. 229 (1976). Although *Washington v. Davis* prevented the "effects" approach from becoming ascendant, the cases of the type I am going to discuss undercut its rationale and force in contexts in which it has previously been well established.

16. *Regents of Univ. of California v. Bakke*, 438 U.S. 265 (1978).

17. Justice Lewis F. Powell, Jr., noted cryptically in *Bakke* that it is "far too late to argue that the guarantee of equal protection to all persons permits the recognition of special wards entitled to a degree of protection greater than that accorded others." Ibid. at 295. To my

mind, the abrogation of a role for the clause that dates back to the end of the Civil War requires more explanation than Justice Powell offers in this opinion.

18. The prototype of this argument may be found in Justice Powell's opinion in *Bakke*, 438 U.S. at 295–97. It is also offered by Justice Sandra Day O'Connor in *City of Richmond v. J. A. Croson Co.*, 488 U.S. 469, 505–6 (1989).

19. See *City of Richmond*, 488 U.S. 469.

20. *City of Richmond*, 488 U.S. at 493; *Bakke*, 438 U.S. at 298.

21. *Bakke*, 438 U.S. at 316–18.

22. *City of Richmond*, 488 U.S. at 493-506.

23. *Shaw*, 113 S. Ct. at 2830–31.

24. *City of Richmond*, 488 U.S. at 503.

25. *Shaw*, 113 S. Ct. at 2827.

26. On the contrary, opponents of race-conscious remedies frequently express concern that these programs will cast negative aspersions on the capabilities of their beneficiaries. See, e.g., *Bakke*, 438 U.S. at 298.

27. This reasoning reaches a high watermark in recent cases such as *Shaw v. Reno*, 113 S. Ct. 2816 (1993), a case challenging the constitutionality of race-conscious electoral districting, in which the Court refers to a "right to participate in a color-blind electoral process," ibid. at 2824, and asserts that even the black voters whose electoral opportunity is enhanced by the districts are disserved by the state's operating assumption that black voters share political interests, ibid. at 2827.

28. The works that helped bring this critique to law include Derrick A. Bell, Jr., *And We Are Not Saved: The Elusive Quest for Racial Justice* (New York: Basic Books, 1987); Martha Minow, *Making All the Difference: Inclusion, Exclusion, and American Law* (Ithaca, N.Y.: Cornell University Press, 1990); Joseph Singer, "The Player and the Cards: Nihilism and Legal Theory," *Yale Law Journal* 94 (November 1984): 1–70; Kimberle Crenshaw, "Race, Reform, and Retrenchment: Transformation and Legitimation in Anti-Discrimination Law," *Harvard Law Review* 101 (May 1988): 1331; Richard Delgado, "The Imperial Scholar," *University of Pennsylvania Law Review* 132 (March 1984): 561; Mac-Kinnon, "Feminism, Marxism, Method, and the State." This critique is not entirely unprecedented in law, as certain of its elements were previewed in the work of legal realists. For a thought-provoking discussion of the relation between legal realism and critical legal theory, see Joseph Singer, "Legal Realism Now," *California Law Review* 76 (March 1988): 465, 531.

29. See Catharine MacKinnon, *Feminism Unmodified* (Cambridge: Harvard University Press, 1987), 32–45.

30. Bell, *And We Are Not Saved*. The chronicle in which Bell challenges this tension most explicitly is "The Chronicle of the DeVine Gift"; the ostensible tension between affirmative action and meritocracy is only one of the many premises of conventional anti-discrimination doctrine contested in this pathbreaking book.

31. Patricia Williams, "Spirit-Murdering the Messenger: The Discourse of Fingerpointing as the Law's Response to Racism," *Miami Law Review* 42 (September 1987): 127.

32. Patricia Williams, "The Obliging Shell: An Informal Essay on Formal Equal Opportunity," *Michigan Law Review* 89 (August 1989): 2128.

33. Charles Lawrence, "The Id, the Ego, and Equal Protection: Reckoning with Unconscious Racism," *Stanford Law Review* 39 (January 1987): 317.

34. See Vicki Schultz, "Telling Stories about Women and Work: Judicial Interpretations of Sex Segregation in the Workplace in Title VII Cases Raising the Lack of Interest Defense," *Harvard Law Review* 103 (June 1990): 1749.

35. Both Justice O'Connor's majority opinion and Justice Ruth Bader Ginsburg's con-

currence in the recent *Harris* case support this view of the harm of sexual harassment. See *Harris v. Forklift Systems*, 114 S. Ct. 367 (1993).

36. See generally Dorothy Roberts, "Punishing Drug Addicts Who Have Babies: Women of Color, Equality, and the Right of Privacy," *Harvard Law Review* 104 (May 1991): 1419.

37. Judy Scales-Trent, "Commonalities: On Being Black and White, Different, and the Same," *Yale Journal of Law and Feminism* 2 (Spring 1990): 305.

38. Similar insights have been communicated by scholars writing about gender, sexuality, and sexual orientation. They suggest that categories such as male/female, gay/straight are far more ambivalent than antidiscrimination doctrine, or mainstream political views, suggest. See, e.g., Katherine Franke, "The Central Mistake of Sex Discrimination Law: The Disaggregation of Sex from Gender," *University of Pennsylvania Law Review* 144 (November 1995): 1; Mary Anne Case, "Disaggregating Gender from Sex and Sexual Orientation: The Effeminate Man in the Law and Feminist Jurisprudence," *Yale Law Journal* 105 (October 1995): 1; Francisco Valdez, "Queers, Sissies, Dykes, and 'Tomboys' Deconstructing the Conflation of 'Sex,' 'Gender,' and 'Sexual Orientation' in Euro-American Law and Society," *California Law Review* 83 (January 1995): 1; Abrams, "Title VII and the Complex Female Subject." See generally Ruth Colker, "Bi," *Ohio State Law Journal* 56, no. 1 (1995): 1.

39. Patricia Williams, *The Alchemy of Race and Rights* (Cambridge: Harvard University Press, 1990).

40. Kimberle Crenshaw, "Whose Story Is It Anyway? Feminist and Antiracist Appropriations of Anita Hill," in *Race-ing Justice, Engender-ing Power*, ed. Toni Morrison (New York: Pantheon, 1992).

41. See, e.g., Crenshaw, "Demarginalizing the Intersection of Race and Sex"; Patricia Cain, "Feminist Jurisprudence: Grounding the Theories," *Berkeley Women's Law Journal* 4, no. 2 (1989–90): 191.

42. Crenshaw, "Whose Story Is It Anyway?"

43. For an interesting discussion of the pros and cons of pure class-based affirmative action, see Joanne Barkin, "Symposium: Affirmative Action," *Dissent* 42 (Fall 1995): 461, 462–63.

44. See Roberts, "Punishing Drug Addicts Who Have Babies"; Michelle Oberman, "Sex, Drugs, Pregnancy, and the Law: Rethinking the Problems of Pregnant Women Who Use Drugs," *Hastings Law Journal* 43 (March 1992): 505.

45. Roberts, "Punishing Drug Addicts Who Have Babies," 1434.

46. See ibid.; Oberman, "Sex, Drugs, Pregnancy, and the Law."

47. See *Brown v. Board of Education*, 347 U.S. 483 (1954) (n. 11).

48. See Charles L. Black, "The Lawfulness of the Desegregation Decisions," *Yale Law Journal* 69 (1960): 421.

3

Civil Rights Reform in Historical Perspective

Regulating Marital Violence

REVA B. SIEGEL

In the nineteenth century, and again in the twentieth century, the American feminist movement has attempted to reform the law of marriage so as to secure for wives equality with their husbands. In each century, the movement's efforts have produced significant changes in the law structuring marriage. The status of married women has improved, but wives still have not attained equality with their husbands—if we measure equality as the dignitary and material "goods" associated with the wealth wives control, or the work they perform, or the degree of physical security they enjoy. The legal system continues to play an important role in perpetuating these status differences, although, over time, the role that law plays in enforcing status relations has become increasingly less visible.

As this essay will show, efforts to reform a status regime do bring about change—but not always the kind of change advocates seek. When the legitimacy of a status regime is successfully contested, lawmakers and jurists will both cede and defend status privileges—gradually relinquishing the original rules and justificatory rhetoric of the contested regime and finding new rules and reasons to protect such status privileges as they choose to defend. Thus, civil rights reform can breathe "new life" into a body of status law by pressuring elites to translate it into a more contemporary, and less controversial, social idiom. I call this kind of change in the rules and rhetoric of a status regime "preservation through transformation," and I illustrate this modernization dynamic in a case study of domestic assault law as it evolved in rule structure and rationale from a law of marital prerogative to a law of marital privacy.

The Anglo-American common law originally provided that a husband, as master of his household, could subject his wife to corporal punishment or "chastisement" as long as he did not inflict permanent injury on her. During the nineteenth century, an era of feminist agitation for reform of marriage law, courts in England and in the United States declared that a husband no longer had the right to chastise his wife. Yet for a century after courts repudiated the right of chastisement, the American legal system continued to treat wife beating differently from other cases of assault and battery. Although authorities denied that a husband had the right to beat his wife, they rarely intervened in cases of marital violence; a husband who assaulted his wife was granted various formal and informal immunities from prosecution in order to protect the privacy of the family and to promote domestic harmony.

As the nineteenth-century feminist movement protested a husband's marital prerogatives, it helped bring about the repudiation of chastisement doctrine; but in so doing, the movement also precipitated changes in the regulation of marital violence that "modernized" this body of status law. Instead of reasoning about marriage in the older, hierarchy-based norms of the common law, lawmakers began to justify the regulation of domestic violence in the language of privacy and love associated with companionate marriage in the industrial era. Once translated from an antiquated to a more contemporary gender idiom, the state's justification for treating wife beating differently from other kinds of assault seemed reasonable in ways the law of chastisement did not.

As the evolution of domestic violence law illustrates, political opposition to a status regime may bring about changes that incrementally improve the welfare of subordinated groups. With the demise of chastisement law, the situation of married women improved—certainly, in dignitary terms, and perhaps materially as well. At the same time, the story of chastisement's demise suggests that there is a price for the dignitary and material gains that civil rights reform may bring. If a reform movement is at all successful in advancing its justice claims, it will bring pressure to bear on lawmakers to rationalize status-enforcing state action in new and less socially controversial terms. This process of adaptation can actually revitalize a body of status law, *enhancing* its capacity to legitimate social inequalities that remain among status-differentiated groups. Examined from this perspective, the reform of chastisement doctrine can teach us much about the dilemmas confronting movements for social justice in America today.

Reforming Spousal Assault Law: From Prerogative to Privacy

The Right of Chastisement and Its Critics

Until the late nineteenth century, Anglo-American common law structured marriage to give a husband superiority over his wife in all aspects of the relationship. By law, a husband acquired rights to his wife's person, the value of her paid and unpaid labor, and most property she brought into the marriage. A wife was obliged to obey and serve her husband, and the husband was subject to a reciprocal duty to support his wife and represent her within the legal system. According to the doctrine of marital unity, a wife's legal identity "merged" with her husband's, so that she was unable to file suit without his participation, whether to enforce contracts or to seek damages in tort. The husband was in turn responsible for his wife's conduct—liable, under certain circumstances, for her contracts, torts, and even some crimes.[1]

As master of the household, a husband could command his wife's obedience and subject her to corporal punishment or "chastisement" if she defied his authority. In his treatise on the English common law, William Blackstone explained that a husband could "give his wife moderate correction,"

> [f]or, as he is to answer for her misbehaviour, the law thought it reasonable to intrust him with this power of restraining her, by domestic chastisement, in the same moderation that a man is allowed to correct his apprentices or children; for whom the master or parent is also liable in some cases to answer. But this power of correction was confined within reasonable bounds, and the husband was prohibited from using any violence to his wife.[2]

As Blackstone suggested, the right to give corporal punishment was subject to legal and customary limits. The master of the household might chastise his wife (or children or servants), but he could not inflict permanent injury on them without risking indictment for assault and battery.

Blackstone's *Commentaries* played an important role in shaping American legal culture;[3] and early American law treatises described chastisement as one of the husband's marital prerogatives.[4] Records of chastisement law in America are scant, however. The practice of wife beating was more frequently addressed in popular culture than in published judicial decisions of the era. Yet cases in a number of states, particularly in the southern and mid-Atlantic region, recognized a husband's prerogative to chastise his wife.[5]

By the middle of the nineteenth century, a variety of political and economic forces had begun to erode the common law of marital status in which the right of chastisement was situated.[6] Two of the most powerful reform movements of nineteenth-century America, the movements against slavery ("abolition") and alcohol ("temperance"), gave rise to the first organized movement for women's rights. Although membership in this new reform movement was relatively small, it was well connected to social elites both within and without government. In 1848, when the "woman's rights" movement held its first convention, it denounced the law of marriage in a formal "Declaration of Sentiments":

> He has made her, if married, in the eye of the law, civilly dead.
> He has taken from her all right in property, even to the wages she earns.
> *... In the covenant of marriage, she is compelled to promise obedience to her husband, he becoming, to all intents and purposes, her master—the law giving him power to deprive her of her liberty, and to administer chastisement.*[7]

By mid-century, legislatures in a number of states had begun to enact statutes that modified the common law of marital status; these first statutes typically allowed wives to hold property in their own names. Passage of the married women's property acts inaugurated a gradual process of reform that continues to the present day. At no point was there a categorical repudiation of the doctrine of marital unity; rather, with feminists continually protesting the law of marital status, legislatures and courts modified the common law in piecemeal fashion, giving wives the right to hold property in marriage, the right to their earnings, and the rudiments of legal agency: the right to file suit in their own names and to claim contract and tort damages.[8]

During this period, the right of chastisement was subject to two kinds of criticism. Criticism of the prerogative began indirectly. As the temperance movement protested the social evils of alcohol, it drew public attention to the violence that drunken husbands so often inflicted on their families. The movement's conventions, newspapers, poems, songs, and novels featured vivid accounts of women and children who had been impoverished, terrorized, maimed, and killed by drunken men.[9] Temperance protest was simultaneously radical and conservative in tenor. Condemning alcohol provided reformers an outlet for criticizing the social conditions of family life, in the name of protecting the sanctity of family life. Initially, at least, temperance activists preached one remedy for the family violence they so graphically depicted: prohibiting the sale of alcohol.

The woman's rights movement differed from the temperance movement, both in its diagnosis of family violence and in the social remedies it proposed. As woman's rights advocates attacked the hierarchical structure of marriage, they challenged the husband's authority over his wife, which the prerogative to chastise practically and symbolically embodied. The woman's rights movement thus broke with the temperance movement by depicting wife beating as a symptom of fundamental defects in the structure of marriage itself. The movement's 1848 "Declaration of Sentiments" identified chastisement as part of a political system of male dominance, an analysis that feminists continued to elaborate in the ensuing decades.

For woman's rights advocates, a structural diagnosis of male violence against women dictated a structural remedy. In the 1870s, one of the movement's newspapers argued that domestic violence exposed the "fiction of Woman's protection by man" and thus demonstrated "the necessity that women should have increased power, social, civil, legal, political and ecclesiastical, in order to protect themselves."[10] "These horrors," another writer contended, "result inevitably from the subjection and disfranchisement of women, just as similar outrages used to result from the subjection and disfranchisement of negroes. Equal Rights and Impartial Suffrage are the only radical cure for these barbarities."[11] But some in the movement proposed more immediate remedies. Beginning in the 1850s, a vocal minority in the temperance and woman's rights movement argued that wives should be allowed to divorce drunken, violent husbands.[12]

Formal Repudiation of the Right of Chastisement

The American legal system did respond to these criticisms of chastisement law— but it did so in complex ways. Decades of protest by temperance and woman's rights advocates, combined with shifting attitudes toward corporal punishment and changing gender mores, worked to discredit the law of chastisement. By the 1870s, there was no judge or treatise writer in the United States who would defend the right of chastisement. Thus, when wife beaters were charged with assault and battery, judges refused to entertain the claim that a husband had a legal right to strike his wife. Instead judges pronounced chastisement a "quaint" or "barbaric" remnant of the past and allowed the criminal prosecution to proceed. As an Alabama court explained in 1871: "The wife is not to be considered as the husband's slave. And the privilege, ancient though it be, to beat her with a stick, to pull her hair, choke her, spit in her face or kick her about the floor, or to inflict upon her like indignities, is not now acknowledged by our law."[13] In several states, legislatures enacted statutes specifically prohibiting wife beating; three states even revived corporal punishment for the crime, providing that wife beaters could be sentenced to the whipping post.[14]

Thus the law governing wife beating began to change. But if lawmakers and jurists unanimously repudiated the law of chastisement, they did not adopt legal rules that would necessarily constrain wife beating.

For example, during the late nineteenth century, the legal system remained largely unresponsive to feminist demands for reforms that might assist battered wives in protecting themselves. Feminist efforts to secure for the battered wife the right to separate from her husband, or to divorce him, were largely unsuccessful: reform proposals of this sort were disparaged as threatening the sanctity of marriage and family. In this period, states did begin to grant divorce on grounds of cruelty, but the standards for securing such a divorce were quite difficult to satisfy. Typically, a battered wife was required to prove that her husband acted with "extreme" and "repeated" cruelty.[15] Moreover, the evidence required to prove "extreme cruelty" varied by class, on the assumption that violence was a common, and normal, part of life among the married poor.[16] At the same time, a husband could defeat his wife's divorce petition either by showing that she misbehaved in some way that "provoked" his violence or by showing that she delayed petitioning for divorce and so forgave and "condoned" his violence.[17] In short, the law of divorce still assumed that a wife was obliged to endure various kinds of violence as a normal—and sometimes deserved—part of married life.

Just as marriage law changed to allow divorce on grounds of cruelty while continuing to tolerate significant amounts of violence in the marital relationship, so the criminal law also changed to prohibit chastisement while continuing to allow much violence in marriage to go unchecked. Here, too, class played an important role in discourses about marital violence. In the closing decades of the nineteenth century, commentators regularly depicted wife beating as the practice of lawless or unruly men of the "dangerous" classes. More particularly, they demonized the wife beater as a racial "other," whom authorities needed to control in order to secure social stability. Statistics on arrests and convictions for wife beating during this era demonstrate that criminal assault law was enforced against wife beaters only sporadically and then most often against African Americans and immigrant ethnic groups.[18]

The reforms of the 1870s did not mark the beginning of more fundamental change. Instead, for the ensuing century, the American legal system continued to tolerate violence in marriage as it did not in other relationships. As we will see, it was possible for lawmakers and jurists to condone wife beating even as they condemned the chastisement prerogative because lawmakers and jurists had begun to reason about the regulation of marital violence in a new conceptual framework.

Regulating Domestic Violence in an Era of Companionate Marriage

In the world of Blackstone's *Commentaries*, marriage was a hierarchical relationship in which a husband ruled over his wife and other members of the household. Yet by the nineteenth century, this authority-based conception of marriage had begun to lose its persuasive power—a development that clearly contributed to the demise of the chastisement prerogative. For example, treatise author James Schouler observed in 1870 that there was a tension between the hierarchical premises of chastisement doctrine and contemporary conceptions of marriage: "In a ruder state of society the husband frequently maintained his authority by force. . . . *But [in recent times] the wife has been regarded more as the companion of her husband*; and this right of chastisement may be regarded as exceedingly questionable at the present day. *The rule of love has superseded the rule of force.*"[19] The shift in popular understandings of marriage that Schouler's treatise registers had important consequences for the way in which jurists reasoned about a husband's marital authority. Nineteenth-century jurists did not deny that a husband had authority over his wife; instead, as Schouler's treatise illustrates, they insisted that a husband rule his household by love rather than by force. This mingling of authority and affect-based conceptions of marriage shaped the body of marital status law that emerged in the wake of chastisement's demise.

As jurists began to reason about domestic violence within the discourse of companionate marriage, they developed a new framework for analyzing the regulation of wife beating. Judges who would no longer defend the husband's right to inflict corporal punishment on his wife began instead to emphasize that the law should promote *domestic harmony* between husband and wife and protect the *privacy* of the marriage relationship.

THE DISCOURSE OF AFFECTIVE PRIVACY IN DOMESTIC ASSAULT LAW

The discourse of affective privacy, a new mode of reasoning about the regulation of marital violence, made its earliest appearance in American case law as a *justification* for the right of chastisement. For example, when North Carolina upheld the right of chastisement in *State v. Black*,[20] the court justified the prerogative on two grounds: the husband's authority over his wife ("[a] husband is responsible for the acts of his wife, and he is required to govern his household") and the need to shield domestic conflicts from public scrutiny ("the law will not invade the domestic forum or go behind the curtain").[21] In *Black*, the traditional hierarchy-based rationale for chastisement law was intermingled with new rationales couched in the discourse of affective privacy: "public exhibition in the court-house of such quarrels and fights between man and wife widens the breach, makes reconciliation almost impossible, and encourages insubordination."[22]

Such arguments began to play an even more prominent role in the regulation of marital violence when North Carolina repudiated the doctrine of chastisement in the 1868 case of *State v. Rhodes*.[23] In *Rhodes*, the North Carolina Supreme Court declined to enforce an assault and battery charge against a man who assaulted his wife. The court repudiated the chastisement prerogative but then granted the wife beater immunity from criminal prosecution, justifying this new immunity policy in the rhetoric of affective privacy:

> [H]owever great are the evils of ill temper, quarrels, and even personal conflicts inflicting only temporary pain, they are not comparable with the evils which would result from raising the curtain, and exposing to public curiosity and criticism, the nursery and the bed chamber. Every household has and must have, a government of its own, modelled to suit the temper, disposition and condition of its inmates. Mere ebullitions of passion, impulsive violence, and temporary pain, affection will soon forget and forgive; and each member will find excuse for the other in his own frailties. But when trifles are taken hold of by the public, and the parties are exposed and disgraced, and each endeavors to justify himself or herself by criminating the other, that which ought to be forgotten in a day, will be remembered for life.[24]

As the court summed up the new doctrine six years later in a much-quoted opinion: "If no permanent injury has been inflicted, nor malice, cruelty nor dangerous violence shown by the husband, *it is better to draw the curtain, shut out the public gaze, and leave the parties to forget and forgive.*"[25] Thus, North Carolina courts abrogated a husband's prerogative to chastise his wife but supplanted it with an immunity from prosecution that coincided with the scope of the former prerogative. The law of chastisement was thus translated into a body of doctrine that comported with the logic of companionate marriage.

The concern for privacy that appears in these North Carolina cases does not seem to have played a significant role in the development of criminal law in the late nineteenth century—perhaps because criminal prosecution of wife beaters during this era was focused on controlling men of the "lower classes," men whose privacy needs elites scarcely recognized, much less sought to protect. But privacy-based reasoning about domestic violence did shape the development of private law in the late nineteenth century, playing a key role in the law of intentional torts as it emerged from reform by the married women's property acts. It was in the law of torts that privacy-based reasoning about marital violence flourished before returning to shape the criminal law during the early twentieth century.

PRIVACY IN THE EMERGING LAW OF
INTERSPOUSAL TORT IMMUNITY

While it was clear by the second half of the nineteenth century that wife beating was a crime, it was not at all clear that this same conduct constituted a tort. A criminal prosecution for wife beating was brought against a husband by the state, whereas a tort claim was prosecuted by the married woman herself. Could a battered wife bring suit against her husband in order to vindicate her own injuries without depending on the state to intervene and protect her? The question was startling to those versed in common-law understandings of marriage. The same body of common law that vested a husband with the prerogative to chastise his wife also denied a married woman the right to file suit without her husband's consent and joinder.[26] Interspousal litigation violated fundamental precepts of the doctrine of marital unity.

But if the prospect of a wife's suing her husband contravened the most basic common-law concepts of marriage, it was also an inevitable outgrowth of common-law reform in the mid-nineteenth century—a period when the doctrine of marital unity was undergoing statutory modification under the pressure of feminist advocacy. Courts asked to determine whether wife beating was a tort had to interpret the marriage reform legislation whose enactment the woman's rights movement had advocated. Among the many rights these laws gave married women was the right to file suit without their husbands' joinder and the right to collect tort damages for injuries to their persons and property. Under these reform statutes, could a wife now bring a tort suit against a husband who assaulted her and collect money damages? The question presented women as agents of their own vindication in a dual sense: a plaintiff sought redress for her injury without relying on the state to protect her, and she did so under the authority of legislation enacted in response to feminist advocacy.

The law of torts differed from the criminal law in one other respect relevant to our analysis of the development of modern domestic assault law. A wife was likely to bring a suit for money damages against a husband who assaulted her only in circumstances in which there were assets to redistribute within the family. Thus, as jurists would surely recognize, it was married men of the middle and upper classes who might face tort claims for wife beating—precisely those men who were unlikely to face criminal prosecution for wife beating during the late nineteenth century.

With these gender- and class-salient features to recommend it, the new tort claim was not well received. Regardless of whether a husband beat, choked, stabbed, or shot his wife, all courts that heard such tort claims initially rejected them. (This doctrine of "interspousal tort immunity" survived well into the twentieth century and still remains law in a number of states today.)[27]

The Supreme Court of Maine was one of the first to synthesize the "domestic harmony" and "privacy" rationales in a tort case decided in 1877. In *Abbott v. Abbott*, a woman sued her ex-husband in tort, alleging that he violently assaulted her. The Maine court ruled that the plaintiff could not recover tort damages from her ex-husband. The court acknowledged that "there has been for many years a gradual evolution of the law going on, for the amelioration of the married woman's condition, until it is now undoubtedly, the law of England and of all the American states that the husband has no right to strike his wife, to punish her, under any circumstances or provocation whatever."[28] Yet, after repudiating the right of chastisement, the court declared that a husband was immune from tort liability for assaulting his wife. To support this view, the court quoted an opinion of the North Carolina Supreme Court explaining why a husband should be immune from criminal prosecution for beating his wife : " '[I]t is better to draw the curtain, shut out the public gaze, and leave the parties to forget and forgive.' ''[29] Asserting that a tort remedy was not "desirable" as a wife could seek relief in the criminal courts, or seek a divorce on grounds of cruelty, the court observed that "[i]t would be a poor policy for the law to grant the remedy asked for in this case," for "[t]he private matters of the whole period of married existence might be exposed by suits" and "this would add a new method by which estates could be plundered."[30]

When the U.S. Supreme Court construed the District of Columbia's married woman's property act in 1910, it invoked both a "privacy" and a "domestic harmony" rationale for interspousal tort immunity.[31] The Court asserted that Congress had not intended to give spouses the capacity to sue each other;[32] it then observed that allowing intramarital suits would "open the doors of the courts to accusations of all sorts of one spouse against the other, and bring into public notice complaints for assault, slander and libel" and questioned whether "the exercise of such jurisdisction would be promotive of the public welfare and domestic harmony."[33] By the early twentieth century, numerous state supreme courts had barred wives from suing their husbands for intentional torts typically on the grounds that "the tranquility of family relations" would be "disturbed by dragging into court for judicial investigation at the suit of a peevish, fault-finding husband, or at the suit of the nagging, ill-tempered wife, *matters of no serious moment, which if permitted to slumber in the home closet would silently be forgiven or forgotten.*"[34]

It is important to observe that courts developed the doctrine of interspousal tort immunity in response to the *reform* of the common law. As the common law was slowly modified by statute and judicial decision, courts had to explain anomalies in the law of marital status that simply did not exist before. At common law, a wife lacked capacity to sue anyone without her husband's joinder, so her inability to sue her husband was hardly in need of explanation. But once a married woman was granted the right to sue in tort for injuries to property or person, courts had to decide whether she could sue her husband and, if not, to explain why not. All courts that faced the claim initially ruled against it, with some explaining the emergent law of interspousal tort immunity by invoking the doctrine of marital unity. But because the doctrine of unity was itself under attack, courts sought *new* grounds on which to justify the immunity bar. "Privacy" supplied grounds on which to justify interspousal tort immunity—grounds that were seemingly independent of the increasingly discredited language of marital hierarchy. And so the discourse of marital status began to shift from the rhetoric of "marital unity" to the rhetoric of "privacy" and "domestic harmony."

Thus, judges seeking to explain the modified structure of marital status law increasingly drew upon gender concepts of the industrial era to explain the law of marriage in more contemporary and socially credible terms. Rather than represent marriage in the biblical discourse of "one flesh," as a relation that "merged" wife with husband, courts instead discussed marriage as it was understood in nineteenth-century America: as a companionate relationship based on an affective bond that flourished best in a sphere separate from civil society. Some judges even went so far as to depict the marriage relation as situated in a home with heavily curtained windows: thus, a court would not hear a wife's suit for damages against a husband who battered her because public policy counseled that "it is better to draw the curtain, shut out the public gaze, and leave the parties to forget and forgive."[35] With this shift to privacy talk, a husband's marital prerogatives could be preserved in new juridical form—as legal immunities.

Once courts ceased to rely on the rhetoric of marital unity and began to discuss marriage in the language of privacy and affect, they no longer had to explain the law of marriage as enforcing relations of hierarchy. Instead, courts could explain the law of marriage as preserving relations of *altruism*. If a wife suffered a beating at the hands of her husband, "it is better to . . . leave the parties to forget and forgive."[36] As the North Carolina Supreme Court observed: "[The law] drops the curtain upon scenes of domestic life, preferring not to take cognizance of what transpires within that circle, to the exposure of public prosecution. It presumes that acts of wrong committed in passsion will be followed by contrition and atonement in a cooler moment, and forgiveness will blot it out of memory."[37] In short, it was no longer necessary to justify a husband's acts of abuse as the lawful prerogatives of a master. Rather, the state granted a husband immunity to abuse his wife in order to foster the altruistic ethos of the private realm. In this way, laws that protected relations of domination could be justified as promoting relations of love. The regulation of marital violence was thus translated into the language of companionate marriage prevailing during the industrial era.

PRIVACY IN THE CRIMINAL LAW OF
DOMESTIC ASSAULT

By the beginning of the twentieth century, this new mode of reasoning about marital violence traveled from tort law to criminal law and found institutional expression in the criminal justice system. During this period, cities began to establish special domestic relations courts staffed by social workers to handle complaints of marital violence; by 1920 most major cities had such courts. The family court system sought to decriminalize marital violence. The underlying theory of this special court system, a New York City judge explained, was that "domestic trouble cases are not criminal in a legal sense."[38] Rather than arrest or punish those who assaulted their partners, the judge and social workers urged couples to reconcile, providing informal or formal counseling designed to preserve the relationship whenever possible. Battered wives were discouraged from filing criminal charges against their husbands, urged to accept responsibility for their role in provoking the violence, and encouraged to remain in the relationship and rebuild it rather than attempt to separate or divorce. The police adjusted their arrest procedures to accord with the new philosophy of the domestic relations courts, channeling family violence cases out of the criminal justice system and into counseling whenever possible. In this institutional framework, physical assault was not viewed as criminal conduct; instead, it was viewed as an expression of emotions that needed to be adjusted and rechanneled into marriage.

Regulation of marital violence continued in this "therapeutic" framework for much of the twentieth century. There was no formal immunity rule as in tort law, but the criminal justice system developed a set of informal procedures for handling marital violence—which it justified in the discourse of affective privacy. In the 1960s, for example, the training bulletin of the International Association of Chiefs of Police offered the following instructions for handling "family disturbances":

For the most part these disputes are personal matters requiring no direct police action. However, an inquiry into the facts must be made to satisfy the originating complaint. . . . Once inside the home, the officer's sole purpose is to *preserve the peace . . . [a]ttempt to soothe feelings, pacify parties . . .* [s]uggest parties refer their problem to a church or a community agency. . . . In dealing with family disputes *the power of arrest should be exercised as a last resort. The officer should never create a police problem when there is only a family problem existing.*[39]

Until the last decade, this set of instructions was quite typical of police procedure in American cities. For example, in California, the Oakland Police Department's 1975 "Training Bulletin on Techniques of Dispute Intervention" asserted that *"[t]he police role in a dispute situation is more often that of a mediator and peacemaker than enforcer of law. . . .* Normally, officers should adhere to the policy that that arrests shall be avoided . . . but when one of the parties demands arrest, you should . . . encourage the parties to reason with each other."[40]

It was not until the late 1970s that the contemporary women's rights movement mounted an effective challenge to this regime. Today, after numerous protest activities and lawsuits, there are shelters for battered women and their children, new arrest procedures for police departments across the country, and even federal legislation making gender-motivated assaults a civil rights violation.[41] Yet as the U.S. surgeon general recently found, battering of women by husbands, ex-husbands, and lovers remains the single largest cause of injury to women in the United States today.[42]

Notwithstanding profound changes in the laws and mores of marriage since the turn of the century, Americans still reason about marital violence in terms of privacy. O. J. Simpson invoked this tradition in 1989 when he shouted at police who had responded to his wife's call for help: "The police have been out here eight times before, and now you're going to arrest me for this? *This is a family matter. Why do you want to make a big deal out of it when we can handle it?*"[43] The chief justice of the United States invoked this discourse of the private when he objected to provisions in the new Violence against Women Act[44] that create a federal cause of action for gender-motivated violence. The bill's "broad definition of criminal conduct is so open-ended, and the new private right of action so sweeping," Chief Justice William H. Rehnquist complained, "that the legislation *could involve the federal courts in a whole host of domestic relations disputes.*"[45]

Civil Rights Reform and the Modernization of Status Discourse

In this essay I have attempted to demonstrate that some kinds of privacy talk are properly understood as modern expressions of the putatively discredited doctrine of marital unity. There is no necessary connection here, only a historically contingent one. But the connection is terribly important to observe for just that reason. Status talk is mutable and remarkably adaptable: it will evolve as the rule structure of a status regime evolves. In the ensuing sections I reflect briefly on the significance of this observation for our understanding of civil rights reform, both historical and contemporary.

Historical Perspectives

Status regimes are not static but dynamic—revitalized from time to time as they are reshaped by diverse political forces and draw on evolving social mores. For example, in the decades after the Civil War, a regime of racial status built on the law of chattel slavery evolved in rule structure and rhetoric into the form of American apartheid known as "Jim Crow." The law of de jure segregation differed from chattel slavery in its constitutive rules (so that former slaves were subject to a different set of labor codes and restrictions on their civil liberties); it is less commonly observed that the law of de jure segregation also differed from chattel slavery, at least in part, in the rhetorics employed to justify its constitutive rules. During the aptly named "Reconstruction" era, overtly hierarchy-based justifications offered for chattel slavery began to give way to justifications for apartheid that drew upon racial discourses of the private. Thus, in *Plessy v. Ferguson*, the Supreme Court upheld racial segregation under the Fourteenth Amendment by reasoning that racial equality did not require "an enforced commingling of the two races":[46]

> The object of the amendment was undoubtedly to enforce the absolute equality of the two races before the law, but in the nature of things it could not have been intended to abolish distinctions based upon color, or to enforce social, as distinguished from political equality, or a commingling of the two races upon terms unsatisfactory to either. . . . If the two races are to meet upon terms of social equality, it must be the result of natural affinities, a mutual appreciation of each other's merits and a voluntary consent of individuals.[47]

The racial discourse of the private that the Court invoked in *Plessy* differed from the discourses of affective privacy employed to rationalize elements of marital status law during the same period but functioned in strikingly similar ways: to explain laws enforcing status privileges, once justified in overtly hierarchy-based discourses, with reference to other, less contested, social values.

There were significant differences in the rules and rhetoric that were employed to enforce racial status relations under chattel slavery and under Jim Crow. Yet it plainly would be wrong to overlook the elements of continuity between regimes. During Reconstruction, the legal system still played a significant role in maintaining the differences in material and dignitary privilege that constituted "the two races," although it now did so by means of a new cluster of rules and rhetorics. In short, Jim Crow was a successor to chattel slavery that enforced the status relations we call "race" by somewhat less formalized means. I call this dynamic of preservation through transformation in the structure of a status regime "deformalization" or "modernization."

Modernization of a status regime occurs when a legal system enforces social stratification by means that change over time. One commonly recognized way that law enforces social stratification is by according groups hierarchically differentiated entitlements and obligations. In antebellum America, the law of slavery and marriage enforced race and gender hierarchy by such overt means. But by the Reconstruction era, the law of race and gender status had begun, slowly, to evolve, in diverse ways eschewing the overtly hierarchical forms of the antebellum period. In this era, the legal system continued to draw distinctions on the basis of race and gender, but it now began to emphasize formal equality of entitlements in relationships once explicitly organized as relationships of mastery and subordination and to repudiate openly caste-based justifications for such group-based distinctions as the law continued to enforce. While the American legal system continued to distribute social goods and privileges in ways that favored whites and males, it now began self-consciously to disavow its role in doing so. The new interest in rule equality and the energy devoted to explaining law without recourse to overtly caste-based justifications mark an important shift in the mode of regulating race and gender relations, a deformalization and concomitant modernization of status law.

Civil rights agitation plays a significant role in precipitating the modernization of status regimes. Abolitionist protest (and a civil war) contributed to the modernization of racial-status law during the Reconstruction era, just as the woman's rights protest contributed to the modernization of gender-status law during this same period. If successful, protest of this sort will draw the legitimacy of a status regime into question and so bring pressure to bear on lawmakers and other legal elites to cede status privileges. In such circumstances, legal elites may begin to cede status privileges, but they will also defend them. They will initially defend privileges within the traditional rhetoric of the status regime—but because the traditional rhetoric of the status regime is now socially contested, they will begin to search for "new reasons" to justify those status privileges they choose to defend. As reform of the common-law marital-status rules illustrates, this process of ceding and defending status privileges will result in changes in the constitutive rules of the regime and in its justificatory rhetoric—with the result that, over time, status relationships will be translated from an older, socially contested idiom into a newer, more socially acceptable idiom. In short, civil rights reform is an important engine of social change. Yet civil rights reform does not simply abolish a status regime; in important respects, it modernizes the rules and rhetoric through which status relations are enforced and justified.

The dynamic of preservation through transformation that I am describing need not arise through the conspiratorial or malevolent motivations of the legal elites directing reform. Indeed, we can posit for purposes of argument that the legal elites who implement these changes in the constitutive rules and rhetoric of a status regime are acting in "good faith." For example, I assume that the judges who repudiated marital chastisement, yet developed the interspousal tort immunity doctrine to constrain interpretation of the married women's property acts, did not snicker in the robing room in gleeful appreciation of their interpretive sophistry. They could well have harbored the good-faith conviction that privacy and domestic harmony were important social values that required protection as they superintended the marriage relation through a period of turbulent legal transformation. Thus, as judges contemplated the question of whether the reform statutes granting married women a tort claim for injury to their persons and property should be construed to enable wives to sue their husbands, judges could well have decided, in all sincerity, that considerations of "public policy" warranted interpreting the statutes to bar the claim.

Yet it also seems clear that, as educated, propertied men, judges reasoned about this question within certain legal traditions and from a certain social position that predisposed them to certain legal conclusions. Judges who initially adopted the tort immunity rule openly embraced it as preserving elements of the doctrine of marital unity; only as the doctrine of marital unity was progressively discredited did courts come to rely exclusively on justifications couched in the discourse of affective privacy. Moreover, given the social position from which judges reasoned about "public policy," they were far more likely to appreciate the benefits of the tort immunity rule (to propertied husbands) than to register its costs (to battered wives)—a phenomenon Paul Brest has elegantly dubbed "selective sympathy and indifference."[48] Of course, we can assume that at least some of these judges had the critical faculties to discern, and thus to correct for, the biases to which their deliberative processes were subject. Sometimes, however, critical oblivion is bliss, especially when it is interest-convergent.

Does this inquiry into the modernization of status regimes turn out to be a story about stasis after all? Is Jim Crow slavery by another name and the network of formal and informal immunities for wife beating that emerged during Reconstruction the functional equivalent of chastisement? As I indicated at the outset of this discussion, I believe that the dynamic I am describing can fairly be called one of preservation through transformation or characterized in any way that indicates that elements of continuity *and* change are at stake in the process. A body of status law is modernized when its rules and rhetoric are reformed, and yet the law continues to distribute material and dignitary privileges in ways that maintain the distinctions constituting the regime (e.g., "race" or "gender") in relatively continuous terms. Modernization of a status regime may nonetheless bring about perceptible, even significant, changes in status relations. For example, we can posit that African Americans were "better off" under a regime of Jim Crow than a regime of chattel slavery, certainly in terms of dignitary values and possibly in terms of their material welfare as well. Similarly, we can posit that married women were "better off" under a regime of formal and informal immunities for wife beating, certainly in terms of dignitary values and possibly in terms of their material welfare as well.

There is, however, one way in which members of each group were indisputably worse off: in their capacity to achieve further, welfare-enhancing reform of the status regime in which they were subordinated. By the mid-nineteenth century, slavery and marital-status law (chastisement, in particular) were socially contested and substantially discredited practices. They lacked legitimacy in the eyes of many. But once racial-status law and marital-status law were reformed in the Reconstruction era, each status regime gained substantially in legitimacy. As each regime was translated from contested rules and rhetorics into more contemporary rules and rhetorics, each was again "naturalized" as just and reasonable, in significant part because each was now formally and substantively distinguishable from its contested predecessor: each could be justified in terms of social values that were distinct from the orthodox, hierarchy-based norms that characterized its predecessor (slavery, marriage) as a regime of mastery. Considered from this perspective, we can see that civil rights reform may alleviate certain dignitary or material aspects of the inequalities that subordinated groups suffer; *but we can also see that civil rights reform may enhance the legal system's capacity to legitimate residual social inequalities among status-differentiated groups.*

Of course, struggle persists, and oftentimes subordinated groups can exploit the semantic instability of status discourses for their own resistance purposes. After many decades, the rhetoric of separate but equal was turned against Jim Crow, and the discourse of privacy developed a constitutional life that would have startled the nineteenth-century judiciary. It might seem that such developments would tend ultimately to destabilize regimes of race and gender status. Yet the dynamic runs in both directions. Protest or resistance discourses are semantically unstable as well, with the result that rhetorics employed by recent civil rights movements to challenge laws enforcing race-and gender-status relationships are now being turned to *status-preserving* ends. As the recent life of the color-blindness trope illustrates, civil rights rhetoric can supply "legitimate," "nondiscriminatory" reasons for opposing affirmative action and other group-conscious initiatives intended to remedy racial and gender inequalities. This change in the political valence of civil rights discourse—a phenomenon Jack Balkin calls "ideological drift"[49]—occurs as those who oppose current efforts to rectify race and gender stratification seek to justify their opposition in terms that can be differentiated from a naked interest in preserving race and gender stratification. Although many justifications might suffice for these purposes, claiming fidelity to principles of equality would seem to provide an unimpeachable reason for opposing group-conscious efforts to rectify race and gender stratification. The language of color-blindness can now be appropriated for these purposes, because the rule structure of contemporary race- and gender-status law has changed in response to demands for color-and sex-blindness that have been advanced by the civil rights movement over the last several decades, and government rarely employs race-and gender-conscious regulation any more, except for the purpose of alleviating social stratification. Under such circumstances, old protest discourses (such as color-blindness) are especially susceptible to capture, "drift," or co-optation, as they justify adherence to the status quo in terms that are especially difficult to impugn. As I observed at the outset of this discussion, status talk is mutable and remarkably adaptable and will evolve as the rule structure of a status regime evolves.[50]

Contemporary Perspectives

To what extent is the legal system responsible for the continuing race and gender stratification of American society? Today it is commonplace to distinguish between de jure and de facto discrimination—and to attribute some aspects of race and gender stratification to state action and others to "social" factors that might reflect "the continuing effects of past discrimination." Largely unarticulated in such accounts of de jure and de facto discrimination is any theory about what kinds of state action are discriminatory, or status enforcing. Most often it is tacitly assumed that race- or gender-specific state action is status enforcing, whereas so-called facially neutral state action is not.

This way of reasoning about the de jure–de facto distinction has its roots in equal protection doctrines requiring "heightened scrutiny" of race- or gender-specific state action. Under the pressure of this constitutional requirement, laws that only recently were cast in race- or gender-specific terms have been revised so that they are now cleansed of any race- or gender-specific references. As a consequence, the persisting race and gender stratification of American life is commonly (and often legally) attributed to "the continuing effects of past discrimination" rather than to current, "facially neutral" forms of state action.

There is little in contemporary equal protection doctrine that challenges this view. The Court will hear arguments that race- or sex-based state action is discriminatory; otherwise it requires plaintiffs to prove that facially neutral state action is motivated by a discriminatory purpose.[51] Yet the Court has construed "discriminatory purpose" to be a state of mind akin to malice,[52] and, as the Court itself has acknowledged, it is exceedingly difficult to prove "discriminatory purpose" once it is defined in this way: lawmakers can always articulate socially benign (or at least nonmalicious) reasons for policies they adopt that may "incidentally" perpetuate status inequalities among groups. Cumulatively, this body of equal protection doctrine has given lawmakers a strong incentive to change the rule structure of policies that long enforced racial or gender stratification and to articulate "legitimate, nondiscriminatory reasons" for those policies in order to immunize them from further equal protection challenge.

Thus, the civil rights revolutions of the 1960s and 1970s precipitated a shift in the rule structure and justificatory rhetoric of laws that long played a role in enforcing race- and gender-status relations. Given that today most state action has been cleansed of race- and gender-specific references, can we assume, as both the Supreme Court and the American public seemingly have, that by virtue of these reforms, the state has generally withdrawn from the business of enforcing race- and gender-status relations?

We might consider this question by examining how equal protection doctrines of heightened scrutiny have affected law enforcement policies regulating marital violence. Although general criminal assault statutes were often used to regulate "domestic disturbances," it was also commonplace for judicial opinions, statutes, and law enforcement policies to refer to the conduct as "wife beating" or otherwise to discuss the parties involved in gender-specific terms. After 1976, when the Court decided in *Craig v. Boren*[53] that sex-based state action would be subject to a heightened or intermediate standard of review under the equal protection clause of the Fourteenth Amendment, all this began to change. Residual gender-specific references were deleted from the law and replaced with gender-neutral language, with the result that the conduct is now generally referred to as "spousal assault" or "domestic violence." (To be sure, in this era many feminists advocated the use of gender-neutral language in domestic violence policies, *in the course of seeking reform of their substantive norms*; lawmakers readily adopted the gender-neutral language and moved far more slowly to revise the constitutive norms and procedures of their domestic violence policies.)

Now, when litigants challenge law enforcement policies providing lesser degrees of protection to victims of domestic violence, they have great difficulty proving that the policies are sexually discriminatory—despite the fact that it is women who are overwhelmingly the targets of assaults between intimates.[54] A number of federal circuit courts have ruled that facially neutral spousal assault policies are not subject to heightened standards of review under the equal protection clause (although such policies may constitute discrimination against married persons or cohabitants, subject to more deferential or "rational relation" review).[55] Because such policies are couched in gender-neutral terms, plaintiffs seeking to prove that the policies were animated by a sexually discriminatory purpose would have to show that they were adopted "at least in part because of, and not merely in spite of," their impact on women.[56] Similar problems in proving sex discrimination occur with equal protection challenges to the doctrine of interspousal tort immunity (which, as we have seen, was couched, from the outset, in formally gender-neutral terms), or to the exemption for "spousal" rape, or to rules giving "spouses" rights to the value of labor performed in the household.

In this way, modern doctrines of equal protection are effacing the gender-specific (or race-specific) antecedents of state policies that in their current, facially neutral form may well continue to enforce relations of gender or racial inequality. While modern equal protection law has served to disestablish certain forms of status-enforcing state action, in many cases, the changes equal protection doctrines effected were at best superficial.[57]

Consider the domestic violence policies we have examined. The threat of equal protection litigation prompted the deletion of gender-specific references from the law; once "sanitized" in this way, such policies have become exceedingly difficult to challenge with existing constitutional tools, even when their historically rooted norms remain intact and substantially unquestioned. Under the case law we have just surveyed, a municipality defending a facially neutral domestic violence policy against an equal protection claim need show only that the policy is rationally related to some legitimate state purpose and was not adopted "because of" its "adverse effects" on women. To say the least, this showing does not require municipalities to make significant changes in the structure of their policies—even if the facially neutral policies continue to treat victims of assaults by intimates differently than other victims of assault. In *Siddle v. City of Cambridge*,[58] the court found that the city's proffered justifications did in fact pass the rational-basis test:

> The state puts forth several justifications for any differences that may exist. These justifications fulfill the rational basis test, and reach the level of an important state objective. *The first is that the criminal area may not be the best place to resolve marital problems of this sort. The government needs flexibility so that all of its resources, including mental health agencies, can rectify the situation.* Often criminal sanctions alone are ineffective. *Moreover, domestic violence situation [sic] are different from other forms of criminal behavior in their complex emotional causes of behavior....* The government need not treat cases as the same, because it would be unproductive, and possibility counter-productive, to do so.[59]

The justifications accepted by this court as satisfying the rational relation (and even intermediate scrutiny) test should be quite familiar. The reasons supplied are conventional expressions of the discourse of affective privacy, which has been used to justify criminal law policies on domestic violence since the Progressive Era— *reasons for affording informal immunity to assaults between intimates that would not obtain in other contexts.* The analytical framework of equal protection cases such as these merely serves to rationalize a body of laws whose normative roots can be traced to the ancient doctrine of marital chastisement. For close to two decades now, the modern feminist movement has protested the inadequacy of domestic violence policies but, in the course of this work, has received considerably less assistance from the Constitution's promise of equal protection of the laws than the lineage of the policies would seem to warrant.

There are certain modifications to equal protection doctrine that could make it supple enough to police for bias in the new forms of "facially neutral" state action it has helped bring into being. For instance, the Court might revise the doctrinal criteria that define race-and sex-based state action for purposes of triggering heightened scrutiny. Given the lineage of "spousal" assault policies, why should the mere use of gender-neutral language immunize the policies from heightened scrutiny? Or the Court might revise the much-criticized doctrines of discriminatory purpose that plaintiffs must use to challenge facially neutral policies and practices. Given the history of marital violence regulation, why must a plaintiff show that a facially neutral spousal assault policy was adopted "because of" its "adverse effects" on women? This requirement seems especially perverse in an "equal rights" era, when policymakers conventionally supply "legitimate, nondiscriminatory" reasons for their actions.

Unfortunately, as currently constituted, the Court shows scant interest in revising equal protection doctrines of heightened scrutiny and discriminatory purpose. This body of constitutional law once served to dismantle status-enforcing state action, but, because of its very success in precipitating the reform—*and modernization*— of status-enforcing state action, the doctrines often serve to rationalize rather than scrutinize the new, facially neutral forms of status-enforcing state action they helped bring into being.

Conclusion

As this essay has demonstrated, status law is dynamic and evolves in rule structure and rhetoric under the pressure of civil rights reform. In the nineteenth century, when judges repudiated a husband's common-law prerogative to chastise his wife, they began to grant wife beaters a variety of formal and informal immunities from public and private prosecution. Just as the doctrine of chastisement was rationalized by rhetorics of hierarchy, this new regime of immunity rules was rationalized by rhetorics of interiority: by a discourse of affective privacy that invoked the feelings and spaces of domesticity to justify the law of marital status in an era of companionate marriage.

In short, as this essay has illustrated, emotions have a history, and their discursive roots can be traced—if only in small part—to the nineteenth-century courtroom, where the discourse of affective privacy served to make "reasonable" marital-status doctrines when talk of marital unity no longer could. There, judges invoking the discourse of affective privacy translated the hierarchy-based chastisement doctrine into immunity rules couched in a more modern idiom: "If no permanent injury has been inflicted, nor malice, cruelty nor dangerous violence shown by the husband, *it is better to draw the curtain, shut out the public gaze, and leave the parties to forget and forgive.*"[60] The American antidiscrimination tradition pays scant attention to these chameleon-like qualities of status talk; it has reified the phenomena it calls "sex discrimination" and "race discrimination," without attending to their dynamic character. But this study of marital violence law demonstrates that status discourse is mutable, evolving as it is contested over the course of the centuries. If civil rights reform is to be effective, civil rights law must continually adapt, striving to remain in critical dialogue with the evolving rules and rhetoric of any status regime it aspires to disestablish.

NOTES

This chapter is drawn in part from " 'The Rule of Love': Wife Beating as Prerogative and Privacy," *Yale Law Journal* 105 (1996): 2117–2207.

1. William Blackstone, *Commentaries*, vol. 1 (Chicago: University of Chicago Press, 1979), 441; see, e.g., Norma Basch, *In the Eyes of the Law: Women, Marriage, and Property in Ninetenth-Century New York* (Ithaca: Cornell University Press, 1982), 51–52.

2. Blackstone, *Commentaries*, 444.

3. See Daniel Boorstin, *The Mysterious Science of the Law: An Essay on Blackstone's Commentaries* (Cambridge, Mass.: Harvard University Press, 1941), 1.

4. See, e.g., James Kent, *Commentaries on American Law*, vol. 2 (New York: E. B. Clayton, 1840), 180; Francis Wharton, *A Treatise on the Criminal Law of the United States* (Pittsburgh: James Kay, Jr. & Brother, 1846), 314.

5. For early American cases recognizing the right of chastisement, see *Helms v. Franciscus*, 2 Bland 544, 562 n. (Md. Ch. 1840) (quoting *Bread's Case*, Chancery Proceedings, lib. C.D. fol. 319 [1681]; *Bradley v. State*, 1 Miss. (Walk.) 156, 158 (1824); *State v. Black*, 60 N.C. 262 (1864); *State v. Buckley*, 2 Del. (2 Harr.) 552 (1838); *Richards v. Richards*, 1 Grant's Cases 389, 392–93 (Pa. 1856); *Adams v. Adams*, 100 Mass. 365, 369–70 (1868).

6. For an overview of the historiography on the reform of marital status law in nineteenth-century America, see Reva Siegel, "The Modernization of Marital Status Law: Adjudicating Wives' Rights to Earnings, 1860–1930," *Georgetown Law Journal* 82 (1994): 2127, 2132–41.

7. *Report of the Woman's Rights Convention, Held at Seneca Falls, N.Y., July 19 & 20, 1848* (Rochester, N.Y.: John Dick, 1848), 6 (emphasis added).

8. For an illustration of the slow progress of common-law reform, see Siegel, "Marital Status Law," 2149–57; Reva Siegel, "Home As Work: The First Woman's Rights Claims Concerning Wives' Household Labor, 1850–1880," *Yale Law Journal* 103 (1994): 1073, 1167–77.

9. Jerome Nadelhaft, "Wife Torture: A Known Phenomenon in Nineteenth-Century America," *Journal of American Culture* 10 (1987): 39, 42.

10. C. C. H. of East Orange, New Jersey, "Crimes against Women," *Woman's Journal* (December 25, 1875): 413.

11. Henry B. Blackwell, "Crimes of a Single Day," *Woman's Journal* (January 29, 1876): 34.

12. Elizabeth Pleck, *Domestic Tyranny: The Making of American Social Policy against Family Violence from Colonial Times to the Present* (New York: Oxford University Press,

1987), 100; Elizabeth Pleck, "Feminist Responses to 'Crimes against Women,' 1868–1896," *Signs* 8 (1983): 451, 462–65.

13. *Fulgam v. State*, 46 Ala. 143, 146 (1871).

14. Elizabeth Pleck, "The Whipping Post for Wife Beaters, 1876–1906," in *Essays on the Family and Historical Change*, ed. David Levine et al. (College Station: Texas A&M University Press, 1983), 127.

15. See, e.g., Chester Vernier, *American Family Laws*, vol. 2, sec. 66 (London: Oxford University Press, 1932) (quoting, by state, statutory definitions of cruelty as grounds for divorce).

16. See, e.g., *Bailey v. Bailey*, 97 Mass. 373, 379 (1867) ("Among the lower classes, blows sometimes pass between married couples who in the main are happy, and have no desire to part. Amidst very coarse habits . . . a word and a blow go together") (quoting Shelford, *Marriage and Divorce*, sec. 764, at 428).

17. On the defense of provocation, see, e.g., *Knight v. Knight*, 31 Ia. 451 (1871). On the defense of condonation, see, e.g., *Davies v. Davies*, 37 N.Y. 45, 46, 48 (1869).

18. See, e.g. Pleck, "The Whipping Post," 135–36. For more extended discussion of race and class bias in the prosecution of wife beaters in this era, see Reva B. Siegel, " 'The Rule of Love': Wife Beating as Prerogative and Privacy," *Yale Law Journal* 105 (1996): 2117, 2134–41.

19. James Schouler, *A Treatise on the Law of Domestic Relations; Embracing Husband and Wife, Parent and Child, Guardian and Ward, Infancy, and Master and Servant* (Boston: Little, Brown & Co., 1870), 59 (emphasis added).

20. 60 N.C. 262 (1864).

21. Ibid.

22. Ibid.

23. 61 N.C. (Phil. Law) 453 (1868).

24. Ibid. at 457.

25. *State v. Oliver*, 70 N.C. 60, 61–62 (1874) (emphasis added).

26. See Joseph Story, *Commentaries on Equity Pleadings, and the Incidents Thereof, According to the Practice of the Courts of Equity, of England and America*, 7th ed. (Boston: Little, Brown & Co., 1865), 54–55.

27. Carl Tobias, "Interspousal Tort Immunity in America," *Georgia Law Review* 23 (1989): 359, 383.

28. 67 Me. 304, 307 (1877).

29. Ibid. (quoting *State v. Oliver*, 70 N.C. 60, 61–62 [1874]).

30. Ibid. at 308.

31. *Thompson v. Thompson*, 218 U.S. 611 (1910).

32. Ibid. at 617.

33. Ibid. at 617–18.

34. *Drake v. Drake*, 177 N.W. 624, 625 (Minn. 1920) (emphasis added).

35. *Abbott v. Abbott*, 67 Me. 304, 307 (1877) (quoting *State v. Oliver*, 70 N.C. 60, 61–62 [1874]).

36. Ibid.

37. *State v. Fulton*, 63 S.E. 145, 145 (N.C. 1908) (quoting *State v. Edens*, 95 N.C. 693) (spousal tort immunity for slander).

38. Pleck, *Domestic Tyranny*, 137 (quoting Judge Bernhard Rabbino of New York City Court of Domestic Relations).

39. International Association of Police Chiefs, *Training Key No. 16, Handling Disturbance Calls* 1968–69), 94–95, quoted in Sue E. Eisenberg and Patricia L. Micklow, "The Assaulted Wife: 'Catch 22' Revisited," *Women's Rights Law Reporter* 3 (1977): 138, 156 (emphasis added).

40. Del Martin, *Battered Wives* (1981), 93–94 (emphasis added).

41. See Violence Against Women Act, Pub. L. No. 103-322, 108 Stat. 1796 (1994) (codified at 42 U.S.C. § 13,981 [1994]).

42. Joan Zorza, "The Criminal Law of Misdemeanor Domestic Violence, 1970–1990," *Journal of Criminal Law and Criminology* 83 (1992): 46, 46 (quoting Nikki R. Van Hightower and Susan A. McManus, "Limits of State Constitutional Guarantees: Lessons from Efforts to Implement Domestic Violence Policies," *Public Administrative Review* 49 [1982]: 269, 269).

43. Josh Meyer, "Police Records Detail 1989 Beating That Led to Charge; A Bloodied Nicole Simpson, Hiding in Bushes after 911 Call, Told Officers: 'He's Going to Kill Me.' Judge Overruled Prosecutors' Request That Simpson Serve Jail Time," *Los Angeles Times*, 17 June 1994, pt. A, 24 (emphasis added).

44. 42 U.S.C. § 13,981 (1994).

45. William Rehnquist, "Chief Justice's 1991 Year-End Report on the Federal Judiciary," *Third Branch*, January 1992, 3 (emphasis added), quoted in "Developments in Law: Legal Responses to Domestic Violence," *Harvard Law Review* 106 (1993): 1498, 1545–46.

46. 163 U.S. 537, 551 (1896).

47. Ibid. at 544, 551.

48. Paul Brest, "The Supreme Court, 1975 Term—Foreword: In Defense of the Antidiscrimination Principle," *Harvard Law Review* 90 (1976): 1, 7–8.

49. J. M. Balkin, "Ideological Drift and the Struggle over Meaning," *Connecticut Law Review* 25 (1993): 869, 872–73.

50. Of course, nothing in the account of modernization I offer requires that new status discourses be generated out of co-opted protest discourses. On the other hand, my account of the modernization of status regimes does explain why old protest discourses are especially attractive candidates for co-optation into status discourses. As I indicate in the text, old protest discourses provide seemingly unimpeachable grounds for defending the structure of a status regime when its legitimacy is under attack.

51. See *Washington v. Davis*, 426 U.S. 229 (1976).

52. See *Personnel Adm'r v. Feeney*, 442 U.S. 256, 279 (1979).

53. 429 U.S. 190 (1976).

54. The Justice Department has estimated that 90% to 95% of domestic violence victims are women. "Laws Mandating Reporting of Domestic Violence: Do They Promote Patient Well-Being?" *Journal of the American Medical Association* 273 (1995): 1781 (quoting U.S. Department of Justice, Bureau of Justice Statistics, *Violence between Intimates* [1994]).

55. The leading case in this area is *Hynson v. City of Chester Legal Dep't*, 864 F.2d 1026, 1031 (3d Cir. 1988).

56. See *Personnel Adm'r v. Feeney*, 442 U.S. 256, 279 (1979).

57. Making a race- or gender-specific law facially neutral may have very different consequences, depending on a variety of factors, including the nature of the law, the nature of the social practice it regulates, and the ways in which the regulated practice allocates dignitary and/or material privileges. Although the topic is far too vast to explore in the present context, the following examples should suffice to illustrate my point. Removing racial distinctions from a school assignment policy may facilitate the integration of a school system but will have less of an integration effect if the policy endorses "neighborhood" school assignments under conditions of residential segregation. Removing gender distinctions from a law conscripting persons for military service will facilitate the integration of the armed forces but will have less of an integration effect if the conscription policy specifies height, weight, and strength requirements that relatively few women can meet. Removing gender

distinctions from the law of rape will not much alter the social conditions under which rapes are practiced; nor will removing gender distinctions from domestic violence law much alter the practice of "spouse beating." Making such laws facially neutral does not alter the constraints on men who assault women; rather it extends the scope of the prohibition to include women. Presumably this reform will have a marginal deterrent effect on women's conduct but none on men's conduct. Nor is it clear what "symbolic" message is communicated by making gender-specific laws regulating gender-salient practices into gender-neutral laws. To disrupt the subordinating practice in these cases, it is necessary to alter the norms of the laws that regulate it. In short, formal equality will disrupt certain subordinating practices and leave others relatively undisturbed—possibly even masking the nature of the harm they are inflicting.

58. 761 F. Supp. 503 (S.D. Ohio 1991).

59. Ibid. at 512 (emphasis added).

60. *State v. Oliver*, 70 N.C. 60, 61–62 (1874) (criminal immunity case) (emphasis added), quoted in *Abbott v. Abbott*, 67 Me. 304, 307 (1877) (tort immunity case).

4

The Illusory Distinction between Equality of Opportunity and Equality of Result

DAVID A. STRAUSS

Our society should guarantee equality of opportunity, but not equality of result.''
The idea is a familiar one. Usually it is offered as part of a general attack on
government measures that redistribute wealth. The idea appears to be that the government's role is to ensure that everyone starts off from the same point, not that
everyone ends up in the same condition. If people have equal opportunities, what
they make of those opportunities is their responsibility. If they end up worse off,
the government should not intervene to help them.[1]

I want to suggest that the distinction between equality of opportunity and equality
of result is not a useful one. I do not mean to say that the notion of equality of
opportunity is an empty one; on the contrary, it is potentially a powerful and
important ideal. It is, however, much more complex than the proponents of the
distinction between ''opportunity'' and ''result'' acknowledge.

The most natural conception of equality of opportunity, which I discuss in the
second section of this chapter, is that equality of opportunity requires the elimination of barriers to advancement that are in some sense arbitrary. This conception
of equality of opportunity, however, requires large-scale redistributions of resources—perhaps not literal equality of results, in the sense that every person must
have the same resources, but a much closer approximation to that state than the
advocates of ''equality of opportunity, not result'' might suspect (and probably
much closer than anyone would desire). The central idea is familiar: talents and
abilities, the qualities that (ideally) are responsible for inequalities in results, are
in an important sense no less arbitrary than the barriers that any advocate of equality
of opportunity would want to eliminate.

In the third section, I will discuss a different conception of equality of opportunity, one that is perhaps closer to what the advocates of ''equality of opportunity,
not result'' have in mind. This conception sees equality of opportunity as a mer-

itocratic principle that allows, roughly speaking, the free operation of the market. According to this view, government actions that alter outcomes produced by the market derogate from equality of opportunity and can be viewed only as efforts to promote equality of result.

My argument is that the market-oriented meritocratic conception of equality of opportunity, although a coherent view, is an ideal of equality only in a limited and somewhat counterintuitive sense. More important, the form of equality that characterizes well-functioning market processes also characterizes well-functioning democratic processes. Therefore, in principle, there is no difference between the equality manifested in market-oriented meritocracy (so-called equality of opportunity) and the equality characteristic of a well-functioning democracy that alters market outcomes (so-called equality of result). It follows that the distinction between opportunity and result is an unhelpful and misleading way to categorize social institutions.

Equality of Opportunity as the Elimination of Arbitrary Barriers to Advancement

Formal Equality of Opportunity

One indisputable aspect of equality of opportunity is what might be called formal equality of opportunity.[2] I believe that those who rely on the distinction between equality of opportunity and equality of result have this principle in mind as at least the minimum content of equality of opportunity.

The principle of formal equality of opportunity holds, in the classic formulation, that careers should be open to talents.[3] The law should not bar a person from an occupation or a position of prestige just because—as the principle would have been stated at a time when it was more controversial than today—that person was born into a family that does not belong to the aristocracy.[4] Today the equivalent example would probably be not birth into a nonaristocratic family but birth into a certain racial group. A law that bars members of a racial minority from certain jobs, for example, denies them equality of opportunity.

Why are formal barriers to opportunity unacceptable? Perhaps the most obvious reason is the intuition that a person's fortunes should not depend on such arbitrary circumstances as race or family background. These are accidents of birth that are beyond an individual's control. It is therefore unfair to the individual to allow these factors to be so influential. There are other plausible arguments against formal barriers, of course. For example, one might say that formal equality of opportunity is desirable not because it is fairer to the individual but because it maximizes social well-being. I consider those arguments below. At least the most obvious and immediate argument for equality of opportunity is based on the idea that it is unfair to allow arbitrary factors to have a dramatic effect on a person's life.

This argument for equality of opportunity, however, quickly leads to arguments for much more than the elimination of formal barriers. The call for "equality of opportunity, not equality of result'' is sometimes offered as a reason for opposing welfare state measures.[5] But if the basis of equality of opportunity is the unfairness of allowing arbitrary factors to affect a person's chances in life, it is immediately apparent that equality of opportunity might require extensive government welfare and redistribution programs.[6] This is an important theme of John Rawls's *Theory of Justice*—that the principles that justify well-established liberal institutions, such as toleration, also entail substantial redistribution of resources.

The reasoning is familiar. Even without formal barriers, a person with as much talent and initiative as another may not do as well if he or she has had, for example, an inferior education or inferior health care. Indeed, because family background has such a powerful influence on people's fortunes, true equality of opportunity probably would require a degree of intervention into the family that we would find unacceptable.[7] For example, parents' willingness to play an active role in their children's education surely affects the children's prospects in life. But having parents interested in one's welfare is as much an arbitrary factor as having parents descended from King Arthur. Therefore, the idea of equality of opportunity as elimination of arbitrary barriers, if extended logically, would require that the interests and abilities of parents be equalized among families. No one would accept that conclusion.

The government might, however, do many things short of that to equalize opportunity. It could ensure, for example, equal schooling and equal access to health care without unacceptably interfering in the family. The notion of equal schooling is more complex than it might appear at first: some might dispute, for example, whether the government should provide the same resources to all or special educational benefits to those with special needs.[8] In any event, this conception of equality of opportunity would still require substantial government activity, in the nature of welfare state measures.

It does not follow that the distinction between equality of opportunity and equality of result is useless. It is plausible and coherent to say that the government should ensure that no one's fortunes in life will suffer because he or she did not have access to health care or education as good as anyone else's but that if opportunities are equalized in that way, the government must not correct any differences in results. Those differences, it might be said, are caused by differences in talent or initiative, not differences in opportunities.

Talents and Abilities as Accidents of Birth

The difference between equality of opportunity and equality of result begins to collapse when one recognizes that differences in talent are as much an accident of birth as skin color or aristocratic pedigree.[9] Of course, people can develop their talents through initiative and determination. But it is not obvious that such qualities as initiative and determination should be considered to be within an individual's control. Even assuming that those qualities are not considered accidents of birth, and even taking the most expansive view of how much people can develop, there is undeniably a substantial component of ability that a person cannot, on any view, control.[10] It is the result not just of heredity but of childhood and other environmental influences that cannot be plausibly attributed to the individual any more than race can be.

If equality of opportunity means that people's fortunes should not be determined by factors over which they have no control, then allowing their talents to affect their fortunes violates equality of opportunity. "There is no more reason to permit the distribution of income and wealth to be settled by the distribution of natural assets than by historical and social fortune. . . . From a moral standpoint the two seem equally arbitrary."[11] Once we take this step, however, the difference between equality of opportunity and equality of result begins to disappear. Differences in talent and ability, to the considerable extent that they are not within a person's control, should no more be permitted to affect a person's fortunes than differences in race or social class.

Three related objections might be made to this argument.

FORMAL VERSUS INFORMAL BARRIERS

First, it might be said that distinctions based on race or family status create explicit formal barriers. By contrast, no law says that untalented people may not seek certain positions. People with lesser talents, unlike the victims of formal barriers, are free to seek their fortunes as best they can. They will not do as well, but that is not the result of barriers erected by the government. It is just the result of "the way the world is"—specifically, it is the result of a multitude of decisions made by private individuals and reflected in the operation of various markets. Certain attributes are rewarded; others are not. But that is different from the government's decreeing that some categories of people will be barred entirely from certain opportunities.

This distinction is an important one for many purposes. Indeed, there must be some difference between a market system that rewards the untalented less than the talented and a system of formal barriers that excludes, for example, racial minorities: there is strong public consensus against the latter,[12] but few people entirely oppose the former.

But this difference between the formal barriers of racially exclusionary laws and the market barriers to those lacking certain talents has nothing to do with whether the influential factor is an accident of birth. The only difference is that one appears as an explicit legal barrier and the other seems to be an incident of the operation of a market economy. In both instances, society has made a decision to allow an arbitrary factor to affect a person's fortunes. A market, no less than a formal barrier, is created and maintained by the government: the government defines and maintains property rights, punishes theft and fraud, and so on. The government can do those things in a way that rewards talents (as it does, in a sense, when it maintains a market economy); or it can do those things in a way that rewards some other characteristics, of a kind we do not think should be rewarded. Those two kinds of action by the government are obviously not equally justifiable. But they are both actions by the government, even if only one consists of what we would call a formal barrier.[13] In either case, the government's action results in a person's fortune being determined by an accident of birth.

THE SUPPOSED INEVITABILITY OF
INEQUALITY IN TALENTS

The second objection is that talents, unlike such things as education or health care, cannot be distributed equally. Talents have already been distributed unequally by nature. (Indeed, that is the foundation of the argument that foreclosing opportunities on the basis of talents is no less arbitrary than foreclosing them on the basis of race or family background.) Barriers resulting from formal exclusionary laws can be eliminated by the stroke of a pen. Barriers resulting from unequal education, health care, and the like are more difficult to eliminate, but the government can at least ameliorate them. Talents cannot be equalized even in theory. Indeed, the objection would continue, the government cannot even reduce the differences in talent. Therefore, the barrier to equal opportunity resulting from unequal talents cannot be compared to either formal barriers or unequal education.

To be sure, the objection would conclude, some day we might be able to engineer people genetically so as to equalize talents. Then we would have to face the question whether it would be worth doing so in order to equalize opportunity. The answer would surely be no, but at least we would be aware that we were overriding the interest in equality of opportunity in favor of more fundamental values. But until we can do such things, it might be said, inequalities of talent simply do not raise the question of equality of opportunity because there is nothing we can do about them.

This argument, too, is mistaken, for two reasons. First, although we cannot transplant talents, it does not follow that nothing can be done to equalize them. People might be educated differentially so as to minimize disparities in talent.[14] Equality in education does not necessarily mean that everyone receives the same education; it might mean that educations should be tailored for those with special needs (as is required in certain cases by the Individuals with Disabilities Education Act).[15] Or the idea of ''special needs'' might be generalized: equal education might mean that education is tailored for the talents of each person (or, more realistically, each category of people) so as to minimize the effects of inequalities of talent. There are many possible arguments against such an approach to education.[16] But for present purposes, it is enough that such a form of education is theoretically possible. That possibility shows the error of saying that inequalities in talent are simply a given that cannot be altered.

The notion that nothing can be done about inequalities of talent is mistaken for a further reason. Equality of opportunity, according to the conception I am discussing, requires that people's fortunes in life not be affected by arbitrary factors over which they have no control. One way to achieve this is to eliminate or equalize the arbitrary factors. But if those factors cannot be eliminated, another way of providing equality of opportunity is to ensure that those factors do not affect people's chances in life. Racial differences, like differences in talent, cannot be elim-

inated: the way we ensure equality of opportunity in the face of racial differences
is to have institutions that eliminate the influence of race.

At this point, however, equality of opportunity collapses more or less completely
into equality of result. Talent is an arbitrary factor; nature distributes it unequally,
and, let us assume, education cannot equalize it. But equality of opportunity requires that arbitrary factors not determine people's fortunes. The only way to satisfy
equality of opportunity, therefore, is to equalize people's fortunes so that they do
not reflect the irreducible inequalities of talent—that is, to bring about equality of
result. If we do not take major steps toward equality of result, then the arbitrary
difference in talents will produce a difference in fortunes. Therefore equality of
opportunity, faithfully pursued, requires substantial equalization of results.

This argument does not establish that equality of opportunity requires complete
equality of result: the difference in fortunes is partly the result of what individuals
have done with their talents, and there might be a sense in which that is under
their control. Of course it is unclear—and a very complex question—exactly what
it means for something to be under a person's control.[17] But even if we gave the
largest plausible scope to the category of factors that are thought to be under
people's control, many of the things that determine people's fortunes would still
not be under their control. Equality of opportunity, understood as the requirement
that fortunes not be determined by arbitrary factors, would still require a great
equalization of results, even if not complete equality. Indeed, even assuming that
the objective of a regime of equality of opportunity is to prevent only those factors
that are unquestionably beyond people's control from affecting their fortunes in
life, that regime would require the elimination of inequalities of fortune on a massive scale. It would require something approaching equality of result far more
closely than the critics of the welfare state would like.

If this argument is correct, distinguishing equality of opportunity from equality
of result serves no purpose. Equality of opportunity entails, if not complete equality
of result, substantial equality of result. The interesting question is not the choice
between equality of opportunity and equality of result. It is how much equality of
opportunity we want. To what extent do we want the leveling entailed by the
proposition—which I am taking to be definitional of equality of opportunity—that
fortunes should not depend on arbitrary circumstances? That is a difficult question
in many ways. But the claim that equality of opportunity is superior to equality of
result does not help resolve it.

ESSENTIAL VERSUS INESSENTIAL ATTRIBUTES

The third objection to the view that talents and abilities are factors just as arbitrary
as race or aristocratic background is related to the quite different conception of
equality of opportunity that I discuss in the section below. The objection is that
talents and abilities are different because they are essential rather than incidental
to the individual. They are constitutive of an individual's identity in a way that
race and social class are not.[18] Genetic engineering to equalize talents and abilities
is an unthinkable invasion of individual autonomy. Redistributing the fruits of those
talents and abilities is obviously less invasive but, in principle, suffers from a

similar flaw: it amounts to depriving a person of something that is an essential aspect of his or her identity.

The difficulty with this argument lies in the justification offered for its central claim about the constituents of personal identity. Some societies regard race as a central constituent of a person's identity.[19] (Some would say it is so regarded in our society.) Historically, some societies regarded social class as far more central to one's identity than talents or abilities as we define them.[20] Race is as unalterable as ability, and in some cultures, social class is no more easily alterable. Nothing inherent in any of these qualities suggests that one is more central to human identity than the other. Different societies define the constituents of human identity differently.

Again, there are good reasons for considering ability to be more central to a person's identity than family background. But those reasons concern the consequences of doing so. In particular, talents and abilities, at least in a market-oriented society, relate to the capacity of people to produce goods and services that satisfy others' desires. But talents and abilities remain arbitrary factors in the sense that they are beyond the person's control, and allowing them to determine the person's fortunes remains inconsistent with equality of opportunity (as I have defined that term for now). There are good reasons for departing from equality of opportunity in this respect, but a departure from equality of opportunity is exactly what is involved. To the extent we do not depart from equality of opportunity, we are necessarily committed to trying to bring about a large measure of equality of result.

Equality of Opportunity as a Meritocratic Principle

The Meritocratic Conception

Equality of opportunity might be understood in a fundamentally different way. The barriers that must be eliminated, according to this understanding, are arbitrary not in the sense that they are beyond people's control but in the sense that we cannot give adequate reasons for them.[21] There is no good reason to allow a person's fortunes to turn on race or social class. But talents and abilities are not arbitrary in the crucial sense because they correspond to the capacity to produce value in society. Rewarding them, therefore, is not inconsistent with equality of opportunity.

By contrast, barriers based on factors like race and social class diminish the amount of value produced in society and therefore should be eliminated. Those barriers are arbitrary in the sense that they are irrational; no good reason can be given for them, and a good reason can be given for eliminating them. When such a formal barrier prevents talented people from reaching the positions for which they are best suited, society loses the benefits of their talents.[22] Multiplied across a large number of people held back by formal barriers, the effects on the total well-being of society can be enormous. Formal barriers based on race or class are arbitrary in this sense of being unreasoned, not in the sense that those factors are accidents of birth.

The point of equality of opportunity, on this view, is to guarantee that people go as far as their abilities, talents, initiative, and dedication take them. (I refer simply to "merit" to denote that complex of characteristics; later I discuss the complexities of the notion of merit.) So understood, equality of opportunity appears to be a principle that justifies, and perhaps requires, inequality of results. There should be equality among those people with the same level of merit, but there is no reason for equality among those with different levels of merit. Because abilities differ, as do the willingness and capacity to use them, results will differ. Equality of result seems antithetical to this conception of equality of opportunity because equality of result seems to call for leveling the differences in condition that are produced by different levels of merit. I refer to this conception of "equality of opportunity, not equality of result" as the meritocratic conception; those with the most merit ought to do better.

The Justification for the Meritocratic Conception

Part of the intuitive appeal of this conception of "equality of opportunity, not equality of result" stems from the analogy that can be drawn to a game.[23] If a game is well designed and its rules are enforced, each of the competitors can be said to have an equal opportunity to win even though some will have more of the requisite abilities. To insist that the results be equalized to compensate for differences in abilities among the competitors would be inconsistent with the whole idea of playing the game.

As the analogy suggests, however, we must justify the game that is being played. In our society, people who succeed in the marketplace, roughly speaking, are rewarded. But why should we play the market-oriented game to which we are accustomed instead of, for example, a game that rewards physical strength and courage or hereditary ties to famous families? Those games would be lost by many people who win the market game and would be won by many people who do not succeed in the market.

Today the most common justification for the market game is consequentialist. On this view, "merit" is rewarded because it makes society better off. We reward people who produce things that other people value; people succeed according to their abilities to satisfy others' desires. That is what "merit" is. There is no fixed catalog of capacities that are rewarded, and no one is rewarded for the mere possession of an unexercised capacity. It all depends on what will benefit society. The "barriers" that face the untalented simply reflect their lack of the capacities that bring value to others in society.

According to the meritocratic conception, then, equality of opportunity exists when everyone is allowed to compete equally to satisfy others' desires, as those desires are revealed in the market. When the government alters the results of that competition, it promotes equality of result, not equality of opportunity.[24] There is much to say, of course, about the justification for the market game. Most would agree today, I believe, that market mechanisms should play an important role in distributing wealth, but few would say that market distributions are inviolate. My purpose here, however, is to analyze the conception of equality of opportunity that corresponds to this game and to determine its relationship to the notion of equality of result. My argument is that the kind of *equality* involved in the market-oriented meritocratic regime of equality of opportunity is not meaningfully distinguishable from the kind of equality involved in government actions to "equalize results" by altering the distributions produced by the market.

THE NATURE OF MERITOCRATIC EQUALITY

Leaving aside the distinction between opportunity and result for a moment, it is not clear why a market-oriented meritocracy should be characterized as one of equality at all, in anything but a Pickwickian sense. In a game, everyone has an equal opportunity to succeed only if "equality" is defined by the rules of the game. In a sport, a person lacking the relevant athletic ability obviously does not have the same opportunity to succeed as an athletically gifted person.[25] Why should not the market-oriented meritocratic regime be characterized as one of *in*equality of opportunity? People with certain talents have a much better chance to succeed than others. The inequality of opportunity may be justified by the way in which the market operates to satisfy desires. But inequality of opportunity remains a more accurate description.

Suppose, for example, there were a society that valued not the satisfaction of desires as revealed in the market but the production of human specimens of great physical beauty and strength; suppose that society showered riches on the few people who had such characteristics because it thought that doing so would propitiate the gods. We would not regard such a society as one characterized by equality of opportunity. If we did so regard it, then any society could be so regarded. But in what sense does that society have less equality of opportunity than a market-oriented meritocratic society? Anyone who became extremely strong or beautiful could succeed spectacularly; in that sense there would be equality of opportunity. Of course, characteristics beyond people's control would powerfully affect their chances of success. But that is true of the meritocratic conception as well. As in the meritocratic society, people in the society that valued beauty and strength could do something to improve their chances. Some might be able to "pull themselves up by the bootstraps" and succeed despite being born without the greatest natural attributes of beauty or strength. Most others who lacked good fortune would not succeed, no matter how hard they worked. There would be differences from a modern market economy but only differences in degree.

In this light, there is something puzzling about the association of market regimes with any kind of equality. Nonetheless, there is a persistent intuition that a market-oriented meritocratic regime is characterized by equality of opportunity in a way that is not true of other regimes, such as the hypothetical one I just described or an aristocratic regime. Three related aspects of the market regime seem to account for this.

First, in the market regime many people have the impression that they have a significant degree of control over whether they succeed. Many people feel that even though they may in the end be defeated by their lack of talents, their fate is in their own hands to some degree. If they work hard and are enterprising, they have a chance. Obviously not everyone holds this view, and in significant ways it is an illusion. Nevertheless, it is a commonly held view and may account to some degree for the perception that a market-oriented regime is one of equality of opportunity.

Second and related, in a market regime there may be a sense, within certain classes, that almost anyone can succeed. All a person has to do is to figure out a way to appeal to large numbers of people—to build a better mousetrap—and that person will succeed. In an aristocratic regime, by contrast, it will be clearer for many more people at an early point in their lives that they are destined not to succeed because they were born into the wrong family.

Third, in a market-oriented regime the specific criteria of value are fluid. The path to success is not obvious and can change overnight. In addition, no single person has the power to determine which capacities will be rewarded. Value is the result of a multitude of private decisions. All of these factors contribute to the sense that few people are permanently closed out. Moreover, failure will seem, even to someone who failed, to be the result of that person's own shortcomings rather than the fiat of another person. In a regime of equality of opportunity, the explanation for failure is: "I had a chance, but I wasn't good enough." In a regime with unequal opportunity, the complaint is: "I never had a fair chance; so-and-so [a person or group] closed the door on me."

Of course, each of these intuitions about a market regime is to a significant extent incorrect. People often do not have control in any meaningful sense (even leaving aside controversial questions about what "control" might mean) over whether they succeed in the market. While we cannot identify winners and losers at birth to the same degree we can in certain other regimes, we do know from the outset that many people will be losers. (And we can probably identify more market losers at birth than the official rhetoric would acknowledge.) Finally, in a market regime the criteria of value are, in fact, dictated by others, of course; the only reason we might think they are not is that the others are numerous, and they dictate through a large number of decisions that are often visible only in the aggregate.

At the same time, however, these intuitions reveal something significant about the notion of equality of opportunity—something that begins to give some content to the notion of equality of opportunity, although it undermines any effort to draw an easy contrast between equality of opportunity and equality of result. The apparent fluidity and unpredictability of markets are a result of what might be described as their democratic character. In a market-oriented meritocracy, the forces that determine success or failure are democratic in the sense that they are the products of a multitude of personal decisions, not the act of a dictatorial person or group. The intuition that this is a regime of equality derives from the sense that everyone is subject to these forces; no one person can control them, and no one is exempt from them.

It is in this sense that the market-oriented meritocratic regime can be said to be one of equality of opportunity. It is manifestly untrue that everyone has an equal chance to succeed or that everyone has an equal chance to control his or her destiny. It is true, however, that no identifiable person or, if the markets are operating as they should, self-conscious group of persons can dictate another's fate.[26]

Democratic Equality in Markets and Governments

In the end, therefore, the so-called equality of opportunity in a market-oriented meritocratic regime is not that everyone has an equal chance to succeed but that no one has a greater chance than anyone else to determine who will succeed. In practice, of course, this will often not be true; some individuals will have power in the market. But the meritocratic conception is an ideal: there is equality of opportunity when markets operate perfectly. There is inequality only to the extent that markets are imperfect.

This understanding of equality of opportunity begins to give some definite content to that notion, in the face of the Rawlsian challenge that all factors producing inequality are as arbitrary as the formal barriers that everyone agrees are inconsistent with equality of opportunity. Equality of opportunity exists if identifiable individuals do not determine one's fortunes. On this account, there is an important sense in which equality of opportunity might be said to exist in a market-oriented society but not in an aristocratic regime.

But the distinction between equality of opportunity and equality of result is not yet rehabilitated. The claim of those who contrast equality of opportunity and equality of result is that equality of opportunity, conceived as a market-oriented meritocratic principle, is different from equality of result, understood as a government action designed to offset the effects of the market. In fact, however, the kind of equality involved in the two cases is, potentially at least, the same.

Once we understand that the equality of a meritocracy is equality not in the chance to succeed but in the chance to influence others' abilities to succeed, there is nothing distinctive about meritocracy. The same democratic characteristics that arguably make a meritocracy a regime of equality are present elsewhere. Most notably, of course, these characteristics are present in a well-functioning democratic government. In a well-functioning democracy, as in a well-functioning market economy, decisions are impersonal in the sense that they are not the products of the will of an identifiable individual.

Specifically, in a well-functioning democracy, every person has an equal opportunity to succeed by persuading fellow citizens to provide him or her with benefits—in the same sense that, in a well-functioning market economy, every person has an equal opportunity to create a new mousetrap. In both cases, some will fail. But in both cases, success will be determined by apparently impersonal forces rather than by the will of an identifiable individual. This is the only sense in which markets provide equality of opportunity. Democratic decisionmaking provides equality in exactly the same sense. The same kind of equality that is a characteristic of well-functioning markets is present in well-functioning democracies as well.

What does it mean to refer to a ''well-functioning'' democracy? Under either of two conceptions of democracy, democratic decisions (including decisions that equalize results) afford the same kind of equality as the so-called equality of opportunity that characterizes market-oriented meritocracy. It is not necessary to assume that a democratic system always pursues the public interest or to reject ''public choice'' accounts that treat political outcomes as the products of self-interested behavior.[27] If democracy is a pluralist struggle among self-interested groups, then democratic decisions will provide the same kind of equality as a market, as long as no one group or coalition can entrench itself in power.[28] Indeed, the pluralist view is deliberately modeled after the theory of the market.[29]

Alternatively, if democratic politics is characterized by an effort to promote the public interest, conceived in a way that treats everyone fairly, then this form of equality of opportunity is again present.[30] Specifically, in either of these forms of democratic society, people will have an opportunity to persuade their fellow citizens to advance their interests—just as in the market, people have an opportunity to succeed by satisfying others' desires. Some efforts at persuasion will fail—some will be doomed from the start—but that is true of efforts in the market as well. In a well-functioning democracy, under either the pluralist or public-interest model, outcomes are not dictated by individuals or cohesive groups of individuals. Outcomes are the result of forces that cannot be identified with any individual: either the market-mimicking dynamic of pluralist democracy or the disinterested inquiry into the public interest.

Of course, democracy can function badly in a variety of ways. "Equality of result" might be imposed by a dominant group. Then the kind of equality found in well-functioning markets will be absent. But markets can also be imperfect— not just when there is concentration in an industry but in more routine cases of agency and information costs that allow, for example, a bureaucratic superior to exercise unwarranted power over a subordinate. This problem is commonplace in employment markets: sexual harassment is a notorious example.

There is much room for debate (and of course much debate) over whether the market or democracy is more likely to malfunction, how often, and how badly. Those are complex questions that depend heavily on empirical knowledge. But the dichotomy—equality of opportunity is characteristic of market-oriented meritocracy, while equality of result is characteristic of democratic decisionmaking—is misconceived. When markets function well, they are characterized by something that can plausibly be called equality of opportunity. But that same kind of equality is present in well-functioning democratic decisionmaking. When both markets and democratic governments function correctly, the kind of equality displayed in the markets is also present in the government.

Conclusion

Equality of opportunity is a powerful ideal. It is, however, more complex than it first appears, and the contrast between equality of opportunity and equality of result is not a useful one. Understood in perhaps the most natural sense—as a requirement that a person's fortunes not be determined by accidents of birth or other factors over which he or she has no control—equality of opportunity has very powerful implications. It calls for the large-scale equalization of results.

Understood in a different sense—as a characteristic of a market-oriented meritocratic regime—equality of opportunity does not necessarily call for such dramatic measures. But the meritocratic conception of equality of opportunity is a conception of equality only in a very specialized way. People have equal opportunities only in the sense that their chances for success are not dictated by identifiable others. The same kind of equality inheres in well-functioning democratic political arrangements that bring about equality of result by altering market outcomes. Arguments for equality of opportunity and equality of result rest on the same foundations, and the rhetoric that contrasts them is more misleading than valuable.

NOTES

I thank Neal Devins, Elana Kagan, Lawrence Lessig, Geoffrey Stone, and Cass Sunstein for their helpful comments on earlier drafts. The Russell Baker Scholars Fund and the Lee and Brena Freeman Faculty Research Fund at the University of Chicago Law School provided financial support.

1. The literature on equality of opportunity is of course very extensive. For a recent exchange, see *Boston Review* 20 (April/May 1995): 3–16. Recent collections on the subject include Ellen Frankel Paul et al., eds., *Equal Opportunity* (Cambridge: Basil Blackwell, 1987); Norman Bowie, ed., *Equal Opportunity* (Boulder: Westview Press, 1988). For the use of the "equality of opportunity, not result" slogan to oppose welfare state measures, see, e.g., Michael Novak, *The Spirit of Democratic Capitalism* (New York: S & S Trade, 1982), 123–25 (1982); Thomas Sowell, *Civil Rights: Rhetoric or Reality?* (New York: W. Morrow, 1984), 37–60.

2. This principle has been stated by many. For a prominent example, see Henry Sidgwick, *The Methods of Ethics*, 7th ed. (Indianapolis: Hackett Publishing, 1907), 285 n.1.

3. Ibid.

4. For a well-known account of the historical development of this principle, see Richard H. Tawney, *Equality*, 4th ed. (New York: Barnes & Noble, 1964), ch. 3, sec. 2.

5. See, e.g., Novak, *Democratic Capitalism*, 123–25; Sowell, *Civil Rights*, 37–60.

6. This is a familiar point. See, e.g., John Rawls, *A Theory of Justice* (Cambridge, Mass.: Belknap Press, 1971); Robert Haveman, *Starting Even* (New York: S & S Trade, 1988); see also Robert Nozick, *Anarchy, State, and Utopia* (New York: Basic Books, 1974), 235–38 (criticizing equality of opportunity on ground that it requires redistribution).

7. This is a principal theme of James Fishkin, *Justice, Equal Opportunity, and the Family* (New Haven: Yale University Press, 1983). See ibid., 1–10.

8. See text accompanying notes 14–16.

9. See Rawls, *Theory of Justice*, 73–74; see also Douglas Rae, *Equalities* (Cambridge: Harvard University Press, 1981), 64–81.

10. See Rae, *Equalities*, 70; Sidgwick, *Methods of Ethics*, 285 n.1.

11. Rawls, *Theory of Justice*, 74–75; see also Bernard Williams, "The Idea of Equality," in *Problems of the Self* (Cambridge: Cambridge University Press, 1973), 230, 239–49.

12. Even opponents of the antidiscrimination laws acknowledge this point. See, e.g., Richard A. Epstein, *Forbidden Grounds* (Cambridge: Harvard University Press, 1992), 1–9.

13. See, e.g., Cass R. Sunstein, *The Partial Constitution* (Cambridge: Harvard University Press, 1993), especially ch. 3; Robert L. Hale, "Coercion and Distribution in a Supposedly Non-Coercive State," *Political Science Quarterly* 38 (1923): 470–74.

14. See Amy Gutmann, "Distributing Public Education in a Democracy," in *Democracy and the Welfare State*, ed. Amy Gutmann (Princeton: Princeton University Press, 1988), 107, 110–111 (discussing Fishkin, *Justice, Equal Opportunity, and the Family*).

15. 20 U.S.C. §§ 1400–1485.

16. See, e.g., Gutmann, *Democracy and the Welfare State*, 111–12.

17. This problem is addressed by John E. Roemer, "Equality and Responsibility," *Boston Review* 20 (April/May 1995): 3, and by many of the responses to Roemer's article in that issue of the *Boston Review*. See, in particular, Samuel Scheffler, "Another Unfunded Mandate," *Boston Review* 20 (April/May 1995): 10.

18. This position is suggested by writers disparate in their ultimate views, e.g., Michael Sandel, *Liberalism and the Limits of Justice* (Cambridge: Cambridge University Press, 1982), and Nozick, *Anarchy, State, and Utopia*.

19. See, e.g., Louis Dumont, *Homo Hierarchius*, trans. Mark Sainsbury et al. (Chicago: University of Chicago Press, 1970), 33–200 (discussing caste system in India); Donald L. Horowitz, *Ethnic Groups in Conflict* (Berkeley: University of California Press, 1985), 95–288 (discussing ethnic conflict generally).

20. See, e.g., Stanley I. Binn and Richard S. Peters, *The Principles of Political Thought* (New York: Free Press, 1965), 132.

21. On the connection between equality and the ability to give reasons for differences among people, see Williams, *Problems of the Self*, 240–41.

22. See ibid., 242–45.

23. This analogy is in the nontechnical sense of a game played for amusement, not in the more technical sense in which "game" is used in microeconomics to refer to certain kinds of interactions between people. See, e.g., Rae, *Equalities*, 65–66.

24. For this conception, see Daniel Bell, "On Meritocracy and Equality," *Public Interest* 29 (1972): 29, 40–41.

25. These points are advanced to support a different conclusion in Peter Westen, "The Concept of Equal Opportunity," *Ethics* 95 (1985): 837.

26. In fact, even if markets operate as they should, they reward people only for satisfying desires as those desires are revealed in the market. Many important kinds of desires are not adequately accounted for in the market. For a well-known discussion, see Amartya K. Sen, "Rational Fools: A Critique of the Behavioral Foundations of Economic Theory," *Philosophy and Public Affairs* 6 (1977): 317.

27. See generally Dennis C. Mueller, *Public Choice II* (Cambridge: Cambridge University Press, 1989).

28. A well-known description of this form of pluralist democracy is found in Robert A. Dahl, *A Preface to Democratic Theory* (Chicago: University of Chicago Press, 1956).

29. See, e.g., Anthony Downs, *An Economic Theory of Democracy* (New York: Harper Collins, 1957); Joseph A. Schumpeter, *Capitalism, Socialism and Democracy*, 5th ed. (New York: Harper Collins, 1950), chs. 21–23.

30. See, e.g., Rawls, *Theory of Justice*, 359–61.

5

The Word "American" Ends in "I Can"

The Ambiguous Promise of the American Dream

JENNIFER L. HOCHSCHILD

[I]n the beginning," wrote John Locke, "all the world was America."[1] Locke was referring specifically to the absence of a cash nexus in primitive society, but the sentence evokes the unsullied newness, infinite possibility, limitless resources that are commonly understood to be the essence of "the American dream." The idea of the American dream has been attached to everything from religious freedom to a home in the suburbs, and it has inspired emotions ranging from deep gratification to disillusioned fury. Nevertheless, the phrase elicits for most Americans some variant of Locke's fantasy—a new world where anything can happen and good things might.

Millions of immigrants moved to America and internal migrants moved around within it in order to fulfill their version of the American dream.[2] By objective measures and their own accounts, many came astonishingly close to success.[3] Just as many were probably defeated and disillusioned.[4] My purpose is to examine what the American dream has done for and meant to various migrants, focusing especially on African Americans, who did not come to America to fulfill their dreams. The American dream is, however, an ideology whose power extends far beyond my particular interests in race. It has been Americans' dominant ideology at least since the early nineteenth century. Americans' beliefs about happiness, freedom, personal and collective responsibility, and equality can all be understood in the context of the American dream and perhaps only in that context. Opponents, embittered former believers, and boosters alike all shape their assumptions and actions in response, one way or another, to the enticing promise of the dream.

In this chapter I provide an extended definition of the American dream and discuss its virtues and drawbacks as a dominant ideology. I conclude by drawing implications for the ideal and practice of equality, American style.

The Meaning of Success

What is the American dream? It consists of tenets about achieving success. Let us first explore the meaning of "success" and then consider the rules for achieving it.

Former president Ronald Reagan stated, "[W]hat I want to see above all is that this country remains a country where someone can always get rich. That's the one thing that we have and that must be preserved."[5] Most people agree with President Reagan that success means a high income, prestigious job, and economic security. Material well-being, however, is only one form of accomplishment. People seek success in arenas ranging from the pulpit to the stage of the Metropolitan Opera House, from membership in the newest and hottest dance club to membership in the Senate. Indeed, if we believe oral histories, people define success as "a right to say what they wanta say, do what they wanta do, and fashion a world into something that can be great for everyone"[6] as often as they think of it in terms of wealth and status.

Different kinds of success need not, but often do, conflict. A classic plot of American family sagas is the children's rejection of the parents' hard-won wealth and social standing in favor of some "deeper," more meaningful form of accomplishment.[7] The conflict need not be intergenerational, however, and the rejection may work in reverse, as Cotton Mather sadly reported:

> There have been very fine settlements in the north-east regions; but what is become of them? I have heard that one of our ministers once preaching to a congregation there, urged them to approve themselves a religious people from this consideration, "that otherwise they would contradict the main end of planting this wilderness"; whereupon a well-known person, then in the assembly, cryed out, "Sir, you are mistaken: you think you are preaching to the people at the [Plymouth] Bay; our main end was to catch fish."[8]

Mather "wished, that something more excellent had been the main end of the settlements in that brave country,"[9] but the ideology of the American dream itself remains agnostic on the definition of "excellent."

No matter what it consists of, success can be measured in three ways, the choice among which results in profoundly different normative and behavioral consequences. First, success can be absolute. In this case, achieving the American dream implies reaching some threshold of well-being, perhaps higher than where one began but not necessarily dazzling. One of the first American civil engineers thus explained westward migration: "Every man will endeavor to improve his circumstances by a change of occupation or by a change of place. He fixes a standard mark of enjoyments by comparison of his present situation with what the new and unpeopled district holds out to him."[10] Rock star Bruce Springsteen provided a more recent instance: "I don't think the American dream was that everybody was going to make . . . a billion dollars, but it was that everybody was going to have an opportunity and the chance to live a life with some decency and some dignity and a chance for some self-respect."[11]

In the ideology of the American dream, absolute success is in principle equally available to everyone although guaranteed to no one. As Springsteen continued, "I dreamed something and I was lucky. A large part of it came true. But it's not just for one; it's gotta be for everyone, and you've gotta fight for it every day."[12] To the degree that a society makes it possible for most people to become better off—to achieve absolute success, in my terms—the society is structured to promote equality of results without any hint of identity of results.

Second, success can be relative. By this measurement, the American dream means becoming better off than some point of comparison. That point may be one's own childhood, people in the old country, one's neighbors, a character from a book, another race or gender—anything or anyone that one chooses to measure oneself against. Relative success implies no threshold of well-being and may or may not entail continually changing the comparison group as one achieves a given level of accomplishment. Memoirist James Comer captured a benign version of relative success in his depiction of a "kind of competition . . . we [his parents] had . . . going on" with "the closest friends that we had":[13]

> When we first met them, we had a dining room and they didn't. They went back and they turned one of their bedrooms into a dining room. . . . After that we bought this big Buick car. And we came to their house and they had bought another car. She bought a fur coat one year and your dad bought me one the next. But it was a friendly thing, the way we raced. It gave you something to work for, to look forward to. Every year we tried to have something different to show them what we had done, and they would have something to show us.[14]

In 1736, William Byrd II articulated a more malign version: slaves "blow up the pride, and ruin the industry of our white people, who seeing a rank of poor creatures below them, detest work for fear it should make them look like slaves."[15]

As Byrd suggested, relative success implies a rather different understanding of equality than does absolute success. It contains no hint of equality of outcomes; rather it calls for, at most, equal chances for all to do better than some standard. It implies, in short, a "soft" form of equal opportunity.

A third form of success is competitive. Success in this context consists not of reaching a threshold or doing better than some standard but of achieving victory over someone else. My success implies at the least your lack of success and, at the most, your failure. One's competitors are usually people, whether known and concrete as opponents in a tennis match or unknown and abstract as all other applicants for a job. For example, *U.S. News and World Report*, in an article celebrating success in the roaring '80s, pictured a businessman with flying tie and bulging briefcase striding over four prone colleagues, with the caption, "Like it or not, success often means stepping over others."[16] One's opponent may, however, be entirely impersonal—a hurricane, a disease, or a mountain. John Henry, "the steel-drivin' man," is famed for beating a machine, and Paul Bunyan, for taming the primeval forest. This form of success rejects equality of results, and competitors generally do not worry about whether their opponent starts with an equal chance for victory. Thus competitive success implies, at most, a "hard" form of equal opportunity.

Rules for Achieving Success

Success can be material, spiritual, or otherwise; it may be available to all or a few. One person's success may enable the success of others or come at their expense. How is it to be sought and achieved? The bundle of commonly understood, even unconsciously assumed, tenets about achieving success are what make up the ideology of the American dream.

As I construe it, the ideology has four related but distinct premises. They answer the questions: *Who* may pursue the American dream? In *what* does the pursuit consist? *How* does one successfully pursue the dream? And *why* is the pursuit worthy of our deepest commitment? The answer to "who" in the standard ideology is "everyone, regardless of ascriptive traits, family background, or personal history." The answer to "what" is "the reasonable anticipation, though not the promise, of success, however it is defined." The answer to "how" is "through actions and traits under one's own control." The answer to "why" is "true success is associated with virtue." Let us consider each rule in turn.

The first tenet, that all people may always pursue their dreams, is the most direct connotation of Locke's statement that "in the beginning, all the world was *America.*"[17] The idea extends, however, beyond the image of a pristine state of nature waiting for whoever "discovers" it; even in the distinctly nonpristine, nonnatural world of Harlem in New York City and Harlan County, Kentucky, anyone can pursue a dream. A century ago, one moved to the frontier to hide a spotted past and begin afresh. As one woman from that period put it, Montana frontierswomen "never ask[ed] women where they [had] come from or what they did before they came to live in our neck of the woods. If they wore a wedding band and were good wives, mothers, and neighbors that was enough for us to know."[18] Today one appeals to the Equal Employment Opportunity Commission to overturn racial, gender, or age discrimination. In effect, Americans believe they can create in their own lives a ministate of nature that will allow them to slough off the past and invent a better future.

The second tenet, that one may reasonably anticipate success, suggests a more guarded promise. After all, "reasonable anticipation" is far from a guarantee, as all children on the morning of their birthdays know. Reasonable anticipation, however, is also much more than simply longing; most children are not silly or crazy to expect at least some of what they wish for on their birthdays. Immigrants most clearly articulate this hope: "All my life I am thinking to come to this country. For what I read in the magazines, and the movies. . . . I would have a beautiful castle in the United States. I will have a thousand servant. I will have five Rolls-Royces in my door. . . . We thinking everybody has this kind of life. . . . I have this kind of dream."[19]

The third premise, that success results from action's under one's own control, explains how one is to achieve the success that one anticipates. Ralph Waldo Emerson is uncharacteristically succinct on the point: "There is always a reason, in *the man,* for his good or bad fortune, and so in making money."[20] Lest we smile at the quaint optimism, or crude propaganda, of our ancestors, consider a recent advertisement from Citicorp Bank. It shows a carefully balanced group of shining faces—young and old, male and female, black, Latino, WASP, and Asian—all gazing starry-eyed at the middle distance over the words:

FROM SEA TO SHINING SEA, THE WILL TO SUCCEED IS PART OF THE AMERICAN SPIRIT. The instant you become an American, whether by birth or by choice, you are guaranteed . . . the freedom to succeed. You are free to dream your own dream of success, to study, to work, to create and discover and build, for yourself and your children, the success you want.[21]

Implicit in this flow of oratory is the fourth tenet of the American dream, that the pursuit of success warrants so much fervor because it is associated with virtue. "Associated with" has at least four more precise meanings: virtue leads to success, success makes a person virtuous, success indicates virtue, or apparent success is not real success unless one is also virtuous. Benjamin Franklin provides the most famous aphorisms on this point: "[N]o Qualities were so likely to make a poor Man's Fortune as those of Probity & Integrity." Conversely, "Proverbial Sentences, chiefly such as inculcated Industry and Frugality," are included in *Poor Richard's Almanack* as "the Means of procuring Wealth and thereby securing Virtue, it being more difficult for a Man in Want to act always honestly, as . . . *it is hard for an empty Sack to stand upright.*"[22]

If we consider these four premises of the American dream in light of the varying meanings of success described earlier, we can see the full richness—and seductiveness—of the ideology. Different understandings of success do not much affect the first tenet, the norm of universal participation and endless chances to start over. However, such understandings do affect the other three tenets.

If success is defined as achieving some absolute threshold of well-being, the ideology portrays America as a land of plenty and Americans as "people of plenty."[23] Hard work and virtue (combined through most of our history with plenty of purportedly uninhabited land in the West) allow everyone to anticipate success even in the face of continued adversity. This is the great theme, of course, of one of the most powerful children's sagas ever written in America, Laura Ingalls Wilder's *Little House in the Big Woods* series. Many years—and eight volumes—of grasshopper plagues, ferocious blizzards, cheating and cowardly railroad bosses, and even hostile Indians cannot prevent Pa and his girls from eventually "winning their bet with Uncle Sam" and becoming prosperous homesteaders.[24]

If success is defined competitively, however, the ideology portrays a rather different America. Hard work and virtue combined with scarce resources produce winners who are successful and good and losers who have failed and are bad. This theme appears in John Rockefeller's Sunday school address: "The growth of a large business . . . is merely a survival of the fittest.. . . .The American Beauty rose can be produced in the splendor and fragrance which bring cheer to its beholder only by sacrificing the early buds which grow up around it. This is not an evil tendency in business. It is merely the working out of a law of nature and a law of God."[25]

As the perennial popularity of the *Little House* series indicates, Americans prefer the self-image of universal achievement to the self-image of a few stalwarts triumphing over weaker contenders. However, more important than any single image are the enormous elasticity and range of the ideology of the American dream. People can encourage themselves with softer versions, congratulate themselves with harder ones, and exult with the hardest, as their circumstances and characters warrant.

Thus, the American dream is in many ways an enormously successful ideology. It has for centuries lured people to America and moved them around within it and has kept them striving in horrible conditions against impossible odds. Most Americans celebrate it unthinkingly, along with apple pie and motherhood; criticism typically is limited to imperfections in its application. But like apple pie and motherhood, the American dream upon closer examination turns out to be less than perfect. Let us turn, then, to flaws intrinsic to the dream.

Defects in the American Dream

The First Tenet: Equal Participation

Each premise, and the overall dream, is problematic.[26] The first tenet, that everyone can participate equally and can always start over, is troubling to the degree that it is not true. It is, of course, never true in the strongest sense because people cannot shed their existing selves as snakes shed their skin. So the myth of the individual ministate of nature is just that—a fantasy to be sought but never attained.

Nothing is wrong with fantasies as long as people understand that that is what they are. For that reason, a weaker formulation of the first tenet—people start the pursuit with varying degrees of advantage, but no one is barred from the pursuit—is more troubling because its falsity is much less clear. For most of American history, being a woman, Native American, Asian, black, or pauper has barred people from all but a very narrow range of possible futures. The constraints of ascriptive traits arguably have weakened over time, but until recently no more than about a third of the population was able to take seriously the first premise of the American dream.

This flaw has implications beyond the evident ones of racism and sexism. The emotional potency of the American dream has made people who *were* able to identify with it the norm for everyone else. White men, especially European immigrants able to ride the wave of the Industrial Revolution to comfort or even prosperity, became the epitomizing demonstration of America as the bountiful state of nature. Those who did not fit the model disappeared from the collective self-portrait. Thus the irony doubles: not only have most Americans been denied the ideal of universal participation, but also our national self-image denies the very fact of this denial.

This double irony creates deep misunderstandings and correspondingly deep political tensions. Consider as an example racial discrimination. Whereas the proportion of whites who believe that racial discrimination is declining rose from three-tenths to nine-tenths over the past twenty-five years, the analogous proportion of blacks *declined* from between 50 and 90 percent in the mid-1960s to between 20 and 45 percent by the 1990s.[27] To cite only one specific instance of these dramatically different perceptions, in 1995, 72 percent of blacks but only 38 percent of whites agreed that past and present discrimination is a "major reason" for the problems faced by African Americans.[28] About the same proportions agreed that "racism is a big problem in our society today."[29]

Most blacks, in short, do not believe that the first tenet of the American dream applies to them. Most whites deny this disbelief.[30] As a consequence of these very different starting points, blacks and whites typically disagree on the policies needed to enable blacks to realize the claim of the first tenet of the American dream. The most vocal disagreement is over affirmative action policies, but debates over spending on urban infrastructure, management of social welfare, access to higher education, and other topics all stem from divergent assumptions about whether the premise of equal access to the dream really holds true.

The Second Tenet: Reasonable Anticipation of Success

The flaws of the second tenet of the American dream, the reasonable anticipation of success, stem from the close link between anticipation and expectation. That link presents little problem as long as enough resources and opportunities exist so that everyone has a reasonable chance of having some expectations met. Indeed, panegyrists of the American dream always expound on the bounty and openness of the American continent. For example, South Carolina governor James Glen typified the eighteenth-century entrepreneurs of colonization by promising:

> Adventurers will be pleased to find a Change from Poverty and Distress to Ease and Plenty; they are invited to a Country not yet half settled, where the Rivers are crouded with Fish, and the Forests with Game; and no Game-Act to restrain them from enjoying those Bounties of Providence, no heavy Taxes to impoverish them, nor oppressive Landlords to snatch the hard-earned Morsel from the Mouth of Indigence, and where Industry will certainly inrich them.[31]

These fantasies are innocuous as long as the resources roughly balance the dreams for enough people enough of the time. If, however, they do not—or worse, if they used to but do no longer—then the dream rapidly loses its appeal. The particular circumstances that cause resources to no longer balance dreams vary, ranging from the closing of the frontier to an economic downturn to a rapid increase in the number of dreamers. The general point, though, always holds: no one promises that dreams will be fulfilled, but the distinction between the right to dream of success and the right to succeed is psychologically hard to maintain. Maintaining the distinction is especially hard because the dream sustains Americans against daily nightmares only if they believe that they have a significant likelihood, not just a formal chance, of reaching their goals.

In short, the right to aspire to success works as an ideological substitute for a guarantee of success only if it begins to approach a guarantee. When it becomes clear that chances for success are slim or getting slimmer, the whole tenor of the American dream changes dramatically.

The general problem of scarcity varies slightly depending on what form of success people anticipate. It is most obvious and acute for those focused on compet-

itive success, in which, by definition, resources and opportunities are insufficient
to satisfy all dreamers. Scarcity may, however, be more problematic for those who
look forward to relative success, if only because there are more such people and
because they have no a priori reason to assume that many will fail. Thus, journalists
worry that "for the first time in living memory, America's children have less hope
of attaining a higher standard of living than their parents did."[32] The problem of
scarcity may be most devastating for people anticipating absolute success because
they have the least reason to expect that some will fail.[33] Losers of this type have
an unmatched poignancy: "I don't dream any more like I used to. I believed that
in this country, we would have all we needed for the decent life. I don't see that
any more."[34]

Conversely, the availability of resources and opportunities may shape the kind
of success that people dream of. If resources are profoundly scarce as in a famine,
or inherently limited as in election to the presidency, people almost certainly envision competitive success. If resources are moderately scarce, people will be concerned about their positions relative to those of others, but they will not necessarily
see another's gain as their loss. When resources and opportunities seem wide
open—anyone can achieve salvation, get an "A" on the exam, claim 160 acres of
western prairie—people are most free to pursue their own dreams and measure
their achievements by their own absolute standards.

This logic suggests a dynamic: as resources become tighter, people are likely to
shift their hopes for success from absolute to relative to competitive. For example,
before the 1980s, according to one journalist, "there was always enough to go
around, plenty of places in the sun. It didn't even matter much about the rich—so
long as everyone was living better, it seemed the rich couldn't be denied their
chance to get richer." But "today that wave [of prosperity] has crested. . . . Now
when the rich get richer, the middle class stagnates—and the poor get decidedly
poorer."[35]

The risks of anticipating success do not stop with anticipation. Attaining one's
dreams can be surprisingly problematic as well. From Jane Austen to Theodore
Dreiser to John Updike, writers have limned the loneliness of being at the top, the
spiritual costs of cutthroat competition, the shallowness of a society that rewards
success above all else. Alexis de Tocqueville characteristically provided one of the
most eloquent of these admonitions: "[Americans] never stop thinking of the good
things they have not got. It is odd to watch with what feverish ardor the Americans
pursue prosperity and how they are ever tormented by the shadowy suspicion that
they may not have chosen the shortest route to get it."[36] Tocqueville continued by
pointing out that the obsession with ever more success threatens not only the individual soul but also the body politic, noting that "[t]hey find it a tiresome in-
convenience to exercise political rights which distract them from industry. . . . The
role of government is left unfilled."[37]

The problems of success, however, pale beside the problems of failure. Because
success is so central to Americans' self-image, and because they expect as well as
hope to achieve it, Americans are not gracious about failure. Others' failure reminds
them that the dream may be just that—a dream, to be distinguished from waking

reality. Their own failure confirms that fear. Assistant professors denied tenure thus report contracting a sudden case of "leprosy"; their friends back away from them, and their own bodies betray their internal selves. Once Dreiser's G. W. Hurstwood loses his job as manager of Chicago's most fashionable saloon, he cannot prevent himself from sinking into lethargy, sloth, and utter destitution.

Furthermore, the better the dream works for other people, the more devastating failure is for the smaller and smaller proportion of people left behind. Thus in World War II, members of military units with a high probability of promotion were less satisfied with advancement opportunities than were members of units with a much lower probability of promotion because failure to earn promotion in the former case was both more salient and more demonstrably a personal rather than a systemic flaw.[38] In short, the ideology of the American dream includes no cushion for failure; a failed dream denies the loser not only success but even a shred of dignity to cover or soften the loss.

The Third Tenet: Success Is within One's Own Control

The nakedness of failure is made more stark by the third premise of the American dream—the belief that success results from actions and traits under one's own control. Logic does not support the reasoning that if success results from individual volition, then failure results from lack of volition. All one needs in order to see the logical flaw here is the distinction between "necessary" and "sufficient." But that distinction is not obvious or intuitive, and in any case the psycho-logic of the American dream differs from strict logic. In the psycho-logic, if one may claim responsibility for success, one must accept responsibility for failure.

Americans who do everything they can and still fail may come to understand that effort and talent alone do not guarantee success, but they have a hard time persuading others. After all, they are losers—why listen to them? Will we not benefit more by listening to winners, who seldom challenge the premise that effort and talent breed success? Americans are thus much less willing than Europeans to ascribe poverty to structural flaws or wealth to the prior ownership of wealth. For example, in 1985 only 31 percent of Americans agreed that "[i]n America what you achieve in life depends largely on your family background,"[39] compared with 51 percent of Austrians, 52 percent of Britons, and 63 percent of Italians.[40] Germans resemble Americans on this question; only 35 percent agreed.[41] However, three-quarters of American respondents compared with only half of the Germans agreed that "differences in social standing between people are acceptable because they basically reflect what people made out of the opportunities they had."[42] Similarly, 85 percent of Americans and 72 percent of Germans agreed that "America (Germany) has an open society. What one achieves in life no longer depends on one's family background, but on the abilities one has and the education one acquires."[43] In short, people who fail not only challenge the implicit promise of the American dream, but also are stigmatized because they presumably manifest—to winners more than to losers, to be sure—weakness of will or lack of talent.

The Fourth Tenet: Success Equals Virtue

The final blow to people who fail to achieve their dreams comes from the ideology's fourth tenet, the association of success with virtue. By the psycho-logic just described, if success implies virtue, failure implies sin.

American history and popular culture are replete with demonstrations of the connection between failure and sin. In the 1600s, indentured servants—kidnapped children, convicts, and families impoverished by the enclosure movement alike—were met on the shores of the New World with the assumption that they were all "strong and idle beggars, vagabonds, egyptians, comon and notorious whoores, theeves, and other dissolute and lousy persons."[44] A century later, even revolutionaries assumed that "only the 'shiftless, diseased, or vicious' were 'labourers, . . . who look to the earning of today for the subsistence of tomorrow.' " Members of nineteenth-century reform societies concurred, stating that fallen women were typically "the daughters of the ignorant, depraved and vicious part of our population, trained up without culture of any kind, amidst the contagion of evil example, and enter upon a life of prostitution for the gratification of their unbridled passions, and become harlots altogether by choice."[45]

Small wonder that by the late twentieth century, even the poor blame the poor for their condition. Despite her vivid awareness of exploitation by the rich, an aging cleaning woman insists that many people are poor because they "make the money and drink it all up. They don't care about the kids or the clothes. Just have a bottle on that table all the time."[46] In 1985, 60 percent of poor people, compared with 61 percent of the nonpoor, agreed that often "welfare encourages husbands to avoid family responsibilities."[47] Even more startling, 64 percent of the poor, but only 44 percent of the nonpoor, agreed that often "[p]oor young women have babies so they can collect welfare."[48]

The association of success with virtue obviously harms losers. The association, though, creates equally important if less obvious problems for winners. On the one hand, if I believe that virtue produced my success or that success has made me even more virtuous, I am likely to become insufferably smug. That may not bother me much, but the fact that people around me feel the same way will. In addition, this equation raises the stakes very high for further rounds of endeavor. If I continue to win, all is well; if I falter, I lose my amour propre as well as my wealth or power. On the other hand, if I recognize that my success is due partly to my lying to a few clients, evading a few taxes, or cheating a few employees, then I am likely to take on considerable guilt. This guilt might induce reform and recompense, but it may just as well induce drinking to assuage the unease, persecution of other nonvirtuous winners, attempts to show that losers are even more sinful, or simple hypocrisy.

These problems intensify when patterns of group success rather than the idiosyncrasies of individual success are at issue. If members of one group are seen as disproportionately successful, that group acquires a halo of ascribed virtue. For example, consider an article titled "The Great Jewish Invasion" that appeared in *McClure's Magazine* in 1907.[49] The author's ethnicity, the publication, the date, and the article's title all lead one to expect an anti-Semitic diatribe, at best only thinly veiled. The first few pages seem to confirm that expectation, pointing out that the success of New York's Jews is "remarkable" because most Jewish New Yorkers "are not what are commonly regarded as the most enlightened of their race,"[50] being from eastern rather than western Europe.[51] After all "[n]o people have had a more inadequate preparation, educational and economic, for American citizenship."[52] The article, nevertheless, goes on to describe in careful and admiring detail how these dirt-poor, ignorant, orthodox immigrants work, save, cooperate, sacrifice for their children—and end up wealthy beyond anyone's wildest imaginings.[53] In his highest possible accolade, the author even insists that the Russian Jew's "enthusiasm for America knows no bounds. He eagerly looks forward to the time when he can be naturalized."[54] In short, in one generation the East European Orthodox Jewish immigrant had gone from an unassimilable, bovine drag on the American spirit to the epitome of all of the American virtues. Nothing succeeds like success.

The contemporary equivalent of Burton Hendrick's "amazing" Jews are Southeast Asians. A half century ago, Americans could hardly derogate Chinese and Japanese immigrants enough. Now, newspapers have a seemingly endless supply of rags-to-riches stories about the daughter of destitute boat people who became the high school valedictorian a scant five years after arriving in the United States and is now in a premed program at Stanford. Such success is inevitably due to hard work, self-discipline, family support, and refusal to follow the bad example set by American-born peers.[55] This journalistic trend has become so powerful that spokespeople for Asian immigrants feel impelled to insist publicly that not *all* Asians escape poverty, crime, and discrimination and that even the most successful pay a heavy emotional cost.[56]

To argue that excessive praise is as bad as racism or ethnic slurs would be churlish. The problem is that the newly anointed group is often used to cast aspersions, implicit or explicit, on some other equally despised group that has not managed to fulfill the American dream. In Hendrick's case, the main negative reference group is the Irish, who drink and gamble, yield their productive jobs to Jews, and, worst of all, band together in labor unions, in the "Irish vote," and in political party machines.[57] In the case of immigrant Asians, the usual—if slightly more subtle—message is, "Why can't American blacks do the same thing? After all, they at least speak English when they start school." This dynamic adds yet another component to the nightmare of a failed American dream. Members of a denigrated group are disproportionately likely to fail to achieve their goals; they are blamed as individuals, and perhaps blame themselves, for their failure; and they carry a further stigma as members of a group that cannot help itself as other groups have done.

Defects in the Overall Dream

Finally, consider several problems inherent in the ideology of the American dream as a whole rather than in any single tenet. The American dream need not, but often does, take on a radically individualist cast. Achievers mark their success by moving away from the tenement, ghetto, or "holler" of their impoverished and impotent youth, thus speeding the breakup of their ethnic community. This is a bittersweet phenomenon. The freedom to move up and out is desirable, or at least desired; however, certainly those left behind, probably those who leave, and arguably the nation as a whole lose when groups of people with close cultural and personal ties break those ties in the pursuit of "the bitch-goddess, success."[58] The line between autonomy and atomism is hard to draw.

American culture is full of stories about the ambivalent effects of success on communities and their residents. A Polish folksong tells of a man who emigrated to America, worked for three years in a foundry, returned home with "gold and silver,"[59] but found that "my children did not know me, [f]or they fled from me, a stranger."[60] The emancipated children may be as distressed as the abandoned parents. In 1933 five brothers complained to the *Jewish Daily Forward*: "Imagine, even when we go with our father to buy something in a store on Fifth Avenue, New York, he insists on speaking Yiddish. We are not ashamed of our parents, God forbid, but they ought to know where it's proper and where it's not."[61]

The second problem is more conceptual than behavioral. The American dream need not be individualistic in the narrow sense, given that one can under its rubric pursue success for one's family or community as well as for oneself. But it is highly *individual*, in that it leads one to focus on people's behaviors rather than on economic processes, environmental constraints, or political structures as the causal explanation for social orderings. That focus is not itself a flaw; it is simply an epistemological choice with methodological implications for the study of American politics. But to the degree that the focus carries a moral message, it points to a weakness at the very heart of the dream.

The idea of the blank slate in the first tenet, the almost-promise of success of the second, the reliance on personal attributes in the third, the association of failure with sin in the fourth—all of these elements of the dream make it extremely difficult for Americans to see that everyone cannot simultaneously attain more than absolute success. Capitalist markets require some firms to fail; elections require some candidates and policy preferences to lose; status hierarchies must have a bottom in order to have a top. But the optimistic language of and methodological individualism built into the American dream *necessarily* deceive people about these societal operations. We need not invoke hypocrites out of Mark Twain or "blue-eyed white devils" in order to understand why some people never attain success; hypocrisy and bias only enter the picture in determining *who* fails. Our basic institutions are designed to ensure that some fail, at least relatively, and the dream does nothing to help Americans cope with or even to recognize that fact.

A final problem of the American dream results from its very dominance. Americans have few models and little historical sanction for simply opting out of the drive for wealth, status, or power. We do not lack for eloquent arguments against the success drive. Henry David Thoreau's *Walden* has, ironically, become an icon. At the height of the Jacksonian celebration of opportunities for the common man, James Fenimore Cooper sniffed, "A people that deems the possession of riches its highest source of distinction, admits one of the most degrading of all influences to preside over its opinions."[62] Even in the "me-decade" of the 1980s, George Will based a thriving journalistic career on the claim of being among the last of the old-time Tories, expounding on "the disappointment many people feel about affluence. Envy has increased while society has become more wealthy."[63]

Most Americans, however, honor this alternative vision more in the breach than in the observance, if then. We have no powerful ascetic tradition comparable to that of Hindus, Buddhists, and Native Americans. We have instead Thoreau, the Shakers, and 1960s hippies—curiosities from whom we take aphorisms, furniture, and hair styles once they are distant enough not to challenge our daily lives. We have similarly little in our ideological tool kit to help us see "small is beautiful" and "social limits to growth" as attractive alternatives rather than dystopias to be staved off as long as possible. Socialism has never enjoyed more than a tiny foothold among the American electorate.

Conclusion

Tocqueville assured his readers that "up to now the Americans have happily avoided all the reefs I have just charted."[64] Arguably we continue, 150 years later, to sail free, and perhaps we always will. If the United States does hit the reefs, however, the ideology of the American dream will not be of much help. Just as individuals whose dreams fail are left with precious few emotional and material resources, so a society that stakes so much on a dream of ever-expanding success is deeply vulnerable to natural, social, or demographic boundaries.

This point brings us back to the beginning—the meaning of the American dream and its implications for Americans' belief in and practice of equality. In the end, the ideology boils down to a profession of hope. It is profoundly egalitarian in at least three ways: it offers that hope to all individuals, at every point in their lives; it posits that all have the means at hand to realize their hopes; and it accepts all wishes as equally deserving and equally precious. It is, however, profoundly inegalitarian also. Its endorsement of inequality is most obvious when success is defined competitively, but the endorsement does not stop there. Losers, whether individuals or groups, have no value in the ideology except insofar as they are object lessons or potential winners sometime in the future. The harshness of this judgment has always been masked by the fact that most people win at least a little bit or are simply written out of the game as nonplayers. The draconian judgment is never far from the profession of hope, however, and one cannot understand the profoundly ambiguous nature of the American dream unless both its egalitarian and inegalitarian sides are kept simultaneously in view.

NOTES

I would like to thank Deborah Baumgold, Albert Hirschman, Kristie Monroe, Noah Pickus, and members of the 1991–92 School of Social Sciences Seminar at the Institute for Advanced Study for their help on earlier drafts of this chapter. Support for this research was provided in part by the Spencer Foundation, the Center for Advanced Study in the Behavioral Sciences, and the Institute for Advanced Study. This chapter is a revision of chapter 1 of

Facing Up to the American Dream: Race, Class, and the Soul of the Nation (Princeton: Princeton University Press, 1995).

1. John Locke, *Second Treatise of Government*, ed. Thomas P. Peandon (New York: Macmillan Co., 1952), 29.

2. Immigration Act of 1990, Pub. L. No. 101-649, § 101, 104 Stat. 4978, 4981–82 (1990) (codified at 8 U.S.C. § 1151 [Supp. II 1990]) (limiting number of legal immigrants to 700,000 for 1992–94 and to 675,000 thereafter).

3. For example, Andrew Carnegie, who immigrated to America from Scotland in 1848, became a millionaire and patron of the arts. See Burton J. Hendrick, *The Life of Andrew Carnegie* (New Brunswick, N.J.: Transaction Publishers, 1932).

4. See generally Upton Sinclair, *The Jungle* (New York: Airmont, 1906) (telling the story of exploited immigrants); George C. Harring, "America and Vietnam: The Unending War," *Foreign Affairs* 70 (Winter 1991): 104 (noting that many Vietnamese immigrants remain unassimilated and live below the poverty line).

5. Ronald Reagan, *Weekly Compilation of Presidential Documents* 19 (28 June 1983), 938, 943.

6. Studs Terkel, *American Dreams: Lost and Found* (New York: Ballantine Books, 1980), 236 (quoting Ed Sadlowski, son of Polish immigrants, who became the youngest district director of United Steel Workers of America).

7. Two recent examples are David Chandler and Mary Chandler, *The Binghams of Louisville: The Dark History behind One of America's Great Fortunes* (New York: Crown, 1987), and Adam Hochschild, *Half the Way Home: A Memoir of Father and Son* (New York: Viking Penguin, 1987).

8. Cotton Mather, *Magnalia Christi Americana*, ed. Raymond J. Cunningham and Frederick Ungar (1702; reprint, New York: Continuum, 1970), 27.

9. Ibid., 27–28.

10. Loammi Baldwin, *Thoughts on a Study of Political Economy* (New York: Kelley, 1809), 15, quoted in Stanley Lebergott, *The Americans: An Economic Record* (New York: Norton, 1984), 85.

11. Quoted in Dave Marsh, *Glory Days: Bruce Springsteen in the 1980s* (New York: Dell, 1984), 264.

12. Ibid.

13. James P. Comer, *Maggie's American Dream: The Life and Times of a Black Family* (New York: NAL-Dutton, 1988), 83–85. James Comer is an African American raised in poverty in Barbour County, Indiana, who became a physician. His book recaptures the life and dreams of his mother, Maggie Comer.

14. Ibid.

15. Byrd II to Lord Egmont, 12 July 1736, in *American Historical Review* 1 (1985): 88–90, quoted in Michael Greenberg, "William Byrd II and the World of the Market," *Social Studies* 16 (1977): 454.

16. Lawrence D. Maloney, "SUCCESS! The Chase Is Back in Style Again," *U.S. News and World Report*, 3 October 1983, 60.

17. See Locke, *Treatise on Government*, 29.

18. Quoted in Julie R. Jeffrey, *Frontier Women: The Trans-Mississippi West 1840–1880* (New York: Hill & Wang, 1979), 141.

19. Miguel Cortéz, quoted in Terkel, *American Dreams*, 131.

20. Ralph Waldo Emerson, "Wealth," in *The Conduct of Life* (Boston: Ticknor & Fields, 1860), 71, 86.

21. Citicorp advertisement, *Time*, 21 August 1989, 44–45.

22. Benjamin Franklin, *Autobiography, in Writings*, ed. J. A. Leo Lemay (New York: Library of America, 1987), 1392, 1397.

23. David M. Potter, *People of Plenty: Economic Abundance and the American Character* (Chicago: University of Chicago Press, 1954).

24. See, e.g., "Pa's Song": "I'm sure in this world there are plenty of good things enough for us all. . . . It is only by plodding and striving . . . that you'll ever be thriving, which you'll do if you've only the will." Laura Ingalls Wilder, *The Long Winter* (New York: Harper & Row, 1940), 334.

25. W. J. Ghent, *Our Benevolent Feudalism* (New York: Macmillan, Co. 1902) (quoting Rockefeller).

26. For an earlier formulation of the defects of the American dream, see Jennifer L. Hochschild, "The Double-Edged Sword of Equal Opportunity," in *Power, Inequality, and Democratic Politics*, ed. Ian Shapiro and Grant Reeher (Boulder: Westview Press, 1988), 168–200.

27. See William Brink and Louis Harris, *Black and White: A Study of U.S. Racial Attitudes Today* (New York: Simon & Schuster, 1966), 222–31; Thomas E. Cavanagh, *Inside Black America* (Washington, D.C.: Joint Center for Political Study, 1985), 3; CBS News/New York Times Poll, *The Kerner Commission—Ten Years Later* (New York: New York Times, 1978), 8; Philip E. Converse et al., *American Social Attitudes Data Sourcebook, 1947–1978* (Cambridge: Harvard University Press, 1980), 79; Louis Harris et al., *A Study of Attitudes toward Racial and Religious Minorities and toward Women* (New York: Louis Harris & Associates, 1978), 56; Gary T. Marx, *Protest and Prejudice: A Study of Belief in the Black Community* (New York: Harper and Row, 1967), 5–11, 220; Media General/Associated Press, *Public Opinion Poll*, at tables 1, 2 (New York: Associated Press, 1988); Howard Schuman et al., *Racial Attitudes in America* (Cambridge: Harvard University Press, 1988), xiii, xiv, 118–27, 141–43; "Black and White: A Newsweek Poll," *Newsweek*, 7 March 1988, 18, 23; Washington Post, *Washington Post Poll: Race Relations* (Washington, D.C.: Washington Post, 1992); Los Angeles Times, *Judge Thomas, Race Relations, and Ronald Reagan*. Poll #259, (Los Angeles: Los Angeles Times, 1991); Washington Post/Harvard University/Kaiser Foundation, *Survey on Race* (Washington, D.C.: Washington Post, 1995); *Gallup Poll Social Audit on Black/White Relations in the United States*, http://www.gallup.com/poll/special/race/, 10 June 1997.

28. Washington Post, *Survey on Race*, 1995.

29. Ibid.

30. For more extensive analyses of how perceptions of racial discrimination differ by race, see Jennifer L. Hochschild and Monica Herk, " 'Yes, but . . . ' ": Principles and Caveats in American Racial Attitudes," in *Nomos: Majorities and Minorities*, no. 32, ed. John W. Chapman and Alan Wertheimer, (New York: New York University Press, 1990), 308; and Hochschild, *Facing Up to the American Dream*.

31. Message from James Glen (1749), quoted in Warren B. Smith, *White Servitude in Colonial South Carolina* (Colombia: University of South Carolina Press, 1961), 51. A half a century later, J. Hector St. John de Crevecoeur was less instrumental, but no less extravagant: "After a foreigner from any part of Europe is arrived and become a citizen; let him devoutly listen to the voice of our great parent, which says to him, 'Welcome to my shores, distressed European; bless the hour in which thou didst see my verdant fields, my fair navigable rivers, and my green mountains! If thou wilt work, I have bread for thee; if thou wilt be honest, sober, and industrious, I have greater rewards to confer on thee—ease and independence. . . . Go thou and work and till; thou shalt prosper, provided thou be just, grateful, and industrious.' " J. Hector St. John de Crevecoeur, *Letters from an American Farmer* (1782; reprint, New York: Penguin Books, 1981), 89–90.

32. Mark L. Goldstein, "The End of the American Dream?" *Industry Weekly*, 4 April 1988, 77. See also Katherine Newman, *Declining Fortunes: The Withering of the American Dream* (New York: Basic Books, 1993).

33. See notes 10–13 above and accompanying text (defining absolute success).

34. Terkel, *American Dreams*, 116 (quoting Florence Scala, daughter of Italian immigrants who led the fight against city hall to save her old neighborhood on Chicago's near west side).

35. Goldstein, "End of the American Dream," 77.

36. Alexis de Tocqueville, *Democracy in America*, ed. J. P. Mayer and Max Lerner, trans. George Lawrence (1835; reprint, New York: Doubleday & Co., 1966).

37. Ibid., 512.

38. Samuel Stouffer et al., *The American Soldier: Adjustment during Army Life* (Princeton, N.J.: Princeton University Press, 1949), 1.

39. Tom W. Smith, "The Welfare State in Cross-National Perspective," *Public Opinion Quarterly* 51 (1987): 404, 411. All results combine "Agree strongly" and "Agree" categories.

40. Ibid.

41. Ibid.

42. Tom W. Smith, "Public Opinion and the Welfare State: A Cross-National Perspective" (paper presented at the Annual Meeting of the American Sociological Association [1987]).

43. Ibid., 39.

44. Gary B. Nash, *Red, White, and Black: The Peoples of Early America* (New York: Prentice Hall, 1982), 217.

45. Magdalen Society, "First Annual Report of the Executive Committee (1830)," in *The Reform Impulse, 1825–1850*, ed. Walter G. Hugins (Columbia: University of South Carolina Press, 1972), 41–42.

46. Quoted in Jennifer L. Hochschild, *What's Fair? American Beliefs about Distributive Justice* (Cambridge: Harvard University Press, 1981), 113.

47. I. A. Lewis and William Schneider, "Hard Times: The Public on Poverty," *Public Opinion* (June–July 1985): 2, 7.

48. Ibid.

49. Burton J. Hendrick, "The Great Jewish Invasion," *McClure's* 28 (1907): 307.

50. Ibid., 310.

51. Ibid.

52. Ibid., 311.

53. Ibid., 312–21.

54. Ibid., 320–21.

55. E.g., Fox Butterfield, "Why Asians Are Going to the Head of the Class," *New York Times*, 3 August 1986, Education Section, 18–23.

56. See, e.g., Reed Ueda, "False Modesty," *New Republic*, 3 July 1989, 16–17 (noting that group success has led to a model minority image that hides many of the problems currently afflicting Asian American societies).

57. Hendrick, "The Great Jewish Invasion," 321.

58. William James to H. G. Wells, in *The Letters of William James* (Boston: Atlantic Monthly, 1920), 2:260.

59. John J. Bukowczyk, *And My Children Did Not Know Me: A History of the Polish-Americans* (Bloomington: Indiana University Press, 1987): frontispiece.

60. Ibid.

61. Quoted in Loren Baritz, *The Good Life: The Meaning of Success for the American Middle Class* (New York: Knopf, 1989), 136.

62. James Fenimore Cooper, *The American Democrat* (Indianapolis: Liberty Fund, 1838), 138.

63. George Will, "The Hell of Affluence," in *The Pursuit of Happiness and Other Sobering Thoughts* (New York: Harper Collins, 1978), 97, 98.

64. Tocqueville, *Democracy in America*, 513.

6

Racial Divisions and Judicial Obstructions

JEREMY RABKIN

Historians may well look back on 1995 as the year that marked the end of "the civil rights era." It began with the transfer of power in Washington to new conservative majorities in Congress, promising substantial cutbacks in federal interference in American society. Before the year was out, the nation's capital played host to a Million Man March, organized by Nation of Islam leader Louis Farrakhan, a purveyor of hate against Jews, Asian Americans, and whites. It was a fearful counterpart to Rev. Martin Luther King's celebrated March on Washington in the summer of 1963, at the outset of the civil rights era: whereas King had preached to a multiracial crowd on behalf of federal enforcement of civil rights, Farrakhan preached a message of black self-help to an exclusively black crowd—and Farrakhan drew two or three times as large a crowd as King.

Both white and black Americans, in quite different ways, expressed an impatience to move beyond the failed liberal policies of the past three decades. The country must do much soul-searching and rethinking in the years to come. On that, almost everyone is agreed. The rethinking, if it is to succeed, must extend to courts as well. Federal judges were seen as central actors in the early stages of the civil rights struggle, as the landmark decision in *Brown v. Board of Education* launched a long tedious struggle for school desegregation, not only in the South but eventually in the urban school districts of the North as well. In more recent times, debates over affirmative action and racial-preference policies have returned again and again to the federal courts, which have been cast as the ultimate arbiters of racial justice.

But all this may now be past—and well past. It would be a considerable exaggeration to depict federal courts as the main cause of failed social policies in the past generation. But it is no exaggeration to say that social policies of the past generation have indeed failed in their central challenge—the healing of racial divisions in the United States. It is simply a fact that courts have been deeply implicated in the elaboration of those failed policies. Fresh thinking about public policy must return to thinking about judicial policies because many judicial policies threaten to derail promising new policy initiatives, if courts do not "rethink their priorities" (to borrow the phrase that so intimidated judges and other political figures in the 1960s).

Two disclaimers are worth emphasizing at the outset. First, the issue is not whether the courts will uphold constitutional guarantees. That is a piece of childish rhetoric designed to appeal to only the very partisan or the very naive. Fairly put, the issue is whether courts will continue to pursue the particular slant given to constitutional interpretation in the past thirty years—most of it marking a considerable leap beyond earlier interpretation and almost all of it guided by policy visions then in fashion. The issue is not even whether courts will adhere to original intent but whether they will insist on adhering to failed intent of the past generation.

Second, in worrying over judicial obstacles to new policy directions, one must necessarily engage in speculation about potential threats. Policy innovations that have not yet been enacted have not yet been tested in the courts. Policy experiments that are still in their early stages have not received definitive judgment from the Supreme Court. And if one thing is sure, it is that courts have been quite unpredictable in their response to new trends in policy—sometimes jumping on the bandwagon of popular policy ideas, sometimes seeking to console the losers in policy debates by imposing new roadblocks. When we are dealing with jurisprudence that has no serious constitutional anchor—as is so plainly true of most doctrines on civil liberties and civil rights—we cannot predict how restrictive or accommodating the doctrine will prove to be in particular cases. The point is to sound a warning of what may prove troublesome, unless courts do undertake more fresh thinking.

At a higher level of generality, however, some things can be said with some confidence. In what follows, I will elaborate three main arguments. First, the ongoing debate about racial preferences and affirmative action—in which courts have been expected to play a central decisional role—is largely irrelevant to our current problems because these civil rights remedies have not touched the problem of the black underclass, which is at the heart of our current racial discord. Second, new approaches must center on local initiatives, to which law and courts have little to contribute—except to prune earlier doctrines that may inhibit or forestall local initiatives. Third, that the threat to new approaches in older doctrines reflects not just the predictable bias of federal courts—toward legalistic, procedural, and uniform national standards—but also the particular bias of New Deal and Great Society liberalism, which expected to deal with moral, spiritual, and human problems by redistributing material resources under the ongoing supervision of Washington bureaucracies.

The Irrelevance of Traditional Remedies

Having denounced racial segregation in the South during the 1950s, the federal courts played a leading role in the late 1960s and early 1970s in demanding that governments must, after all, take account of race—for "benign" purposes. Since the mid-1970s, the Supreme Court has wrestled with the vexing question of how far racial classification or racial-preference schemes can be pressed before they cease to be "benign."[1] As courts have assumed such a central role in past phases of the debate on civil rights, it is natural to think that courts will ultimately play the decisive role in determining the proper bounds of "affirmative action." It is natural to think this way, but it is almost surely mistaken.

To start with, the Supreme Court has vacillated with such regularity on these issues that vacillation, itself, has come to seem the Court's settled policy.[2] Just on the issue of affirmative action set-asides—by which some portion of contracts or benefits are "set aside" for minorities, outside the normal process of competitive bidding—the Court has landed on every side of the issue over the past fifteen years. It was in favor of federal set-asides for construction contracts in 1980;[3] then it struck down in 1987 a virtually identical program initiated by the city of Richmond;[4] then in 1990 it endorsed a fixed system of racial preferences in the awarding of broadcast licenses by the Federal Communications Commission.[5] The confusion reached a fitting culmination in 1995, as the Court ruled that "strict scrutiny" must be imposed on racial set-aside schemes in the awarding of federal construction contracts, but the Court's opinion hastened to add that such programs might well survive such scrutiny.[6]

The Court's hesitations are understandable. Passions run high on both sides of the general issue. It is hard to say that groups that have long been the victims of discrimination should, at some arbitrary stopping point, suddenly forfeit all claims to special governmental solicitude. It is equally hard to deny that individuals who do not belong to a favored minority group may have a legitimate sense of grievance when the accident of their birth works against them in the bestowal of governmental benefits. So the Court has been threading its way carefully—and indecisively.

But even if the Court steels itself to a more consistent repudiation of the most explicit racial-preference programs, judicial rulings are unlikely to quiet the larger debate about racial favoritism. Very few individuals from the favored minority groups own companies that can bid for governmental contracts or licenses, anyway. Indeed, very few white individuals are in a position to be affected in any direct way by such programs. On the other hand, most employment opportunities and opportunities for higher education, affecting tens of millions of people, are very much affected by existing civil rights regulation. And these nondiscrimination programs have a built-in momentum toward racial favoritism that is most unlikely to be affected by tinkering at the margin with affirmative action programs.

The basic reason is that since the late 1960s, the federal government has tracked racial breakdowns in employment, as well as in admissions to institutions of higher education. These figures may then be used to make out a prima facie case of discrimination. Reliance on a "neutral" decision criterion—such as the presence of a high school diploma—may be challenged unless it is proved to be a "bona fide" qualifying criterion.[7] Proving that any normal indicator is a valid predictor of future performance is a daunting (and extremely costly) effort. Employers and admissions committees are thus under constant pressure to make their resulting numbers look right to governmental monitors. Their behavior can be called "nondiscrimination,'' but the effect is not different from the racial preferences demanded by more explicit affirmative action programs.

Even if the Supreme Court reverses ground and becomes more solicitous of "reverse discrimination" claims—something that should not be relied on—this tendency to hire and admit by the numbers will be with us for a long time. The reason is that affirmative action is now deeply ingrained in the internal culture both of big business and of most academic institutions. Even if the federal government relaxed its pressure for numerical results, much of the business world and many public employers, at federal, state, and local levels, would probably continue to operate some informal system of affirmative action. So would most academic institutions. They would continue with affirmative action because managers in private companies, public agencies, and educational institutions have all become accustomed to operating in this way and remain fearful of accusations—even when divorced from legal sanctions—that they are "racist" or guilty of "institutional racism."[8] So a great many institutions will simply rearrange their decisionmaking criteria to ensure that they produce the desired racially balanced results.[9] To enforce truly color-blind decisionmaking, it would be necessary for governmental agencies (or courts) to decide the precise decisionmaking standards appropriate for a neutral decision. And almost no one favors the radical extension of governmental control that this approach would entail.

Thus, when the California Board of Regents, at the urging of Governor Pete Wilson, issued a directive prohibiting affirmative action preferences within the state's higher education system, the policy was protested by faculties and leading administrators within the University of California system—but most observers predicted it would not make much difference in the end.[10] When a citizens' group tried to launch a ballot initiative in California to impose a wider prohibition on any racial preference in state contracting or state employment, it found much public support in opinion polls—and a nearly total refusal by the business community to provide funding for the task of gathering enough signatures to place this initiative on the state ballot.[11] In Congress, the most "radical" measure to reform racial preferences, a bill sponsored by Republican representative Charles T. Canady in the House in 1995,[12] would prohibit courts from enforcing explicit quotas to remedy past discrimination but would not revise the way "discrimination" is defined or judged in federal litigation.

My own view is that efforts to reduce the extent of race-conscious remedies in the law are worthwhile because the law is a teacher as well as an enforcer. The more explicit the race-conscious element in law, the more it teaches whites that blacks cannot compete on their own and the more it teaches blacks that whites are too irredeemably racist to afford fair treatment to all races without coercion.

But the larger point is that, whatever the prospects for reducing race-conscious remedies, we are likely to retain a good deal of race-conscious policy throughout society. Defenders of this approach, like President Bill Clinton, may argue that it is necessary to ensure that white America does not relax its efforts to ensure equality and to ensure that minority citizens do not give up hope. And yet, as even President Clinton has recognized, it has become not only an intractable conflict but also an increasingly marginal one. Racial-preference programs cannot promise an end to racial tensions. Nor is it plausible, on the other hand, that abandoning such programs will put an end to racial tensions.

Even President Clinton, while insisting that racial-preference programs must be retained, acknowledged in a major speech—delivered on the same day as the Far-rakhan march—that affirmative action was not reaching the deepest roots of division.[13] "Blacks," he said, "are right to think something is terribly wrong when . . . almost one in three African American men in their 20s are either in jail, on parole or otherwise under the supervision of the criminal justice system—nearly one in three." The comparable figure for white males is about 7 percent—that is, little more than one-fifth the rate for young blacks. President Clinton did not, however, pretend that whites, for their part, were wrong to draw fearful conclusions from these statistics. Rather, he rightly called on blacks to "understand and ac-knowledge the roots of white fear in America. There is a legitimate fear of the violence that is too prevalent in our urban areas; and . . . too often [it] has a black face."

The larger truth is that the problems of the inner city have gotten worse, not better, during the civil rights era of the last thirty years. As President Clinton said, we have witnessed "a generation of deepening social problems that disproportion-ately impact black Americans."

Crime is only the most dramatic expression of a larger pattern of social break-down. As late as the mid-1960s, 75 percent of black households with children under eighteen years old were headed by married couples; by the mid-1980s, more than half of such black families were headed by women on their own. At the start of the 1960s, fewer than 25 percent of total births among black mothers were out of wedlock; by the mid-1980s, some 60 percent of black babies were born out of wedlock (compared to 12.5 percent among whites).[14] By the early 1990s, the il-legitimacy rate among blacks was nearly 70 percent (while the rate among whites climbed to 22 percent).[15]

For decades, it has been conventional wisdom among liberal policymakers to trace problems of crime and family breakdown to economic dislocation. No doubt, there is truth in the warnings that cities do not offer the abundance of well-paying manufacturing jobs for unskilled labor that attracted black migrants to the North in the 1940s and 1950s. But it is equally clear that family breakdown makes it far more difficult to seize the opportunities that do exist. Children of unwed mothers are far more likely to drop out of school, to repeat the pattern of unwed pregnancy, and to fall into trouble with drugs and with crime.[16]

Thirty years of civil rights enforcement has proved sadly unequal to dealing with these worsening problems. Affirmative action may well have provided a useful leg up for many blacks. But the persistence of a black underclass continues to have a poisoning effect on race relations.

This trend is well documented in Jennifer Hochschild's 1995 book, *Facing Up to the American Dream*. During the 1960s, pollsters continually found optimism among black Americans about the prospects for increasing racial equality, with anywhere from 50 percent to 80 percent of black respondents professing to see racial equality on the increase. By the 1980s, similar polls found that only 20 percent to 45 percent of black respondents saw themselves on a trajectory toward increased equality, and up to half in some polls claimed that the situation of blacks had actually worsened.[17]

Hochschild's most striking and dismaying finding, however, is what she describes as "the paradox of succeeding more and enjoying it less." It is precisely the black middle class—whether defined by education or by income—that has become more embittered and disillusioned. And this is not simply because more worldly people always lose some illusions on their way up in life. Throughout the 1960s, "lower status blacks perceived more white hostility than did their higher-status counterparts," but "that discrepancy was reversed by the end of the 1970s." Polls since then consistently find more "bitterness about white intentions" among higher-status blacks.[18]

The extent of the disaffection among middle-class blacks has generated some alarming responses. A 1990 poll, for example, found that 67 percent of black college graduates (compared with 42 percent of blacks with less than a high school education and 16 percent of whites) thought it was either "true" or "might be true" that "the Government deliberately makes sure that drugs are easily available in poor black neighborhoods in order to harm black people." Asked to consider whether the AIDS virus was "deliberately created in a laboratory in order to infect black people," 40 percent of black college graduates thought this was "true" or "might be true" (compared with 18 percent of blacks with less than a high school education and 5 percent of whites).[19]

What can account for disaffection so severe as to make even such paranoid fantasies seem plausible? How can it be that those who have benefited most from increasing opportunities are so relentlessly suspicious? Hochschild offers a very plausible interpretation: "Many middle-class blacks feel an acute responsibility to their history, their poorer fellows, their race, and each other. That sense of responsibility may not be growing, but the sense that American society will not allow them to fulfill their responsibility despite new-found wealth and power clearly *is* growing. The new frustration leads to bitterness against other Americans and eventually against the American dream."[20]

After such experience, it is very hard to believe that a redoubled commitment to affirmative action will actually take us on a path to further racial healing.

New Approaches, Old Roadblocks

Racial divisions may add urgency to dealing with the plight of inner cities. But the desperation of inner-city conditions would have an urgent claim on public policy in any case. Because the problems are not distinctively racial, solutions can be framed in nonracial terms. Some may arouse opposition in particular communities more than others. But most things that can be done need to be done at the local level, anyway. There is room for and indeed a basic need for trying different approaches in different places. But in one area after another there are common threats from restrictive court rulings.

Crime control is a good place to start. The prevalence of criminal violence in inner cities may frighten whites. But the main victims tend to be nonwhites, and the toll is staggering. In 1992, for example, African Americans, though only 12 percent of the population, constituted almost half of all murder victims (and 94 percent of their killers were also black).[21] Black males were seven times more likely to be victims of murder than their white counterparts, and the life expectancy of black men in central Harlem was calculated, in the early 1990s, to be lower than that of men in Bangladesh.[22]

Professor John DiIulio of Princeton University, one of the leading scholars on crime control, emphasizes that, beyond the tragedy of the immediate victims, the consequences of such carnage destabilize and demoralize entire communities, so it is hard to be hopeful about anything else in inner cities if we cannot put a decisive check on street violence.[23] DiIulio's main prescription, seeking longer and more predictable sentences, does seem to be bearing results. It is expensive to provide prisons on the necessary scale, however, and there is constant pressure on available capacity. Some judges have responded by demanding more facilities for prisoners, driving up the costs. Others have actually ordered prison release programs to ease crowding. There is certainly a legitimate role for courts in preventing the most abusive prison conditions. It is at least fair to ask, however, whether the rights of prisoners should be purchased at the expense of potential victims of prematurely released criminals.[24] Some judges do not seem to take this question at all seriously. Proposals have been put before Congress, therefore, to limit the power of federal judges to order prison releases,[25] but whether such measures would be accepted by courts remains in question.

But even the staunchest advocates of incarceration do not pretend it is a panacea. Prisons may be cost-effective in reducing the social cost of crime, but the cost of prison construction and maintenance still provokes resistance from weary taxpayers (all the more so because the affluent, who pay more taxes, actually do better at protecting themselves, through various private measures, from the burdens and costs of unchecked violent crime). Moreover, the current scale of incarceration has already begun to generate significant political resistance, especially from minority leaders protesting the extremely disproportionate presence of blacks and Hispanics in the nation's prisons. Yet demographic projections suggest that we are in for a new surge of violent crime over the next few years, as a larger cohort of young people enters the most crime-prone period of life.[26]

Some analysts argue that although it is important to have tough sentences, to put a heavy "price" on crime, it is even more important to make criminal justice swift and certain. So the issue is not just the capacity of prisons but the efficiency of police and of the criminal courts. Critics have argued for some decades that court-imposed burdens on the criminal justice system may significantly inhibit police effectiveness. Evidence is certainly disputed. But it is indisputable that some constitutional doctrines—like the "exclusionary rule" that prohibits the use of improperly obtained evidence in criminal trials—impose burdens that have no direct relation to the primary question of whether the defendant is, in fact, guilty as charged.[27] Whatever reformers may have imagined in the 1960s, it is now a much more urgent question whether the multiplication of technical objections—which rich defendants can exploit and ordinary defendants cannot, in practice, afford to pursue—has actually helped to enhance public confidence in the criminal justice system or simply exacerbated public cynicism.[28]

But even a streamlined criminal justice system and an expanded role for official policing cannot be expected, in themselves, to restore order to communities where violence has become endemic. So advocates of tougher measures—along with those who shrink from tougher measures—also put stress on preventive measures. In particular, there has been renewed interest in mobilizing community efforts to help restore order to chaotic and violent neighborhoods.

An obvious beginning is to make streets safer so that more people are willing to move around openly and to make violent criminals more hesitant to act where there will be more witnesses and perhaps more good Samaritans coming to the aid of potential victims. James Q. Wilson, one of the leading analysts of crime-control policy, has urged that police make periodic sweeps of neighborhoods to disarm criminals. He urges that criminals be frisked and disarmed on the streets.[29] The idea is appealing and seems more promising than gun-control schemes that try to prevent the flow of guns into the community in the first place. The notion is that even though it may be difficult to prevent access to guns, carrying them in the streets can be made dangerous.

One difficulty with this approach, however, is that courts may not stand for it. The Supreme Court held in 1968 that police must have probable cause to make searches of suspects.[30] Courts might apply this in lenient ways, as some seem to have done. But others have been rather strict. Courts can be a serious obstacle if they determine to be. In 1994, for example, the U.S. Court of Appeals for the Seventh Circuit overturned a conviction for illegal firearms possession: Milwaukee police had received an anonymous tip about a suspicious car (a Cadillac with tinted windows) and, when they approached the passengers, found a gun barrel protruding from the defendant's coat. Neither the tip nor the suspicious appearance of the car was sufficient, according to the court, to justify the subsequent successful firearms search.[31] Similar rulings are not hard to find.[32]

A related proposal, urged by Wilson, among others, suggested that cities experiment with "perimeter control" to block off streets in hopes of cutting down on through traffic and making neighborhoods more self-contained.[33] The idea is to provide urban neighborhoods with some of the benefits associated with private gated communities for the affluent. In fact, such measures have been taken in California and a few other places to considerable local satisfaction.[34]

But again there are potential legal obstacles. The Supreme Court ruled in 1972 that state "vagrancy" laws are unconstitutionally vague.[35] The opinion by Justice William O. Douglas rhapsodized about Walt Whitman, drawing poetic inspiration from idling through the streets. It is not likely to be a view that commends itself to people in poor neighborhoods, where drifters are more likely to be armed drug dealers than idling poets. But some judges have been extremely solicitous of drifters. In 1990 a judge ruled that there is a constitutional right to be a panhandler in the New York City subways.[36] In a similar case, a court ruled that an unwashed, muttering homeless person had a constitutional right to remain an "annoying" presence in a public library.[37] Courts have also embraced challenges to laws prohibiting loitering for the purpose of begging.[38] It will not be easy to control access to secured neighborhoods if judges of this sort continue to impose their will on struggling communities.

One finds this inclination over and over among contemporary judges, however. The Bush administration tried to evict drug dealers from federally funded housing projects. The Fourth Circuit ruled that this program violates the due process rights of the drug dealers, who must be allowed to stay in public housing—continuing to deal crack cocaine to children and pregnant women—until given an opportunity to defend themselves in a formal hearing.[39]

If judges are hesitant about going after drug dealers, they may be equally uneasy about going after drug users in systematic ways. James Q. Wilson has urged that routine, frequent drug testing be imposed on former users to ensure that they stay away from drugs. He may be right that legal problems can be avoided by focusing on those with previous drug convictions. But again, notions of "probable cause" and "expectations of privacy" can be quite elastic. A majority of the Supreme Court expressed outright opposition or great uneasiness at a school district's policy of imposing mandatory drug testing on high school athletes.[40]

People with financial means have increasingly sought to insulate themselves from crime by retreating to guarded private enclaves. The poor would face obstacles in trying to follow this example, even if the government or charitable donors helped them to secure some of the necessary resources. Some cities, for example, have experimented with private conservancy groups to care for public parks. The experiment might be extended to private parks, private police. But again, court doctrines from earlier times cast a shadow. Courts remain divided on whether even private property, such as shopping malls, should be considered a "public forum," subject to First Amendment restrictions on regulation.[41] Efforts to impose certain standards of polite behavior in private parks may well run afoul of such doctrines.[42] Hiring private police? One of the most ready sources—church volunteers—may raise First Amendment objections if any government money is involved.[43] But government money may be essential when dealing with public housing projects. A rigorous application of recent doctrines, in other words, may make the poor singularly captive to constitutional fashion.

Schools, Families, Judges

What is true for crime control is equally true for education. Dissatisfaction with public schools is widespread and for understandable reasons. So there is great interest in increasing choice. Middle-class families can escape public schools. Why not provide more choice to poor families? Milwaukee attempted to do just this—and was promptly sued. A federal court declared a school choice program unconstitutional for allowing students into religious schools. But 93 of Milwaukee's 130 private schools happen to be religious schools. Parents participating in the choice program were overwhelming black and Hispanic. Non-Catholic parents were still eager for the discipline and morale available in Catholic schools. They certainly had reason to shun the public schools, where fewer than half the students graduate from high school. The dropout rate is seven times the average for the state of Wisconsin, and of those remaining, 79 percent failed the math-proficiency test required for graduation.[44] But although the public schools were demonstrably failing, a federal judge decided that the students simply could not be allowed an alternative: offering students and their parents a choice would be a threat to civil liberty![45]

The Milwaukee case is simply the most recent and most dramatic illustration of a long-established pattern. Across the country, public school systems have been woefully unsuccessful in teaching reading, spelling, or basic math to inner-city children.[46] Careful studies have long confirmed that parochial schools do much better at teaching basic skills, even while spending much less per pupil than public schools. Evidently parochial schools are better equipped to impart the discipline and self-respect needed for orderly learning. They do better, even with inner-city students, even when they are Catholic schools trying to inspire students from non-Catholic families.[47]

Yet state governmental efforts to subsidize parochial education—aimed at making it more widely available—have repeatedly been struck down by the Supreme Court on the grounds that such subsidies would constitute an establishment of religion, somehow violating the rights of ardent secularists. The Court managed to persuade itself that aid to religious colleges could be squared with its reading of the First Amendment, but aid to elementary and secondary parochial schools—which would be far more relevant to the plight of children in the inner cities—must remain unacceptable.[48] The Court, which was prepared to embark on such bitterly divisive measures as mandatory busing programs for school integration, claimed that aid to religiously affiliated schools (at the elementary and secondary level) would be too "divisive."[49] In an era when almost all other forms of governmental spending are insulated from constitutional challenge, the Court has pursued its opposition to assisting religious schools with relentless energy.[50]

Opponents of subsidizing private schools insist that drawing more ambitious students into private schools will undermine the quality of public schools. Of course, the obvious response is to let public schools compete more effectively. But those who emphasize the need for reforms in the public schools may encounter a new set of judicial obstacles.

One of the main problems is reasserting discipline in public schools. Recently, the president of the American Federation of Teachers, the nation's second largest teacher's union, proposed a series of reforms to make American public schools as effective as their European counterparts. The "first essential element" on his list was "the refusal to tolerate disruptive student behavior that regularly interferes with education." Albert Shanker notes that efforts to remove disruptive students from the classroom are infrequent: "When they occur, advocacy groups mount lengthy, expensive legal challenges. And courts are apt to side with the 'repentant' offender rather than the unseen victims—the other students."[51]

Courts are indeed apt to side with the "repentant" offender. A few years ago, for example, a federal court reviewed the twenty-nine-day suspension of a student who, all parties stipulated, "engaged in verbal and physical temper tantrums which included kicking and scratching teachers and hitting other students." The court, acceding to the parents' insistence on making a federal case out of a temporary suspension, ordered the student reinstated.[52]

Of course, beyond removing the most disruptive students, public schools need to cultivate orderly habits and a sense of academic discipline among the ordinary students. Some educators have urged that it would be helpful to separate boys and girls, particularly in early grades, because boys tend to be much more restless and aggressive, becoming frustrated and repelled by the orderly classroom routines to which girls adapt so readily.[53] Experiments of this kind have shown some promise. But it may not be possible to pursue them. A court has already held that mandatory segregation based on sex is unconstitutional.[54]

Other educators have urged the need for more-restrictive dress codes to discourage distracting competition over styles of dress. There have even been proposals to have public schools require standardized school uniforms, as has been done by many private schools and by public schools in other countries. It might help to encourage a sense of discipline. It might promote a sense that school is serious and not a setting for flamboyant personal display.[55] It might also be held unconstitutional because some courts have held that students have a constitutional right to dress as they like.[56]

If schools venture beyond outward displays of discipline to direct efforts to promote moral training, they will again risk judicial scrutiny and interference. Public schools can be slapped down for even the most indirect reference to religious authority. The Supreme Court itself ruled in 1980 that display of the Ten Commandments in public schools would be constitutionally intolerable pedagogy.[57] Even a moment of silent reflection at the beginning of the day was judged by the Supreme Court to be intolerably burdensome to the religious liberty of students.[58] The Court not only condemns such indirect acknowledgment of religious authority but also has condemned straightforward educational decisions—like removing books from school libraries—when it suspects a religious motivation.[59] So lower courts have gotten into the business of determining which books need to be on the shelves of public school libraries and even which school practices, suspected of having been banned by religiously motivated school boards, must be restored to public schools under the banner of assured secularism.[60]

The point hardly requires belaboring. Federal courts have displayed remarkable confidence in their ability to dictate the proper path of public education. Some of the school districts most closely managed by federal judges have deteriorated most dramatically. After more than a decade of micromanaging public schools in Boston, a federal court left the school system more racially segregated than before, while reading and math scores had also fallen lower.[61] Kansas City had much the same experience after decades of judicial management of its public schools.[62] There is much legitimate disagreement about the proper approach to educating poor children with low motivation or inadequate parental support. There needs to be much experiment. Experience suggests, however, that judges are the very last people from whom to expect any constructive help. If they make things worse, after all, they can simply shrug their shoulders, walk away, and chalk it all up to the obligations of "the law." Schools will do better when they are more accountable to parents rather than to judges.

Improving the capacities of parents is surely the most important and most difficult challenge facing public policy. But here, too, judges figure mostly as potential obstacles to necessary reforms.

The most obvious and immediate way to improve parenting is to increase the number of people involved: two is almost always better than one. Single-parent households—meaning, in practice, children reared by unwed mothers—have become the norm in inner cities. It is difficult to know how to break this dreadful pattern at such an advanced stage. It is always difficult to influence private, intimate behavior. It is particularly difficult when policymakers have to worry about not punishing children for the sins of their parents. But serious efforts must be made.

One obvious place to start is with the welfare system. Though the point is certainly disputed among social scientists, there is growing recognition that the welfare system has offered perverse incentives to illegitimacy. Many scholars argue that the generous terms of the Aid to Families with Dependent Children Act (together with related services, such as Medicaid and food stamps) offer more reward than minimum-wage employment, encouraging motherhood as a sort of career—from which the fathers are, by the rules of the system, excluded.[63] It is certainly true that without this "safety net," very young women would have to be vastly more cautious about becoming pregnant without a reliable breadwinning partner—as women were, in black communities and elsewhere in America, before the 1960s.

We are now entering an era in which a Republican Congress seeks to offer much wider discretion to the states to experiment with new approaches to welfare. It remains to be seen whether courts will go along. An early experiment in New Jersey, denying additional financial support to families that have additional children while on welfare, has been upheld by a lower court,[64] but the litigation continues. And it is surely only the beginning. Conditions attached to welfare eligibility may require intrusive monitoring and subjective or contentious judgments by local officials regarding individual cases. (Was the client *genuinely* trying to stay in a training program, *genuinely* trying to take proper care of the children, and so on?) The Supreme Court held in 1970 that welfare payments are an entitlement, requiring comparable procedural protections as private property.[65] Although the doctrine has been subject to considerable erosion, it might well resurface as the instrument by which activist judges seek to put brakes on state experiments in welfare reform.

Other experiments in trying to restore the strength of family obligation will generate even more controversy and more litigation. Congressman Newt Gingrich stirred much controversy when he urged that states and localities might want to reopen orphanages for children who were intolerably neglected by the parents. In fact, the suggestion made by James Q. Wilson was for state-run "homes" for mothers and children, providing a structured program along with food and shelter.[66] Could assignment to such a "home" be made compulsory? We don't yet know.

Some states are seeking to impose financial obligations on fathers of minor children, even if they have not married the mother and even if they have never previously assumed financial responsibility for the mother. Can the mother be forced to identify the father? Can suspected fathers be forced to submit to blood tests and DNA tests? Can their earnings be forcibly garnished until the children have reached adulthood? What happens to the mothers in the meantime? Can more extreme sanctions—such as imprisonment—be applied if the fathers fail to generate any earnings to meet their financial obligations? Litigation is certain. Only the ultimate attitude of the courts is not.

Other efforts may be made to stigmatize unwed motherhood more directly. Only a few decades ago, it was routine to remove pregnant students from schools or at least from regular classes with other students. The idea was to remove a bad example and to stigmatize it. Whether this would still be helpful in discouraging teen pregnancy may be debated. It is at present illegal, under federal regulations interpreting a statute prohibiting sex discrimination.[67] If the regulations are lifted by federal authorities, some local school districts may want to experiment with a return to older approaches. But lower courts have found constitutional objections to discrimination against unwed mothers.[68] Other means of stigmatizing unwed motherhood—or providing special acknowledgment for married mothers—will face similar hurdles.

No one can be sure how courts will respond to such policies. But less than a decade ago, four justices of the Supreme Court insisted that the Constitution guaranteed the right to participate in homosexual practices—or, rather, guaranteed a wide sphere of autonomy for sexual conduct between consenting adults.[69] More recently, the Supreme Court held that it was not ''rational'' to exclude ''homosexual orientation'' from the personal attributes covered by state or local antidiscrimination measures, prompting speculation that the Court is now prepared to proclaim broad constitutional protection for homosexual conduct.[70] The Court has repeatedly reaffirmed a broad right to abortion. It is certainly possible to argue that government may not interfere in ''reproductive choice'' and to argue at the same time that once the choice to have children is made, the government has considerable authority to enforce parental standards of proper care for children. It is certainly possible to argue that single individuals should have broad autonomy to conduct their sex lives as they see fit, but that special burdens or restrictions may apply to parents. It is possible to argue such things. But cases affirming a constitutional right to sexual freedom certainly generate a doctrinal momentum that militates against stern restrictions in the name of protecting family life. And over the past two decades, the Supreme Court has on a number of occasions expressed mistrust of governmental measures that seem to enshrine a particular definition of ''the family'' (as the traditional two-parents-with-children family).[71]

As with crime-control measures and with educational reform measures, we cannot be sure what will work in policies to restore the primacy of family life, what will receive public support, and what will have serious influence on behavior. We cannot be sure how much will be achieved by symbolic measures, aimed at rallying salutary opinion and reinforcing sound moral convictions. We may never be able to gauge the contribution of particular policies or gestures, amid a mass of other policies. But we will never gain any clarity at all without trying new approaches. And we will not be able to do even much of that if courts insist on blocking the way.

Judicial Pride and Inner-City Despair

One might charitably interpret these court decisions as reflecting the judicial commitment to civil liberty. One might say, that is, that an overriding regard for civil liberty has motivated courts to resist efforts at crime control, to oppose efforts to expand school choice and tighten school discipline, and to hobble efforts to revive public morals.

Even when viewed in these terms, however, the stance of the courts is not easy to defend. The Constitution speaks of securing "the blessings of liberty." The framers were perfectly aware, however, that when taken to extremes, liberty could be something quite other than a blessing. *The Federalist* notes that chaotic government "poisons the blessings of liberty, itself."[72] Indeed, *The Federalist* warns, quite explicitly, that "liberty may be endangered by the abuses of liberty as well as by the abuses of power; and ... the former rather than the latter is apparently most to be apprehended by the United States."[73] In fact, the thought is not altogether alien to the current Supreme Court. The Court is quite comfortable sanctioning abridgments of commercial liberty, including those once thought to have been protected by the Constitution, in order to secure what is conceived to be the greater good.

The truth is that the central thrust of contemporary jurisprudence has only been incidentally concerned with liberty. Rather, it has been most of all concerned with a certain view of equality. Ronald Dworkin, one of the most celebrated legal commentators of the past generation, argued quite explicitly that the main constitutional principle must be equality rather than liberty. And he argued that the constitutional promise of equality must be understood as an obligation of government to provide "equal concern and respect": government "must not constrain liberty on the ground that one citizen's conception of the good life ... is nobler or superior to another's."[74]

For some decades, the federal courts have pursued a vision of "equality" that is reasonably well captured in Dworkin's formulations. The Court has sanctioned a vast amount of intrusive governmental constraints on private activity. But it has sought to reassure itself that in all of this, government is simply controlling harmful effects and never expressing moral approbation for one way of life over another. It is hard to explain the Court's allergic response to public acknowledgment of religion—and its general resistance to public assistance to religious schools—except in terms of some formula such as this: religion makes the most authoritative claims about the right way of life; government may therefore spend public funds with no serious constitutional check—except when it comes to religion.[75]

On occasion, the justices themselves put aside legal technicalities to proclaim the vision quite openly. Only recently, three justices—then viewed as the very center of the Court—signed their names to the following declamation: "At the heart of liberty is the right to define one's own concept of existence, of meaning, of the universe, and of the mystery of human life."[76] Liberty, to these justices, has no necessary or intrinsic connection with independence, with personal responsibility, or even with human dignity or the sacredness of the human person. "*At the heart of liberty*" is the cosmic freedom to reconceive the universe in any way one likes—with government and the broader community entirely on the sidelines.

No justice of the Supreme Court, of course, actually has the foolhardy courage of this sophomoric conviction. Were it true that this credo represented "the heart of liberty," it would follow that laws against pornography and narcotics, for example, would be unconstitutional because their main purpose and effect are to stigmatize the view of "meaning" and "the universe" that identifies empty orgasms and drug-induced stupors with the aim of human "existence." There are highly respectable legal commentators who argue that a proper view of the Constitution does entail a constitutional right to all manner of sexual satisfactions (at least among consenting adults) and all manner of narcotic consumption. Suicide, too, has been defended as a constitutional right—as it is a most logical response to a certain despairing concept of "existence" and of "the mystery of human life."[77]

It may be that such consistency is a luxury of tenured professors that judges, even with life tenure of their own, cannot quite afford. More likely, the justices do not have the time or inclination to reflect on the full implications of their own (or their young law clerks') rhetoric. To some extent, they are, like all politicians, prisoners of the phrasemakers. But once set in play, the logic of the doctrine has a certain irresistible force—even though for all that, it frequently is resisted, whether from political necessity or unreflective habit. Much that the Court does can only be explained by the current liberal view that government must never prefer one way of life to another or one moral outlook to another.

Such relentless moral relativism is totally at odds with the common sense of the ordinary citizen. The ordinary citizen thinks it is very wrong to have children when you cannot care for them, very wrong to desert your children and the mother of your children, very wrong to drop out of school and become dependent on governmental handouts. The ordinary citizen would not dream of saying that such "ways of life" are entitled to "equal concern and respect." Of course, it would be dangerous or impractical to give government the power to force everyone to lead a fully virtuous life. But it defies common sense to suppose that government should be indifferent to whether citizens will try to lead more responsible and productive lives.

Why do courts so often set themselves against common sense? One reason, surely, is that it strikes them as too common. For decades, liberal opinion has puffed itself with pride at being more "understanding" than the common person. Judges seem to be particularly tempted by such moral vanity. If judges were not more "understanding" than the ordinary person, after all, why would they be given such large powers with such little accountability? There is the additional consideration that such superior "understanding" has been deployed to justify ever-larger claims of power by federal judges: if the views of ordinary citizens were more to be trusted, there would be less excuse for judges to exert control over schools, prisons, and a range of other institutions, previously left to the good judgment of elected local officials.

It is not a straight line from the formulaic, academic nihilism of the professors and the judges to the nihilistic self-destructiveness of real life in the inner cities.

But there is surely a connection. The crisis of the inner cities is primarily a moral and spiritual crisis. In the depths of the Great Depression, even amid segregation and open racism, there was nothing like the pattern of violence and family breakdown that is reflected in current statistics. There was not the same level of violence and moral anarchy because there was not the same level of utter despair.

For some decades, liberal judges have hewed to the philosophy that shrugs off moral despair as nothing much to worry about—nothing that can't be cured with a little more welfare spending. So the Supreme Court did its best to impose national standards for welfare support in 1969 on the premise that welfare handouts are essential to life.[78] Almost simultaneously it embarked on a program of containing religious education as dangerous and divisive, while raising questions about family obligations at every turn.

In such stances, the courts reflected a strong current of elite opinion, and no doubt they helped to give it more confidence and wider effect.[79] By now, the failure of liberal policy prescriptions has vastly reduced the number of elected officeholders who still adhere to this outlook. One can be sure that the liberalism of the 1960s and 1970s is doomed. One can even be sure that it will be in retreat (as it may already be) within the courts and must eventually give way to sounder views. But one cannot be sure it will happen soon.

Vast social problems will not soon be remedied, in any case. But it remains a matter of some interest whether judges will continue to contribute to the problem. Unlike elected politicians, judges may perpetuate delusions through a life term on the bench.

NOTES

1. Andrew Kull, *The Color-Blind Constitution* (Cambridge: Harvard University Press, 1992), offers a useful survey of the Court's move into "benign" racial remedies in the late 1960s and its struggles to place some limits on racial-preference measures ever since.

2. As Kull remarks, "In the constitutional cases on affirmative action . . . the Court has produced—at enormous length—a record of its inability to agree on any decisive legal principle." Ibid., 207–8. For a detailed review of the Court's recent vacillations, see Neal Devins, "*Adarand Constructors, Inc. v. Pena* and the Continuing Irrelevance of Supreme Court Affirmative Action Decisions," *William and Mary Law Review* 37 (Winter 1996): 673.

3. *Fullilove v. Klutznick*, 448 U.S. 448 (1980).

4. *City of Richmond v. J. A. Croson Co.*, 448 U.S. 469 (1989).

5. *Metro Broadcasting, Inc. v. FCC*, 497 U.S. 547 (1990).

6. *Adarand Constructors, Inc. v. Pena*, 515 U.S. 200 (1995).

7. The development of this system and the operational premises behind it are usefully described in Nathan Glazer, *Affirmative Discrimination* (New York: Basic Books, 1978). A more recent survey concludes that the system holds employers guilty of "discrimination" when their "only sin is hiring the best employees they can find." Stuart Taylor, "Clinton and the Quota Game," *Legal Times*, 28 December 1992, 23.

8. See Anne B. Fisher, "Businessmen Like to Hire by the Numbers," *Fortune*, 16 September 1985, 26 (describing internal affirmative action officers who monitor corporate compliance with proportional hiring goals and nurture internal constituencies for maintaining

such policies). Similar officers exist at all universities. For a more recent survey confirming corporate complacency about proportional hiring programs, see Steven A. Holmes, "Affirmative Action Plans are Part of Business Life," *New York Times*, 22 November 1991, sec. A, 20. For the counterpart tendencies among local government employers, see Stephen Engelberg, "Attack on Quotas Opposed by Cities," *New York Times*, 4 May 1985, sec. A, 1.

9. For an account of how this was done by the University of Texas (Austin) School of Law in response to a reverse discrimination suit demonstrating explicit racial admissions quotas, see Michael Greve, "Segregation Now," *Weekly Standard*, 15 December 1995, 31–35.

10. Bill Small, "Wilson Steps Up Attack on Affirmative Action," *Los Angeles Times*, 19 July 1995, sec. A, 3.

11. John Miller and Abigail Thernstrom, "Losing Race," *New Republic*, 26 June 1995, 17.

12. Equal Opportunity Act of 1995, H.R. 2128, introduced 27 July 1995 (with 72 cosponsors), 104th Congress.

13. Remarks by the president to the Carpenter Lectureship in the Humanities and Sciences, University of Texas, Austin, October 16, 1995.

14. Gerald D. Jaynes and Robin M. Williams, Jr., eds., *A Common Destiny: Blacks and American Society* (Washington: National Research Council, 1989), 518, 528.

15. Bureau of the Census, *Statistical Abstract of the United States 1994* (Washington, D.C., 1994), 80.

16. For a review of the evidence, see Irwin Garfinkel and Sara S. McLanahan, *Single Mothers and Their Children: A New American Dilemma* (Washington, D.C.: Urban Institute Press, 1989).

17. Jennifer Hochschild, *Facing Up to the American Dream* (Princeton: Princeton University Press, 1995), 60–61.

18. Ibid., 74–75.

19. Ibid., 106.

20. Ibid., 140.

21. U.S. Department of Justice, *United States Crime Reports 1993* (Washington, D.C.: Government Printing Office, 1993), 17.

22. Bob Herbert, "Who Will Help the Black Man?" *New York Times Magazine*, 4 December 1994, 74.

23. John DiIulio, "The Question of Black Crime," *Public Interest*, no. 117 (Fall 1994): 4.

24. See John DiIulio, *Courts, Corrections, and the Constitution: The Impact of Judicial Interventions on Prisons and Jails* (New York: Oxford University Press, 1990).

25. Stop Turning Out Our Prisoners Act, H.R. 554, introduced 18 January 1995, 104th Congress.

26. James Q. Wilson, "Crime in America," *Commentary* (February 1995): 20.

27. See, e.g., the recent book by Judge Harold J. Rothwax of New York arguing that the exclusionary rule requires considerable modification to avoid perverse results in the criminal justice system: *Guilty: The Collapse of the Criminal Justice System* (New York: Random House, 1996).

28. Richard Parker, "The Coming Legal Backlash," *New Republic*, 20 March 1995, 21.

29. James Q. Wilson, "Just Take Away Their Guns," *New York Times*, 6 March 1994, sec. G, 47; James Q. Wilson, "Why Falling Crime Statistics Don't Make Us Feel More Secure," *Los Angeles Times*, 25 September 1994, sec. M, 1.

30. *Terry v. Ohio*, 392 U.S. 1 (1968).

31. *United States v. Packer*, 15 F.3d 654 (1994).

32. See, e.g., *United States v. Scopo*, 814 F. Supp. 292 (E.D.N.Y. 1993) (suppressing

evidence of handgun possession because police, after trailing defendant from a stakeout of site used by Colombo crime family, had stopped defendant's car for failing to signal a lane change and then found handgun on his person after frisking him—but not, the court ruled, with "adequate cause").

33. James Q. Wilson, "Human Nature and Social Progress" (paper presented at Bradley Lecture, American Enterprise Institute [1991]).

34. R. Marshall Elizer and Nazir Lalani, "Facing Up to a Street Closure Epidemic," *Public Works* 125 (May 1994): 38, reviews some examples, noting that "increasing crime rates have triggered moves by cities in Southern California to close streets to reduce gang and drug related activities from being conducted in residential neighborhoods," but such efforts sometimes generate local protests for increasing traffic congestion. See also Ronald Brownstein, "The Mean Streets: Cities Are Reclaiming Besieged Areas by Erecting Traffic Barriers and Cracking Down on Panhandlers and Loitering; Some Fear Loss of Freedom," *Los Angeles Times*, 4 May 1994, sec. A, 1 (noting that local residents have praised such efforts but "civil libertarians and homeless advocates" have denounced them in places as "authoritarian").

35. *Papachristou v. City of Jacksonville*, 405 U.S. 156 (1972). See the similar ruling in *Palmer v. City of Euclid*, 402 U.S. 544 (1971), and the parallel reasoning in *Kolender v. Lawson*, 461 U.S. 352 (1983). On the basis of these and similar federal precedents, a New York state court held the state's antiloitering law unconstitutional in *People v. Bright*, 520 N.E.2d 1355 (N.Y. Ct. App. 1988).

36. *Young v. New York City Transit Authority*, 729 F. Supp. 341 (S.D.N.Y. 1990), *rev'd on other grounds*, 903 F.2d 146 (2d Cir. 1990).

37. *Kreimer v. Bureau of Police*, 765 F. Supp. 181 (D.N.J. 1991), *rev'd*, 958 F.2d 1242 (3d Cir. 1992).

38. *Loper v. New York City Police Dep't*, 766 F. Supp. 1280 (S.D.N.Y. 1991).

39. *Richmond Tenant Organization v. Kemp*, 956 F.2d 1300 (4th Cir. 1992).

40. *Veronica School District v. Acton*, 115 S. Ct. 2386 (1995). Justices John Paul Stevens III, Sandra Day O'Connor, and David H. Souter dissented outright; Justices Ruth Bader Ginsburg and Stephen Breyer expressed reservations about extending the testing program in a concurring opinion.

41. See Curtis J. Berger, "Pruneyard Revisited: Political Activity on Private Lands," *New York University Law Review* 66 (June 1991): 633.

42. See, e.g., the New Jersey state court ruling in *State v. Kolz*, 276 A.2d 595 (1971) (holding that courts must enforce First Amendment guarantees against a private retirement village lest they "create a political 'isolation booth' "). Ibid. at 600. For an extended argument for the applicability of constitutional restrictions to private residential associations, see "Note: The Rule of Law in Residential Associations," *Harvard Law Review* 99 (December 1985): 472.

43. Contracts with the Nation of Islam, to provide security patrols in public housing projects, have generated grateful support from local residents and charges from outside advocacy groups that they threaten the separation of church and state. See Clarence Page, "Should the CHA Turn for Security to Nation of Islam?" *Chicago Tribune*, 16 February 1994, 17; Brian Blomquist, "City Praised for Involving Nation Security; Police to Work with Farrakhan's Men," *Washington Times*, 13 October 1995, sec. C, 7; Meyer Eisenberg, "Statement of Anti-Defamation League on Federally Funded Security Services Provided by Affiliates of the Nation of Islam," in *Hearing before Committee on Banking and Financial Services, Subcommittee on General Oversight and Investigations*, U.S. House of Representatives, 2 March 1995.

44. George F. Will, "What School Choice Could Do in Milwaukee," *Washington Post*,

10 September 1995, sec. C, 7; John Norquist, " 'Choice' about Parental Power," *Wisconsin State Journal*, 26 February 1995, 2B.

45. Kimberly J. McClarin, "Court Bars Voucher Plan in Religious Schools," *New York Times*, 26 August 1995, sec. 1, 8.

46. John Chubb and Terry Moe, *Politics, Markets, and America's Schools* (Washington, D.C.: Brookings Institution, 1990), offers much statistical evidence on these tragic patterns.

47. James S. Coleman, *High School Achievement: Public, Catholic, and Parochial Schools Compared* (New York: Basic Books, 1982), 186–91.

48. Compare *Tilton v. Richardson*, 403 U.S. 672 (1971), with *Lemon v. Kurtzmann*, 403 U.S. 602 (1971).

49. *Lemon*, 403 U.S. at 622 ("[P]olitical division along religious lines was one of the principal evils against which the First Amendment was intended to protect. . . . [Debate over religious issues would] tend to confuse and obscure other issues of great urgency").

50. In *Aguilar v. Felton*, 473 U.S. 402 (1985), for example, the Court found that even allowing public school reading teachers to offer special remedial services in parochial schools would constitute excessive governmental "entanglement" with religion. It appears, however, that governmental fire departments will still be allowed to put out fires in religious schools. Only educational services to students in religious schools rattle the Court.

51. Albert Shanker, "Education Contract with America," *Wall Street Journal*, 15 September 1995, sec. A, 14.

52. *John Doe, Jr. v. Rockingham County School Board*, 658 F. Supp. 403 (W.D. Va. 1987). A recent study concludes that "the amount of litigation on the issue in recent years suggests continuing uncertainty as to precisely what process is due students facing possible expulsion." James W. McMasters, "Mediation: New Process for High School Disciplinary Expulsions," *Northwestern University Law Review* 84 (Winter 1990): 737. Twenty years ago, the cost of a formal proceeding for expulsion was calculated at about half the cost of a total year's education for one pupil. David Kirp, "Proceduralism and Bureaucracy: Due Process in the School Setting," *Stanford Law Review* 28 (May 1976): 859–60.

53. For recent endorsements of this view, see Jon Glass, "Separated, Boys and Girls May Learn Better; Controversial Approach Limits Intimidation, Classroom Distractions," *Virginian-Pilot* (Norfolk), 4 January 1995, sec. A, 1; Eric Wee, "School Board Approves Experiments; Same-Sex Classes to Expand," *Washington Post*, 4 May 1995, 6; Richard Rothstein, "Single Sex Schools: Why Ruin Good Experiments with Politics?" *Los Angeles Times*, 21 January 1996, sec. M, 6; Richard Cowen, "Experimental Class," *Record* (Bergen County, N.J.), 29 April 1994, sec. C, 1; Daniel Gardnswartz, "Public Education: An Inner City Crisis! Single Sex Schools: An Inner City Answer?" *Emory Law Journal* 42 (Spring 1993): 591; Sharon K. Mollman, "The Gender Gap: Separating the Sexes in Public Education," *Indiana Law Journal* 68 (Winter 1992): 149; "Note: Inner-City Single-Sex Schools: Educational Reform or Invidious Discrimination?" *Harvard Law Review* 105 (May 1992): 1741.

54. *Vorchheimer v. School District*, 532 F.2d 880 (3d Cir. 1976), upheld a *voluntary* program of single-sex high schools, but the ruling was upheld by only a 4–4 vote of the Supreme Court. 430 U.S. 703 (1977). A mandatory program of this kind was held unconstitutional in *United States v. Hinds School Board*, 560 F.2d 619 (5th Cir. 1977).

55. The suggestion was endorsed by President Clinton in his January 1996 State of the Union Address.

56. See, e.g., *Arnold v. Carpenter*, 459 F.2d 939 (7th Cir. 1972) (striking down school hair-code requirements); *Bannister v. Paradis*, 316 F. Supp. 185 (D.N.H. 1970) (striking down prohibition on dungarees); *Johnson v. Joint School District No. 60*, 508 P.2d 547 (Idaho 1973) (striking down requirement for girls to wear dresses).

57. *Stone v. Graham*, 449 U.S. 39 (1980).

58. *Wallace v. Jaffree*, 472 U.S. 38 (1985).

59. *Island Trees v. Pico*, 457 U.S. 853 (1982).

60. See, e.g., *Virgil v. School Board of Columbia City*, 677 F. Supp. 1547 (M.D. Fla. 1988) (upholding removal of works by Aristophanes and Chaucer from school curriculum); *Brown v. Woodland Joint Unified School District*, 27 F.3d 1373 (9th Cir. 1994) (upholding use of books on "witchcraft" and "voodoo" in school curriculum); *Delcarpio v. St. Tammany Parish School Board*, 865 F. Supp. 350 (E.D. La. 1994) (ordering school district to reverse policy under which it removed books on voodoo spells from school library); *Clayton v. Place*, 690 F. Supp. 850 (W.D. Mo. 1988) (ordering restoration of school dances, allegedly discontinued by school authorities based on religious objections to dancing).

61. Allan Gold, "Boston Schools Set to Overhaul Busing Policies," *New York Times*, 28 December 1988, sec. B, 6.

62. See *Missouri v. Jenkins*, 495 U.S. 33 (1995).

63. For a recent, quite accessible symposium of social scientists on the connections between welfare eligibility standards, family breakdown, and the culture of poverty, see "Sex, Families, Race, Poverty, and Welfare," *American Enterprise*, January 1995.

64. *C. K. v. Shalala*, 883 F. Supp. 991 (D.N.J. 1995) (denying motions for summary judgment).

65. *Goldberg v. Kelly*, 397 U.S. 254 (1970).

66. Wilson, "Crime in America." A similar suggestion by John DiIulio calls for government-sponsored "boarding schools," which "would be formally connected to churches and be frankly and unapologetically religious in character." He says, "Let perverted civil libertarians and others who have worked to prevent inner-city blacks from target-hardening their communities (erecting concrete barriers, metal detectors in high schools, automatically evicting drug dealers from public housing) scream bloody murder about the church-state issues this ostensibly poses." "White Lies about Black Crime," *Public Interest*, no. 118 (Winter 1995): 40.

67. Title IX, Education Amendments of 1972, codified at 20 U.S.C. § 1681 (1972); regulations governing "marital or parental status" (including "pregnancy and related conditions") at 10 C.F.R. § 1040.43 (1972).

68. See, e.g., *Andrews v. Drew School District*, 507 F.2d 611 (5th Cir. 1975) (striking down, on constitutional grounds, school-district rule against employing parents of illegitimate children); *Moore v. Board of Education of Chidester School District No. 59*, 448 F.2d 709 (8th Cir. 1971) (disallowing, on constitutional grounds, dismissal of teacher on grounds of unwed pregnancy); *Ordway v. Hargraves*, 323 F. Supp. 1155 (D. Mass. 1971) (overruling, on constitutional grounds, exclusion of unwed mother from regular attendance at public high school); *Perry v. Grenada Mun. School District*, 300 F. Supp. 748 (N.D. Miss. 1969) (overturning, on constitutional grounds, school-board policy excluding unwed mothers from admission to high school).

69. *Bowers v. Hardwick*, 478 U.S. 186 (1986).

70. *Romer v. Evans*, 116 S. Ct. 1620 (1996).

71. See, e.g., *Moore v. East Cleveland*, 431 U.S. 494 (1977) (overturning local ordinance restricting residency to "families" related by blood or marriage); *New Jersey Welfare Rights Organization v. Cahill*, 411 U.S. 619 (1973) (overturning statute limiting welfare benefits to families in which parents are "ceremonially married"); *U.S. Dep't of Agriculture v. Moreno*, 413 U.S. 508 (1973) (overturning federal statute excluding food stamp eligibility from households with unrelated individuals).

72. James Madison, *The Federalist, No. 62*, ed. Jacob Cooke (Middletown, Conn.: Wesleyan University Press, 1961), 421.

73. Ibid., *No. 63*, 428.

74. Ronald Dworkin, *Taking Rights Seriously* (Cambridge: Harvard University Press, 1977), 273.

75. Compare the decision granting standing to taxpayers complaining of governmental aid to religious schools in *Flast v. Cohen*, 392 U.S. 83 (1968), with subsequent denials of taxpayer standing to challenge any other sort of spending on the basis of any other putative constitutional restriction on spending, as, for example, in *United States v. Richardson*, 418 U.S. 166 (1974) (complaining of secret appropriations for the Central Intelligence Agency, contrary to the requirement in Article I, Section 9, that "a regular statement and account of . . . expenditures of all public money shall be published from time to time").

76. Opinion of Justices Souter, O'Connor, and Kennedy, *Planned Parenthood of Southeastern Pennsylvania v. Casey*, 505 U.S. 833, 851 (1992). It should be noted that this was not a throwaway line in a marginal decision. It was a central part of the argument by which the three centrist justices (all Reagan or Bush appointees) sought to put an end to ongoing national debate about abortion in what they themselves characterized as a decision of "rare importance."

77. For examples of all three positions, see David Richards, *Drugs, Sex, Death, and the Law: An Essay on Human Rights and Overcriminalization* (Totowa, N.J.: Rowan & Littlefield, 1982).

78. *Shapiro v. Thompson*, 394 U.S. 618 (1969) (holding that waiting period to go on welfare after moving to another state would deny "right to travel" to the indigent).

79. For one attempt to sketch the line from liberal opinion—through court rulings—to inner-city demoralization, see Myron Magnet, *The Dream and the Nightmare: The Sixties' Legacy to the Underclass* (New York: Morrow & Co., 1993).

7

The Politics of Clientele Capture

Civil Rights Policy and the Reagan Administration

HUGH DAVIS GRAHAM

This chapter uses the Reagan administration as a case study of national policy-making in the post-1960s American state. Specifically examined is the attempt by conservative Republican policymakers during Reagan's presidency to narrow the reach of federal civil rights enforcement. As a presidential candidate opposing Jimmy Carter in 1980, Ronald Reagan declared: "We must not allow the noble concept of equal opportunity to be distorted into federal guidelines or quotas which require race, ethnicity, or sex—rather than ability and qualifications—to be the principal factor in hiring or education."[1] The 1980 Republican platform criticized "bureaucratic regulations which rely on quotas, ratios, and numerical requirements to exclude some individuals in favor of others."

Reagan conservatives, claiming a national mandate that in 1981 gave Republicans control of the White House and the Senate and, consequently, effective control of appointments to the federal courts, objected to the expansion since 1964 in all three branches of government of civil rights policies that privileged some Americans over others on the basis of traits they were born with. To conservatives, the development during the 1970s of affirmative action requirements based on minority preferences violated both the letter and spirit of the Civil Rights Act of 1964, which prohibited discrimination against any individual on account of race, national origin, or sex. Consequently the Reagan administration launched a counterattack to narrow the range of governmental intrusion in all three branches—the federal agencies, the judiciary, and the Congress. In the executive agencies, where White House control was greatest, Reagan conservatives replaced Carter appointees and attempted to limit the authority of Washington bureaucrats over business firms, state and local governments, and educational institutions. In the federal courts, Justice Department officials held that the Constitution was color-blind and required equal treatment of all citizens irrespective of their race or ethnicity. In the legislative branch, the Reagan White House asked Congress to loosen Washington's regulatory grip not only over airlines, trucking, and banking—a policy of economic deregulation begun by the Carter administration—but also over employers burdened by affirmative action requirements in hiring and promotions. By the end of the 1980s, when President Reagan left office, the results were mixed, but most of Reagan's counteroffensive had been defeated.[2]

This chapter examines civil rights policies during the Reagan presidency not to assess their efficacy in reversing policies inherited from the Carter administration but rather to illuminate the underlying structure of the American regulatory state as it relates to equality that developed following the Civil Rights Act of 1964. Despite internal divisions and policy ambivalence, the Reagan administration launched an ideological counterattack without precedent against the affirmative action regime built during the presidencies of Lyndon Johnson, Richard Nixon, Gerald Ford, and Jimmy Carter. As this list of presidents implies, the construction of a coherent system of race-conscious remedies was a bipartisan effort, with Nixon providing the breakthrough initiatives and Carter presiding over administrative consolidation. The Reagan assault against the affirmative action regime, like explosives detonated in searching for oil deposits, sent shock waves echoing through the substrata of government, the productive economy, and the institutions of civil society. Their refraction, viewed from the perspective of the late 1990s, clarifies foundation structures and fault lines in the new regulatory order that previously had remained hidden.

In the civil rights policies developed by the elected branches of government from the Civil Rights Act in 1964 to the election of a Republican congressional majority in 1994, one finds more policy continuity than change consequent to the Reagan revolution. The Reagan counterattack against the affirmative action regime was spirited, but it was overwhelmed by the deeper forces driving the tide of civil rights regulation during 1964–94. Behind the accumulation and clutter since 1964 of specific civil rights statutes, executive orders, court decisions, and agency regulations, three new developments in the American regulatory state combined to increase the power of the civil rights coalition and weaken the hand of conservative opponents. This chapter examines all three in the light cast by Reagan's battle against them.

The first was the expansion of public law litigation, a new form of policymaking pioneered by the National Association for the Advancement of Colored People (NAACP) in *Brown v. Board of Education*. In public law litigation, the policy process is driven not by elected and appointed government officials but instead by private, public-interest organizations (such as the NAACP). To force change, they sue government agencies (school boards, cabinet departments) on behalf of class-action clients (minority schoolchildren, people with disabilities) to win court-ordered remedies (school desegregation orders, minority-hiring directives). The second new development was a pattern of policy replication developed by Congress in the 1970s, a kind of legislative cloning process, whereby Congress copied the statutory language of Title VI of the Civil Rights Act of 1964, used by agencies during the Johnson and Nixon administrations to develop affirmative action programs for African Americans, and applied it to benefit new advocacy groups.

Third was a new pattern of clientele capture. Federal agencies created to deal with civil rights policy—for example, the Civil Rights Commission, the Equal Employment Opportunity Commission (EEOC), and new offices of civil rights regulation in the Departments of Justice, Labor, and Health, Education, and Welfare (HEW)—developed close coalition ties with benefiting clientele groups. Conservatives complained that regulatory agencies, like courts, should not be captured by advocacy groups that benefited from their decisions. These three paths of institutional development in civil rights enforcement were complex, gradual, and obscure. They were parallel and interdependent yet followed no blueprint. They depended so heavily on processes largely unknown to voters but familiar to insiders—lobbyists for advocacy groups, lawyers for public-interest law firms, policy entrepreneurs in legislative committees—that they were difficult for Reagan conservatives to attack through populistic appeals to voter resentment.

Civil Rights Regulation: The Carter Legacy

The minority-preference policies that most offended Reagan conservatives traced their origins to the affirmative action language attached to federal nondiscrimination requirements in the 1960s.[3] In 1964 the Civil Rights Act banned discrimination on account of race, and the Johnson administration, in enforcing Titles VI (contract compliance) and VII (job discrimination), avoided minority preferences. In the wake of the urban riots of 1965–68, however, the Nixon administration shifted the emphasis of equal employment policy to minority-conscious remedies. Most controversial was the Philadelphia Plan of 1969, which attacked labor union discrimination by requiring proportional representation of workers in federally assisted construction projects. By 1972 federal agencies were enforcing a new regimen of civil rights regulation in contract compliance keyed to the "adverse impact" standard championed by the Leadership Conference on Civil Rights.[4] This standard prohibited any employment test or job requirement, such as a high school diploma, that produced a disproportionately negative impact on minorities unless the test or requirement was justified by employers as a business necessity.

During the 1970s, presidents of both parties in the White House cooperated with Congress in an additive process that extended the remedies designed for African Americans to a widening array of mobilized rights-based groups, including women, Hispanics, Asians, Native Americans, people with disabilities, and the elderly. From 1977 to 1981 the Carter administration reorganized and enlarged the federal enforcement machinery, consolidating regulatory responsibilities and jurisdiction under a strengthened EEOC and Office of Federal Contract Compliance Programs (OFCCP) in the Labor Department.[5] During this period, moreover, an accumulation of appellate decisions under the Burger Court rationalized and codified the requirements of affirmative action enforcement.[6] By 1980 the Leadership Conference, widely respected for its lobbying effectiveness, defended the liberal legacy of the Warren and Burger Courts in civil rights policy as "settled law."[7]

The Reagan Counterattack against Civil Rights Regulation

In 1981 the Reagan administration inherited a maturing system of civil rights regulation. Given the margin of Reagan's victory over Carter, including Republican control of the Senate, the Reagan revolutionaries in 1981 planned sharp changes in civil rights policy. As conservative reformers, the Reagan revolutionaries faced three routes to changing regulatory policy: (1) changing priorities and procedures in the enforcement agencies; (2) changing the federal judges who interpreted the law and the Constitution; and (3) changing the law in Congress. The first route, changing enforcement leaders and policies, is the shortest and quickest, but successor regimes may find it easiest to reverse. Reagan was most successful, especially during his first term when Republicans controlled Senate confirmations, in appointing conservatives to senior posts in the regulatory and mission agencies.[8] Although environmental and consumer deregulation claimed priority under Reagan, the deregulatory campaign included civil rights components. But the well-organized civil rights coalition, contesting each initiative, exacted a high price for limited changes.

In pursuing the first route, which offered employers immediate administrative relief from affirmative action regulation, the Reagan administration was moderately successful in curbing civil rights regulation by the two main enforcement agencies—the EEOC, especially under the chairmanship of Clarence Thomas, and the obscure but more potent OFCCP in the Labor Department. Both agencies shifted enforcement emphasis from class-action proceedings to conciliation and lawsuits seeking make-whole relief for identified victims of discrimination. In both agencies the shift in regulatory strategy was accomplished not through formal, notice-and-comment procedures but through internal policy directives.[9] In addition, the administration slowed regulatory activity by cutting the agency budgets and by requiring agencies to obtain clearance from the president's Office of Management and Budget (OMB) before proposing regulations in the *Federal Register*. These measures, however, were inherently vulnerable to reversal by successor administrations. More significant was the prospect of changing the civil rights regulations administratively. In the Reagan presidency, this effort centered on revising Executive Order No. 11246, the Johnson directive of 1965 that Nixon had used in the Philadelphia Plan to authorize minority-preference requirements in governmental contracts.

The second pathway to conservative reform, changing the ideological makeup of the federal judiciary, was a high priority for the Reagan administration but one that offered the least immediate payoff. The third pathway, changing civil rights statutes in Congress, was the most difficult because Democrats retained large majorities in the House and because the Leadership Conference had built effective majority coalitions in both chambers.[10] The opportunity for change arose in 1984, partly as a consequence of Reagan's judicial appointments, when the Supreme Court's opinion in *Grove City College v. Bell* triggered a legislative battle that Reagan could not avoid and thus sought to turn to his own advantage.

The Campaign to Rewrite the Affirmative Action Executive Order

Reagan's smashing electoral victory in 1980 meant that rewriting the affirmative action order, at least theoretically, could be accomplished shortly after the inauguration—with the proverbial stroke of a pen. The drive to revise Executive Order 11246 was led by William Bradford Reynolds, assistant attorney general for civil rights, and supported by Edwin Meese III, White House counselor during Reagan's first term and, after February 1985, Reagan's attorney general. In January 1984 Reynolds, frustrated by the unwillingness of Labor secretaries Raymond J. Donovan (1981–85) and, after April 1985, William E. Brock III to abandon minority-preference policies inherited from the Carter administration, launched a major campaign to revise the executive order.[11] Meese, who chaired the Domestic Policy Council of the cabinet, won support for revising the executive order from Secretaries Donald Hodel (Interior), William J. Bennett (Education), and John Herrington (Energy) and from OMB director James C. Miller III.

Leading the cabinet-level opposition to rewriting Executive Order 11246 was Labor secretary Brock, whose department had risen in authority and esteem since 1965 largely on the strength of its status as the government's leading agency in contract compliance. Joining Brock in defending the affirmative action status quo within Reagan's cabinet were Secretaries George Shultz (State), James Baker (Treasury), Margaret Heckler (Health and Human Services), Elizabeth Dole (Transportation), and Samuel Pierce (Housing and Urban Development).[12] Brock's resistance stemmed partly from within the Labor Department bureaucracy, where the rights revolution of the 1960s and 1970s, by adding the Office of Federal Contracts (OFCC) in 1965 and the Occupational Safety and Health Administration (OSHA) in 1970, had transformed a once-feeble mission agency into a powerful, two-fisted engine of social regulation. Shultz, as Nixon's first Labor secretary, had led the campaign to adopt the Philadelphia Plan.[13] Dole and Heckler had political ties to organized women's groups; Pierce, the lone African American in Reagan's cabinet, was attentive to urban constituencies.

Resistance in Reagan's cabinet to changing the executive order had political as well as bureaucratic origins. It reflected Republican uneasiness over attacking affirmative action, reinforced by the reluctance of the nation's large employers to plunge into unknown legal waters.[14] The Associated General Contractors and the U.S. Chamber of Commerce supported Reynolds and his conservative battalion in the campaign for color-blind antidiscrimination enforcement. But the National Association of Manufacturers supported Brock. Big business, strongly Republican and supporting deregulation elsewhere, preferred the known routines of underutilization analysis and minority hiring requirements to the unknown perils of reverse-discrimination lawsuits.[15]

At a cabinet meeting on 22 October 1985, Brock mounted a stout defense against the revisionists. He argued that the Labor Department's goals were not quotas, that enforcement abuses inherited from the Carter years were being corrected administratively, and that a political war over affirmative action would damage Republicans in the 1986 and 1988 elections. Meese, a supporter of cabinet government, was unwilling to take directly to the president an issue on which his cabinet was so deeply divided. Nor was White House chief of staff Donald Regan, who screened President Reagan from the entire dispute. In March 1986 Reynolds released a report documenting alleged quota requirements from OFCCP correspondence with contractors. This action, however, only stiffened the resistance of Brock and his allies, who resented such intramural attacks from the Justice Department. When Congress recessed for the 1986 elections, Reynolds's campaign was dead.[16]

Appointing Conservatives to the Federal Courts

The second pathway to curbing affirmative action enforcement, appointing youthful conservatives to the federal courts, was a priority of the Reagan revolution. In his first year in the White House, Reagan appointed Sandra Day O'Connor, the first woman to sit on the high bench, to replace retiring Associate Justice Potter Stewart. In 1986, on the retirement of chief justice Warren E. Burger, Reagan won confirmation of William H. Rehnquist as Chief Justice and Antonin Scalia as associate justice. In 1987, Democrats regained control of the Senate and rejected Reagan's nomination of Robert H. Bork, a conservative he earlier named to the appellate court. Reagan subsequently won Senate confirmation for Anthony M. Kennedy to fill the vacancy created by the retirement of Justice Lewis F. Powell, Jr. By the end of his eight years in the White House, Reagan had filled 338 judgeships on the district and appeals courts—about half the total.[17]

The payoff, however, was slow in coming. Reagan's conservative judicial appointments did not turn the tide against the Warren Court legacy until after Reagan left the White House. Despite the claims of Reynolds in the Justice Department that the Supreme Court had confined affirmative action remedies to actual victims of illegal discrimination, the Court in a series of civil rights opinions during Reagan's second term continued by a narrow margin to support the claims of minority and female plaintiffs.[18] Conservatives were disappointed by the Supreme Court's unwillingness during the Reagan years to overturn liberal precedents, especially in constitutional interpretation, involving affirmative action, abortion rights, school prayer, and rights of the criminally accused. On certain statutory issues, however, the Supreme Court provided better leverage for attacking the growth of regulation from Washington.

The Storm over Grove City College

The third way for the Reagan administration to reduce civil rights regulation, changing the law itself, was opened unexpectedly in February 1984 by the Supreme Court in the *Grove City College* decision. The dispute began in 1977 when Grove City College, a private, coeducational institution in Pennsylvania dedicated to providing a liberal arts education within a Christian framework, refused to sign form 639A, an assurance of compliance sent by HEW officials. These were blank-check promises routinely required by contract-compliance officials, whether acting under the authority of Executive Order 11246, as in the Labor or Defense Department, or of Title VI, as in HEW's Office of Civil Rights (OCR), policing federal grants to colleges and universities or state and local governments. School officials who signed form 639A, for example, agreed to comply with Title IX of the Education Amendments of 1972 "and all applicable requirements imposed by or pursuant to the Department's regulation" to the end that "no person in the United States shall, on the basis of sex, be . . . subjected to discrimination under any education program or activity for which [it] receives or benefits from Federal financial assistance from the Department."[19]

Jealous of its independence from public authorities, Grove City College had never accepted financial assistance from the government, including direct student tuition grants and loans that most American colleges and universities routinely processed through their financial aid offices. Grove City College did, however, enroll students who themselves obtained tuition grants from government offices or loans from banks with government guarantees.[20] Faced with Grove City College's refusal, federal education officials in 1978 obtained from an administrative law judge an order suspending all aid to Grove City students. The college and four students whose aid was terminated (two women and two men) then filed suit against HEW secretary Patricia Roberts Harris.[21] Throughout the six-year process of trial and appeal, all courts rejected Grove City's contention that indirect aid through students did not constitute federal financial assistance and hence did not bring the college under OCR regulations. The courts disagreed, however, on whether the "education program or activity" losing federal funds was the entire college or only the program receiving the aid—in Grove City's case, the financial aid office.[22]

Grove City College appealed to the Supreme Court, which decided the case on 28 February 1984. Agreeing with Solicitor General Rex Lee of the Reagan administration, the Court in a 6–3 opinion upheld the circuit court ruling that indirect aid triggered Title IX coverage and that the department could terminate the students' tuition grants.[23] But the majority in *Grove City* rejected the view, previously supported by U.S. government officials but not by Reagan's solicitor general, that the entire college was the "education program or activity" receiving the federal financial assistance. By ruling in *Grove City* that indirect aid triggered institutional coverage but that aid to one program did not bring entire institutions under regulation, the Supreme Court in 1984 expanded the reach of Title IX regulations to virtually every school and college in the country, while limiting its effect to the particular educational program aided.

The victory for the Reagan Justice Department in *Grove City* prompted a great outcry from the civil rights coalition. The Leadership Conference on Civil Rights, speaking for 165 member organizations, took the lead in coordinating a bipartisan congressional drive to overturn *Grove City* legislatively, attacking the decision as a radical shift that reversed twenty years of enforcement practice under the Civil Rights Act. Liberal critics claimed that *Grove City* stripped away federal protections against discrimination in campus departments of history or athletics because they did not receive earmarked federal aid. In June 1982 the Democratic-controlled House easily passed a bill (by a vote of 375–32) stipulating that a dollar of federal assistance to any program brought the entire institution under federal regulatory control. But a parallel bill remained stalled in the Republican-controlled Senate when the 98th Congress adjourned for the elections of 1984.[24]

Early in 1985 a split developed within the civil rights coalition over the obligation of educational institutions to include abortion services in their medical care coverage. The U.S. Catholic Conference of Bishops, a pillar of the coalition when the rights of racial and ethnic minorities were at issue, opposed any legislation that might extend abortion rights coverage to Catholic hospitals and educational institutions. As a result, neither chamber could pass a bill that the civil rights coalition called a "restoration" bill. In January 1988, with the reluctant concurrence of the Leadership Conference, the Senate accepted an amendment by Republican John Danforth of Missouri that nullified existing regulations requiring educational institutions to provide abortion as well as pregnancy and childbirth services under health insurance and leave policies. This compromise, though opposed by the National Organization of Women (NOW), defused the abortion issue sufficiently to permit passage by both houses in 1988 of the Civil Rights Restoration Act.

Reagan, claiming that the bill greatly extended the reach of civil rights regulation before *Grove City* rather than merely restoring it, vetoed the bill. In this claim Reagan was partly correct. Under the guise of "restoration," the Leadership Conference and its allies in Congress had broadened the scope of federal regulation. The Grove City bill narrowed exemptions involving religious schools and smaller businesses, for example, and extended to the housing industry a presumption of governmental regulatory jurisdiction. For four years the Reagan administration and its congressional allies, led in the Senate by Republican Orrin G. Hatch of Utah, marshaled a parade of horribles to discredit the Grove City bill. White House aide Michael Horowitz, one of the more creative of the conservative alarmists, warned that under the Restoration Act, farmers and ranchers receiving agricultural subsidies, churches and synagogues running day-care centers, and mom-and-pop grocers participating in the food stamp program would all fall under the boot heel of civil rights bureaucrats.[25]

Voters, however, remained unmoved by and uninterested in conservative horror stories about abuses in federal contract compliance, argued in the arcane language of the *Federal Register*. In March 1988 Congress overrode the president's veto by margins humiliating to Reagan—73–24 in the Senate and 292–133 in the House.[26] Of the Senate's forty-five Republicans, twenty-one abandoned their president in the showdown over the Grove City bill.[27] The Reagan revolution, so effective in building majorities for new tax and defense policies, was swept aside by three deeper currents when challenging the post-1964 regulatory state.[28] The first of these, the development of public law litigation, was spawned by the civil rights revolution itself.

Public Law Litigation

Unlike traditional disputes in the civil law involving private parties, in public law litigation, advocacy groups sue the government on behalf of public-interest clients. As public-interest advocacy groups multiplied in the 1960s, courts were drawn deeply into the policymaking process, often trumping the decisions of elected officials. Appointed judges, sheltered from political pressures associated with raising and spending tax funds, offered quick results. Public law litigation exploded during the 1970s, led by race-centered lawsuits like the *Adams* suit over school desegregation. In *Adams* a federal district judge in Maryland for twenty years negotiated school desegregation regulations between the OCR, an expanding list of plaintiffs and intervenors, and state and local officials representing thousands of school districts and higher education systems. Begun by the NAACP Legal Defense and Educational Fund (LDF) in 1970, the *Adams* case soon drew in the Mexican American Legal Defense and Education Fund (MALDEF), the Women's Equity Action League (WEAL), and other public-interest organizations. In addition to civil rights constituencies—racial minorities, women, language minorities, children, people with disabilities, the elderly—*Adams* in its remarkable twenty-year lifespan included public-interest plaintiffs suing on behalf of environmental protection, consumer rights, workplace and transportation safety, and other causes.

Public law litigation pulled the courts into ongoing policy negotiations between plaintiffs' lawyers, federal and state mission agencies, federal regulatory agencies, and trial judges. Presidential control of executive agencies, weakened by the thickening of bureaucracy that accompanied the growth of government programs following World War II, was further weakened by the encroachments of courts, where court-ordered injunctions and court-approved consent decrees bound agencies and preempted presidential authority. Lawsuits like *Adams*, lasting far longer than any presidency, limited the ability and often the willingness of agency officials to follow the president's policy directives.

In such a closed, expert-oriented process, voter awareness is curtailed and public accountability is blurred. In recent studies of the *Adams* case, viewed from different perspectives by political scientist Stephen Halpern and historian William A. Link, presidents, congresses, and cabinet secretaries come and go, remote from the quadrilateral bargaining between plaintiffs' lawyers, enforcement officials in federal agencies, state and local government officials, and federal district judges.[29] Such an insider game, following paths forged by the LDF, MALDEF, the American Civil Liberties Union, Nader's Raiders, the Environmental Defense Fund, and similar organizations, offered little leverage during the 1970s and 1980s for conservatives attempting to shift the direction and shrink the control of government.

Cloning Title VI

A second source of advantage for the civil rights coalition was the congressional practice, adopted quietly during the 1970s, of using the contract-compliance language of Title VI, originally designed for African Americans, to provide similar, adverse impact remedies for other rights-based groups. By the end of the 1960s the OCR, backed by federal courts, had demonstrated the leverage provided by cross-cutting regulations. These rules obliged recipients of federal dollars for whatever purpose (antipoverty, clean water, school lunches) to comply with regulations serving other purposes (school desegregation, bilingual education, birth-control counseling). The effectiveness of the Title VI model of cross-cutting regulation in winning impressive gains in employment and education for racial and ethnic minorities was not lost on the leaders of other movements, most notably feminist groups, people with disabilities, and the elderly. By 1975 advocacy groups representing all four of these constituencies had persuaded Congress to borrow the language of Title VI and apply it to their own regulatory needs.[30]

Feminist groups such as NOW and WEAL, having persuaded President Johnson in 1967 to include sex discrimination in the executive order program enforcing Title VI, won similar inclusion of women from the OFCC in its Revised Order No. 4 in 1971. In 1972 Congress by voice vote passed Title IX, amending the education statutes to bar federal financial assistance to any educational program or activity that practiced sex discrimination. The following year, 1973, Congress in section 504 of the Rehabilitation Act reshaped the familiar language of Title VI to read as follows: "No otherwise qualified handicapped individual in the United States shall, solely by reason of his handicap, be excluded from participation in, be denied the benefits of, or be subject to discrimination under, any program or activity receiving Federal financial assistance."[31] In the Age Discrimination Act of 1975, Congress again borrowed the language of Title VI and filled in the modifier blank with "age" discrimination.

These extensions of the Title VI device during the 1970s differed from the pioneering efforts of the 1960s in several respects. In each instance a far-reaching expansion of cross-cutting regulation occurred with little grassroots pressure from constituency movements, little attention in the media, little congressional debate, and little opposition. Working quietly with advocacy-group lobbies, policy entrepreneurs in Congress extended Title VI's cross-cutting formula to protect new groups, often "with virtually no discussion or debate about the similarities and differences in the forms of discrimination faced by different groups and the types of remedies that might prove most effective in dealing with them."[32] Section 504 of the Rehabilitation Act, taken almost verbatim from Title VI and enacted without hearings, demonstrated an important difference between regulatory laws on behalf of civil rights constituencies (racial and ethnic minorities, women, the elderly, people with disabilities) and legislation governing other forms of social regulation (consumer fraud, health and safety, environmental protection).

In the detailed statutes governing the Enviromntal Protection Agency (EPA) or OSHA, for example, Congress stipulated precise standards for agency enforcement. In the protected-class extensions based on Title VI, on the other hand, Congress delegated wide discretion to the enforcement agencies. In section 504 of the Rehabilitation Act, for example, Congress surely did not mean what it appeared to say (that blind individuals could drive taxis as long as they were "otherwise qualified").[33] What section 504 *did* require would be decided later, mainly by staff lawyers in the OCR and the OFCC, working in consultation with disability rights organizations. By 1980 their regulations, following the path of federal aid, would cover every school system in the country, most colleges and universities, more than 200,000 private businesses and nonprofit organizations, and 23 million employees.

By the time Reagan entered the White House, the additive or cumulative model of civil rights regulation had built a muscular coalition of protected-class constituencies. The roster of the Leadership Conference, listing more than 165 member organizations, read like a Who's Who of organized African Americans, women,

Hispanics, labor unions, Protestant denominations, the Roman Catholic hierarchy, Jewish civic groups, disability rights organizations, and so on. The *Grove City* decision, and Reagan's legislative campaign to defend it, threatened and hence united them. In an inside-the-beltway contest like the Grove City contest, with the general public largely disengaged, victory went to the best organized coalition of interest groups. In that kind of competition, the Leadership Conference, led by the able Ralph Neas, had no peer.[34] By comparison, the organized interests supporting President Reagan—the U.S. Chamber of Commerce, the Associated General Contractors, the American Farm Bureau Federation, the National Apartment Association, the American Association of Bible Colleges—were badly outnumbered and outgunned.

The New Clientele Capture

The third institutionalized process advancing the regulatory agenda of the civil rights coalition was a new form of a traditional phenomenon—agency capture. The practice is as old as Jacksonian democracy, in which party patronage ruled the civil service and mission agencies were expected to cater to the needs of their organized constituencies—farmers, veterans, laborers, educators, businesspeople. Federal regulatory agencies, however, unlike traditional mission departments, were designed by reformers to remain independent and represent the public interest. In the original, pessimistic model of capture, developed from studies of the independent regulatory agencies created by the progressives and the New Dealers, the industries to be regulated—railroads, shippers, airlines, broadcasters, and power companies—tended to win control of the commissions or boards designed to regulate economic behavior in the public interest. In the new civil rights regulation of the 1960s, however, capture took a different twist. Routinely, newly created regulatory offices, such as the EEOC, OCR, and OFCC, were dominated not by the employers and organizations being regulated but by representatives of the constituencies being served. Redistributionist policies enforced by the new regulatory agencies for civil rights would benefit the protected-class designees—African Americans in the 1960s and Latinos, women, people with disabilities, and other groups in the 1970s.[35]

By time-honored practice in American government, interest groups have sought a dominant voice in programs and agencies that affect their welfare—farmers in the Department of Agriculture, veterans in Veterans Affairs, ranching, mining, and timber interests in Interior, unions in Labor, and small business in Commerce. What was new about the social regulation of the 1960s and 1970s, however, was that the benefits of affirmative action affected the entire economy and hence all government departments, not just targeted program sectors. The legislation of 1964–68 mandating equal opportunity in a society deeply rooted in discriminatory norms had made civil rights enforcement a rapid growth field. In 1970 the civil rights bureaucracies in Washington included the Civil Rights Division (including its Voting Rights Section) in the Justice Department; an independent investigatory commission, the Civil Rights Commission; an independent regulatory commission, the EEOC; twenty-seven contract-compliance offices in the mission agencies, including most notably the OFCC in Labor and the OCR in HEW; and the Office of Minority Business Enterprise (OMBE) in the Department of Commerce. Outside the Washington bureaucracy and its regional outposts were overlapping layers of equal opportunity offices in state, county, and municipal jurisdictions; in public school districts and higher education systems; in foundations and nonprofit organizations; and in large business and professional firms.

The simple-capture notion has always lent itself to caricature and misuse. Of particular significance, one of the most striking changes in the politics of policy and regulation in the post-1964 era was seen in the schizophrenic behavior of capture in the new social regulation. In the 1970s the pessimism of liberal reformers over agency capture and regulatory decay gave way to optimism that the new social regulation was structurally resistant to capture. The new agencies of environmental and consumer protection did not seem threatened by capture. But in a development that has not received sufficient scholarly attention, the civil rights component of the new social regulation diverged from this trend. The explanation for this difference between civil rights regulation on the one hand and environmental, consumer, and safety regulation on the other lies in the way outside interests are arrayed in the political environment. In James Q. Wilson's analysis of the politics of regulation, the political environment surrounding most forms of environmental, consumer protection, and transportation safety regulation is characterized by widely distributed benefits (clean air and water, safe drugs and highways) and narrowly concentrated costs (pollution abatement equipment, toxic waste disposal, air-bag requirements).[36] This kind of regulation is popular with consumers and voters, but its concentrated costs bring strong resistance from regulated industries hostile to its goals. In social regulation of occupational health and safety, in which both costs and benefits are highly concentrated, agencies such as OSHA are subject to competing pressures from rival interest groups—organized labor seeking expensive improvements in the workplace environment and business firms resisting costs not tied to productivity. In these political environments, agency capture by regulated interests is difficult. Regulation cuts widely across industrial sectors (environmental protection, pure food and drugs, transportation safety) or rival interests (business, labor) to keep the agency erect (OSHA, National Labor Relations Board).

In modern civil rights regulation, however, benefits (jobs, promotions, admissions, contract set-asides) are narrowly concentrated among protected-class clienteles (racial and ethnic minorities, women, people with disabilities) while costs are widely distributed. Agencies in this environment face a dominant interest group or coalition of advocacy groups favoring its goals. Wilson calls this pattern *client* politics. It is long familiar to us in the folklore of economic regulation, in which regulated industries (railroads, shippers, airlines, motor carriers) captured "client agencies" (Interstate Commerce Commission [ICC], Civil Aeronautics Board [CAB], Federal Communications Commission). The mechanistic metaphors of agency capture and self-serving "iron triangles" linking agencies, legislative committees, and beneficiary groups have always oversimplified institutional and interest-group relationships, and space does not permit addressing that complexity here. Nonetheless, the deregulation movement of the late 1970s built a formidable empirical case against the cozy environment of client protection found at agencies like the CAB and the ICC. Similarly, by the 1970s, clientele groups representing the interests of minorities, women, and people with disabilities (the NAACP, MAL-DEF, NOW, WEAL, the American Coalition of Citizens with Disabilities) lobbied intensely and effectively to shape the regulatory agenda of agencies like the EEOC, OFCC, OCR, Voting Rights Section in the Justice Department, Office of Bilingual Education and Minority Language Affairs, and their counterpart agencies in thousands of federal, state, county, and municipal governments.

The political power of advocacy groups within the civil rights enforcement agencies, backed by the lobbying of the Leadership Conference in Congress and generally supported by the federal courts into the middle 1980s, pushed the agencies to adopt aggressive compliance standards. The OCR's desegregation guidelines, the OFCC's affirmative action program, the EEOC's guidelines on employee selection procedures and race-normed test scores, and the Justice Department's standards for "minority-majority" electoral districts highlight the power of civil rights interests over executive agencies. Agencies such as the OCR, whiplashed between aggressive clientele groups, congressional oversight committees, federal courts in semipermanent lawsuits like the *Adams* case, the political pressures of election campaigns, and shrinking budget resources, often had difficulty pleasing any constituency.[37] Nonetheless, the success of the civil rights coalition in controlling the legislative agenda during the Reagan and Bush administrations, reversing in Congress the Supreme Court's restrictive statutory rulings—in *Grove City College v. Bell* as well as in significant voting rights and employment discrimination decisions[38]—testifies to the advantages of the client model in the politics of regulation.

1994: End of a Thirty-Year Era?

The passage of the Civil Rights Act of 1991 and the election of Bill Clinton in 1992, returning the presidency and Congress to Democratic control in 1993, suggested for a season that the post-1964 regime of rights regulation had weathered the counterattack of the Reagan years.[39] Indeed, in the congressional elections of 1994, the Republican "Contract with America," a ten-point credo of conservative policy goals, nowhere mentioned civil rights. Then came the earthquake of 1994: insurgent Republicans led by House minority leader Newt Gingrich won control of Congress; California voters, resenting the burden of immigration entitlements in a deteriorating economy, passed Proposition 187; Republican leaders with records supporting affirmative action, most notably Senate majority leader Bob Dole and California governor Pete Wilson, attacked minority-preference programs. Equally significant, a conservative majority on the Supreme Court shocked the civil rights coalition in 1995 by narrowing federal minority set-aside programs (*Adarand Constructors, Inc. v. Pena*) and racial gerrymandering in legislative districts (*Miller v. Johnson*).

With hindsight we can see premonitory symptoms of the conservative revolt of the mid-1990s. In 1985, Democratic pollster Stanley Greenberg reported growing disaffection in Michigan among white working-class voters over minority job preferences. Subsequent national surveys by Gallup, ABC News–*Washington Post*, the

University of Michigan's Institute for Social Research, the *New York Times*, and NBC News–*Wall Street Journal* showed growing resentment of affirmative action among whites of both sexes.[40] In *The Scar of Race*, Paul Sniderman and Thomas Piazza found whites by increasing margins supporting not only antidiscrimination policies but also governmental programs to provide income, services, and training to improve the economic and social circumstances of blacks. But on issues of school busing for racial balance and affirmative action preferences, white Americans of both sexes were massively opposed.[41]

Resentment of group-based preference policies was fanned by economic stress—falling real wages, polarizing income distribution, declining job security—and by massive immigration. Following the family reunification reforms of 1965, 25 million immigrants came to the United States. Three quarters of them were from Latin America or Asia and hence qualified under many affirmative action programs for protected-class status on the basis of ancestry. During the 1970s and 1980s the Small Business Administration, for example, in its 8(a) program of subsidized loans and grants, approved minority-preference status for individuals on the basis of ancestry from Indonesia, Sri Lanka, India, Pakistan, China, and Japan, ethnic communities whose history in the United States varies widely but whose average family income and education by the 1990s considerably exceeded that of "white" families.[42]

It is too early to draw conclusions about the direction of change in the mid-1990s. Conservative majorities on the Supreme Court and Republican majorities in Congress are changing the ground rules that governed the 1964–94 era. President Clinton, reelected in 1996, was the first Democrat reelected to the White House since Franklin Roosevelt. Yet his campaign featured issues and proposals (family values, free trade, welfare reform, balancing the budget, policing crime) previously emphasized by Republicans.

We can begin to draw conclusions, however, about the dynamics of the era that seems to be passing. Paradoxically, as the power of the civil rights coalition and the security of affirmative action programs increased, the perceived legitimacy of minority-preference remedies decreased. As the civil rights coalition grew by extending protected-class status to an expanding array of advocacy groups, it purchased insider bargaining power at the price of weakening public claims to fairness. The tension between power and legitimacy thus produced a kind of equilibrium cycle. By populating the federal judiciary with a generation of young conservatives, Reagan and Bush ultimately transformed the face of civil rights enforcement. Reagan's civil rights counterrevolution, however, did not bring with it a fundamental change in policies and programs. As a result, the Reagan revolution did little to deflect the shift of civil rights regulation from individual to group-based claims during 1964–94.

NOTES

1. Quoted in Gary L. McDowell, "Affirmative Inaction: The Brock-Meese Standoff in Federal Racial Quotas," *Policy Review* 48 (Spring 1989): 32.

2. Norman C. Amaker, *Civil Rights and the Reagan Administration* (Washington, D.C.:

The Urban Institute Press, 1988); Robert R. Detletsen, *Civil Rights under Reagan* (San Francisco: Institute for Contemporary Studies, 1991).

3. Hugh Davis Graham, *The Civil Rights Era: Origin and Development of National Policy, 1960–1972* (New York: Oxford University Press, 1990); Hugh Davis Graham, "Race, History, and Policy: African-Americans and Civil Rights since 1964," *Journal of Policy History* 6 (1994): 12–39.

4. Hugh Davis Graham, "Richard Nixon and Civil Rights: Explaining an Enigma," *Presidential Studies Quarterly* 26 (Winter 1996): 93–106.

5. U.S. Commission on Civil Rights, *The Federal Civil Rights Enforcement Budget: Fiscal Year 1983* (Washington, D.C: Government Printing Office, 1982), 14–54.

6. See Paul Brest, "Race Discrimination," *The Burger Court: The Counter-Revolution That Wasn't*, ed. Vincent Blasi (New Haven: Yale University Press, 1983), 113–31.

7. Michael Pertschuk, *Giant Killers* (New York: Norton, 1986), 148–80.

8. Jeremy Rabkin, "The Reagan Revolution Meets the Regulatory Labyrinth," in *Do Elections Matter?* ed. Benjamin Ginsberg and Alan Stone (Armonck, N.Y.: M. E. Sharpe, 1986), 221–39.

9. See Alfred W. Blumrosen, *Modern Law: The Law Transmission System and Equal Opportunity* (Madison: University of Wisconsin Press, 1993), 267–74.

10. Although Republicans gained 33 House seats in the 1980 elections, Democratic majorities in the 97th Congress (1981–83) were 243–192 and in the 98th Congress (1983–85), 269–165.

11. James C. Miller III to Orrin G. Hatch, 14 September 1981, White House Office files (WHORM), HU 011-12, Ronald Reagan Library (RRL), Simi Valley, Calif.; Augustus F. Hawkins to the President, 16 October 1984, WHORM PE 002, RRL; William Bradford Reynolds to Mayor W. Wilson Goode, 12 December 1985, WHORM HU 010, RRL; memo, Ralph G. Neas to members of the press, "Update on the Executive Order on Affirmative Action," 15 February 1986, Leadership Conference on Civil Rights Papers (LCCRP), Manuscript Division, Library of Congress, Washington, D.C.

12. *Newsweek*, 30 December 1985; Daniel Seligman, "It Was Foreseeable," *Fortune*, 22 July 1985; McDowell, "Affirmative Inaction," 32–37.

13. Hugh Davis Graham, *Civil Rights and the Presidency* (New York: Oxford University Press, 1992), 150–69.

14. Memo, Mel Bradley to Jack Svahn, 23 October 1984, WHORM PE 002, RRL; memo, John G. Roberts to Diana G. Holland, 10 April 1986, WHORM PQ 341, RRL.

15. Daniel Seligman, "Affirmative Action Is Here to Stay," *Fortune*, 19 April 1982; Anne B. Fisher, "Businessmen Like to Hire by the Numbers," *Fortune*, 16 September 1985; Steven A. Holmes, "Affirmative Action Plans Are Part of Business Life," *New York Times*, 22 November 1991.

16. Memo, Robert M. Kruger to Peter J. Wallison, 7 April 1986, Kruger files OA 18389, RRL.

17. Walter F. Murphy, "Reagan's Judicial Strategy," *Looking Back on the Reagan Presidency*, ed. Larry Berman (Baltimore: Johns Hopkins University Press, 1990), 207–37.

18. Neal Devins, "Affirmative Action after Reagan," *Texas Law Review* 68 (December 1989): 353.

19. *Grove City College v. Bell, Secretary of Education*, 465 U.S. 555, 560–61 (1984).

20. At the time of the suit, Grove City College enrolled approximately 2,200 students, 140 of whom received federal tuition grants and 342 of whom had obtained federally guaranteed (and interest-subsidized) tuition loans. All parties to the Grove City dispute agreed that the college, half of whose students were women, had not engaged in discrimination by sex, race, or any other form prohibited by federal or state law.

21. *Grove City College v. Harris*, 500 F.Supp. 253 (W.D. Pa. 1980).

22. *Grove City College v. Harris*, 687 F.2d 684 (1982).

23. *Grove City College v. Bell*, 465 U.S. 555 (1984).

24. Robert Pear, "Bill Draws Criticism from Administration," *New York Times*, 23 May 1984; Nadine Cohodas and Janet Cook, "Civil Rights Bill Approved by Two House Committees," *Congressional Quarterly Weekly Report*, 26 May 1984, 1229; Spencer Rich, "Administration Accused of Trying to Sidetrack Key Rights Bill," *Washington Post*, 14 August 1984.

25. See, e.g., memo, Mike Horowitz to David Stockman et al., 4 May 1984, Christena Bach files, OA 12739, RRL.

26. Mark Willen, "Congress Overrides Reagan's Grove City Veto," *Congressional Quarterly Weekly Report*, 26 March 1988, 774–76; Courtney Leatherman, "Congress Overrides President's Veto of Civil Rights Bill," *Chronicle of Higher Education*, 30 March 1988.

27. Liberal Republicans, though shrinking in numbers, were prominent supporters of the Civil Rights Restoration Bill. Senators Lowell P. Weicker (Connecticut) and Bob Packwood (Oregon) joined Democrat Edward Kennedy as cosponsors. Robert Dole of Kansas, Senate majority leader in the 99th Congress, campaigned against Reagan's Grove City policy from the outset, and Senator Pete Wilson of California voted to overturn Reagan's veto.

28. Charles O. Jones, *The Presidency in a Separated System* (Washington, D.C.: Brookings Institution, 1994), 140–43.

29. Stephen C. Halpern, *On the Limits of the Law: The Legacy of Title VI of the Civil Rights Act* (Baltimore: Johns Hopkins University Press, 1995); William A. Link, *William Friday: Power, Purpose, and American Higher Education* (Chapel Hill: University of North Carolina Press, 1995), 249–337.

30. U.S. Advisory Commission on Intergovernmental Relations, *Regulatory Federalism* (Washington, D.C.: ACIR, 1984), 70, 91. In 1970, Hispanic advocacy groups persuaded the OCR under its Title VI authority to issue the "May 25 Memorandum" requiring federally aided school districts to provide bilingual education plans. See Coleman Brez Stein, Jr., *Sink or Swim: The Politics of Bilingual Education* (New York: Praeger, 1986), 36–44.

31. Edward D. Berkowitz, "A Historical Preface to the Americans with Disabilities Act," in *Civil Rights in the United States*, ed. Hugh Davis Graham (University Park: Pennsylvania State University Press, 1994), 102–3.

32. U.S. Advisory Commission on Intergovernmental Relations, *Federal Regulation of State and Local Governments: The Mixed Record of the 1980s* (Washington, D.C.: ACIR, 1993), 9.

33. On section 504, see Richard K. Scotch, *From Goodwill to Civil Rights* (Philadelphia: Temple University Press, 1984); Edward D. Berkowitz, *Disabled Policy: America's Programs for the Handicapped* (New York: Cambridge University Press, 1987).

34. See letter, Benjamin L. Hooks and Ralph G. Neas to members of Congress, 25 April 1984, LCCRP. Among the more than 160 member organizations of the Leadership Conference were the NAACP, National Council of Churches, AFL-CIO, League of Women Voters, ACLU, National Urban League, United Auto Workers, NOW, American Jewish Congress, MALDEF, National Education Association, Children's Defense Fund, American Coalition of Citizens with Disabilities, National Catholic Conference for Interracial Justice, and American Council of the Blind.

35. James Q. Wilson, ed., *The Politics of Regulation* (New York: Basic Books, 1980); Michael Reagan, *Regulation: The Politics of Policy* (Boston: Little, Brown & Co., 1987).

36. James Q. Wilson, *Bureaucracy* (New York: Basic Books, 1989), 72–89; Wilson, *Politics of Regulation*, 357–94.

37. In a few celebrated instances (school desegregation guidelines for Mayor Richard

Daley's Chicago, school dress codes and hair-length codes, school-busing requirements for racial balance), OCR regulations were repudiated even by Democratic-controlled Congresses. In others (banning boys choirs and father-daughter school dinners), public ridicule forced bureaucratic retreat. See, e.g., Joseph A. Califano, *Governing America* (New York: Simon & Schuster, 1981), 219–26; Jeremy Rabkin, *Judicial Compulsions* (New York: Basic Books, 1989), 147–81.

38. *City of Mobile, Alabama v. Bolden*, 446 U.S. 55 (1980) (voting rights); *Grove City College v. Bell*, 465 U.S. 555 (1984); *Ward's Cove Packing Co. v. Antonio*, 109 S. Ct. 2115 (1989) (employment discrimination).

39. See, e.g., William C. Berman, *America's Right Turn: From Nixon to Bush* (Baltimore: Johns Hopkins University Press, 1994).

40. Seymour Martin Lipset, "Equal Chances versus Equal Rights," *Annals* 523 (September 1992): 63–74; Seymour Martin Lipset, "Affirmative Action and the American Creed," *Wilson Quarterly* (Winter 1992): 52–62.

41. Paul M. Sniderman and Thomas Piazza, *The Scar of Race* (Cambridge, Mass.: Belknap Press, 1993), 5.

42. George R. LaNoue, "Split Visions: Minority Business Set-Asides," *Annals of American Academy of Political and Social Science* 523 (September 1992): 104–16; George R. LaNoue and John C. Sullivan, "Presumptions for Preferences: The Small Business Administration's Decisions on Groups Entitled to Affirmative Action," *Journal of Policy History* 6 (1994): 439–67.

8

The Convergence of Black and White Attitudes on School Desegregation Issues

CHRISTINE H. ROSSELL

In its pursuit of racial equality in the schools in the four decades since *Brown v. Board of Education*, the civil rights leadership has made various assumptions about the attitudes and policy preferences of black and white parents. From 1968 to the present, the plaintiffs' attorneys initiated class-action suits on behalf of black students and their parents that demanded the achievement of racial balance throughout the school system by means of mandatory reassignments. In addition, the plaintiffs' attorneys argued that white opposition to mandatory reassignment should be ignored by the courts because it was caused by racism. Most federal district courts appear to have been convinced by these arguments since, from 1968 through 1981, they overwhelmingly ordered the implementation of the mandatory reassignment plans demanded by the attorneys who claimed to be representing the interests of black students and their parents. The opinion data offered in this chapter, however, show that these suppositions about the attitudes and opinions of black and white parents have been wrong and suggest that the civil rights establishment has not always reflected the views of its constituency. Contrary to popular belief, black attitudes toward mandatory reassignments are not very favorable and never have been. In addition, there is considerable evidence calling into question the assumption that white opposition to busing stems solely from racism. In short, the civil rights leadership's almost singleminded pursuit of mandatory reassignment plans in school desegregation litigation from the late 1960s through the early 1990s has either ignored or disregarded the attitudes of ordinary parents. It is thus time to rethink our policies on equality in education because, at least with regard to school desegregation, they have been out of sync with what black parents, and indeed parents of all races, actually believe and want for their children.

The Evolution of School Desegregation Plans

From 1954 to 1968, the criterion for convicting a school district of intentional segregation was the existence of government-mandated segregation, and the only remedy required was that states rescind their segregation laws and that school districts stop assigning children to schools solely on the basis of their race. Neighborhood schools were considered a legitimate desegregation tool because they were race neutral—that is, students were assigned to schools on the basis of their residence, not their race. In the *Brown* litigation, the court explained that although one of the schools in Topeka was "inhabited entirely by colored students, no violation of any constitutional right results because they are compelled to attend the school in the district in which they live."[1] Nevertheless, in the South of the 1950s, neighborhood schools were considered quite revolutionary and thus were fiercely resisted since they could result in black children attending the same school with white children.

As an alternative to race-neutral assignment policies such as neighborhood schools, school districts in the South during the 1950s and early 1960s adopted court-approved "pupil placement laws" and "freedom of choice" plans that were generally believed to be delaying tactics. If these devices were delaying tactics, they appear to have worked; southern schools remained racially imbalanced throughout most of the 1960s. Intellectuals and the courts believed this lack of integration was due solely to the coercion of blacks. It was simply taken for granted that most, if not all, blacks wanted to go to school with whites, even if it meant crosstown busing or other inconveniences. Civil rights advocates did not bother to ask black parents—the injured parties—if this was the remedy they wanted, nor did they question the assumption that busing would achieve more integration than neighborhood schools or any voluntary techniques.

The 1968 Supreme Court decision in *Green v. County Board of Education*[2] marks a watershed in southern desegregation plans because it required that school districts not only stop discriminating but also actually achieve integrated schools. As a result of this decision and subsequent court decisions—in particular the Supreme Court's 1971 decision in *Swann v. Charlotte-Mecklenburg Board of Education*,[3] which established the principle of racial balance and approved crosstown busing to achieve it—the public schools of the Deep South were substantially integrated between 1970 and 1972 by court orders that, at least on paper, reassigned students within a district so that the racial composition of each school was roughly equal to that of the school district as a whole. These plans, popularly called "forced busing," produced protests and white and middle-class flight of varying intensity in every school district in which they were implemented.

As a result of these unintended negative outcomes, by the mid-1970s courts began permitting a second type of voluntary desegregation plans that included such incentives as magnet schools. These magnet-voluntary desegregation plans allowed students to stay at their neighborhood schools if they chose to do so but tried to entice them to opposite-race schools by means of special programs called magnets. Typically, the options to transfer also included a majority to minority (M to M) transfer program in which any student in the school district could transfer from any school in which his or her race was in the majority to any school in which his or her race was in the minority.[4] In general, only minority students participated in the majority to minority program because even today whites will not voluntarily transfer to schools in minority neighborhoods without an incentive in the form of a magnet program.[5]

Controlled choice is the third of the three basic types of desegregation plans (mandatory reassignment, voluntary magnet, and controlled choice) implemented. Controlled-choice plans came into existence in the early 1980s as mandatory reassignment plans grew out of favor with the courts, other policymakers, and minority parents. The academics and policymakers who embraced controlled choice were those who remained uneasy over the freedom of parents in voluntary plans to keep their children in neighborhood schools. Controlled choice thus represents a compromise desegregation strategy partway between mandatory reassignment plans that reassign everyone and completely voluntary plans that allow students to remain in their neighborhood schools if they so desire.

The basic foundation of all controlled-choice desegregation plans is that, at a minimum, parents of entering students or those changing schools are *required* to rank a number of schools in the school system in order of preference and no one is guaranteed a neighborhood school or any other school. The school administration, while trying to give parents their first-choice school, reserves the right to assign students to any school it wants them to go to (typically one where their attendance will satisfy racial-balance requirements). Anywhere from 10 to 40 percent of students do not receive their first-choice school, and more important, many parents refuse to stick around to see if they get a good school assignment in the lottery. Thus, these same plans have produced significant white flight.[6]

The voluntary and controlled-choice plans are virtually the only new plans implemented in the last decade. Indeed, since 1981, only two new mandatory reassignment plans have been ordered by courts, both in Mississippi.[7] This dearth of mandatory reassignment plans has not been a retreat from school desegregation and the pursuit of equality in education, however, since there have been numerous desegregation plans implemented in the last decade and a half, and virtually every school district charged with intentional school segregation has been convicted. Rather, the lack of mandatory reassignment plans represents a retreat from one type of desegregation plan—the type that produces the most opposition and white flight.

Thus, school segregation remedies have almost come full circle. Although the voluntary plans implemented after *Brown* were considered ineffective because no whites ever transferred to black schools—prompting the courts to approve only mandatory reassignment plans from 1968 to 1975—these courts did occasionally point out that voluntary plans per se were not unconstitutional and were to be evaluated in terms of their results. When freedom of choice offered a *real* promise of achieving a unitary, nonracial system, there was no objection to it. What has changed in the years since *Swann* is the willingness of the courts to entertain the possibility that voluntary plans might ultimately achieve more integration at less social cost than mandatory plans. This shift in the courts is thus not a retreat from the principle of equality of education but a retreat from a strategy that came to be viewed as an inefficient and counterproductive means of achieving equality.

Attitudes toward Desegregation

Most people now agree that white attitudes toward desegregation strategies, like white behavioral response, appear to be influenced by two characteristics of plans: the extent of parental choice and the right to remain at one's neighborhood school. The plaintiffs arguing on behalf of mandatory reassignment plans, however, have assumed that these issues were *not* important to black parents. Indeed, with few exceptions, it has been an almost unquestioned assumption of intellectual writing and court opinions in the 1970s that black parents were demanding the mandatory reassignment plans that forced them out of their neighborhood schools to opposite-race schools across town. During this period, while almost universally ordering the plaintiffs' mandatory reassignment plans to be implemented, few courts questioned the plaintiffs' attorneys on whether black parents really wanted to abandon the race-neutral assignment policies of *Brown* for the race-conscious assignment policies of *Green* and *Swann*.

Attitudes on Principles

The *Brown* decision was made at a time when whites were evenly split on the principle of school integration. Only 50 percent believed that white and black students should go to the same school.[8] By 1963, one year before the Civil Rights Act, a clear majority of whites—64 percent—believed in the principle of integration. By 1982 fully 90 percent of whites believed in the principle of integration. By 1985 this belief had reached its peak of 93 percent, causing the National Opinion Research Center (NORC) to stop asking the question because there was so little variation on it. This broad white support for the principle of integration has continued since 1985.[9] One could easily believe that only the lunatic fringe—about 6 percent of the white population—is opposed to the principle of school integration.

This support for the principle of school integration is also true of blacks. Indeed, the only difference between blacks and whites on this issue is that blacks have always had high support for the principle of school integration, at least since they were first asked this question in a national poll in 1972. By 1991 there was only a 2 percentage point difference between whites and blacks in their attitudes toward school integration, with more than 90 percent of both blacks and whites supporting school integration. Thus, despite dire predictions of a resurgence of segregationist attitudes among blacks and whites, these data show no retreat on this principle.

Figure 8.1 elaborates on parental attitudes toward integration by demonstrating the willingness of parents to send their children to integrated schools of three different racial mixtures: a few blacks, half black, and majority black. Although in 1959 more than 70 percent of southern whites objected to sending their children to a school with a few blacks, in contrast to fewer than 10 percent of nonsouthern

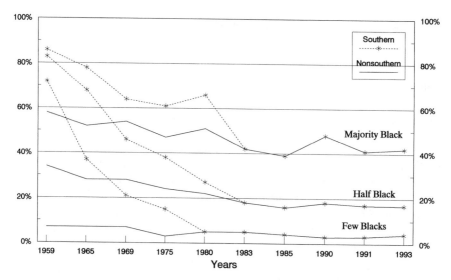

Sources: Gallup Polls, 1959–80, by region; NORC General Social Science Survey, 1983–93.
Note: No regional breakdown was available for NORC survey, 1983–93.

FIGURE 8.1. Percentage of Whites Objecting to Schools with a Few Blacks,
Half Black Schools, Majority Black Schools

whites, by 1980 there was no regional difference and by 1993 only 4 percent of
whites objected to sending their children to a school with a few blacks.[10]

In 1968 almost 85 percent of southerners and 35 percent of northerners objected
to sending their children to a school that was half black. In 1980, the last year a
regional breakdown was available, southerners were only 5 percentage points more
likely than northerners to object to sending their children to a school that is half
black. By 1993, only 17 percent of whites objected to sending their children to a
school that was half black, despite the fact that nationally blacks are only 12 percent
of the population.

The changes over time in white parents' willingness to send their children to an
integrated school that is majority black are even more extraordinary. Although in
1968 almost 90 percent of southerners and 60 percent of northerners objected to
sending their children to a school that was majority black, by 1980 there was only
a 15 percentage point difference between southerners and northerners. By 1993,
only 42 percent of whites objected to sending their children to a school that was
majority black.

The national surveys can be criticized on the grounds that they are a random
sample of adults, most of whom either do not have children or do not live in a
school district with a sizable black population. Thus for many of these respondents,
questions regarding the racial composition of a school they would be willing to
send their children to are abstract or irrelevant.

Armor and Rossell conducted surveys of public school parents in school districts
around the United States faced with adopting a school desegregation plan under

court order.[11] The parent survey data, however, show similar results. From 1977 to 1991, on average, only 13 percent of white parents (4 percentage points fewer than in the NORC national survey) and as much as 5 percent of black parents objected to sending their children to their neighborhood schools if they became half black/Hispanic. Moreover, only 33 percent of white parents (8 percentage points fewer than in the NORC national survey) and as much as 14 percent of black parents objected to sending their children to their neighborhood schools if they became predominantly black/Hispanic.

Given the fact that this question taps issues of power and control, not just race, it is quite remarkable that a majority of white adults and white public school parents do not object to having their children in schools where their race is not in the majority as long as they are their neighborhood schools. It is also interesting that a 50–50 racial composition is more desirable to black parents than is a predominantly minority composition, although the increase in objection to a predominantly minority school is less than is the white increase in objection.

Thus, these data suggest that the civil rights movement has been extraordinarily successful in achieving its symbolic goals. Almost no one is upset if there are a few blacks in his or her child's school. The Little Rock crisis and others like it, in which angry white mobs protested a handful of black children entering their schools, are gone forever. More surprisingly, most white parents do not object to their children being in a racial minority in their neighborhood schools. Blacks are no longer "official pariahs" and racial prejudice in the old-fashioned sense is simply, for all but a tiny minority of whites and blacks, socially unacceptable. This change is a remarkable revolution in white attitudes that must be credited to the moral leadership of the civil rights movement.

Attitudes on Implementation Techniques

At the same time that racial intolerance and support for segregation were declining, however, post-*Swann* mandatory reassignment plans were producing an increase in white enrollment losses in the North from an average annual 2.4 percent loss before desegregation to a 10 percent loss with the implementation of a plan.[12] In the South, white enrollment losses increased from an average 0.8 percent loss predesegregation to a 7.5 percent loss with implementation of a plan.[13] The southern loss is even more dramatic because it occurred in the kinds of school districts thought to be most immune to white flight—countywide districts already encompassing the suburban areas to which whites would normally be expected to flee.

White flight is not inconsistent with white attitudes. Although whites support the principle of integration, they overwhelmingly oppose the most widely used method of desegregating schools—mandatory reassignment or "busing." The Institute for Social Research (ISR) at the University of Michigan asked the following question in 1972, 1974, 1976, 1980, and 1984:[14]

There is much discussion about the best way to deal with racial problems. Some people think achieving racial integration of schools is so important that it justifies busing children to schools out of their own neighborhoods. Others think letting children go to their neighborhood schools is so important that they oppose busing. Where would you place yourself on this scale, or haven't you thought much about this?

1. Bus to achieve integration (1–4)
2. Keep children in neighborhood schools (5–7)
3. Haven't thought much about this.

As shown in figure 8.2, the ISR survey demonstrates a consistent lack of support for busing to achieve integration on the part of whites—rarely greater than 10 percent—when the alternative is keeping children in their neighborhood schools. Black respondents are, however, not exactly supportive of the concept of busing to achieve integration. Indeed, they are clearly split on this issue with only a minority or a bare majority supporting mandatory reassignment. By 1984, only 40 percent of blacks supported busing for integration over neighborhood schools.

Figure 8.2 also shows the Armor and Rossell parent survey results for the years 1977, 1981, 1986, 1988, 1989, 1990, and 1991 in school districts considering desegregation plan alternatives. The question was worded differently from the ISR survey question in that parents were asked only whether they support a mandatory reassignment plan for their school districts. They were not asked to compare such a plan directly to neighborhood schools as in the ISR survey.[15] When black *parents* were asked about a mandatory reassignment plan for the school system in which their children were enrolled, however, there was, on average, about the same lack of support as in the ISR national surveys of black adults.

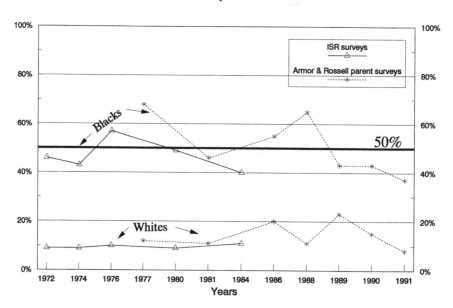

Sources: Institute for Social Research (ISR) surveys, 1972–84; Armor and Rossell district parent surveys, 1977–91.

FIGURE 8.2. Percentage Supporting Busing for Integration rather than Neighborhood Schools

The parent surveys generally show declining support for mandatory reassignment among black parents from a high of almost 70 percent in Los Angeles in 1977 to a low of less than 40 percent in Knox County, Tennessee, in 1991. The exception to this trend is the 65 percent support in Natchez, Mississippi, in 1988. In comparison to the national surveys, however, the low percentage in Knox County is only slightly lower than the percentages shown by the ISR surveys in every year except 1976. Therefore, black support for mandatory reassignment not only has declined since 1972 but also has rarely enjoyed majority support.

White support for mandatory reassignment shows a different trend. Although there is some fluctuation depending on the district or year, the level of white support for mandatory reassignment varies from 10 to 20 percent and there seems to be no trend over time as with black support.

As shown in figure 8.3, on average, black and white parents agree that the most desirable desegregation policy alternative for their districts is neighborhood schools with choice[16] followed by the redrawing of attendance zones of adjacent schools ("Change Zones").[17] What they least want for their children is a mandatory reassignment plan—although controlled choice has even less support among black parents. Interestingly, only a minority of parents of both races support controlled-choice plans, although they provide a lot of choice, perhaps because the plans do not guarantee children the right to attend their neighborhood schools or to be assigned to their first-choice schools.[18] Thus, the inclusion of choice and neighborhood schools explains not only white (and middle-class black) behavioral responses (e.g., protest and white flight) to school desegregation plans but also both black and white attitudinal support for desegregation alternatives.

Figure 8.4 shows the behavioral intentions of black and white public school

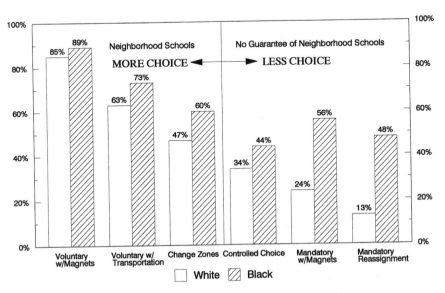

Sources: Armor and Rossell surveys, 1986, 1988, 1990, 1991; Armor survey, 1989.

FIGURE 8.3. Percentage of Parents Supporting Alternative Desegregation Plans

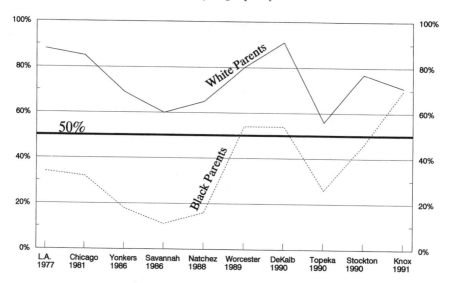

Sources: Armor surveys, 1977, 1981, 1989; Armor and Rossell surveys, 1986, 1988, 1990, 1991.

FIGURE 8.4. Percentage of Parents Not Going Along With Mandatory Reassignment of Own Child

parents if a mandatory reassignment plan were adopted in their school districts and their children were reassigned to an opposite-race school. The percentage of white parents who would not go along with a mandatory reassignment plan declines over time but increases for black parents until, by 1991 in Knox County, Tennessee (which at the time of the survey was about 85 percent white), 71 percent of white parents and 70 percent of black parents would not go along with a mandatory reassignment plan that assigned their children to an opposite-race school.

Even more surprising is the low willingness of black parents to transfer their children voluntarily out of their own schools to an opposite-race school, even when that school has a special magnet program. Given all of the publicity about the poor quality of black schools and the high level of support for neighborhood schools with magnets, it is surprising that only 33 percent of black parents, on average, would definitely choose to transfer their children to a magnet school in an opposite-race neighborhood.

These findings are, however, consistent with black parents' perceptions of the extent of racial "discrimination" in education that exists in their districts. On average, only 35 percent of black parents believe that black students get a worse education in their public schools than do white students.[19] Thus, contrary to the assumption of most of the court decisions of the 1970s and the academic writing on this subject, only a minority of black Americans support mandatory reassignment and a majority would not go along with a mandatory reassignment of their own children to an opposite-race school. Most black parents, like most white parents, prefer their neighborhood schools to being bused out to a school they did not choose, and even more surprising, a large majority of black parents prefer their neighborhood schools to a special school that they could choose, perhaps because most of them believe that black children are currently receiving an education that is at least as good as white children receive.

Given these survey results, it is not unreasonable to ask why the civil rights community has ignored black parents and their preferences. In "Serving Two Masters," Derrick Bell, a black law professor at New York University,[20] concludes that it is because the National Association for the Advancement of Colored People (NAACP) Legal Defense and Educational Fund (LDF), the major plaintiffs' attorney in school desegregation cases, have a conflict of interest. The LDF ignores its clients' preferences because it has to answer to the middle-class blacks and whites who provide financial support for the organization and who not only believe fervently in school integration but also believe in a kind of "domestic domino theory" in which failure on the busing issue would trigger a string of defeats in other civil rights arenas. Its local clientele, black parents, have little or no contact with the LDF once it has solicited them as plaintiffs for litigation. Ron Edmonds, another black educational expert and scholar, agrees with Bell on this point.[21]

Nathaniel Jones, NAACP general counsel, defends the group's behavior with the argument that "it would be absurd to expect that each and every black person should be polled before a lawsuit is filed, or a plan of desegregation is proposed."[22] In a private conversation, Jones said that he did not need to ask black parents about their preferences because he himself was black and could draw on his own life experiences.[23] But he cannot possibly know his clients' preferences, which is precisely the problem with class-action suits—lawyers are a highly educated, highly paid, elite group who, regardless of their origins, are not capable of knowing what their clients want without asking them.[24]

One watchdog group charges that the reason class-action suits often do not represent the preferences of the attorneys' clients is not just because of a conflict of interest but because of egotism. Class-action suits "have the capacity to provide large sources of narcissistic gratification . . . and the psychological motivations which influence the lawyer in taking on 'a fiercer dragon' through the class action may also underlie the tendency to direct the suit toward the goals of the lawyer rather than the client."[25]

Indeed, it is interesting to note that in the Chicago, Yonkers, Worcester (Massachusetts), and Stockton (California) cases, the legal counsel for the plaintiffs offered a mandatory reassignment plan supported by only a minority of black parents, and in none of the desegregation court cases in the school districts noted in Figure 8.4 did the plaintiffs' attorneys offer the plan most supported by black parents—a neighborhood school plan with magnets—despite being given the results of the parent surveys showing that the attorneys were not representing the preferences of their "clients."[26]

Explanations for Rejection of Busing and Acceptance of Integration

What accounts for the preferences of black and white parents, in particular the high level rejecting busing and supporting neighborhood schools? Unfortunately, because of the fascination with white racism in America and the disinterest of the intelligentsia in the opinions of ordinary black parents,[27] almost all of the research and writing have focused on an explanation for white attitudes and opinions.

Black Attitudes

I know of only a few social scientists, most notably Howard Schuman, Charlotte Steeh, and Lawrence Bobo[28] and Lee Sigelman and Susan Welsh,[29] who have even acknowledged, let alone analyzed, declining black support for mandatory reassignment and other governmental strategies for forcing racial equality in American society. Schuman, Steeh, and Bobo offer two hypotheses to explain this phenomenon. Their first hypothesis is that after the incredible energy blacks put into the civil rights movement of the 1960s, there had to be some "natural falling away during the 1970s as the salience of these issues decreased."[30] They see this decline as part of a cyclical psychological pattern—a burst of energy must be followed by exhaustion and alienation. Their second hypothesis is that some blacks may have retreated from the use of federal force for desegregation because of their perception that it was so intensely opposed by whites as to be impractical. In short, white opposition to busing and its resulting flight and protest, rather than blacks own preferences, may have caused the decline in black support.[31]

But Schuman, Steeh, and Bobo admit they find neither explanation satisfactory, and there is little evidence to support either hypothesis. At the very least, however, they believe the gap between blacks' support for the principle of school integration and their opposition to or conflict over *forcing* people to integrate can help us interpret white trends. They conclude: "In their attitudes, as in their lives more generally, blacks and whites in the United States are inescapably connected in many ways, and these connections are easily missed when only one group is considered at a time."[32] Sigelman and Welch agree that the fact that the rejection of busing occurred in tandem for whites and blacks makes it difficult to interpret it as an indication of growing prejudice against blacks. They argue there are some good reasons why black parents might reject busing. For one thing, it diverts attention from what is most important to them: the quality of education of their children. In addition, it is inconvenient, deprives black parents of choice, contravenes the principle of neighborhood schools, and may lower their child's self-esteem. "Thus, many blacks have good reason to suspect that busing to integrate may harm their children."[33]

White Attitudes

Two major theories of the determinants of political attitudes and behavior have been used to explain white opposition to busing. The first theory is that whites are motivated by diffuse attitudes formed in early childhood. In other words, racism explains white opposition to busing. This theory has been offered in several guises—one Schuman, Steeh, and Bobo[34] call "superficial tolerance" from the works of Mary Jackman,[35] and the other they call "symbolic racism" from the work of David Sears and his colleagues and John McConahay.[36]

Jackman's "superficial tolerance" theory argues that the "implementation" questions demonstrate a genuine commitment to integration, whereas the "principle" questions show only a superficial commitment to integration. The problem with her argument, however, is that it ignores the fact that implementation techniques can have varying success in achieving the goals of the civil rights movement and that both blacks and whites might be capable of perceiving this. It also ignores the very real change in white tolerance for half black, and even majority black, schools in their own neighborhoods—a level that is now so high it can hardly be called "superficial" tolerance.

The "symbolic racism" theory in general argues that white racial attitudes are formed in early childhood, but because racism is less socially acceptable today, this racism is expressed covertly in opposition to busing, to a black candidate, or to preferential treatment for blacks. Thus, these opinions on issues are symbolically related to deep-rooted attitudes regarding the racial inferiority of blacks or to fear of them and their effect on society. The evidence for the symbolic racism theory is that in national surveys of white adults, opposition to busing is moderately correlated with a variety of more obvious measures of prejudice (such as support for segregation in general), and it has little relationship to whether an adult has a school-age child—presumably a measure of self-interest.

The major problems with the symbolic racism research[37] are that (1) the absolute levels of opposition to busing are so high that virtually the entire white population must be labeled racist,[38] which ignores not only the change in and currently high level of tolerance for half black and majority black schools but black opposition to busing as well; (2) although opposition to busing is correlated with prejudice, prejudice does not need opposition to busing as a vehicle for expression, as demonstrated by the 6 percent of the white population that still maintains that white and black students should go to separate schools and the 70 percent that at one time maintained it; (3) the size of the correlation between the researchers' racial intolerance scale and a seven-point antibusing item is .36, leaving much of the variation unexplained so that one might reasonably conclude that all racists may oppose busing but not everyone opposed to busing is a racist; and (4) the researchers' definition of self-interest is too narrow in assuming that busing has no cost to those without children, a fact that the childless residents of cities beset by protest, white flight, and unhappy neighbors, relatives, and friends would probably dispute. Indeed, if one thinks of self-interest in terms of collective as well as individual interest, it is quite possible for a group that thinks of itself as distinct to view as a personal threat something that happens to only some members of the group.[39]

Moreover, if whites do lie on surveys, the fact that they feel they now have to lie, not just in public but in a semiprivate situation, and that prior to *Brown* they could openly express blatant racist opinions suggests a fundamental change in American norms that cannot be ignored. Indeed, the only question is exactly how much this enormous social change has truly affected individual attitudes. It would be hard to imagine that it has had no effect.

The second general theory explaining white opposition to busing is that whites express attitudes and behave in ways that are in their own self-interest. In other words, white parents oppose busing because it entails real costs and burdens for them and their children (or their future children and current friends, relatives, and neighbors' children) and the benefit does not appear to be greater than the cost. Self-interest can also be expressed in terms of the kind of society one wants to live in. For example, Seymour Lipset and William Schneider reviewed a wide range of survey questions and concluded that there is a powerful consensus in American society against discrimination that disappears when issues of compulsory integration or preferential treatment are raised because the former is viewed as a threat to freedom and the latter is seen as another form of discrimination.[40]

In short, there is a basic conflict between two important values held by Americans—individual freedom and egalitarianism—that are at the core of our conception of a good society. This value-conflict theory would suggest that most blacks are opposed to busing not only because of the costs in terms of white resentment but also because they, too, resent being forced to go to a school they did not choose by a government they do not particularly trust for an ideal they are not sure produces the benefits claimed for it using a strategy that obviously has some serious costs.

Indeed, Derrick Bell, a black legal scholar, personifies this when he writes:

> Yet, the remedies set forth in the major school cases following *Brown*—balancing the student and teacher populations by race in each school, eliminating one-race schools, redrawing school attendance lines, and transporting students to achieve racial balance— have not in themselves guaranteed black children better schooling than they received in the pre-Brown era. . . . Plans relying on racial balance to foreclose evasion have not eliminated the need for further orders protecting black children against discriminatory policies, including resegregation within desegregated schools, the loss of black faculty and administrators, suspensions and expulsions at much higher rates than white students, and varying forms of racial harassment ranging from exclusion from extracurricular activities to physical violence. . . . The educational benefits that have resulted from the mandatory assignment of black and white children to the same schools are also debatable. If benefits did exist, they have begun to dissipate as whites flee in alarming numbers from school districts ordered to implement mandatory reassignment plans.[41]

Conclusions

The survey data reviewed above strongly suggest that most blacks perceive busing as not in their self-interest. If that is true, then why is this not also possible for whites who have seen trumpeted in the media allegations by the plaintiffs' attorneys that black schools are inferior and that white racists will ensure that desegregation is accompanied by protest and violence and who furthermore were raised to believe that neighborhood schools are the best kind of schools because they allow local control and parent participation in the education of their children? In short, there are some real benefits to neighborhood schools and real costs to mandatory reassignment out of one's neighborhood to a school not of one's choice that both black and white parents are probably capable of perceiving.

Moreover, the superiority of mandatory reassignment plans in simply achieving integration is just not evident. By the fall of 1996, the Boston public schools, for example, were 83.2 percent minority twenty-two years after the original mandatory reassignment order. Indeed, there was almost half the interracial exposure in 1996—14.9 percent white in the average minority child's school—than the 24 percent white in the average minority child's school that existed before the first mandatory reassignment plan was implemented in 1974. Nor is this an isolated occurrence. Most of the big cities of the United States that implemented mandatory reassignment plans have almost no whites left in the public schools. Although their desegregation plans only caused, on average, about half of the long-term decline in white enrollment, few people seem able or willing to make this distinction. They see the "forced busing" plans as completely responsible for the fact that there are few whites, or middle-class parents of other races, left in the public schools of these big cities.

Nor do the national trends demonstrate the superiority of mandatory reassignment plans. As shown in Rossell and Armor (1996), school districts that had never had a formal desegregation plan continue to have greater interracial exposure— that is, a higher proportion white in the average black child's school—than school districts that implemented a formal desegregation plan.[42] In addition, school districts that only implemented a voluntary desegregation plan (neighborhood schools with majority to minority transfer programs or magnet options or freedom of choice) have greater interracial exposure than school districts that implemented mandatory reassignment plans, although they had no initial advantage in the percentage of white students[43] or interracial exposure. Controlled choice seems to have had no effect at all on interracial exposure.[44]

Thus, after forty years of desegregation plans, many of them massive racial balance/busing schemes with serious costs not only to communities but also to individuals, particularly the poorest families who do not have the alternatives available to the affluent, there is no evidence to support the conclusion that mandatory reassignment plans do a better job of achieving school integration than doing nothing formal (beyond not discriminating or modifying attendance zones of adjacent schools or placing new schools so they will be racially balanced) or letting people stay in their neighborhood schools and offering them the chance to transfer to an opposite-race school if they so choose. While white and black parents may not have the image in their minds of national trends in desegregation outcomes when they respond to survey questions regarding their desegregation preferences, they do have a sense, thanks to the national media and their own experiences, of the probability that mandatory reassignment plans will drive out whites and middle-class blacks and produce little or no benefits in the places where blacks are most likely to live—medium and large cities.

It would thus seem that the validity of the racism explanation is diminished and that of the self-interest explanation increased by the lackluster empirical evidence on positive outcomes and the current agreement between black and white parents

on desegregation implementation strategies and their behavioral intentions if forced
to desegregate. If black parents overwhelmingly support neighborhood schools with
voluntary magnet options and would not go along with the mandatory reassignment
of their own children to an opposite-race school and if only a minority even want
to voluntarily transfer to a magnet school in a white neighborhood or believe that
whites are getting a better education, then why is white sentiment along these lines
suspect?

Paul M. Sniderman and Thomas Piazza argue that too many cynics have missed
the fact that race is today largely (although not completely) an issue of politics. In
the years after *Brown*, intellectuals and civil rights activists had come to believe
that Americans' reactions to public policies dealing with blacks reflected how they
felt about blacks. After four decades of experimenting with public polices aimed
at overcoming the evils of slavery and segregation and achieving a just and decent
society, however, we have learned enough to be able to have rational disagreements
about what policies work best.[45] Indeed, the evidence presented in this chapter
suggests that disagreements over the desirability of busing or affirmative action do
not have to be covert racism; they can be rational and realistic assessments of the
efficiency, effectiveness, and equity of alternative strategies in achieving the principle of a just and color-blind society. The agreement between black and white
parents on principles and strategies of school integration evidenced in both the
national trend data and our parent surveys in districts considering desegregation
plans suggest that Sniderman and Piazza are correct when they conclude that although ''prejudice is part of the politics of race . . . a larger part is politics itself.
. . . Today there *is* a politics to issues of race. Racial policies themselves—the
specific goals they are intended to serve, and the particular means by which they
propose to accomplish those goals—define significantly the structure of conflict
over race.''[46]

And that is the legacy of *Brown*—black Americans are no longer a subject of
public debate; it is policies designed to *help* them that are the subject of debate.
Even if whites are lying about their feelings about blacks, the fact that they feel
they have to lie demonstrates an enormous change in social norms since *Brown*.
This is not to say, however, that we have even come close to solving the race
problem in the United States; but only that we have made substantial progress in
agreeing on goals, and in one policy area—integrated schools—on the means.
School integration should be voluntary, and neighborhood schools should be maintained.

Unfortunately, these research findings make the public policy arena enormously
complex because they mean that if we want school integration, we are going to
have to accomplish it indirectly, and thus slowly, by the elimination of the social
class and cultural differences between blacks and whites that still keep us largely
in different neighborhoods and, at least part of the time, in different worlds. The
solution is no longer simple, but perhaps it will actually achieve the goals black
Americans had in 1954 of *freedom*, dignity, and equality in American life. At the
very least we will be focused on the cause, not the symptom, of black/white inequality. Moreover, if nothing else is achieved, these survey data suggest that black
parents will be happier.

NOTES

I am indebted to Dr. David Armor, the original creator of the school district parent surveys in 1976, for his pioneering work in this field and his generosity in collaborating with me on these projects beginning in 1986. He is also the coprincipal investigator of the national survey of school districts, "Magnet Schools and Desegregation, Quality, and Choice" (May 1993), cited in this chapter. I am also grateful to Tom Smith of the National Opinion Research Center for his generous willingness to do special computer runs to provide me with the most up-to-date survey findings.

1. *Brown v. Board of Education*, 139 F. Supp. 468, 470 (D. Kan. 1955).
2. 391 U.S. 430 (1968).
3. 402 U.S. 1 (1971).
4. Some school districts, particularly those that are predominantly of one race, use as their standard for the sending school whether a student's race is above the district percentage. Similarly, the standard for the receiving school is whether a student's race is below the district percentage.
5. Christine H. Rossell, "The Carrot or the Stick for School Desegregation Policy?" *Urban Affairs Quarterly* 25, no. 3 (1990): 474–99; Christine H. Rossell, *The Carrot or the Stick for School Desegregation Policy: Magnet Schools vs. Forced Busing* (Philadelphia: Temple University Press, 1990).
6. See Christine H. Rossell and David Armor, "The Effectiveness of School Desegregation Plans, 1968–1991," *American Politics Quarterly* 24 (July 1996): 267–302; Christine H. Rossell, "Controlled Choice Desegregation Plans: Not Enough Choice, Too Much Control?" *Urban Affairs Review* (formerly *Urban Affairs Quarterly*) 31 (September 1995): 43–76.
7. These plans are in the Hattiesburg School District and the Natchez-Adams School District. In the latter case, a parent survey was introduced into evidence showing that black parents overwhelmingly preferred neighborhood schools with voluntary integration techniques over mandatory reassignment. The plaintiffs and the court in ordering mandatory reassignments ignored the survey.
8. The question was "Do you think white students and black students should go to the same schools or to separate schools?" This question was asked by the National Opinion Research Center (NORC) at the University of Chicago from 1942 through 1985 in their General Social Science Survey. The NORC data for 1942 through 1982 are from Howard Schuman, Charlotte Steeh, and Lawrence Bobo, *Racial Attitudes in America* (Cambridge: Harvard University Press, 1985), 74–75. Data for 1984 and 1985 are provided by Tom Smith at the National Opinion Research Center.
9. The data after 1985 come from the Armor and Rossell parent surveys in individual districts asking a question identical to the NORC one. The districts in which parents were asked this question are DeKalb, Georgia (1990); Topeka, Kansas (1990); Stockton, California (1990); and Knox County, Tennessee (1991).
10. The question was "Would you yourself have any objection to sending your children to a school where a few of the children are (Negroes/blacks)?" Gallup and NORC used the following definition of the South: Alabama, Arkansas, Delaware, Florida, Georgia, Kentucky, Louisiana, Maryland, Mississippi, North Carolina, Oklahoma, South Carolina, Tennessee, Texas, Virginia, West Virginia, and the District of Columbia.
11. Armor and Rossell parent survey results are from Los Angeles, California (1977); Chicago, Illinois (1981); Worcester, Massachusetts (1989); DeKalb, Georgia (1990); Topeka, Kansas (1990); Stockton, California (1990); Knox County, Tennessee (1991).

12. This loss is calculated as follows: white enrollment in one year is subtracted from white enrollment the previous year, and that sum is divided by white enrollment the previous year. This figure is then multiplied by 100 to produce a percentage. These data come from Christine Rossell, "Assessing the Unintended Impacts of Public Policy: School Desegregation and Resegregation" (report to the National Institute of Education, Washington, D.C., 1978).

13. Ibid.

14. The Institute for Social Research (ISR) responses from 1972 through 1980 are quoted in Schuman, Steeh, and Bobo, *Racial Attitudes in America*, 88–89, 144–47. The ISR responses for 1984 are cited as the American National Election Study (ANES)—the opinion study directed by the ISR—in Lee Sigelman and Susan Welsh, *Black Americans' Views of Racial Inequality: The Dream Deferred* (New York: Cambridge University Press, 1991), 124.

15. The question asked in the parent surveys from 1986 on varies slightly from district to district but generally informs public school parents that the school district is considering options or ideas for school desegregation and wants their opinions of these options. For each desegregation alternative, parents were asked whether they strongly support, somewhat support, strongly oppose, or somewhat oppose the described alternative. In the case of mandatory reassignment plans, the question usually asked was how they feel about mandatory busing of students in order to attain racial integration.

16. The question generally began with wording similar to the following: "As you may know the _____ public schools are considering ways to improve school integration. I am going to read you a few ideas that could improve school integration in the _____ public schools, and I would like you to tell me if you strongly support, support somewhat, oppose somewhat, or strongly oppose each idea." The voluntary techniques described were "What about voluntary transfers to other schools to improve racial integration, with free transportation?" "What about a voluntary program in which children can attend integrated schools with special programs like intense computer or science studies, which are called magnet schools?"

17. The question was "What about improving integration by changing attendance boundaries of adjacent schools?"

18. The question was generally worded: "Another method for racial and ethnic integration is called a controlled-choice plan. In this type of plan, all neighborhood attendance zones are eliminated and no one is guaranteed a neighborhood school. Instead, all parents choose what schools they would like their children to attend, which could include your current neighborhood school. The administration would make school assignments, and it would try to give everyone their first choices. But it would also have to make sure each school was integrated, so some students would be assigned to schools their parents did not choose. Free transportation would be provided if you chose or were assigned to a school other than your neighborhood school."

19. Armor and Rossell parent survey results.

20. Derrick A. Bell, Jr., "Serving Two Masters: Integration Ideals and Client Interests in School Desegregation Litigation," *Yale Law Journal* 85 (March 1976): 470–516.

21. Ron Edmonds, "Advocating Inequity: A Critique of the Civil Rights Attorney in Class Action Desegregation Suits," *Black Law Journal* 3 (1974): 178, quoted in Bell, "Serving Two Masters," 490.

22. Nathaniel Jones to Derrick A. Bell, Jr., 31 July 1975, cited in Bell, "Serving Two Masters," 492.

23. Nathaniel Jones, conversation with author, Williamsburg, Virginia, 17 May 1994.

24. Nor is listening to parent activists a good substitute. As any political scientist knows, activists have different attitudes and opinions from ordinary citizens.

25. Council on Legal Education for Professional Responsibility, Inc., *Lawyers, Clients & Ethics*, ed. M. Bloom, 101 (1974), quoted in Bell, "Serving Two Masters," 493.

26. In Stockton, an 80% minority school district, the plaintiffs' attorneys finally agreed after months of negotiations to enter into a settlement agreement offering educational enhancements but only because the changing demographics of the school district eventually caused them to conclude that desegregation was no longer achievable, not because it was not supported by their "clients." In Knox County the plaintiff organization was not a black civil rights legal defense group but the Office for Civil Rights, and its position on mandatory reassignment was not very clear. The only thing that was clear was that the district's prior majority to minority transfer plan and other voluntary efforts were considered inadequate.

27. It is telling that the first national survey of the attitudes of black Americans on the principle of school integration and their opinions on school desegregation implementation techniques was in 1972, eighteen years after *Brown,* four years after *Green,* and one year after *Swann,* all court decisions that produced major innovations in legal principles governing school segregation and, in *Swann,* innovations regarding strategies to eliminate it. These innovations apparently did not need to be informed by information regarding what black parents wanted. Indeed, I am not aware of *any* advocate of mandatory reassignment who has polled black parents on this issue.

28. See Schuman, Steeh, and Bobo, *Racial Attitudes in America.*

29. See Sigelman and Welch, *Black Americans' Views of Racial Inequality.*

30. See Schuman, Steeh, and Bobo, *Racial Attitudes in America,* 159.

31. Ibid.

32. Ibid., 161.

33. See Sigelman and Welch, *Black Americans' Views of Racial Inequality,* 126.

34. See Schuman, Steeh, and Bobo, *Racial Attitudes in America,* 171–88.

35. Mary R. Jackman, "General and Applied Tolerance: Does Education Increase Commitment to Racial Integration?" *American Journal of Political Science* 22 (1978): 302–24; Mary R. Jackman, "Education and Policy Commitment to Racial Integration," *American Journal of Political Science* 25 (1981): 256–69; Mary R. Jackman and Michael J. Muha, "Education and Intergroup Attitudes: Moral Enlightenment, Superficial Democratic Commitment, or Ideological Refinement," *American Sociological Review* 49 (1984): 751–69.

36. Donald R. Kinder and David O. Sears, "Prejudice and Politics: Symbolic Racism vs. Racial Threats to the 'Good Life,' " *Journal of Personality and Social Psychology* 40 (1981): 414–31; David O. Sears et al., "Self-Interest vs. Symbolic Politics in Policy Attitudes and Presidential Votings," *American Political Science Review* 74 (1980): 670–84; David O. Sears, Carl P. Hensler, and Leslie K. Speer, "Whites' Opposition to 'Busing': Self-Interest or Symbolic Politics?" *American Political Science Review* 73 (1979): 369–84; John B. McConahay, "Self-Interest versus Racial Attitudes as Correlates of Anti-Busing Attitudes in Louisville," *Journal of Politics* 44 (1982): 692–720; John B. McConahay, Betty B. Hardee, and Valerie Batts, "Has Racism Declined in America? It Depends on Who Is Asking and What Is Asked," *Journal of Conflict Resolution* 25 (1981): 563–79.

37. Much of my discussion here draws on Schuman, Steeh, and Bobo's criticisms, *Racial Attitudes in America,* 178–79.

38. Moreover, it produces a variable that is so skewed that what Sears and his colleagues are really measuring is symbolic "antiracism."

39. As Schuman, Steeh, and Bobo point out, almost all blacks were opposed to the Reagan administration and its policies, but only a few of them were directly affected by those policies. Schuman, Steeh, and Bobo, *Racial Attitudes in America.*

40. Seymour Martin Lipset and William Schneider, "The *Bakke* Case: How Would It Be

Decided at the Bar of Public Opinion?'' *Public Opinion* (March/April 1978): 38–44, quoted in Schuman, Steeh, and Bobo, *Racial Attitudes in America*.

41. Derrick A. Bell, Jr., *"Brown v. Board of Education* and the Interest-Convergence Dilemma,'' *Harvard Law Review* 93 (1980): 531.

42. Rossell and Armor, ''Effectiveness of School Desegregation Plans.''

43. In 1968 both the districts with voluntary and those with mandatory plans had 69% white students. The districts that never had a plan had 80% white students, and those with a controlled-choice plan had 78% white students.

44. The lack of superiority of the mandatory reassignment plans or controlled choice is not due to the fact that they were less extensive than the voluntary plans. Indeed, there is almost no difference between voluntary and mandatory plan districts in their 1991 racial imbalance, and the controlled choice plans have a bit less racial imbalance. See also Rossell, ''Controlled Choice Desegregation Plans.''

45. Moreover, as Sniderman and Piazza demonstrate in some experiments alternating the order of questions, the mere mention of policies that are thought of as fundamentally unfair, such as affirmative action, can actually increase white prejudice against blacks. In short, rather than racism causing opposition to policies designed to help blacks, policies designed to help blacks can increase racist attitudes. Paul M. Sniderman and Thomas Piazza, *The Scar of Race* (Cambridge: Harvard University Press, 1993).

46. Ibid., 175.

9

Brown Blues

Rethinking the Integrative Ideal

DREW S. DAYS III

More than forty years have passed since the Supreme Court's *Brown v. Board of Education*[1] decision, declaring unconstitutional state-imposed segregation of public schools. One would have thought that by now American society would have arrived at a consensus with respect to the substance and scope of *Brown*. The truth is otherwise. Even in the education sector of our national life that *Brown* specifically addressed, deep differences remain over what changes that decision was designed to effect.

Of course, opposition to *Brown* by whites committed to the maintenance of racial segregation in public education has been a daily reality from the moment the decision was announced. Over the years, that opposition has taken a variety of forms both simpleminded and sophisticated. However, it was generally thought that one group, African Americans, was uniformly supportive of *Brown* and committed to its full implementation in education. After all, *Brown* was the culmination of a long campaign by the National Association for the Advancement of Colored People (NAACP) to overturn the "separate but equal" doctrine. It also ushered in, without doubt, more than a generation of court decisions and legislation that eradicated all vestiges of formal segregation in America. Blacks seemed to agree with the Supreme Court's pronouncement in *Brown* that children are unlikely to function effectively in America's pluralistic society unless they live and learn with people of different races from an early age.[2]

Several developments in recent years suggest, however, that growing numbers of blacks may be turning away from this integrative ideal. Four examples of this shift are worth noting: first, black parents now express support for school board efforts to end desegregation plans that involve busing, favoring instead a return to neighborhood schools, even though this would result in increases in the number of virtually all-black schools in the inner city;[3] second, at the urging of black parents, school boards in a number of major cities have attempted to create all-black male academies;[4] third, black administrators, faculty, students, and alumni of historically black colleges in the South have joined state officials in opposition to court-ordered higher education desegregation plans;[5] and fourth, black students on predominantly white college campuses have urged administrators to provide special facilities for black students' social and cultural events.[6] Some critics have dismissed these developments as perverse efforts by blacks to return to a ''separate but equal'' regime. In fact, these developments raise serious and complex questions about the future of race relations in America that deserve careful analysis, not simplistic characterization. This chapter is an attempt to contribute constructively to that process.

Blacks and Neighborhood Schools

The school desegregation process has not been unproblematic, to say the least. More than forty years after *Brown*, there is still active litigation alleging constitutional violations. There is no gainsaying, however, that as a result of *Brown* and its progeny, thousands of black, white, and Hispanic children have been able to receive integrated educations and develop both educational and social skills that will stand them in good stead in later life. At the very least, the mandatory presence of white children has saved some black and other minority children from the physically inferior facilities—and inferior resources—to which they had been assigned under segregation.

Acknowledging the important gains of desegregation, however, should not blind us to the continuing legacy of segregation within desegregated systems. In many schools, racially segregated classes make it unlikely that children of different races will have meaningful interaction during the school day. Moreover, the black community has paid, in some instances, a high price for desegregation. For example, schools that served not only as educational institutions but also as community centers in predominantly black neighborhoods have been closed;[7] the burden of busing has fallen disproportionately on black children;[8] black teachers and administrators have been dismissed and demoted disproportionately;[9] and black students have encountered increased disciplinary action in recently desegregated schools.[10]

Most important, perhaps, given the initial hope that desegregation would increase the quality of educational opportunity for black students, is the fact that the desegregation process has not necessarily brought about improvements. Indeed, in some cases, desegregation has limited opportunity. For example, where magnet schools offering innovative educational programs have replaced formerly all-black facilities, black student enrollment in the special programs has been limited by the need to maintain racial balance.[11] This record establishes, contrary to common assumptions, that desegregation has not been an unmitigated benefit to previously segregated black students, teachers, and administrators.

We need not conclude that these negative consequences are the inevitable result of desegregation, however, and that the black community might have been better off seeking to improve educational opportunities within a segregated system. The more plausible explanation is that the same racist tendencies in America that created and maintained segregated schools did not disappear overnight once desegregation was mandated. Rather, they merely found new opportunities in this new arrangement to disadvantage the black community.

Whatever the pros and cons of desegregation, however, the reality is that demographic changes in the United States since 1954 have produced a pattern of residential segregation.[12] This makes further progress in school desegregation in certain areas difficult to envision. Urban centers across the nation are predominantly black and Hispanic; the suburbs and rural areas are predominantly white.[13] Even in those cities where the white population exceeds the minority, the public school populations are predominantly black and Hispanic. This latter phenomenon can be explained by the presence of childless white couples, older white couples, and white families with children enrolled in private and parochial, rather than public, schools.

Although some litigation efforts to achieve metropolitan-wide desegregation have been successful, the Supreme Court's 1974 decision in a Detroit school desegregation case[14] effectively limited the availability of that remedy in most urban areas. A few large cities have adopted voluntary desegregation plans involving urban and suburban communities,[15] but their impact on inner-city segregation has been modest, largely because those participating in such programs have been disproportionately black. The result has been, therefore, a one-way rather than a two-way process, with urban blacks heading out to suburban schools but relatively few suburban whites coming into the city.[16]

It is true that some predominantly black and Hispanic school districts have been able to obtain significant resources from their states based on a second Supreme Court ruling involving Detroit schools.[17] Still, the educational experiences of many black and Hispanic students in America will occur in one-race schools in poorly funded urban communities that have been abandoned by large numbers of white— as well as middle-class black—families.[18] Even in those districts where it is still possible for blacks and whites to attend school together, some members of the black community have begun to question whether the result achieved is worth the time and expense that desegregation entails.

There is also a sense among some blacks that although some desegregation plans no longer produce meaningful numbers of whites and blacks studying together, the plans are maintained because of the mistaken belief that blacks cannot learn unless whites are sitting next to them in class. The blacks who challenge the continuation of such plans argue that a return to neighborhood school assignment makes more sense because parental and community involvement in the schools would be more likely to increase. Moreover, governmental resources expended on busing could be redirected to increasing the quality of materials and instruction available at those schools.

Blacks and whites who oppose efforts to roll back desegregation plans do so for a variety of reasons. First, they fear that such proposals are yet another attempt by school boards guilty of past intentional segregation to escape any further role in avoiding resegregation. Second, they suspect blacks who support such rollbacks of acting more in their own political and economic interests than in the interests of black children. What roll-back proponents seek, in fact, are more and better jobs for black administrators and teachers in exchange for reduced pressure for increasing or maintaining desegregation levels. Third, roll-back opponents fear that a return to all-black schools will result in "benign neglect" of those schools in terms of resources allocated for facilities, materials, and personnel.[19]

This debate, although perhaps the subject of greater media focus in recent years, is not a new one. Blacks, having seen the bad, along with the good, of desegregation, have for some time questioned whether the process should be extended to the limits that the Supreme Court precedents allowed. This attitude has been particularly prevalent with respect to desegregation plans that require extensive busing. These voices of restraint often had no effective forum, however, because they were often white school boards correctly viewed as inherently untrustworthy spokespersons for this point of view. The major civil rights organizations representing the plaintiffs in desegregation cases, on the other hand, strongly reject any thought of stopping short of what the Constitution would permit.

The debate has taken on a new dimension, however, because black mayors, city council members, and school superintendents have begun to express similar concerns about the wisdom of what they see as "desegregation at any cost." Courts are justifiably perplexed over how to evaluate the views of this group because their authority, as elected and appointed blacks, to speak for the black community certainly is equal to, if not greater than, that of plaintiffs and their lawyers in school desegregation cases. Although some might dismiss their views as perversely malevolent toward black students, the positions of black elected and appointed officials deserve an evaluation as expressions of concern about the most effective approach to educating black children under daunting circumstances.

For these and other reasons, blacks increasingly support efforts by school districts under court desegregation orders to return to neighborhood school arrangements, even though such modifications inevitably will return certain facilities in the black community to largely one-race status.[20] Of course, we must not lose sight of the fact that constitutional rights are individual. Whether a school district has satisfied its responsibility under *Brown* and its progeny to dismantle a dual system is not subject to resolution by referendum. The difficult legal question, one with which the Supreme Court continues to grapple, is how we determine whether the dual system is still in place.[21] Meanwhile, debates over modifications of desegregation plans continue.

Proponents of modification argue that once the school board has done all it can to eradicate the vestiges of its previously dual system, it has satisfied constitutional requirements. Continued segregation, they contend, is not the school board's fault but rather the consequence of residential segregation caused by private choice and market forces. Opponents of rolling back desegregation plans argue that the school board has a duty to continue making adjustments until the results of the pattern of segregation it created have been eradicated. They take the position that demographics cited by the board as an explanation of continued segregation are not adventitious but rather the consequence of past school board practices. Under current Supreme Court doctrines, the proponents of modification are likely to prevail because the Court consistently has refused to consider the extent to which segregative actions by governmental agencies other than school boards might justify maintenance of desegregation plans when modification would result in resegregation. Consequently, school desegregation plaintiffs are left with a wrong in search of a remedy.[22] As they witness schools that were all black before desegregation return to that status once the board's modifications go into effect, it must seem to them that years of effort have been in vain.

Schools for Black Males

Media attention and public debate over the past few years have also focused on proposals to establish public schools or programs exclusively for black male students.[23] In Milwaukee, for example, the school board planned to designate two schools as all-black or virtually all-black facilities in which special attention would be given to the educational and developmental needs of black males. These "immersion schools" would offer features unavailable in other Milwaukee facilities: school days one hour longer and less rigidly structured than normal, a multicultural curriculum, and mandatory Saturday classes held in cooperation with the local branch of the Urban League. Weekend sessions would focus on nonacademic subjects, such as "what it means to be a responsible male," "how to save and invest money," and "the practicalities of cooking and cleaning." The students would also be required to wear uniforms.

As a result of actual or threatened litigation, Milwaukee's proposal and similar ones in other urban school districts were modified to include female and white students who wished to participate.[24] The legal and political debate continues, however. At the core of the controversy is the question of whether a school that admits only blacks is any more constitutional than the ones that *Brown* outlawed because they admitted only whites.

At one level, they clearly are not comparable. The system of state-imposed racial segregation in public education that *Brown* declared unconstitutional was designed to ensure that blacks remained a second-class, subjugated race in American society. Schools established for black males, in contrast, are not designed to subjugate whites or deny them first-class citizenship. Rather, they address what most people would acknowledge is the critical plight of young black males in urban America. The premise of the theory is that "one of the most obvious psychosocial deficits in the environment of inner-city black boys is the lack of consistent, positive, literate, black *male* role models."[25]

At another level, however, our history counsels us to be wary of *any* racial classifications. For that reason, the Supreme Court has mandated that any use of racial criteria by government must be for the purpose of achieving a compelling interest and must be necessary to achieve that purpose. Dual school systems under segregation failed that test because maintaining segregation of the races did not constitute a compelling governmental interest. All-black academies, in contrast, concededly are designed to meet a compelling interest—saving black males from educational and social disaster.[26] However, the case has not been made persuasively that this is an interest that *necessarily* requires the exclusion of whites.

The fact that the school district might be able to achieve its goals more efficiently employing a racially exclusive approach is no justification for such a system. Expedience cannot legitimize racial segregation. Even taking the proponents of all-black academies at their word, there is little evidence to support the view that mentoring, counseling, extended school days, small classes, and a curriculum that gives proper recognition to the contributions of blacks to American society will improve black male educational and social functioning *only* in a racially segregated setting. Such an enriched educational environment is likely to produce positive effects *irrespective* of the racial setting.

Proponents may contend that only experimentation will determine the effectiveness of such programs. Racial classifications, however, are not proper subjects for experimentation. Of course, in many urban settings, the likelihood that whites will be enrolled in center-city schools and thereby be displaced to accommodate the all-black academies is slim. Similarly, whites likely will not apply to attend such schools. Under these circumstances, as a practical matter, school districts can set up programs for all-black student bodies without imposing any bar to whites.

Proposals to create all-black male academies have attracted adherents largely in those districts where a number of schools in the center city, as in Milwaukee, cannot feasibly be desegregated. Under these circumstances, it is hard to fault black parents and sympathetic school officials who do not believe that black male students can await the integration millennium. Consequently, they have joined forces to develop a structure that they hope will save black males. Such approaches clearly reflect disenchantment with the *Brown* integrative ideal and may be educationally misguided. However, to the extent that whites and females may participate, the programs would not appear to violate constitutional limits.

Historically Black Colleges and Universities

Lawyers for the NAACP prepared for their ultimate assault on the "separate but equal" doctrine in *Brown* by challenging successfully the exclusion of blacks from all-white graduate and professional schools.[27] Indeed, it was in one of those earlier cases that the Supreme Court acknowledged the "intangible" inequality caused by segregation that would figure so prominently in its 1954 decision.[28] The Court made clear shortly after *Brown II*,[29] the desegregation implementation decision in 1955, that southern higher education officials could not delay opening their institutions by invoking the "all deliberate speed" doctrine.[30] Consequently, efforts by blacks to enroll in previously all-white colleges and universities during the late 1950s and early 1960s found support in the courts, as well as in the executive branch. In a few instances, the government even called out troops to ensure the admission of blacks.[31]

Meanwhile, almost no attention was being given to the fact that southern and border states were continuing to operate dual systems of higher education. This arrangement was dictated, in large part, by the federal government's promotion in 1862, under the First Morrill Act,[32] of state land grant colleges for whites and then in 1890, under the Second Morrill Act,[33] parallel institutions for blacks. Thereafter states systematically discriminated against black institutions in the allocation of funds for a period that extended well beyond 1954.[34]

The historically black institutions, as a group, nevertheless, achieved remarkable success educating students from segregated and inferior secondary schools. They developed programs that provided their students with instruction and nurturing sufficient to prepare them to function effectively in society after graduation. In many cases, their graduates have pursued graduate and professional training at prestigious universities in the North and West.

Early attempts to challenge dual systems of higher education produced court orders that seemed to embrace a "freedom-of-choice" approach. State officials successfully argued that college students were not assigned to institutions but rather were free to select a college or university based on considerations of curriculum, location, cost, and admissions requirements. Consequently, as long as states did not preclude students from attending an institution because of their race, the courts determined that dual systems did not offend the Constitution.

In the early 1970s, however, black plaintiffs initiated litigation in *Adams v. Richardson*, charging federal officials with illegally providing funds to states that maintained dual systems of higher education.[35] As a result of this suit, the court ordered the Department of Health, Education, and Welfare (HEW)—and later the Department of Education—to launch an enforcement campaign to dismantle those systems. Central to that campaign was the premise that the states in question had a constitutional duty to act affirmatively to remedy the conditions that created and perpetuated separate black and white institutions at the postsecondary level.[36]

Unlike earlier court decisions, federal administrative directives rejected the notion that "freedom of choice" was the proper remedial model.[37] They recognized that students' choices were shaped powerfully by the effects of long-standing mandated segregation and discriminatory resource allocations between black and white institutions. One example of this was the placement of new institutions with parallel curricula in communities where previously only historically black public institutions existed. These parallel institutions effectively provided white students with segregated alternatives.[38]

Black higher-education groups were at odds with federal agencies and the NAACP Legal Defense and Educational Fund, which brought the *Adams* suit, regarding the wisdom of pressing desegregation of public colleges and universities.[39] Black college presidents, faculty, and alumni were undoubtedly mindful of the burdens the black community had been forced to bear during desegregation of public primary and secondary systems. They feared that desegregation of higher education would result, at best, in whites displacing black teachers and administrators, as well as black students. At worst, given the relative inferiority of their institutions, desegregation might result in the closing of schools or the absorption of traditionally black institutions into historically white schools. In either event, institutions important to the black community would lose their identity, and opportunities in higher education for black administrators, faculty, and students would be significantly diminished.

Despite similar concerns, however, proponents of desegregation in higher education believed that both litigation and administrative enforcement could increase resources available to historically black institutions. Reducing program duplication and forcing the states to locate especially attractive academic programs at traditionally black schools would also enhance the schools' long-term viability.[40]

It is fair to say that this desegregation effort has not been very successful. Significant segregation between historically black and white institutions is still apparent. Since 1973, state officials have effectively utilized the administrative process to delay meaningful change. Ultimately, the Court of Appeals for the District of Columbia Circuit dismissed the *Adams* litigation on technical grounds.[41] As a result, the federal government is able to decide on the nature, scope, and timing of enforcement largely free of court oversight.

Two higher-education desegregation efforts, one involving Louisiana and the other Mississippi, were severed from the *Adams* administrative process and referred by HEW to the Justice Department for judicial enforcement. Little systemic desegregation has occurred in either case over the many years they have been in court. The Supreme Court recently ruled on Mississippi's higher-education desegregation case.[42]

The case presented the Court with an opportunity to define a state's constitutional duty to dismantle formerly dual systems of higher education, a question that had produced conflicting answers in the lower federal courts. Some courts had taken the position that higher-education authorities had an affirmative responsibility, similar to that imposed on school boards in the case of primary and secondary school desegregation, to eradicate the vestiges of their dual systems.[43] Like the HEW in the *Adams* proceedings, these courts believed that this responsibility must be discharged by addressing a variety of practices that affect students' decisions about which institutions they attend, such as admissions standards, program duplication, institutional resources, and governance.[44] Other courts rejected the notion that primary and secondary school desegregation doctrines had any applicability to higher education, principally because college and university attendance is not mandated by the state but depends on individual student choice.[45] Consequently, these courts—including both the trial and appellate courts in the Mississippi case—concluded that a state's constitutional responsibility ends once the state has removed all racial bars to students' attending the college or university of their choice.[46]

In *United States v. Fordice*,[47] the Supreme Court essentially embraced the former "affirmative duty" doctrine and reversed the lower courts' determination that Mississippi had met its constitutional responsibility. The Court found that in at least four areas—admission standards, program duplication, institutional mission assignments, and continued operation of all eight public universities—the state had failed to show that the "policies and practices traceable to its prior system that continue to have segregative effects" had "sound educational justification" and could not "be practicably eliminated."[48] The case was then returned to the lower courts for evaluation of the Mississippi system against the Court's newly articulated standard.

The Court's decision leaves in limbo, however, the future of Mississippi's three historically black institutions. Although the Court acknowledged that "closure of one or more institutions would decrease the discriminatory effects of the present system,"[49] it declined to find such action constitutionally required. However, it flatly rejected the notion that Mississippi had a constitutional duty to upgrade the historically black institutions, as such. Rather, it left to the lower courts the question of whether "an increase in funding is necessary to achieve a full dismantlement."[50] Given this ambiguity, the possibility exists that Mississippi will be able to achieve a unitary higher-education system by closing those institutions.[51]

It is this fear that black institutions will be the inevitable casualties of higher-education desegregation that has complicated the dismantling of dual systems. Take, for example, the ostensibly odd alignment of parties in the Louisiana case. After concluding that Louisiana's desegregation plans were inadequate, the federal court commissioned its own strategy. That plan envisioned, among other things, merging the traditionally black Southern University Law Center into the law school of Louisiana State University (LSU), the state's traditionally white flagship institution.[52] The two law schools are located in Baton Rouge, only a few miles apart.

That the state opposed the merger plan was not surprising. However, it was joined by the Southern University Board of Supervisors, which viewed the court's order as a step backward, rather than forward, for black education in Louisiana.[53] The board claimed that blacks, the victims of the state's history of segregation and discrimination in higher education, were being required to bear a disproportionate burden in rectifying that situation.[54] Specifically, the board contended that the merger of Southern University's law school with LSU's would undoubtedly displace black faculty and staff and curtail opportunities for blacks seeking legal education.[55] The court's plan did not envision LSU's absorbing Southern University's faculty and staff, nor did it require LSU to expand to ensure against a net loss of law school seats for black students after the merger.

In defense of its plan, the court took the position that the merger was required by the Constitution and was in the long-term interests of the citizens of Louisiana, black and white.[56] But for the state's creation and maintenance of segregated higher education, the court pointed out, there would not still be two public law schools in the same city, one white and the other black. The court concluded that desegregation could occur only if one of the institutions closed. Moreover, the court observed that in a fiscally strapped state, maintaining two law schools in Baton Rouge made no economic sense.

Southern University's law school had been denied adequate state support because of its status as a black institution. The condition of its physical plant and the quality of its educational program were, as a result, inferior to those of LSU. Consequently, the court concluded that Southern University's law school should be the one to close.[57] In response to the Southern University Board of Supervisors' concerns about the desegregation process, the court suggested that the board was interested in protecting the jobs of Southern University faculty and administrators rather than in improving educational opportunities for blacks.

This controversy delineates starkly the dilemma confronting proponents of higher-education desegregation. The court clearly was correct that the maintenance of dual, segregated law schools in one city makes no legal or fiscal sense and that merging the institutions would require blacks and whites to study law together rather than apart. But the black opponents of the merger also have compelling arguments. Absent the state's history of discriminatory treatment of Southern University Law Center, the school's facilities and program probably would not be so inferior to those of LSU. Had there been "tangible" equality over the years between the two institutions, white students might have opted to attend Southern University rather than LSU based on "intangible" considerations, such as the presence of particular faculty members or curricular emphases. Moreover, there is no reason why Southern University's board should apologize for seeking to protect the jobs of faculty and administrators. They, too, are victims of the state's segregative practices.

Finally, Southern University Law Center and LSU Law School have different admissions criteria. As a consequence, Southern University has been able to admit some black students who, based on objective indicators such as grade point average and Law School Admission Test scores, would not be competitive candidates at LSU. Southern University, nevertheless, has been able to train and graduate generations of black lawyers who provide competent legal services to poor and minority communities in the state. Unless LSU ensured that black students whom Southern University would have admitted would find seats at LSU, the merger would represent a net loss of educational opportunities for black students in Louisiana.

The Louisiana case eventually was dismissed in light of the Fifth Circuit's ruling in the Mississippi case.[58] Solving the dilemma in Louisiana and in other states where higher-education desegregation is under way will not be easy now that the Supreme Court has vacated that decision.[59] The solution cannot be achieved overnight, however. It must operate within the twin constraints of constitutional requirements and economic reality. At the same time, it must address responsibly the displacement effects of the desegregation process and the ironic price that the black community must pay for desegregation.

Blacks on White Campuses

The proposed merger of Southern University Law Center with LSU undoubtedly raised concerns in the minds of black students about the reception they were likely to receive upon enrolling at LSU. Would the administration be supportive? Would faculty members nurture their intellectual development? Would white students accept them as colleagues and peers? These are questions that many black applicants likely ask when considering a predominantly white college or university anywhere in the country. The alternative for these students is to attend one of a group of public and private historically black institutions with proven track records of providing students with excellent preparation for postgraduate employment or education.

These are not idle concerns. Blacks have always encountered difficulties in predominantly white institutions, as accounts of the "best and brightest" of pioneer black students at prestigious northern institutions attest.[60] They had to overcome both social isolation and a lack of evenhanded administrative and faculty support in order to excel. Even though black enrollment in these institutions has increased over the years, the schools generally have not succeeded in retaining and graduating blacks in proportions equal to those for white students.[61]

Explanations for this disparity range from the failure of such institutions to provide adequate financial support to the academic deficiencies of the students. One of the major variables, however, appears to be black students' perception of the degree to which the institutions will offer supportive environments within which they can grow academically and socially.[62] This concern is not unique to blacks, of course. Students from other racial or ethnic minorities, public school graduates, southerners going north, and northerners going south want to know whether they are going to feel at home in the institutions they are considering. The stakes just seem to be higher for blacks.

The number of black students attending traditionally white institutions surpassed token levels in the late 1960s, largely through a combination of more aggressive recruiting of candidates clearly meeting normal admissions criteria, as well as the establishment of affirmative action programs for qualified but less competitive students. This development was not an unalloyed advance, however, in efforts to increase educational opportunities for black students and reduce racial segregation in higher education. Black students on predominantly white campuses began to express concern about the difficulties of their adjustment, unlike their predecessors, who usually opted to suffer in silence. With varying degrees of insistence, black students asked that college administrators provide facilities specifically to allow them opportunities for greater social interaction than the institutions were affording them.

These requests prompted a range of reactions from blacks and whites, many quite hostile to the idea of black "Afro-Am houses" on campus. Some blacks and whites who had fought to end segregation viewed such developments as striking at the very heart of what *Brown* symbolized. Some administrators wondered why blacks had sought admission to their predominantly white institutions in order to segregate themselves from their white classmates. Whites who would have preferred not to see any black students on campus pointed cynically to the demands for special "houses" to justify their support for social groups, such as Greek societies or eating clubs, that excluded blacks.[63]

These considerations, even the cynical claims of racists, highlight the difficulty of defending university support for racially *exclusive* social clubs and living arrangements that bar nonblacks irrespective of their backgrounds or interests.[64] Blacks-only clubs or dormitories are bad social policy in that they reinforce racial stereotypes and most likely are unconstitutional. Ensuring that a hostile campus environment does not force black students to terminate their studies before graduation may well qualify as a compelling interest that justifies the establishment of such clubs and dormitories. As in the case of all-black academies, however, it is not clear that racially exclusive facilities within the university are *necessary* to achieving that goal.

In contrast, administrative support for *nonexclusive* facilities to benefit black students is sound social policy. They may provide black students with a "safe harbor" from stormy weather, particularly for those who are encountering a predominantly white environment for the first time.[65] When special facilities for blacks first appeared on campuses, some sympathetic observers thought, perhaps naively, that blacks would have decreasing need for such refuges as time passed. However, the ongoing debate over affirmative action issues—from the legality of minority scholarships to whether blacks are stigmatized by such efforts—and the growth of hate speech on college campuses[66] have surely caused black students on predominantly white campuses to feel more embattled than ever before. Black students should not have to subject themselves to undue psychological and emotional stress in order to enjoy the prestige, rich resources, outstanding academic programs, and influential alumni networks that top, predominantly white institutions provide their students. "Afro-Am houses," properly handled, need not be the source of racial divisiveness. Rather, they can serve to promote the healthy integration of black students and black culture into the life of predominantly white institutions. Such integration does not demand black assimilation but instead reflects respect for cultural diversity.

Conclusion

The *Brown* decision and the integrative ideal that it embraced have opened opportunities for black advancement that were previously unthinkable. *Brown* also transformed our entire society in other ways too numerous to recite under these circumstances. As the four developments discussed above suggest, however, the increasing racial polarization and residential segregation in America have put the integrative ideal to the test. Concerns about the burdens blacks have had to carry in the desegregation process, the degree to which integration requires assimilation and rejection of black values and institutions, and the seemingly intractable problems presented for largely black school systems in educational *extremis* are causing growing numbers of blacks to rethink *Brown*'s integrative ideal. These are admittedly difficult questions. Nevertheless, they deserve to be asked—indeed, they cannot be avoided. They must also be answered, although the answers may be uncomfortable and disappointing, at least in the short run, for those of us who hoped that we would see a different America forty years after *Brown*.

NOTES

1. 347 U.S. 483 (1954).
2. Martin Luther King, Jr., "The Ethical Demands for Integration," in *A Testament of Hope: The Essential Writings of Martin Luther King, Jr.*, ed. James M. Washington (New York: Harper Collins, 1986), 117.
3. See, e.g., Gary Orfield and Susan E. Eaton, *Dismantling Desegregation: The Quiet Reversal of Brown v. Board of Education* (1996), 73–114; Steven A. Holmes, "At N.A.A.C.P., Talk of a Shift on Integration," *New York Times*, 23 June 1997, sec. A, 1; and Michel Marriott, "Louisville Debates Plan to End Forced Grade School Busing," *New York Times*, 11 December 1991, sec. B, 13.
4. Dirk Johnson, "Milwaukee Creating Two Schools for Black Boys," *New York Times*, 30 September 1990, sec. A, 1.
5. Peter Applebome, "Separate but Equal Goes Back to Court—A Special Report; Epilogue to Integration Fight: Blacks Favor Own Colleges," *New York Times*, 29 May 1991, sec. A, 1.
6. "Cornell: Opposition Blocks Plan to Improve Dorm Racial Mix," *New York Times*, 12 April 1992, sec. A, 51.
7. See *Bell v. West Point Mun. Separate School District*, 446 F.2d 1362 (5th Cir. 1971).

8. U.S. Commission on Civil Rights, *Fulfilling the Letter and Spirit of the Law* (Washington, D.C.: U.S. Commission on Civil Rights, 1976), 202–6.

9. Senate Select Committee on Equal Education Opportunity, *Desegregation under the Law*, 91st Cong., 2d sess., 1970, 1006–7, 1082–144.

10. U.S. Commission on Civil Rights, *Fulfilling the Letter and Spirit of the Law*, 255–69.

11. Jennifer L. Hochschild, *The New American Dilemma: Liberal Democracy and School Desegregation* (New Haven: Yale University Press, 1984), 77.

12. Gerald D. Jaynes and Robyn M. Williams, Jr., eds., *A Common Destiny: Blacks and American Society* (Washington, D.C.: National Research Council, 1989), 88–91.

13. This pattern of residential segregation has been affected somewhat by decisions of African American urban dwellers to locate in all-black upscale suburban communities. See David J. Dent, "The New Black Suburbs," *New York Times*, 14 June 1992, sec. 6, 18.

14. *Milliken v. Bradley*, 418 U.S. 717 (1974).

15. See, e.g., *Liddell v. Missouri*, 731 F.2d 1294, 1300 (8th Cir.) (en banc), *cert. denied*, 469 U.S. 816 (1984) (discussing a voluntary plan for St. Louis and suburbs).

16. See *Liddell*, 731 F.2d at 1301–2.

17. See *Milliken v. Bradley*, 433 U.S. 267 (1977). But see also *Missouri v. Jenkins*, 115 S. Ct. 2038 (1995) (limitation on further state funding of educational enrichment programs).

18. See William J. Wilson, *The Truly Disadvantaged: The Inner City, the Under-Class, and Public Policy* (Chicago: University of Chicago Press, 1987), 56–58, 102–4, 135–36.

19. See Gary Orfield and Carole Ashkinaze, *The Closing Door: Conservative Policy and Black Opportunity* (Chicago: University of Chicago Press, 1991), 105–12.

20. See David Montgomery and Terry M. Neal, "In P.G., a New School of Thought: Evolving Views on Race, Segregation Lead to Busing Consensus," *Washington Post*, 28 July 1996, sec. B, 1.

21. See *Freeman v. Pitts*, 112 S. Ct. 1430 (1992); *Board of Education v. Dowell*, 111 S. Ct. 630 (1991).

22. See *Swann v. Charlotte-Mecklenburg Board of Education*, 402 U.S. 1, 22–23, 31–32 (1971). For a more complete treatment of this issue, see Drew S. Days III, "School Desegregation Law in the 1980's: Why Isn't Anybody Laughing?" *Yale Law Journal* 95 (July 1986): 1737.

23. Tom Dunkel, "Self-Segregated Schools Seek to Build Self-Esteem," *Washington Times*, 11 March 1991, sec. E, 1.

24. Carol Innerst, "School Geared to Black Boys Attracts Girls," *Washington Times*, 3 September 1991, sec. A, 3; Patrice M. Jones, "A Place All Their Own: Detroit Uses Special Academies to Help Black Boys Overcome Challenges," *Plain Dealer*, 23 April 1996, sec. A, 1.

25. Spencer H. Holland, "A Radical Approach to Educating Young Black Males," *Education Week*, 25 March 1987, 24.

26. In Milwaukee, for example, 50% of the black males entering high school do not graduate. Dunkel, "Self-Segregated Schools," sec. E, 1. Black males make up 27.6% of the school population but account for half of all students suspended. Ibid. In 1990, out of 5,716 black males in the city's public high schools, only 125 had grade point averages above 3.0. Ibid.

27. See Mark V. Tushnet, *The NAACP Legal Strategy against Segregated Education, 1925–1950* (Chapel Hill: University of North Carolina Press, 1987), 105–37.

28. *Sweatt v. Painter*, 339 U.S. 629, 634–35 (1950).

29. *Brown v. Board of Education*, 349 U.S. 294 (1955).

30. *Florida ex rel. Hawkins v. Board of Control*, 350 U.S. 413, 413–14 (1956); see also Charlayne Hunter-Gault, *In My Place* (New York: Farrar Straus Giroux, 1992).

31. James H. Meredith, *Three Years in Mississippi* (Bloomington: Indiana University Press, 1966), 207–14.

32. Ch. 130, § 4, 12 Stat. 503, 504 (1862) (codified as amended at 7 U.S.C. §§ 301–305, 307–308 (1988)).

33. Ch. 841, 26 Stat. 417 (1890) (codified as amended at 7 U.S.C. §§ 321–326, 328 [1988]).

34. For a general review of the Morrill Acts and underfunding of historically black institutions, see Gil Kujovich, "Equal Opportunity in Higher Education and the Black Public College: The Era of Separate but Equal," *Minnesota Law Review* 72 (October 1987): 29, 40–64.

35. 480 F.2d 1159 (D.C. Cir. 1973) (en banc) (per curiam).

36. See ibid. at 1163–65; *Geier v. University of Tennessee*, 597 F.2d 1056, 1065 (6th Cir. 1979).

37. See, e.g., *Federal Register* 43, "Revised Criteria Specifying the Ingredients of Acceptable Plans to Desegregate State Systems of Public Higher Education," 95th Cong., 15 February 1978, 6658–59, 6661 (hereafter cited as "Revised Criteria").

38. See *Geier v. Blanton*, 427 F. Supp. 644 (M.D. Tenn. 1977) (mandating merger of parallel institutions because desegregation was not occurring), *aff'd sub nom. Geier v. University of Tennessee*, 597 F.2d. 1056 (6th Cir. 1979).

39. For a full discussion of these concerns, see Jean L. Preer, *Lawyers v. Educators: Black Colleges and Desegregation in Public Higher Education* (Westport, Conn.: Greenwood Press, 1982), 182–232.

40. "Revised Criteria," 6658–64.

41. *Women's Equity Action League v. Cavazos*, 906 F.2d. 742 (D.C. Cir. 1990).

42. *United States v. Fordice*, 505 U.S. 717 (1992).

43. See *United States v. Louisiana*, 718 F. Supp. 499, 532–35 (E.D. La. 1989).

44. See, e.g., *Geier v. Blanton*, 427 F. Supp. 644, 657–60 (M.D. Tenn. 1977), *aff'd sub nom. Geier v. University of Tennessee*, 597 F.2d 1056 (6th Cir. 1979).

45. See *Allain*, 674 F. Supp. at 1553–54.

46. *Ayers v. Allain*, 914 F.3d 676, 687 (5th Cir. 1990) (en banc), *vacated and remanded, sub nom. United States v. Fordice*, 505 U.S. 717 (1992); *Allain*, 674 F. Supp. at 1554.

47. 505 U.S. 717 (1992).

48. Ibid. at 731.

49. Ibid. at 742.

50. Ibid.

51. Both Justice Thomas, ibid. at 747–48 (Thomas, J., concurring), and Justice Scalia, ibid. at 758–60 (Scalia, J., concurring in judgment and dissenting in part), expressed concern in *Fordice* over the future of historically black institutions.

52. *United States v. Louisiana*, 718 F. Supp. at 514.

53. Marilyn Milloy, "Black School Fights Desegregation," *Newsday*, 19 November 1989, 6.

54. See *United States v. Louisiana*, 718 F. Supp. at 533.

55. See ibid.

56. Ibid. at 532–35; see also ibid. at 508, 513–14 (explaining the need to end duplication of law schools in order to end dual system).

57. Ibid. at 513–14.

58. *United States v. Louisiana*, 751 F. Supp. 606 (E.D. La. 1990), *vacating* 692 F. Supp. 642 (E.D. La. 1988).

59. *United States v. Fordice*, 505 U.S. 717 (1992), *vacating Ayers v. Allain*, 914 F.2d 676 (5th Cir. 1990). For further proceedings in the Louisiana case, see *United States v. Louisiana*, 9 F.3d 1159 (5th Cir. 1993) (remanding it for further proceedings in light of *Fordice*).

60. See, e.g., Gilbert Ware, *William Hastie: Grace under Pressure* (New York: Oxford University Press, 1984), 12–20 (accounting William Hastie's college experience at Amherst in the 1920s). Hastie graduated Phi Beta Kappa, made the *Law Review* at Harvard, and later became the first black federal judge.

61. See Walter R. Allen, "The Color of Success: African-American College Student Outcomes at Predominantly White and Historically Black Public Colleges and Universities," *Harvard Education Review* 62 (1992): 26, 27. See generally Jacqueline Fleming, *Blacks in College* (San Francisco: Jossey-Bass, 1984) (presenting comprehensive study of black students' intellectual development in various settings).

62. Richard C. Richardson and Elizabeth F. Skinner, *Achieving Quality and Diversity: Universities in a Multicultural Society* (Phoenix: Oryx Press, 1991), 33–46.

63. See "University of Minnesota Will Not Recognize or Support Group That Promotes 'White Culture,' " *Chronicle of Higher Education*, 18 March 1992, A34.

64. See "Campus Life; Syracuse: Blacks-Only Group May Soon Forfeit Status and Money," *New York Times*, 9 December 1990, sec. A, 62; Mary Jo Hill, "Do Theme Dorms Sanction Self-Segregation?" *Christian Science Monitor*, 15 July 1996, 12.

65. Carnegie Foundation for the Advancement of Teaching, *Campus Life: In Search of Community* (New York: Carnegie Foundation, 1990), 25–32.

66. See Robert Demmons, " 'We Won't Go Back': The First and Second Assaults on Affirmative Action," in *We Won't Go Back: Making the Case for Affirmative Action*, ed. Charles R. Lawrence III and Mari J. Matsuda (Boston: Houghton Mifflin, 1997). For a collection of campus incidents, see Mari J. Matsuda, "Public Response to Racist Speech: Considering the Victim's Story," *Michigan Law Review* 87 (August 1989): 2320, 2370–73 nn.245–56; see also Carnegie Foundation, *In Search of Community*, 26–34 (giving examples of racial harassment).

10

The Social Construction of
Brown v. Board of Education

Law Reform and the Reconstructive Paradox

RICHARD DELGADO

JEAN STEFANCIC

Fundamental to so much discussion about equality in America has been the Supreme Court's 1954 decision in *Brown v. Board of Education*[1] declaring racially segregated schools unconstitutional. Yet critics have differed as to the success of the Court's *Brown* decision in actually achieving equality in American life. Broadly speaking, there are two views about *Brown*. The conventional view holds that *Brown* is one of the two or three most important cases in American legal history. According to this interpretation, *Brown* supplied the impetus for the modern civil rights movement, demonstrated that courts, at least at times, can assert moral leadership, and emphasized that African Americans are entitled to live in the United States on terms equal to whites.[2]

The other view, that of the revisionists, holds that *Brown* accomplished relatively little, in either the short or the long run.[3] Revisionists argue that *Brown* is the product of a momentary convergence between white and black interests that began to fade soon thereafter.[4] Some argue that landmark cases like *Brown* may even impair the cause of black rights by inducing a mood of unwarranted euphoria among supporters while stiffening resistance on the part of diehards and white supremacists.0[5] Revisionists and conventionalists are apt to differ not only in their understanding of *Brown* but also in their interpretation of how social change occurs. In general, revisionists hold that social reform is difficult to achieve, especially through law, and that gains have a way of slipping back.[6] The more sanguine conventionalists argue that if *Brown* has not brought about racial justice by itself, we can at least move closer to this goal through further effort. *Brown* has certainly helped; and if it has fallen short, what we need is a *Brown III* or a *Brown IV*.[7]

Although these and other differences separate the revisionists and the conventionalists, in one respect they both approach *Brown* in the same manner. Each examines the situation that prevailed before and after *Brown* and asks: Did the landmark decision make a difference? Were the forces that led to the 1960s-era reforms already in motion before *Brown*? Did *Brown* benefit white elites more than it benefited blacks? If it benefited blacks, did it help mostly middle-class blacks, leaving the underclass as badly off as before? Both groups, in short, examine *Brown* longitudinally and temporally, looking for evidence of causation or its lack. The argument has what we might call a vertical character: one lines up the situation that prevailed before *Brown* and after and looks for signs that *Brown* brought about changes.

In this chapter, we argue that an ignored, and equally vital, axis is horizontal.[8] To understand *Brown*'s role, and that of law reform cases generally, one must attend to contemporaneous events in society at the time *Brown* was decided. Focusing on this other dimension enables us to understand why *Brown* was seen as a breakthrough case, even though it failed to have much effect outside the narrow area of school desegregation,[9] and even there, less than one might have hoped.[10] Moreover, focusing on this horizontal dimension allows us to understand law's limitations in propelling social change in general.

We begin by summarizing what *Brown* was and was not able to accomplish, doctrinally and conceptually, employing as our principal illustration the debate over campus hate-speech rules.[11] We argue that society's resistance to reform in this area is just one example of a backward drift in matters of race, and the decisions whose narratives more aptly characterize our time are not *Brown* but the nineteenth-century Supreme Court cases—*Plessy v. Ferguson*,[12] the *Civil Rights Cases*,[13] and *Dred Scott v. Sandford*.[14] Finally, we put forward a *reconstructive paradox* that names and explains why, despite evidence to the contrary, we continue to believe the legal system can bring about significant change in areas such as race when it is in fact capable of bringing about very little.[15]

How *Brown* Failed to Generalize

Many critics have pointed out that *Brown* accomplished relatively little in the way of school desegregation, except in the Deep South, and that black children are as likely today as they were forty years ago to attend predominantly black schools.[16] To this, one could add doctrinal retrenchment in closely related areas. Although subsequent courts have left *Brown* standing, in the sense that they did not expressly overrule it, they have done much to cut back its effect. School districts may not enact metropolitan desegregation plans, at least in the absence of a showing of prior discrimination.[17] Education is not a fundamental interest,[18] nor is poverty a suspect class.[19] States have no obligation to fund property-rich and property-poor districts similarly.[20] Segregation that results from white flight is essentially irremediable.[21] Black male academies are unconstitutional,[22] minority scholarships are under fire,[23] and affirmative action that takes the form of reserving slots in state-funded professional schools is illegal.[24]

Why did *Brown* end up having so little effect, even in the area of school reform? Elsewhere, we have put forward the thesis that social reform through law is relatively ineffective because law's scope is so narrow.[25] Because every social practice is part of an interlocking system of other practices, meanings, and interpretations, changing just one element (e.g., student-assignment rules) leaves the rest unchanged.[26] Thus, when the Supreme Court decided *Brown*, its principle was soon robbed of much effect when, in a myriad of decisions, school officials, lower courts, sheriffs, and others interpreted *Brown* against the familiar background.[27] "Of course, the Supreme Court didn't mean *that*," they would reason in close cases. It is as though legal decisions take place against a gravitational field, with the pull being toward the familiar, toward stasis.[28] Because *Brown* set out to change just one element, leaving the force field itself intact, its effect quickly eroded. For social reform to happen, "everything must change at once," but in the law, doctrines such as stare decisis, standing, mootness, ripeness, and political question mean that the law cannot change everything at once.[29] It can decide only the case before it.

Disbelieving or obstructionist officials are not the only forces that act to rob landmark decisions of much of their effect. If they were, all that would be necessary would be vigilance and determined enforcement. Rather, such decisions fail to establish themselves in the wider legal culture, so that even those who are generally sympathetic to reform fail to see their applications in closely related areas.

Consider, for example, the debate over campus hate-speech rules.[30] Beginning about a decade ago, college and university administrators began noticing an upsurge in the number of racist insults, graffiti, and name-calling taking place on their campuses.[31] At some institutions, the number of students of color began to drop as parents decided to send their sons and daughters elsewhere.[32] Many campuses responded by enacting anti-hate-speech rules that punished certain forms of racial or sexual taunting or name-calling.[33] The rules sparked immediate resistance.

Brown at least had some effect. Today, a school official who might be tempted to assign all the black children to one school and the white ones to another would likely think, "I had better not do that, at least unless I disguise what I am doing." Today's opponents of hate-speech rules, however, show little such hesitation; they proceed as though *Brown* had not taken place at all.[34] Hate-speech rules are in many respects like student-assignment rules.[35] Yet opponents make the same arguments against them, the same rhetorical moves, that we witnessed with the classic resistance to school desegregation.

Under *Plessy v. Ferguson*,[36] schemes that allocated benefits along racial lines were upheld, as long as the benefit blacks received was roughly comparable to that received by whites. In *Plessy*, blacks were forced to ride in one railroad car, whites in another.[37] The Supreme Court upheld the railroad's rule: separate but equal. Whites and blacks were equally disadvantaged: neither could ride in the other's car. A similar situation prevailed in the schools of Topeka, Kansas, at the time *Brown* was decided. Indeed, shortly after the decision was announced, a famous constitutional scholar was prompted to wonder if the decision was principled: Why should the rights of blacks to associate with whites trump that of whites *not* to associate with blacks?[38] One right balanced another, one claim against its perfect reciprocal.

In the debate about hate speech, we find a strikingly similar structure. The white person insists on a right to say whatever is on his or her mind. The black person demands protection when what is on the white's mind is a direct face-to-face racial insult. One claims a right to do X, the other the right not to have X done to him or her. One right emanates from one part of the Constitution—the First Amendment—one, from another—the Fourteenth Amendment.[39] As with separate but equal, today's debate over hate speech features commentators insisting that the black's injury is all in his or her head.[40] This perspective parallels early cases in which the Supreme Court told blacks that the indignity of being herded into separate railroad cars is offensive only if they put that construction on it.[41] Today's opponents of hate-speech rules dismiss the black's injury as merely dignitary and not a real harm.[42] One well-regarded constitutional scholar recently rejected the "silencing" argument by pointing out that it requires mental mediation—the victim decides to remain silent.[43] As with *Brown*, the opposition to hate-speech rules portrays itself as highly principled. It is not in favor of hate speech (heaven forbid). Rather, there are other, higher principles at stake here.[44]

Why *Brown* Failed to Generalize

Brown effected little change in terms of doctrine, consciousness, or the realities of life for black schoolchildren. Yet society has constructed the decision as a breakthrough of momentous proportions. We believe the two observations are related. *Brown*'s sharp departure from the past caused it to stand out, to seem a breathtaking advance. This departure also assured that it would fail to "take"—would succumb to what we called earlier a kind of social gravity.[45] In this section, we spell out in greater detail what that gravity is. We conclude by describing a "reconstructive paradox" that afflicts all reform movements, especially those that rely heavily on the law and litigation.

The Forces That Swallow Social Reform Decisions Like Brown

What we have described as a kind of social gravity that affects all novel social claims, especially legal ones, has at least three components. As we previously mentioned, it includes the system of meanings and interpretations against which the new rule must operate.[46] It also includes a set of narratives, or "stock stories," with which the new ruling is required to harmonize.[47] Last, it includes a set of social practices with which the new command must contend.[48] Each of these components mitigates the new decision's effect. Each is an aspect of what we called the horizontal dimension[49] of a case, that which was taking place in society at the time the case was adjudicated.

MEANINGS AND SOCIAL INTERPRETATIONS

Any text, including legal ones, is interpreted against a background of meanings, presumptions, and preexisting understandings.[50] If a parent tells a child, "Clean up your room," the terms "clean" and "room" have relatively well agreed-on meanings. The child knows he or she is not expected to launder the drapes or vacuum the attic space above the room. If an adolescent tells the parent, "I'll be back by midnight," both understand that "midnight" means tonight, not next week, and that "back" means inside the house. The same is true of legal commands. Thus, when *Brown* ordered school districts to desegregate "with all deliberate speed,"[51] southern officials interpreted the decree in terms of their common sense. In hundreds of close cases, they construed *Brown* to mean the only thing it could mean, consistent with their experience: integration that went not too far and not too fast and that left the school system as intact as possible.[52] Operators of public beaches, restaurants, colleges, and other facilities interpreted *Brown* as a case affecting only schools. Some school officials even took the position that it bound only the districts before the court.[53] To recalcitrant officials, *Brown* looked like an exception, an improbable edict that should naturally be interpreted in that light. The only way to harmonize it with common sense was to construe it narrowly: "Of course, the Supreme Court did not mean that blacks and whites are strictly equal," they told themselves. "It surely didn't mean that we would have to do *this*" (assign black principals to white schools, provide college counseling to all, adopt due process protections in school discipline cases affecting black children facing expulsion, and so on). Because *Brown* was interpreted against the background of a myriad of such understandings, traditions, and expectations and because, unlike a parent, the Supreme Court was not instantly available to clarify what it meant, the case had relatively little impact. It did change one thing, student-assignment rules, but the rest of society remained essentially the same.[54] The gain in this one area was quickly swallowed up by interpretive effects emanating from all of the others.[55]

SOCIAL PRACTICES

A second component of what we have called the gravitational field against which new legal rules must operate is the set of preexisting social practices, most of which the Supreme Court is powerless to change. These practices include friendship patterns, the way a teacher looks at or responds to a black child, and that child's own self-concept and expectations with respect to treatment from whites. They include the ways in which librarians, bus drivers, shop owners, and landlords deal with the young black schoolchild and his or her family. They determine who is chosen for student-body president, the debate team, and the cheerleading squad. If all of these practices remain the same while only student-assignment rules change, a black child's life will not be greatly improved after *Brown* (and may be considerably worse).[56]

Of course, a forced change in one social practice theoretically could prompt reconsideration of all of the others. Because white schoolchildren now are required to attend school in a building that will house some blacks, the other social practices we have mentioned might begin to change. But everything we know about cognitive dissonance and resistance to the unfamiliar suggests the opposite.[57] New practices that are discordant with old ones are resisted and adopted, if at all, slowly and grudgingly.[58] New reasons are found to justify now disputed social practices.[59]

THE ROLE OF NARRATIVES

A final component of the social milieu that affects the reception of a legal decision or rule is the backdrop of narratives or stories against which the new element will be forced to operate.[60] Narratives are the simple, scriptlike interpretive structures—''he hit first,'' ''I didn't know it was yours,'' ''majority rules,'' or ''I've been here longer''—that we use to order our understanding of the world.[61]

In the school desegregation setting, court decrees confront a whole host of narratives and social perceptions that generate resistance. Such narratives include: ''neighborhood schools are best''; ''who are these outsiders trying to tell us what to do?''; ''blacks were happy until . . .''; ''black people just want to push into where they are not wanted''; ''they want things they don't deserve and haven't earned''; ''integration might be okay, but the schools should remain predominantly white, and the curriculum, teachers, and so on, roughly as they are now''; and so on.[62]

As with meanings and social practices, these and other narratives could theoretically change. A person who holds a stock of hundreds of such narratives regarding minority people, neighborhood schools, and ''the way things are'' could radically revise his or her worldview when confronted by the image of a surprisingly nice, intelligent, reasonable black individual at a school or workplace. But narratives change very slowly, in part because we interpret new experiences and new narratives in terms of the old ones—the ones we hold.[63] These old narratives, indeed, form the basis for understanding new experiences, including that of our first close black associate. It is far easier to pronounce the black an ''exception'' than to revise one's entire stock of beliefs.

Eventually, of course, social stories and practices change but much more slowly than we like to think.[64] And when they do, courts and decrees play little role in bringing about the change.[65] Courts are usually distant institutions. Unlike flesh-and-blood persons, they cannot follow up an exchange by saying, for example: ''No, he is not an exception; most of them are like that if you take the trouble to get to know them.'' Courts are not in a position to engage society in the kind of continuing dialogue that could in theory change meanings and practices.[66] Courts can only change one practice at a time. Everything else—the entire system of practices, traditions, and meanings—remains the same, exerting its gravitational tug toward the familiar. In giving obedience to the new decree—something the courts *are* in a position to enforce—hundreds of lower-level bureaucrats, state officials, and lower-court judges will interpret the ringing words according to their commonsense understandings about persons, about relations, and about what is just and deserved.[67]

The Reconstructive Paradox

The combined effect of the forces just mentioned means that any reform measure other than the smallest and most incremental will meet predictable resistance, re-interpretation, and obstruction in ways that the legal system is ill equipped to manage and counter.[68] One perspective from which to view these horizontal forces is in terms of what we call the "reconstructive paradox." After defining the paradox,[69] we illustrate its operation by demonstrating that the current approach to race and race remedies shows the influence of the nineteenth-century cases, especially *Plessy v. Ferguson,* more than that of their more famous twentieth-century rival, *Brown v. Board of Education.*[70]

DEFINING THE RECONSTRUCTIVE PARADOX

Much of what we have said so far can be summarized in the following six steps, constituting what we call the reconstructive paradox:

1. The greater a social evil (e.g., black subordination) the more it is apt to be entrenched in our national life.[71]
2. The more entrenched the evil, the more massive the social effort that will be necessary to eradicate it.[72]
3. The harm of an entrenched evil will be invisible to many because it is embedded and ordinary.[73]
4. The massive social effort will inevitably collide with other social values and things we hold dear (e.g., settled expectations, religion, the family, privacy, and the southern way of life). It will entail dislocations, shifts in spending priorities, new taxes, and changes in the way we speak and relate to each other.[74]
5. These efforts, by contrast, will be highly visible and will spark resistance and accusations that the backers are engaging in totalitarian tactics, siding with big government, dislodging innocent whites, operating in derogation of the merit principle, elevating group over individual relief, reviving old grudges, whipping up division where none existed before, and so on.[75]
6. Resisting these latter complaints will feel right and proper, for the other side will appear to be callously sacrificing real liberty, real security, and real resources for a nebulous goal.[76]

Therefore, reconstruction will always strike many in a society as unprincipled, unwarranted, and wrong. Little surprise, then, that few take up its cause, persist for long in the face of the resistance it calls forth, or even frame their programs and objectives broadly enough so that if they are adopted, they have a chance of remaining in place and achieving some real effects.

BACK TO *PLESSY*: PRESENT-DAY RHETORIC AND EVIDENCE OF THE RECONSTRUCTIVE PARADOX OPERATING IN OUR TIME

Reform through *law alone,* as we mentioned, is apt to have little effect, because legal decrees succumb silently and painlessly to interpretation and other forms of cultural weight.[77] Even when, as happened with the civil rights revolution of the 1960s, legal reform operates in concert with broader social forces to produce undeniable and much-needed gains, resistance is apt to set in at some point. Consider how today we no longer talk in terms of separateness as an inherent injury, of black schoolchildren as victims, or of racism as a harm whose injury "is unlikely ever to be undone." Instead, we speak of the need for formal neutrality, of the dangers affirmative action poses for innocent whites, and of the need for black Americans to look to their own resources.[78] Moderates and conservatives alike have rolled back affirmative action[79] and challenged university and college theme houses, special curricula, and ethnic studies departments,[80] which they see as violations of the merit principle and fair and equal treatment policies. Courts are quick to strike down set-aside programs and affirmative action plans as "quota systems" likely to discriminate against "innocent whites."[81] The narrative of *Plessy v. Ferguson*[82] more aptly characterizes our attitudes with respect to race than do the stirring words of *Brown*.

In *Plessy*, Supreme Court Justice Henry B. Brown could not see anything wrong with a system that required blacks to sit in separate railroad cars and overlooked the unmistakable damage inflicted on blacks' sense of dignity by such a discriminatory system. Indeed, he wrote: "We consider the underlying fallacy of the plaintiff's argument to consist in the assumption that the enforced separation of the two races stamps the colored race with a badge of inferiority. If this be so, it is not by reason of anything found in the act, but solely because the colored race chooses to put that construction upon it."[83]

In a 1981 case, *City of Memphis v. Greene*,[84] Justice John Paul Stevens III declared that a municipal decision to separate a white neighborhood from a black one by allowing the construction of a wall between them to regulate traffic flow was fair and not motivated by an intention to discriminate against blacks but rather by an "interest in protecting the safety and tranquillity of a residential neighborhood."[85] Echoing the earlier opinion of Justice Brown in *Plessy*, Stevens wrote:

> Because urban neighborhoods are so frequently characterized by a common ethnic or racial heritage, a regulation's adverse impact on a particular neighborhood will often have a disparate effect on an identifiable ethnic or racial group. To regard an inevitable consequence of that kind as a form of stigma so severe as to violate the Thirteenth Amendment would trivialize the great purpose of that charter of freedom.[86]

In both cases, separated by nearly a century, during which much progress in race relations was said to have been made, blacks have been presented with a rhetorical legerdemain that tests both their ability to participate in societal self-deception and their inclination to prevail in the face of it.

Other modern-era cases show the same tendency to disregard blacks' longstanding predicament or whites' contribution to it. Because *Brown* only addressed the effects of segregated education on black schoolchildren, remaining silent on the issue of white responsibility, it was perhaps inevitable that the question of fault would become the next hurdle to blacks struggling to achieve social gains. *Washington v. Davis*[87] is perhaps the most well known example, but a number of others vie for consideration. In *Arlington Heights v. Metropolitan Housing Development Corp.*,[88] the Court held that certain zoning regulations that had the effect of excluding blacks were constitutionally valid because they were not enacted with that purpose in mind.[89] In *San Antonio Independent School District v. Rodriguez*,[90] a school finance scheme that caused a great disparity in funding tax-rich and tax-poor schools was upheld despite its serious impact on poor and minority children.[91] And, as mentioned earlier, a traffic control measure that took the form of a wall between white and black neighbors in Memphis was deemed just that, a traffic control measure, despite the way in which it physically and symbolically separated the races.[92]

Each of these cases foreshadows a retreat from the ringing words of *Brown*; each in many ways is reminiscent of the crabbed neutrality and unrealistic refusal to see discrimination that characterized *Plessy*. Not only has our time implicitly resurrected *Plessy* in its approach to racial justice, but a second notorious nineteenth-century case's star is rising as well: the *Civil Rights Cases*.[93] In the *Civil Rights Cases*, the Supreme Court wrote that blacks who were demanding equal access to various types of public accommodation were seriously overstepping and in effect demanding to be afforded special treatment. The Court wrote:

> When a man has emerged from slavery, and by the aid of beneficent legislation has shaken off the inseparable concomitants of that state, there must be some stage in the progress of his elevation when he takes the rank of a mere citizen, and ceases to be the special favorite of the laws, and when his rights as a citizen, or a man, are to be protected in the ordinary modes by which other men's rights are protected.[94]

Cases in our time show much the same attitude. Blacks' demands for justice are considered themselves unjust because they are a form of asking for special treatment and because they encroach on white privilege and settled expectations. One example is *Regents of University of California v. Bakke*.[95] There, the Supreme Court upheld the challenge of a white applicant to a state-sponsored medical school.[96] The plurality opinion cast him in the role of victim. The medical school's affirmative action program, which reserved a small number of slots for African Americans, unconstitutionally violated the rights of applicants such as Bakke.[97] The university's program operated unfairly against "innocent persons in respondent's position."[98] The state's interest in remedying past discrimination was not sufficiently compelling to justify the "special treatment" black candidates received. In language reminiscent of Justice Joseph P. Bradley's in the *Civil Rights Cases*, the plurality opinion painted the university's affirmative action program to increase the number of black doctors as coddling and favoritism.[99] Other recent affirmative action cases have taken a similar position and employed rhetoric nearly as unsympathetic as that of *Bakke*.[100]

The most startling parallel is found in *City of Richmond v. J. A. Croson Co.*,[101] in which the Court struck down a minority set-aside program in the construction industry that had been adopted by the Richmond city council.[102] The majority opinion found the council's action a potential case of "simple racial politics."[103] A concurring opinion went even further, warning that society should be watchful against those who might attempt to "even the score" at the expense of whites.[104]

Societal rhetoric follows suit. A host of commentators today rail against multicultural programs on university campuses;[105] minority-only scholarships are under fire;[106] welfare programs are under sustained attack as disguised giveaways to undeserving, unambitious, and oversexed blacks; and the use of code words like "political correctness" indicates that many in our society believe that blacks have gone too far.[107] They think blacks are now receiving special, not just equal, treatment and that it is time to put a stop to it, just as it is time to begin closing our borders to immigration from Mexico, Haiti, Cuba, and other societies of color.[108]

We believe, then, that dispassionate examination of today's dominant narratives shows that the themes of *Plessy* and the *Civil Rights Cases* are in ascension. We put forward an even more somber prediction: without concerted action or a sharp change in national circumstances, one final step will be taken. Just as the clock of time seems to be rolling backward, a final narrative may soon regain prominence: that of *Dred Scott v. Sandford.*[109]

In *Dred Scott*, the Supreme Court, in a case concerning a runaway slave, held that African Americans have "no rights which the white person is bound to respect."[110] The claim of an African American to citizenship was absurd, both historically and legally: blacks simply were not citizens because they never were such and the framers of the Constitution, "great men," never regarded them that way.[111] *Dred Scott* constitutes, certainly, the nadir of American law's treatment of African Americans, a blot on the record of the American legal conscience. Yet its narrative retains vitality today. We see growing evidence of it in Supreme Court opinions and in popular culture.[112]

Chief Justice Roger B. Taney's opinion depicted blacks as subhumans.[113] Is this shocking portrayal of other races so far from today's range of possibilities? Is the story of the primitive bestial black or Mexican completely missing in today's narratives, both in popular culture and in judicial opinions? Unfortunately, we believe not. Indeed, we believe this account of groups of color is undergoing a resurgence.

Consider, for example, the revival of race-IQ theories, some seconded by well-regarded scientists and writers such as Charles Murray, Richard Herrnstein,[114] Arthur Jensen,[115] and William Shockley.[116] Consider the number of books, such as Ben Wattenberg's *Birth Dearth*,[117] and reports that have urged renewed attention to the question of selective breeding: our "best" citizens have too few children and minorities and the poor, too many, so that the gene pool in the United States is declining. Consider the resurgence of nativism and movements to close the nation's borders particularly to brown-skinned immigrants.[118] Consider also the English-only movement.[119] Much of this attitude is fueled by the conviction that "those people" are not fit to reside here; that their language, customs, and morals are inferior; and that they are and always will be second-class citizens. All of these cultural strands converge around the idea that this is a white country and that nonwhite persons, genes, ideas, languages, and culture are inferior to European ones, a principal theme in *Dred Scott*.

Nor has the legal system been totally divorced from the return of the *Dred Scott* mentality. In the Rodney King case, a Los Angeles–area jury acquitted police officers who were videotaped beating a black motorist while he lay unresisting on the ground.[120] Testimony by the police and later interviews with the jurors showed that the motorist, King, was *seen* as the kind of being who might resist, who might at any moment strike out with tremendous force, and who, because he was caught speeding, deserved whatever penalty the police chose to inflict.[121]

Supreme Court decisions also contain hints of *Dred Scott* and its brusque dis-

missal of African American humanity. In *McCleskey v. Kemp*,[122] the Supreme Court
considered a challenge to Georgia's infliction of the death penalty, which fell disproportionately heavily on blacks, particularly ones whose victims were white.[123]
The Court rejected McClesky's claim, at the same time reprimanding him and his
lawyers for even having brought it.[124] Such claims, based on statistical disparities,
might be raised in virtually any setting, the Court reasoned, resulting in repetitive
demands "based upon any arbitrary variable."[125] Cases brought by poor women—
Wyman v. James[126] (the welfare-search case), *Maher v. Roe*,[127] and other abortion-
funding cases—show the same thinly veiled exasperation on the part of the Court.
These decisions stop barely short of telling poor women that they do not know
their places and what is expected of them—to be as quiet, prudent, nondemanding,
and nonsexual as possible. The demand for privacy in the face of a welfare in-
spection or for an abortion from a state-funded clinic appears outrageous. The
women are chastised for the effrontery of wanting to live life on their own terms.[128]

Many earlier eras, of course, witnessed similar patterns of advance followed by
retrenchment. During Reconstruction, African Americans made great gains, but
these were followed by an era of lynching and Jim Crow laws.[129] *Brown v. Board
of Education* was followed by new resistance in the South.[130] In Europe the broadened vistas and relaxed worker-migration policies of the early European community
years soon were followed by xenophobia, a resurgence of Nazism, and tightened
controls on immigration.[131] We believe the United States is in the middle of such
a retrenchment today. Indeed, it is as though the arrow of time has reversed. We
see the nineteenth-century cases appearing in modern guise before our eyes—first
the *Plessy* line of cases, then the notorious *Civil Rights Cases*, and finally, in the
wings, *Dred Scott v. Sandford.*

What *Brown* and the Reconstructive Paradox Mean for Activists and Reformers: Summary and Suggestions

Brown, like all law reform cases, confronted built-in resistances that deprived it of
the efficacy its supporters hoped for it. Social reform proceeds, if at all, in small
increments; the pendulum swing is as apt to be backward at any given time as
forward. *Brown*'s relatively slight effect is part of a broader form of social response—the reconstructive paradox—which holds that the greater the evil, the
greater the need for reform; the greater the reform effort, the more unprincipled
and unjust the effort will seem and the greater the resistance it will call up. Even
more than other avenues for reform, law is handicapped by its inability to engage
in dialogue with the group whose values and practices need changing. Except in
criminal law, which can put violators in jail, law has little ability to provide the
constant reinforcement necessary to change attitudes or behavior. Indeed, law is
always outnumbered; doctrines such as standing ensure that any wide-ranging legal
edict appears incomprehensible and wrong, evoking the reaction: surely the court
didn't mean *that*.

If we are right, reformers should hesitate to place much faith in the legal system as the primary instrument for their agendas.[132] Law is relatively powerless to effect social revolutions as both theory and history, including the case of *Brown*, demonstrate. Everything must change at once, so that a far greater focus than the merely legal is necessary before reform begins to be possible. Because the reconstructive paradox has greatest force with respect to courts, reformers ought to reserve judicial activism for the later stages of a revolution, using courts for the final mopping-up steps to secure a social advance that society has already begun to accept.

Litigation is expensive and frustrating if resorted to at the wrong time. We urge that reformers reconsider the appropriate time to use it. If employed too early, as it arguably may have been with *Brown*, it leads to false celebration, then disillusionment by persons who, like African Americans, have waited too long to see their just demands met—then betrayed.

Conclusion

Society has constructed *Brown v. Board of Education* as a great case. Yet as we have seen, the opinion failed to generalize and accordingly exercised little influence outside the area of school desegregation. Even within that arena, it brought about relatively few improvements in the lives of black schoolchildren, most of whom today attend schools that are just as segregated and in even greater disarray than the ones they attended in *Brown*'s time.

We believe the two observations are related, indeed dependent on one another. We saw *Brown* as a startling, extraordinary decision—which it was—for the very reasons that brought about its demise, namely, the way in which it challenged and departed from current culture and orthodoxy. Every law reform decision, we pointed out, takes place against a background of beliefs, narratives, meanings, and social practices that constitute a kind of social gravitational field. This field causes the exceptional case to erode quickly, to be resisted, interpreted away, and increasingly ignored. This dissipation has visited *Brown*. Although we afford it lip service and pay attention to its ringing, aspirational message on celebratory occasions, other narratives have turned out to have greater vitality. These more-lasting narratives are those of the nineteenth-century cases, ones that celebrate white superiority and that depict blacks as inferior, subhuman, demanding, and unjustified. As a culture, and as a legal profession, we are rapidly returning to the regime of *Plessy v. Ferguson*'s separate but equal doctrine and the *Civil Rights Cases'* view of blacks as imposers and whiners because they desire to live in American society on the same terms as whites. Moreover, we find some frightening straws in the wind—indications that ought to give pause to any defender of freedom and minority rights. We have reviewed evidence that society generally, and the legal system in particular, are beginning to regress in one final, decisive quantum jump. American society, without the spur of Cold War competition or the need for minority labor or soldiers, is in serious danger of quietly, implicitly readopting a familiar standard from another era: that of *Dred Scott v. Sandford*, in which blacks and other minorities of color have no rights that white Americans are bound to respect.

NOTES

1. 347 U.S. 483 (1954).

2. Books in this general vein include Richard Kluger, *Simple Justice* (New York: Knopf, 1976); Juan Williams, *Eyes on the Prize* (New York: Viking, 1987). For a discussion of the conventional view and its alleged weaknesses, see Michael J. Klarman, "*Brown*, Racial Change, and the Civil Rights Movement," *Virginia Law Review* 80 (February 1994): 7–150.

3. On the revisionist view of *Brown*, see, for example, Klarman, "*Brown*, Racial Change, and the Civil Rights Movement," 7–150. On the revisionist view of law reform generally, see Gerald N. Rosenberg, *The Hollow Hope: Can Courts Bring About Social Change?* (Chicago: University of Chicago Press, 1991); see also Derrick A. Bell, Jr., "*Brown v. Board of Education* and the Interest-Convergence Dilemma," *Harvard Law Review* 93 (January 1980): 518.

4. See, e.g., Bell, "*Brown v. Board of Education*," 3.

5. See Derrick A. Bell, Jr., *And We Are Not Saved: The Elusive Quest for Racial Justice* (New York: Basic Books, 1987), 3, 111; Klarman, "*Brown*, Racial Change, and the Civil Rights Movement," 85 (discussing the way *Brown* inspired a wave of southern resistance).

6. See, e.g., Bell, *And We Are Not Saved*; Richard Delgado and Jean Stefancic, *Failed Revolutions: Social Reform and the Limits of Legal Imagination* (Boulder: Westview Press, 1994).

7. See, e.g., Williams, *Eyes on the Prize*, 2.

8. That is to say, an axis that examines events contemporaneous with a key event rather than ones that came earlier or later.

9. See notes 16–44 below and accompanying text.

10. See notes 16–24 below and accompanying text.

11. See notes 30–44 below and accompanying text. For writing on the issue of hate speech, see, e.g., Mari Matsuda et al., *Words That Wound* (Boulder: Westview Press, 1993); Nadine Strossen, "Regulating Racist Speech on Campus: A Modest Proposal," *Duke Law Journal* (1990): 484.

12. 163 U.S. 537 (1896).

13. 109 U.S. 3 (1883).

14. 60 U.S. 393 (1856).

15. For an earlier treatment of a related mechanism, the *empathic fallacy*, see Richard Delgado and Jean Stefancic, "Images of the Outsider in American Law and Culture: Can Free Expression Remedy Systemic Social Ills?" *Cornell Law Review* 77 (September 1992): 1258.

16. See, e.g., Klarman, "*Brown*, Racial Change, and the Civil Rights Movement," 11–12, 76–86; see also Andrew Hacker, *Two Nations: Black and White, Separate, Hostile, Unequal* (New York: Ballantine Books, 1992); *The Words of Martin Luther King, Jr.*, ed. Coretta S. King (New York: Newmarket, 1987) (hereafter cited as *MLK*); Jerome M. Culp, Jr., "Water Buffalo and Diversity: Naming Names and Reclaiming the Racial Discourse," *Connecticut Law Review* 26 (Fall 1993): 209, 246–47 (discussing the situation in law schools).

17. See, e.g., *Milliken v. Bradley*, 433 U.S. 267 (1977).

18. *San Antonio Indep. School District v. Rodriguez*, 411 U.S. 1 (1973).

19. *James v. Valtierra*, 402 U.S. 137 (1971).

20. *Rodriguez*, 411 U.S. 1; see also *Valtierra*, 402 U.S. 137 (upholding state constitutional provision requiring low-rent housing projects to be approved by a majority of qualified electors).

21. Metropolitan desegregation plans are permissible only if the segregation results from official action, not the aggregate of individual decisions by white families to move to the suburbs. See *Milliken*, 433 U.S. 267.

22. On the difficulties of establishing such schools with public funds, see Jacqueline Conciatore, "Detroit Must Admit Girls to Public All-Male Academies, Judge Says," *Black Issues in Higher Education*, 29 August 1991, 8; "Whites in Detroit Teach Students at Black School a Fourth R: Racism," *New York Times*, 2 December 1992, sec. B, 6.

23. See, e.g., Michael A. Olivas, "Federal Law and Scholarship Policy: An Essay on the Office for Civil Rights, Title VI, and Racial Restrictions," *Journal of College and University Law* 18 (Summer 1991): 21 (articulating the position of the recent Republican administration on this issue).

24. *Regents of Univ. of California v. Bakke*, 438 U.S. 265 (1978).

25. See Delgado and Stefancic, *Failed Revolutions*, 6; see also *MLK*.

26. See, e.g., Delgado and Stefancic, *Failed Revolutions*, 6; Delgado and Stefancic, *Images of the Outsider*, 15.

27. See notes 51–55 below and accompanying text.

28. See Bell, *And We Are Not Saved*, 3 (discussing the way racial breakthroughs erode soon thereafter); see also Richard Delgado, "Derrick Bell and the Ideology of Racial Reform: Will We Ever Be Saved?" *Yale Law Journal* 97 (April 1988): 23 (elaborating on this process); *MLK*, 118–19 (on resistance to civil rights decrees).

29. On these doctrines and the way they limit the range of cases and issues courts may consider, see Ronald D. Rotunda, *Modern Constitutional Law*, 3d ed. (St. Paul: West Publishing Co., 1989), 1026–73.

30. On the problem of hate speech in general, see Matsuda, *Words That Wound*, and Strossen, "Regulating Racist Speech." On campus hate speech, see Richard Delgado, "Campus Antiracism Rules: Constitutional Narratives in Collision," *Northwestern University Law Review* 85 (Winter 1991): 343.

31. Delgado, "Campus Racism Rules," 348–58.

32. Ibid., 376, 386 n.354.

33. For a discussion of some campuses where rules have been enacted, see ibid., 358–61.

34. See notes 40–43 below and accompanying text.

35. For a discussion of these parallels, see Charles R. Lawrence III, "If He Hollers Let Him Go: Regulating Racist Speech on Campus," *Duke Law Journal* (1990): 431; Richard Delgado and Jean Stefancic, "Overcoming Legal Barriers to Regulating Hate Speech on Campuses," *Chronicle of Higher Education*, 11 August 1993, B1; notes 38–44 below and accompanying text.

36. 163 U.S. 537 (1896).

37. Ibid. at 537–39.

38. Herbert Wechsler, "Toward Neutral Principles of Constitutional Law," *Harvard Law Review* 73 (November 1959): 1.

39. For a discussion of these and other similarities, see Delgado, "Campus Antiracism Rules," 345–48; Lawrence, "If He Hollers Let Him Go," 438–40.

40. See Dinesh D'Souza, *Illiberal Education: The Politics of Race and Sex on Campus* (New York: Free Press, 1991), 132–36, 156; Nat Hentoff, *Free Speech for Me but Not for Thee* (New York: Harper Collins, 1992) (stating that minorities are ready to complain of imagined or exaggerated slights).

41. See *Plessy v. Ferguson*, 163 U.S. 537, 551 (1896).

42. See, e.g., Strossen, "Regulating Racist Speech," 498 (characterizing the injury to minorities as merely suffering an unpleasant environment).

43. Cass R. Sunstein, "Words, Conduct, Caste," *University of Chicago Law Review* 60 (Summer/Fall 1993): 795.

44. Strossen, "Regulating Racist Speech" (observing that debate implicates our grand national commitment to free speech, academic freedom, the *true* interests of minorities, and other high-sounding values).

45. See note 28 above and accompanying text.

46. See notes 28–29 above and accompanying text.

47. See Delgado and Stefancic, "Images of the Outsider"; Gerald Lopez, "Lay Lawyering," *UCLA Law Review* 32 (October 1984): 1 (discussing the role of narratives and stock stories in constructing social reality and guiding what we do and do not see).

48. See, e.g., Girardeau Spann, "Pure Politics," *Michigan Law Review* 88 (June 1990): 1971 (discussing the role of social practices in confining the effect of legal decrees).

49. For an explanation of our use of this term, see note 8 above and accompanying text.

50. These background elements often reflect the operation of social power and tradition. See Stanley Fish, *Is There a Text in This Class? The Authority of Interpretive Communities* (Cambridge: Harvard University Press, 1980); Richard Delgado, "Shadowboxing: An Essay on Power," *Cornell Law Review* 77 (May 1992): 813.

51. *Brown v. Board of Education*, 349 U.S. 294, 300 (1955).

52. See, e.g., Derrick A. Bell, Jr., *Race, Racism, and American Law*, 3d ed. (Boston: Little, Brown, & Co., 1992), 552–54, 565–607 (discussing the process of interpretation); Klarman, "*Brown*, Racial Change, and the Civil Rights Movement," 12, 76–85.

53. Bell, *Race, Racism, and American Law*, 118–20, 565–607.

54. See notes 17–26 above and accompanying text; notes 78–81 and 84–92 below and accompanying text.

55. Bell, *Race, Racism, and American Law*; see also Klarman, "*Brown*, Racial Change, and the Civil Rights Movement"; Rosenberg, *Hollow Hope*; Bell, "*Brown v. Board of Education*."

56. See *MLK*, 6 (observing that the costs of racial remedies generally are exacted from blacks); Spann, "Pure Politics."

57. See Leon Festinger, *A Theory of Cognitive Dissonance* (Stanford, Calif.: Stanford University Press, 1962).

58. Ibid.

59. Ibid.

60. See, e.g., Delgado and Stefancic, "Images of the Outsider" (discussing the role of narratives in shaping how we see the world); Delgado, "Campus Antiracism Rules."

61. See, e.g., Delgado and Stefancic, "Images of the Outsider."

62. See Klarman, "*Brown*, Racial Change, and the Civil Rights Movement" (discussing this resistance).

63. See Delgado and Stefancic, "Images of the Outsider," 1259–60 (defining "empathic fallacy" as the belief that we can change our own, and each other's, belief systems quickly and easily by presenting new arguments, stories, or accounts).

64. Ibid.

65. See Rosenberg, *Hollow Hope*; Delgado and Stefancic, *Failed Revolutions*.

66. Communities (large collectivities), by contrast, are essential to the process of forming and sharing meanings. See, e.g., Frank I. Michelman, "Foreword: Traces of Self-Government," *Harvard Law Review* 100 (November 1986): 4; see also Fish, *Is There a Text?* 278–81 (illustrating one court's limited ability to communicate the meaning of statutory language). Federal judges are situated too distantly and remotely to effect rapid change in social meanings.

67. See notes 27–29 and 50–53 above and accompanying text.

68. See Delgado and Stefancic, "Images of the Outsider," 1258–59 (observing that speech and dialogue can effectively correct small, clearly bounded, but not systemic error).

69. See text accompanying notes 71–77.

70. See text accompanying notes 78–130.

71. See, e.g., Delgado, "Shadowboxing"; Delgado and Stefancic, "Images of the Outsider."

72. Racism, for example, is generally agreed to consist of a complex of attitudes and practices that permeate institutions and individuals. See, e.g., *The Sociology of Race Relations: Reflection and Reform*, ed. Thomas F. Pettigrew (New York: Free Press, 1980); Charles R. Lawrence III, "The Id, the Ego, and Equal Protection: Reckoning with Unconscious Racism," *Stanford Law Review* 39 (January 1987): 317 (reconsidering the doctrine of discriminatory purpose).

73. See Derrick A. Bell, Jr., "Racial Realism," *Connecticut Law Review* 24 (Winter 1992): 363 (suggesting that racial equality is unobtainable because of the entrenched racism of Americans).

74. Ibid.; see also Bell, *And We Are Not Saved* (doubting that society will ever undertake such an effort).

75. Bell, "Racial Realism"; Richard Delgado, "Rodrigo's Chronicle," *Yale Law Journal* 101 (April 1992): 1357.

76. Richard Delgado and Jean Stefancic, "Imposition," *William and Mary Law Review* 35 (Spring 1994): 1025.

77. See notes 50–67 above and accompanying text.

78. Delgado and Stefancic, "Imposition" (collecting and evaluating examples of judicial and social rhetoric regarding blacks and other minorities); Thomas Ross, "Innocence and Affirmative Action," *Vanderbilt Law Review* 43 (March 1990): 297.

79. See, e.g., *Bakke*, 438 U.S. 265 (holding that admissions program that reserved positions in medical school class for disadvantaged minority students was unconstitutional). For a discussion of this retrenchment, see Joel Dreyfuss and Charles Lawrence III, *The Bakke Case: The Politics of Inequality* (New York: Harcourt Brace Jovanovich, 1979).

80. See, e.g., D'Souza, *Illiberal Education* (discussing the academic and cultural revolution at American universities).

81. See, e.g., *City of Richmond v. J. A. Croson Co.*, 488 U.S. 469 (1989) (striking down plan requiring city construction contracts to subcontract 30% of each contract to minority-owned businesses); Thomas Ross, "The Richmond Narratives," *Texas Law Review* 68 (December 1981): 381.

82. 163 U.S. 537 (1896).

83. Ibid. at 551.

84. 451 U.S. 100 (1981).

85. Ibid. at 119–20.

86. Ibid. at 128.

87. 426 U.S. 229 (1976) (holding that a test administered to black applicants for employment as police officers was not unconstitutional because the purpose was not discriminatory even though the impact may have been).

88. 429 U.S. 252 (1977).

89. Ibid. at 268–70.

90. 411 U.S. 1 (1973).

91. Ibid. at 54–55.

92. See notes 84–86 above and accompanying text (discussing *City of Memphis v. Greene*, 451 U.S. 100 [1981]).

93. 109 U.S. 3 (1883).

94. Ibid. at 24–25.

95. 438 U.S. 265 (1978).

96. Ibid.

97. Ibid. at 320.

98. Ibid. at 298 (plurality opinion of Powell, J.).

99. Ibid. at 295, 298–99.

100. E.g., *Wygant v. Jackson Board of Education*, 476 U.S. 267, 274–76 (1986) (rejecting role-model argument for affirmative action as dangerous, unproven, and potentially unbounded).

101. 488 U.S. 469 (1989).

102. Ibid.

103. Ibid. at 493.

104. Ibid. at 527–28 (Scalia J., concurring).

105. E.g., D'Souza, *Illiberal Education.*

106. See Olivas, "Federal Law and Scholarship Policy."

107. For examples of various social texts, ranging from editorials to conservative treatises, see Delgado and Stefancic, "Imposition."

108. Ibid., 1032 (discussing immigration issues); Gerald L. Neuman, "Back to *Dred Scott,*" *San Diego Law Review* 24, no. 2 (1987): 485 (reviewing Peter Shuck and Roger Smith, *Citizenship without Consent: Illegal Aliens in the American Polity* [New Haven: Yale University Press, 1985]).

109. 60 U.S. 393 (1856). For other discussions of the rhetorical parallels between *Dred Scott*, other nineteenth-century cases, and today's cases, see Ross, "Innocence and Affirmative Action"; Thomas Ross, "The Rhetorical Tapestry of Race: White Innocence and Black Abstraction," *William and Mary Law Review* 32 (Fall 1990): 1.

110. *Dred Scott*, 60 U.S. at 404–07.

111. Ibid. at 410.

112. See notes 122–28 below and accompanying text.

113. *Dred Scott*, 60 U.S. at 405–10 (depicting history of blacks as chattels).

114. Richard J. Herrnstein, *IQ in the Meritocracy* (London: Allen Lane, 1973); Richard Herrnstein and Charles Murray, *The Bell Curve* (New York: Free Press, 1994).

115. Arthur Jensen, "How Much Can We Boost IQ and Scholastic Achievement?" *Harvard Education Review* 39 (1969): 1.

116. For a discussion of the Nobel Prize–winning scientist's controversial views on race and IQ, see Richard Delgado et al., "Can Science Be Inopportune? Constitutional Validity of Governmental Restrictions on Race-IQ Research," *UCLA Law Review* 31 (October 1983): 128.

117. Ben J. Wattenberg, *The Birth Dearth* (New York: Pharos Books, 1987).

118. E.g., Neuman, "Back to *Dred Scott.*" On the history of U.S. nativism, see *Nativism, Discrimination, and Images of Immigrants*, ed. George Pozzetta (New York: Garland, 1991).

119. For a discussion of this and similar language-purification efforts, see Delgado and Stefancic, "Imposition," 1035; Juan Perea, "Demography and Distrust: An Essay on American Language, Cultural Pluralism, and Official English," *Minnesota Law Review* 77 (December 1992): 269.

120. For a collection of essays on the Rodney King case and the Los Angeles disturbances that followed, see "Symposium, Los Angeles, April 29, 1992 and Beyond: The Law, Issues, and Perspectives," *Southern California Law Review* 66 (May 1993): 1313.

121. Ibid.; see Jerome M. Culp, Jr., "Notes from California: Rodney King and the Race Question," *Denver University Law Review* 70, no. 2 (1993): 199.

122. 481 U.S. 279 (1987).

123. Ibid.

124. Ibid. at 319 (''McCleskey's arguments are best presented to the legislative bodies'').

125. Ibid. at 317.

126. 400 U.S. 309 (1971).

127. 432 U.S. 464 (1977).

128. Delgado and Stefancic, ''Imposition,'' 1033.

129. Bell, *Race, Racism and American Law*, 39–46; Eric Foner, *Reconstruction: America's Unfinished Revolution* (New York: Harper & Row, 1988).

130. E.g., Klarman, ''*Brown*, Racial Change, and the Civil Rights Movement,'' 12–13, 76.

131. E.g., European Parliament Committee of Inquiry on Racism and Xenophobia, *Report on the Findings of the Inquiry* (Luxembourg: Office for Official Publications of the European Communities, 1991); Commission of the European Communities, *Legal Instruments to Combat Racism and Xenophobia* (Brussels: Directorate General, Employment, Industrial Relations and Social Affairs, 1992); ''Italians Examine Fascist History,'' *Denver Post*, 9 April 1994, 21A.

132. Compare our conclusion with similar ones drawn by Girardeau A. Spann, *Race against the Court* (New York: New York University Press, 1993) (observing that Supreme Court litigation is of limited use as an instrument of racial reform), and Bell, *And We Are Not Saved*, 526–50; see also *MLK*, 5 (similar observation about romantic view of law and law's efficacy).

11

The Irrelevant Court

The Supreme Court's Inability to Influence Popular Beliefs about Equality (or Anything Else)

GERALD N. ROSENBERG

American citizens are riveted to certain events. Championship games in sports, for example, are talked about endlessly. Professional football's Super Bowl, played every January, draws enormous television-viewing audiences. Real-life dramas, like O. J. Simpson's 1995 criminal trial or the 1994 California highway chase leading to his arrest, create endless conversations. Autumn debates between the major presidential candidates can catch the attention of large percentages of Americans. When Americans care about an event and the media give it extensive coverage, it can become an important part of the political, social, and cultural life of the United States.

The focus of this chapter is the ability of the U.S. Supreme Court to win the attention of the American public and increase its support for racial and gender equality. When the Court issues opinions about equality, how do Americans react? Are they aware of the decisions? Do they talk about them? Does their thinking about equality change? Or does little change? Are Americans basically unaware of what the Court does, even in landmark cases? Do they form opinions about equality from sources other than the Court? Are their opinions about equality relatively fixed or susceptible to change from Court-induced reflection?

There are good reasons for expecting the Supreme Court to have the power to change people's views. First, the Supreme Court is generally considered the most powerful court in the world. The justices hold their positions for life and exercise the power to invalidate the acts of governmental officials (judicial review). Second, the nine justices are formally independent of electoral constraints and political pressure. Unlike other governmental officials, they are not politically beholden, they can't be thrown out of office for unpopular decisions, and they do not run for reelection. Third, they operate in the world of rights and principles, not policy and preferences. The questions they address are not whether a law or act is good policy or an appropriate response to interest-group demands but whether the law or act is consistent with constitutional requirements or existing legislation. The "above-politics," independent, and principled nature of much Supreme Court decision-making may give Supreme Court decisions a powerful legitimacy.[1]

Many scholars who have written about the Supreme Court emphasize its ability to change opinions. Courts, one writer suggests, can provide "a cheap method of pricking powerful consciences."[2] For Professor Eugene V. Rostow, the Supreme Court is an "educational body, and the Justices are inevitably teachers in a vital national seminar."[3] Professor Alexander Bickel noted that courts have the "capacity to appeal to men's better natures, to call forth their aspirations, which may have been forgotten in the moment's hue and cry"; courts, he suggested, are a "great and highly effective educational institution."[4] More recently, the Supreme Court of the mid-and late twentieth century is generally understood to have played a leading role in creating a more equal America. From civil rights to women's rights, the Court's decisions are widely believed to have led to greater equality. As Aryeh Neier puts it, "[S]ince the early 1950s, the courts have been the most accessible and, often, the most effective instrument of government for bringing about the changes in public policy sought by social protest movements."[5]

In contrast, there are some who believe that courts are epiphenomenal to the process of social change. Perhaps the most celebrated exponent of this view is Alexander Hamilton, who wrote in *The Federalist* of the "natural feebleness of the judiciary," arguing that the courts were by far the weakest of the three branches of government.[6] In more recent times, some writers have stressed the broader environment in which courts exist. In this view, court decisions are part of a social, political, economic, and cultural milieu that gives them meaning. In and of themselves, they are unlikely to change anything or even to be noticed.[7]

Consider, for example, the Supreme Court's infamous *Dred Scott* decision (1857), which denied that African Americans were citizens, invalidated the Missouri Compromise, and upheld the constitutionality of slavery. Since it was delivered as the nation was approaching the Civil War, evidently an aim of its authors was to avoid war by treating the issue of slavery in the territories as a constitutional matter and settling it legally. By all accounts, the decision was a dismal failure. It changed no opinions, and rather than settling the issue, it fanned the flames. Not surprisingly, it was popular in the South but unpopular in the North, where it was widely referred to as a "stump speech."[8] Horace Greeley editorialized that the decision is "entitled to just so much moral weight as would be the judgment of a majority of those congregated in any Washington bar-room."[9] The *New York Independent* wrote, "If the people obey this decision they disobey God."[10] When emotions run high, as they do over issues of equality, one might think it unlikely that the Court's decisions would change opinions.

One reason for skepticism about the view of courts as powerful promoters of equality is that there is little or no evidence that the Court's decisions change people's views. Typically, the effect is simply assumed. But claims about the real world require evidence. If the claims are right, supportive evidence will make them that much stronger. However, if the evidence doesn't support the claims, then they ought to be treated cautiously or rejected.

The Supreme Court and Public Opinion

The modern view sketched above is that courts play an important role in alerting Americans to social and political grievances. According to one defender of the claim, "without the dramatic intervention of so dignified an institution as a court, which puts its own prestige and authority on the line, most middle-class Americans would not be informed about such grievances."[11] For this claim to hold, for courts to affect behavior, directly or indirectly, people must be aware of what courts do. Although this does not seem an onerous responsibility, survey researchers report that most Americans have little knowledge about courts and pay little attention to them. This holds true even for the Supreme Court, the most visible and important American court.

In general, surveys have shown that only about 40 percent of the American public, at best, follows Supreme Court actions, as measured by survey respondents having either read or heard something about the Court. In 1966, for example, nearly 40 percent of the American public could not identify Earl Warren, despite a decade of Court activism in which the chief justice was both loudly praised and vilified. And in 1989, while more than 25 percent of survey respondents identified Judge Joseph Wapner of television's *People's Court*, fewer than 10 percent could name the chief justice of the United States, William Rehnquist. Also, in 1966, despite important Supreme Court decisions on race, religion, criminal justice, and voting rights, 46 percent of a nationwide sample could not recall *anything at all* that the Court had recently done. And when prompted with a list of eight "decisions," four of which the Court had recently made and four of which it had never made, and asked to identify which, if any, the Court had made, only 15 percent of a 1966 sample made four or more correct choices. More recently, despite a "barrage" of media coverage of President Ronald Reagan's nomination of Judge Robert H. Bork for a seat on the U.S. Supreme Court, "surprisingly few citizens expressed concern or formed opinions on the issue."[12]

Among Americans who have some awareness of what the Court does, there is little evidence that its decisions change opinions. That is, people aware of what the Court does may disagree with it. In fact, the more knowledgeable a person is about the Supreme Court, the more likely he or she is to disagree with it. In reviewing the literature, David Adamany writes of the "Court's *incapacity* to legitimize governmental action."[13] Evidence for this conclusion comes from the work of Walter Murphy and Joseph Tanenhaus, who found that only 13 percent of the American public has the knowledge and beliefs about the Court necessary for it to legitimate action.[14] This includes the belief that the Court is a proper, impartial, and competent interpreter of the Constitution. Thus, the potential pool of people who could be influenced by a Supreme Court decision is small. The point is that although in principle law may be a powerful legitimating force in American society capable of changing opinions, in practice, courts, including the Supreme Court, are weak legitimaters.

A possible way in which this general lack of knowledge and barrier to the Court's effectiveness could be overcome is through heightened press coverage. Despite the general findings of the literature, the Supreme Court could influence

Americans through the press. The trouble with this line of reasoning is that there is little evidence that Supreme Court decisions increase press coverage. Numerous studies have documented the media's lack of interest in providing the kind of in-depth and continuous coverage that could lead to greater public awareness and influence opinions about equality. For example, Charles Franklin and Liane Kosaki examined network television news coverage of the Supreme Court over the nine-teen-month period from January 1989 to July 1990. On average, there were 0.25 stories per day involving the Supreme Court (about one every four days), compared to 2.1 stories per day on the president and 1.0 stories per day on Congress.[15] As Franklin and Kosaki put it, the "episodic nature of Court decisions and the irregular coverage it receives means that substantial portions of the public will fail to hear of many decisions."[16] This combination of little interest and knowledge in what the Court does and the lack of media interest in overcoming it suggests that the Court is highly unlikely to play much of a role in influencing views on equality.

In the bulk of this chapter, I examine the question of whether Supreme Court de-cisions involving issues of racial and gender equality influence the opinions Amer-icans hold on these issues. By bringing together public opinion data from a variety of fields, a coherent picture appears. And it's a picture that may surprise the reader.

Racial Equality

When the Supreme Court unanimously condemned racial segregation in public elementary and secondary schools in *Brown v. Board of Education*[17] in 1954, it marked the first time since 1875 that one of the three branches of the federal government spoke strongly in favor of civil rights on a fundamental issue. "Sep-arate educational facilities," Chief Justice Earl Warren wrote for a unanimous Supreme Court, "are inherently unequal."[18] Surely this principled statement of constitutional requirements affected the thinking of Americans about racial equality. "*Brown*," it is claimed, "launched the public debate over racial equality."[19] In the following section I explore the evidence that the Supreme Court through *Brown* increased support for equality.

One important way in which the Court may have changed thinking about racial equality is through inducing increased press coverage of it and balanced treatment of African Americans. However, overall, there is no evidence of such an increase or major change in reporting in the years immediately following *Brown*. In general, newspaper coverage of civil rights was poor until the massive demonstrations of the 1960s. In the South, for example, a study by the Southern Regional Council (SRC) of "representative" white newspapers concluded that they constituted "the greatest single force in perpetuating the popular stereotype of the Negro." The problem, the SRC found, was that "the average white editor believes, rightly or wrongly, that readers want little mention of the Negro which does not fit in with their own concept of colored persons."[20] Numerous studies support this conclusion. C. A. McKnight, executive director of the Southern Education Reporting Service, found that in the years following *Brown*, Supreme Court treatment of segregation received "minimum coverage."[21] This was particularly true in the South, where there was a "paucity" of coverage and where the wire services "seldom reported the story in its full dimensions and meaning."[22] And *Time* magazine criticized southern newspapers for doing a "patchy, pussyfooting job of covering the region's biggest running story since the end of slavery."[23]

The most powerful way to determine if there was a sustained increase in press coverage of civil rights in response to *Brown* is to actually count press stories over time. If the Supreme Court affected thinking about equality, then one would expect to see a sustained increase in media coverage of civil rights. The evidence is presented in figure 11.1. Although press coverage of civil rights, as measured by the number of stories dealing with the issue in the *Reader's Guide to Periodical Literature*, increased moderately in 1954 over the previous year's total, by 1958 and 1959, coverage actually dropped below the level found in several of the years of the late 1940s and early 1950s![24] In addition, if one examines the largest-circulations magazines of the 1950s and early 1960s, *Reader's Digest, Ladies Home Journal, Life,* and the *Saturday Evening Post,* the same general pattern is found. And it was not until 1962 that *TV Guide* ran a story having to do with civil rights. Thus, changes in press coverage provide no evidence that the Court's decision influenced the press to give attention to civil rights.

It is possible, of course, that public opinion is formed more by elites than by ordinary citizens. Thus, it may be that the magazines most likely read by elites, the *New York Times Magazine, Newsweek, Time,* and the *New Republic,* would provide increased coverage of civil rights in the wake of the Court's decision. But this is not the case; these magazines show the same pattern. Even though most did contain more civil rights articles in 1956 and 1957 than in the years before *Brown,*

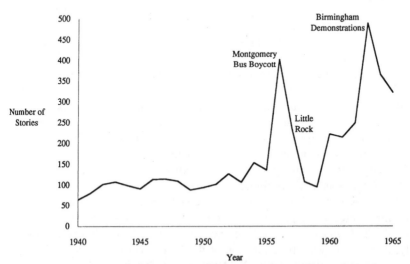

FIGURE 11.1. Magazine Coverage of Civil Rights, 1940–1965 (Reprinted by permission from Gerald N. Rosenberg, *The Hollow Hope: Can Courts Bring About Social Change?* [Chicago: The University of Chicago Press, 1991], © 1991 by The University of Chicago)

this increased coverage is most plausibly due to the factors identified above. In fact, for each of these magazines there was as much, if not more, coverage of civil rights in several of the years of the 1940s as in 1958 or 1959. The same general pattern holds for civil rights coverage in the *New York Times* as measured by the proportion of pages in the *Times Index* devoted to discrimination. In 1952 there was actually more coverage than in 1954 or 1955. Further, coverage in the years 1954, 1955, 1958, and 1959 was barely equal to or actually less than the coverage allotted to civil rights in four of the years of the 1940s! Here again, there is no evidence that the Court's action influenced views of equality by putting civil rights on the political agenda through the press.

Public Opinion

The most straightforward way to examine the Court's ability to influence thinking about racial equality is to examine public opinion. As one scholar has put it, the Supreme Court "pricked the conscience"[25] of white America by pointing out both its constitutional duty and its shortcomings. "Except for *Brown*," Aryeh Neier contends, white Americans "would not have known about the plight of blacks under segregation."[26]

One place to look for evidence is in responses to survey questions about racial equality in general and support for *Brown* in particular. Surprisingly, and unfortunately, there appear to be no polls addressing knowledge of *Brown*. There are, however, polls charting the reaction to *Brown* by southerners over time. In July 1954, just a few months after the decision, 24 percent of *all* southerners approved of the decision and of integrated schools and 71 percent disapproved. Nearly seven years later, in June 1961, the numbers were virtually identical, with 24 percent approving and 69 percent disapproving. Among white southerners, in February 1956, only 16 percent approved. When white southerners were asked in July 1954 whether they would object to sending their children to integrated schools, only 15 percent responded that they would not object. By 1959, support for desegregation actually dropped, with only 8 percent of white southerners responding that they would not object.[27] Given the lack of positive change over time, it is entirely possible that supportive respondents were supportive before the Court acted. If not, then at most the Court influenced about one-quarter of all southerners and about one-sixth of white southerners. But since there was at least some support for desegregated schools in the South before the Court acted, it seems fair to assume that the actual influence was less.

If there is little evidence that *Brown* increased support for school desegregation in the South, perhaps it helped change white opinions more generally. Indeed, a main argument for the Court's influence is that the Court's action pricked the conscience of white America and changed racial attitudes. Ideally, to answer this question, one would look to time-series data on white opinions about civil rights. Support for the Court's influence would be found if there was a sharp increase in supportive attitudes about racial equality after *Brown* or if the rate of change of supportive attitudes increased. Unfortunately, the data are not ideal. Questions were not asked regularly, and the pre-1954 data are sketchy. That being said, throughout the period from the beginning of World War II to the passage of the 1964 Civil Rights Act, whites became increasingly supportive of civil rights. Writing in 1956, Herbert Hyman and Paul Sheatsley found that the changes in attitude were "solidly based" and "not easily accelerated nor easily reversed."[28] Reviewing the available data in 1964, they noted the "unbroken trend of the past twenty years."[29] Further, they found that the changes were not due to any specific event, such as President John Kennedy's assassination or a Supreme Court decision. They found that changes in national opinion "represent long-term trends that are not easily modified by specific—even by highly dramatic—events."[30]

Another way of examining the Court's influence on how Americans view racial equality is to look at how the sensitivity of white Americans to civil rights changed generally. According to one scholar, the "*Brown* decision was central to eliciting the moral outrage that both blacks and whites were to feel and express about segregation."[31] If the Court served this role, it would necessarily have increased awareness of the plight of African Americans. The evidence, however, shows no sign of such an increase. Survey questions about whether most African Americans were being treated fairly resulted in affirmative responses of 66 percent in 1944, 66 percent in 1946, and 69 percent in 1956.[32] By 1963, when Gallup asked if any group in America was being treated unfairly, 80 percent said no. Only 5 percent of the sample named "the Negroes" as being unfairly treated, and 4 percent named "the whites."[33] This result and the change over time hardly show an America whose conscience was aroused.

This lack of sensitivity to the plight of African Americans can be seen most poignantly in the 1957 crisis involving the Court-ordered admission of nine African American children to the all-white Central High School in Little Rock, Arkansas. Governor Orval Faubus of Arkansas gained national attention by repeatedly defying court orders and blocking the desegregation. In December 1958, when Gallup asked its usual question about the most admired men in the world, Governor Faubus was among the top ten![34] If the Court pricked the conscience of white Americans, the sensitivity disappeared quickly. Thus, there does not appear to be evidence supporting the claim that the massive change in the opinions of white Americans about civil rights was an effect of the Court's action. As Burke Marshall, head of the Justice Department's Civil Rights Division, put it, "[T]he Negro and his problems were still pretty much invisible to the country . . . until mass demonstrations of the Birmingham type."[35]

In sum, in several areas in which the Supreme Court would be expected to increase support among white Americans for racial equality, evidence of the effect has not been found. Most Americans neither follow Supreme Court decisions nor understand the Court's constitutional role. It is not surprising, then, that change in public opinion about racial equality appears to be unrelated to the Court.

African Americans

The preceding section focussed on general poll data. In so doing, it left out the possible effect of the Supreme Court on African Americans. Here, a plausible claim is that *Brown* was the spark that ignited the African American revolution. By recognizing and legitimating African American grievances, the public pronounce-ment by the Court could have provided African Americans with a new image and encouraged them to act. *Brown* "begot," one legal scholar tells us, "a union of the mightiest and lowliest in America, a mystical, passionate union bound by the pained depths of the black man's cry for justice and the moral authority, unique to the Court, to see that justice realized."[36] If this is the case, then there are a number of places where evidence should be found.

For *Brown* to have played this role, African Americans must have known about the decision and approved both of its holdings and of the Court's constitutional role. As discussed earlier, there is little evidence that Americans, black or white, credit the Court with a legitimating role. Further, it is not entirely clear that knowl-edge of *Brown* was widespread. For example, during the school desegregation crisis in Clinton, Tennessee, in the fall of 1956, a team of social scientists interviewing people found that "a number" had "never heard of the U.S. Supreme Court de-cision against segregation."[37] A decade after *Brown*, a white volunteer teaching in a Mississippi Freedom School during the summer of 1964 wrote in a letter: "My students are from 13 to 17 years old, and not one of them had heard about the Supreme Court decision of 1954. . . . [T]hey are surprised to hear that the law is on their side."[38]

Part of the reason for this lack of knowledge is clearly Americans' general ignorance of Supreme Court decisions. Part is also due to poor newspaper coverage, as has been discussed. But another possibility is that many African Americans did not approve of the decision. In November 1955, a special Gallup poll found that barely half of southern African Americans (53 percent) approved of *Brown*.[39] Al-though such poll data should be approached cautiously, a poll taken just a few weeks later found that 82 percent of southern African Americans approved of an Interstate Commerce Commission ruling prohibiting segregation in transportation.[40] The large difference between the two approval percentages is striking. Knowledge of, and support for, *Brown* may not have been high.

Brown was not greeted with an outpouring of public support by African Amer-icans. Overall, the reaction within the African American community to *Brown* was muted. After *Brown*, "there were no street celebrations in Negro communities"[41] and no "grand celebrations."[42] Ralph Abernathy understood the lack of public response this way: "[M]ost blacks in the Deep South states looked with curiosity at what was going [on] in the high courts, shrugged their shoulders, and went back to their day-to-day lives. . . . After all, they had waited a lifetime and seen no change at all."[43]

Another possible explanation for the generally moderate response may lie with the African American press. Its coverage of the cases preceding *Brown* showed "understandable caution" and was sometimes "optimistic, though not ecstatic."[44] After *Brown*, responses varied. In some states, like Texas, the decision was strongly supported.[45] In others, like Mississippi, little was said. Although Mississippi is undoubtedly an extreme case, a book-length compilation of studies of the African American press in the eleven southern states and Missouri had only six references to *Brown*.[46] Thus, it is possible that the African American press did not fill in where the white press failed.

Affirmative Action

In the last several decades of the twentieth century, many universities and employers throughout the United States practiced some form of affirmative action. The idea behind affirmative action is that because of both past and present prejudice, members of certain minority groups (and women) are at a disadvantage in competing with others for jobs and admissions. In evaluating qualifications of applicants, educational institutions and employers with affirmative action plans have kept this background in mind and admitted or hired individuals whose test scores or other application materials would normally not have been sufficient.

The Supreme Court entered the area in 1978 in *Regents of University of California v. Bakke.*[47] In *Bakke*, which involved an affirmative action plan at the medical school of the University of California at Davis, the Court upheld the use of race as one factor among many in admissions. Whereas the decision invalidated the use of racial quotas (and invalidated the Davis program), it found nonquota affirmative action plans constitutional. *Bakke* was followed by other decisions like *United Steel Workers v. Weber* (1978),[48] which upheld an affirmative action plan adopted by the United Steel Workers and Kaiser Aluminum, and *Fullilove v. Klutznick* (1980),[49] which upheld the minority set-aside provision of the Public Works Employment Act of 1977.

Because affirmative action is aimed at the disadvantaged, it is seen by its supporters as an equality issue. Its aim is to undo the past and present effects of discrimination, to equalize opportunity, and to help produce greater equality in the United States. If the Court has the power to increase support for equality, then the data should show an increase in support for affirmative action as a result of the Court's action. Table 11.1 presents the data.

In measuring the beliefs of Americans about affirmative action, Gallup asked the following question: "Some people say that to make up for past discrimination, women and members of minority groups should be given preferential treatment in getting jobs and places in college. Others say that ability, as determined by test scores, should be the main consideration. Which point comes closest to how you feel on this matter?" The data show no change in the wake of Supreme Court decisions supportive of affirmative action. White Americans are overwhelmingly opposed to affirmative action plans before and after the Court's decisions. Non-

TABLE 11.1. Support of Affirmative Action

Date	Whites		Nonwhites	
	Ability	Preference to Minorities	Ability	Preference to Minorities
May 1977	86%	8%	64%	27%
November 1977	84	9	55	30
April 1979*	85	10	49	38
May 1981	87	7	57	29
August 1991	84	8	60	24

Source: George H. Gallup, *The Gallup Poll: Public Opinion* (Wilmington, Del.: Scholarly Resources, Inc., 1978–92).

*The 1979 survey was given to "full-time students representing 60 campuses."

whites show a similar but less pronounced pattern. Eight percent of white respondents supported affirmative action in 1977, before the Court's action, and 8 percent of white respondents did so in 1991. Among nonwhites the change was only 3 percentage points (and it moved against affirmative action!). Once again, the data provide no support for the claim that Supreme Court decisions create support for racial equality among Americans.

In sum, while support for racial equality on most issues has grown over time, there is little evidence that the Supreme Court contributed much to this change. But perhaps this finding is unique to racial equality. In order to determine that, the next section explores gender equality.

Gender Equality

The role of women in American society and the opportunities open to them have changed a great deal over the last several decades. Although discrimination continues to exist, many women today have choices that their mothers lacked. On a formal level, the Supreme Court has added to women's equality. In a series of decisions starting in 1971, the Supreme Court struck down many laws that discriminated against women. In 1973, in *Roe v. Wade*,[50] it struck down most prohibitions on abortions. Did these decisions increase support for gender equality?[51]

Salience

It is entirely possible that litigation in abortion and women's rights changed perceptions of the position of women in American society. Indeed, many groups involved in women's rights litigation believe that "litigation, because it attracts television, newspaper, and magazine attention, is critical in raising the consciousness of the American public."[52] If this is the case, then increased press coverage of women's rights and abortion should be seen after the Court entered the field.

Starting with abortion, figure 11.2 shows that while there was a major increase in magazine coverage, it came in 1970 and 1971, well before the Court's action. There was actually less coverage of abortion in the *Reader's Guide* in 1973, the year of the Court's decisions, than in the years 1972, 1971, and 1970! With the nation's largest-circulation magazines, there was no large increase in 1973. Large increases did occur in 1970 and 1971, before the Court's action. And coverage in the *New York Times* shows the same pattern. With women's rights, figure 11.3 reports similar data. A steep increase is recorded, but it is in 1970 and 1971, before any major action by the Court. As with abortion, the major change in large-circulation magazine coverage of women's rights occurred in the years 1970 and 1971, before the Court's action. Again, *New York Times* coverage is similar.

Turning to the four magazines most likely read by political elites, the pattern repeats. There was no increase in abortion coverage in 1973, the year of the Court's decisions. In fact, all four magazines had more abortion stories in previous recent years than in 1973. With women's rights, there was no large increase in coverage in the years 1973 and beyond. The change that did occur came in 1970 and 1971.

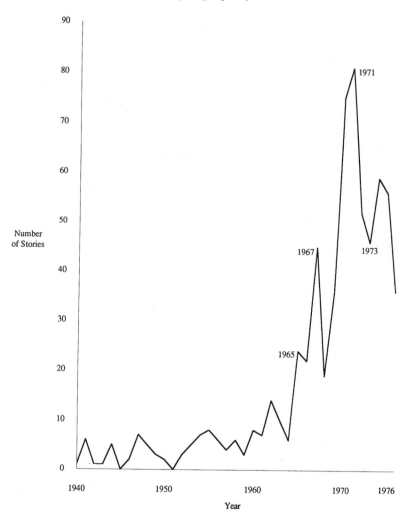

FIGURE 11.2. Magazine Coverage of Abortion, 1940–1976 (Reprinted by permission from Gerald N. Rosenberg, *The Hollow Hope: Can Courts Bring About Social Change?* [Chicago: The University of Chicago Press, 1991], © 1991 by The University of Chicago)

This pattern is particularly pronounced in coverage of the women's liberation movement. The point is clear: the Court's decisions on abortion and women's rights did *not* result in greater coverage of these issues. The argument that the Court's action gave women's rights and abortion salience lacks evidence.

Public Opinion

Media coverage aside, it is still possible that litigation in abortion and women's rights increased support for gender equality. A good place to look for evidence of this is in changes in public opinion. Fortunately, some data are available.

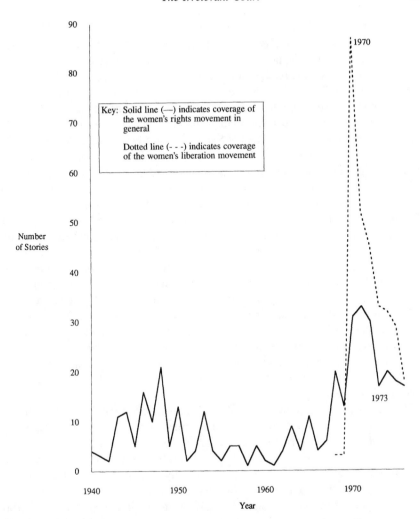

FIGURE 11.3. Magazine Coverage of Women's Rights, 1940–1976 (Reprinted by permission from Gerald N. Rosenberg, *The Hollow Hope: Can Courts Bring About Social Change?* [Chicago: The University of Chicago Press, 1991], © 1991 by The University of Chicago)

Abortion

Abortion is about the equality of women. If women lack the power to control their fertility, they lack the power to control their lives. Regardless of one's view of the constitutionality or the morality of abortion, one can explore changes in public opinion in the wake of Supreme Court decisions. If the Court plays an important role in increasing support for gender equality, then surely the Supreme Court's finding of a constitutional right to choose an abortion increased support for abortion choice.

The evidence does show large increases in support for a woman's right to choose but *before* the Court acted. By the eve of the Court's decisions in 1973, public opinion had dramatically shifted from opposition to abortion in most cases to substantial, if not majority, support. Indeed, in the decades that have followed, opinion on abortion has remained remarkably stable.

Why didn't public opinion change after the Court found a constitutional right for women to choose to terminate their pregnancies? To start, in order for the Court to affect views, people must know about its decisions. However, it appears that many Americans are unaware that the Supreme Court has issued an opinion on the constitutionality of abortion. In 1975, two years after *Roe*, a Gallup poll found that "less than half of American adult respondents were informed about the 1973 decisions."[53] In 1982, nearly a decade after the decisions and two years into the Reagan administration and its loudly proclaimed commitment to end legal abortion, 59 percent of a national survey sample answered either "don't know" or "no" to a question whether the Supreme Court had issued an opinion permitting abortion in the first three months of pregnancy.[54] These results were highlighted in 1990 by eleven teenage focus groups held around the country by the Center for Population Options in Washington, D.C. Summing up their findings, Rebecca Stone and Cynthia Waszak reported: "Many of the participants thought it [abortion] was illegal in most states, although participants seemed to know that abortion was legal in their own state. No participants said that abortion was legal in all 50 states (many were surprised to learn the truth), and only a few of the teenagers could identify *Roe v. Wade* or explain its significance."[55] These data suggest that knowledge of the Court's decisions is low. If citizens don't know that the Court has acted, the Court can't influence their views.

The data support this conclusion of little influence. Summarizing the literature, Judith Blake concludes, "None of our time series on public views regarding abortion indicates that the Supreme Court decisions had an important effect on opinion."[56] Table 11.2 provides data starting in 1975, two years after the decision. The data show that public opinion remained essentially constant for more than a decade until 1989, when it started to move in a more supportive direction.

What happened in 1989 to cause this growth in opinion supportive of abortion choice? Perhaps the Supreme Court issued an abortion decision? Indeed it did, but the Supreme Court's 1989 abortion decision (*Webster v. Reproductive Health Services*)[57] put restrictions on the right! That is, although the Court limited the right to abortion, there was a small but significant growth in pro-choice support. In other words, the Court's pro-choice decisions did not increase public support for abortion choice, but the Court's decision limiting the right seemed to create more, not less, support for it.

These findings may appear startling to many. But they are in line with what students have learned about the Supreme Court and public opinion. Data are lacking on knowledge of other women's rights issues, but it seems likely that if more than half the American public didn't know about *Roe*, then at least that percentage wouldn't know about other, less famous, Court decisions.

In sum, the Supreme Court has not been able to influence the views Americans hold about abortion. Even though there has been major increase in support for legal abortion, it occurred principally before the Court acted. The small change occurring after the Court's action has flowed counter to the Court's decision. That is, when

TABLE 11.2. Support of Abortion: Conditions
under Which It Should Be Legal

Year	Always Legal	Legal in Certain Circumstances	Always Illegal
1975	21%	54%	22%
1977	22	55	19
1979	22	54	19
1980	25	53	18
1981	23	52	21
1983	23	58	16
1988	24	57	17
1989 (July)	29	51	17
1990	31	53	12
1991	33	49	14
1992 (July)	34	48	13

Source: Frank Newport and Leslie McAneny, "Whose Court Is It Anyhow? O'Connor, Kennedy, Souter Position Reflects Abortion Views of Most Americans," *Gallup Poll Monthly*, no. 322 (July 1992): 51, 52.

Note: "No opinion" omitted.

the Court narrowed the right to choose abortion in *Webster*, the public grew somewhat more supportive of the broader right. With abortion, as with the other issues I have examined, the Court appears unable to increase support for equality.

Women's Rights

Another area to examine for evidence of the Court's ability to increase public support for equality is the change in public opinion on women's rights issues other than abortion. Although there is no firm demarcation line, as with abortion, the 1973 abortion decisions are a rough breaking point. If the Court can change views, then major changes in support for gender equality should occur after these dates. However, if change is being driven by other forces, then it should be seen before major Court decisions.

There has been substantial change in public opinion about women's rights, but much of it occurred before the Court's action. Writing in 1972, Lou Harris found that "a swing in attitude—and a dramatic one—is taking place among women in America today."[58] This "dramatic swing" occurred in the late 1960s and early 1970s, before the Court's action.

One area in which the swing was pronounced was in opinions about the place of women in American society. In 1970, for example, 40 percent of women and 42 percent of a national sample favored efforts to strengthen and change women's status in society. By 1972, there was an eight-point gain in the percentage of women supporting efforts for change (48 percent) and a six-point gain in the percentage of the national sample (48 percent).[59] A similar pattern is found with college-educated women in questions of sex-role beliefs. Using surveys from the

1960s and 1970s, Karen Mason, John Czajka, and Sara Arber found that the period 1964–70 saw "rather sizable attitude shifts" among these women. By 1970, they found that "large majorities held relatively egalitarian beliefs about women's dependency on men's plans, about the consequences of maternal employment for children's well-being, and about the differential socialization of boys and girls."[60] The attitudes of college-educated men also appeared to be changing. In 1972, for the first time, fewer than one-half of entering male college freshmen accepted the notion that a woman's place is in the home.[61] Finally, as early as 1962, a Gallup poll found that 90 percent of housewives surveyed did not want their daughters to lead the same type of life they led.[62]

Another indication of growing support for gender equality is found in opinions about married women working. In 1936 only 18 percent of Gallup's respondents said yes to the question "Should a married woman earn money if she has a husband capable of supporting her?"[63] By 1967, opinions had changed a great deal, with 44 percent of the sample responding positively to a similar Roper question.[64] Just two years later, however, the percentage of respondents approving of married women earning money increased to 55 percent.[65] This eleven-point increase in two years was nearly half the increase recorded in the thirty-one years between 1936 and 1967. And it was recorded before any major Court action. Although support has continued to grow, reaching 86 percent in 1993, the pace of change has remained steady, suggesting that it was driven by structural factors within the society.

In sum, in the area of public opinion, abortion, and women's rights, major increases in support for gender equality predate Court action. With women's rights, support did continue to grow in the 1970s, but it "did not occur at a consistently faster pace after 1970 than before."[66] Again, evidence for the Court's ability to increase support for gender equality is lacking.

Equality and Sexual Preference

A final aspect of gender equality to be considered is sexual preference. Unlike the other equality areas that I have examined, the Supreme Court has not been supportive of equality for homosexuals.[67] Indeed, in 1986 in *Bowers v. Hardwick*,[68] the Court denied constitutional protection to consenting adults to engage in private homosexual relations. If the Court's views on equality carry weight with the American public, then one would expect to see growing opposition to equality for gays.

The data that exist do show change, but in the opposite direction from *Bowers*. That is, the American public is becoming more supportive of equality for homosexuals despite the Court's ruling. For example, Gallup has repeatedly asked its respondents the following question: "In general, do you think homosexuals should or should not have equal rights in terms of job opportunities?" In 1977, 56 percent of respondents said "yes" and 33 percent said "no." By 1992, support had increased to 74 percent, with 18 percent opposing. And, in 1993, the percentage of supporters increased again, with 80 percent supporting equality and only 14 percent opposing it.[69]

Most useful for this analysis was a question concerning legalizing homosexual relations. On several occasions Gallup asked respondents whether "homosexual

TABLE 11.3. Support for Legalization of Homosexual Relations between Consenting Adults

Date	Should Be Legal	Should Not Be Legal
July 1977	43%	43%
December 1985	44	47
October 1989	47	36
June 1992	48	44

Source: George H. Gallup, *The Gallup Poll: Public Opinion* (Wilmington, Del.: Scholarly Resources, Inc., 1978–93).

relations between consenting adults'' should or should not be made legal—the very question the Court addressed in *Bowers*. Table 11.3 presents the results.

The data show a small increase of 5 percentage points in supportive responses over a fifteen-year period (1977–92) and essentially no change in negative responses. The key point is that despite the Court's denial of equality in *Bowers*, over time the American public has become more supportive of equality, not less. And this increase has occurred in the context of concern, if not hysteria, about the AIDS virus.

In sum, the Court's antigay views do not appear to have influenced the public. The American public has increased its support of equality regardless of sexual preference despite the Court's reading of the Constitution to deny that equality. This, perhaps, is a bit of good news for believers in equality. The Court may not be able to increase support for equality, but perhaps it can't lessen support either.

Conclusion

This chapter has examined the ability of the Court to influence the views of Americans on equality. The findings are consistent: there is no evidence supporting the power of the Court to increase support for racial or gender equality. Those looking to influence how Americans think about equality need to look elsewhere.

This conclusion should not be surprising. As I suggested at the beginning of this chapter, courts are only one among many institutions, and their decisions compete with other events for the public's attention. Further, to the extent that their decisions are heard, they are heard by people deeply enmeshed in powerful social and cultural networks, be they ethnic, racial, religious, and so on. As anyone who has ever debated issues of racial or gender equality can attest, opinions on such issues are often deeply held. It is naive to expect an institution seen as distant and unfamiliar, shrouded in mystery, and using arcane language and procedures to change people's views. Perhaps what is most surprising is not that the Supreme Court appears unable to increase support for equality but that anyone thinks that it can.

The findings of this chapter also suggest that claims about the real-world effects of court decisions need empirical testing. To debate the merits of judicial opinions is certainly appropriate, but when the discussion turns to the effects of such opinions, those effects must be measured. Sometimes measurement is hard and data are unavailable. What that means to the scholar as opposed to the ideologue is that claims must be put in the form of hypotheses to be tested, tentative suggestions about how people might behave. There is much to be said for principled beliefs, but to confuse them with reality is both bad scholarship and bad politics. And for those of us committed to furthering both equality and scholarship, this confusion is a double mistake.

NOTES

Ronna Landy and Julie Alig provided superb research assistance in the preparation of this chapter.

1. Owen Fiss, "The Forms of Justice," *Harvard Law Review* 93 (1979): 1.

2. Note, "Implementation Problems in Institutional Reform Litigation," *Harvard Law Review* 91 (1977): 428, 463.

3. Eugene V. Rostow, "The Democratic Character of Judicial Review," *Harvard Law Review* 66 (1952): 193, 208.

4. Alexander M. Bickel, *The Least Dangerous Branch: The Supreme Court at the Bar of Politics*, 2d ed. (New Haven: Yale University Press, 1962, 1986), 26.

5. Aryeh Neier, *Only Judgment: The Limits of Litigation in Social Change* (Middletown, Conn.: Wesleyan University Press, 1982), 9.

6. Alexander Hamilton, *The Federalist, No. 78*, ed. Jacob Cooke (Middletown, Conn.: Wesleyan University Press, 1961).

7. For an in-depth exploration of the inability of courts to further equality by producing significant social reform, see Gerald N. Rosenberg, *The Hollow Hope: Can Courts Bring About Social Change?* (Chicago: University of Chicago Press, 1991).

8. Walter F. Murphy, *Congress and the Court* (Chicago: University of Chicago Press, 1962), 30 (discussing *Dred Scott v. Sandford*, 60 U.S. 393 [1856]).

9. Quoted in ibid., 31.

10. Ibid.

11. Neier, *Only Judgment*, 239.

12. Gregory A. Caldeira, "Courts and Public Opinion," in *The American Courts: A Critical Assessment*, ed. John B. Gates and Charles A. Johnson (Washington, D.C.: Congressional Quarterly Press, 1990), 327 n.1. Caldeira bases this conclusion on Gallup poll surveys.

13. David Adamany, "Law and Society: Legitimacy, Realigning Elections, and the Supreme Court," *Wisconsin Law Review* (1973): 791, 807.

14. Walter F. Murphy and Joseph Tanenhaus, "Public Opinion and the Supreme Court: A Preliminary Mapping of Some Prerequisites for Court Legitimation of Regime Change," *Law and Society Review* 2 (1968): 357.

15. Charles H. Franklin and Liane C. Kosaki, "Media, Knowledge, and Public Evaluations of the Supreme Court," in *Contemplating Courts*, ed. Lee Epstein (Washington, D.C.: Congressional Quarterly Press, 1995), 356–57.

16. Ibid., 370.

17. 347 U.S. 483 (1954).

18. Ibid. at 495.

19. Neier, *Only Judgment*, 241–42.

20. Southern Regional Council, *Race in the News* (Atlanta: Southern Regional Council, n.d.), 2.

21. Quoted in Reed Sarratt, *The Ordeal of Desegregation* (New York: Harper & Row, 1966), 263.

22. Pat Watters and Reese Cleghorn, *Climbing Jacob's Ladder* (New York: Harcourt, Brace and World, 1967), 73 n.10.

23. "The Press—Dilemma in Dixie," *Time*, 20 February 1956, 76.

24. The enormous increases in 1956 and 1957 are most persuasively explained not by the Court's action but rather by the Montgomery bus boycott, the violence in Clinton, Tennessee, and the presidential election campaign in 1956, as well as the Little Rock crisis in 1957.

25. Loren Miller, "Very Deliberate Speed," in *The Segregation Era 1863–1954*, ed. Allen Weinstein and Frank Otto Gatell (New York: Oxford University Press, 1970), 281.

26. Neier, *Only Judgment*, 239.

27. American Institute of Public Opinion poll, in Hazel Gaudet Erskine, "The Polls: Race Relations," *Public Opinion Quarterly* 26 (1962): 140, 141.

28. Herbert H. Hyman and Paul B. Sheatsley, "Attitudes toward Desegregation," *Scientific American* (December 1956): 39.

29. Herbert H. Hyman and Paul B. Sheatsley, "Attitudes toward Desegregation," *Scientific American* (July 1964): 23.

30. Ibid., 17.

31. Henry M. Levin, "Education and Earnings of Blacks and the *Brown* Decision," in *Have We Overcome? Race Relations Since* Brown, ed. Michael V. Namorato (Jackson: University of Mississippi Press, 1979), 110.

32. Hyman and Sheatsley, "Attitudes toward Desegregation" (December 1956): 39.

33. George H. Gallup, *The Gallup Poll: Public Opinion 1935–1971*, 3 vols. (New York: Random House, 1972), 3:1825.

34. Ibid., 2: 1548.

35. Quoted in Adam Fairclough, *To Redeem the Soul of America: The Southern Christian Leadership Conference and Martin Luther King, Jr.* (Athens: University of Georgia Press, 1987), 135.

36. Harvie J. Wilkinson III, *From Brown to Alexander: The Supreme Court and School Integration, 1954–1978* (New York: Oxford University Press, 1979), 5.

37. Glen Robinson, "Man in No Man's Land," in *With All Deliberate Speed*, ed. Don Shoemaker (New York: Harper and Brothers, 1957), 183.

38. Quoted in Elizabeth Sutherland, ed., *Letters from Mississippi* (New York: McGraw-Hill, 1965), 93.

39. Gallup, *The Gallup Poll*, 2: 1402.

40. Ibid.

41. Taylor Branch, *Parting the Waters: America in the King Years, 1954–1963* (New York: Simon & Schuster, 1988), 112.

42. Juan Williams, *Eyes on the Prize: America's Civil Rights Years, 1954–1965* (New York: Viking, 1987), 351.

43. Ralph David Abernathy, *And the Walls Came Tumbling Down* (New York: Harper & Row, 1989), 114.

44. Bill Weaver and Oscar C. Page, "The Black Press and the Drive for Integrated Graduate and Professional Schools," *Phylon* 43 (1982): 15, 21, 27.

45. James Smallwood, "Texas," in *The Black Press and the South, 1865–1979*, ed. Henry Lewis Suggs (Westport, Conn.: Greenwood Press, 1983).

46. Ibid.

47. 438 U.S. 265 (1978).

48. 443 U.S. 193 (1978).

49. 448 U.S. 448 (1980).

50. 410 U.S. 113 (1973).

51. This discussion is based on Rosenberg, *Hollow Hope*, especially ch. 8.

52. Karen O'Connor, *Women's Organizations Use of the Courts* (Lexington: Heath, 1980), 120.

53. Judith Blake, "The Supreme Court's Abortion Decisions and Public Opinion in the United States," *Population and Development Review* 3 (1977): 45, 57–59.

54. "Americans Evaluate the Court System," *Public Opinion* 5 (August/September 1982): 25.

55. Rebecca Stone and Cynthia Waszak, "Adolescent Knowledge and Attitudes about Abortion," *Family Planning Perspectives* 24 (1992): 52, 55.

56. Blake, "The Supreme Court's Abortion Decisions," 57.

57. 492 U.S. 490 (1989).

58. Louis Harris and Associates, "The 1972 Virginia Slims American Women's Poll" (n.p., n.d.), 1.

59. Connie De Boer, "The Polls: Women at Work," *Public Opinion Quarterly* 41 (1977): 268–69; Harris, "1972 Virginia Slims American Women's Poll," 2.

60. Karen Oppenheimer Mason, John L. Czajka, and Sara Arber, "Change in U.S. Women's Sex-Role Attitudes, 1964–1974," *American Sociological Review* 41 (1976): 573, 587.

61. Maren Lockwood Carden, *The New Feminist Movement* (New York: Sage, 1974), xiii n.11. The survey, done by the American Council on Education, also found that only about a quarter of women entering college held the notion.

62. Cited in Barbara S. Deckard, *The Women's Movement*, 3d ed. (New York: Harper and Row, 1983), 319.

63. Gallup, *The Gallup Poll*, 1: 39.

64. Hazel Gaudet Erskine, "The Polls: Women's Role," *Public Opinion Quarterly* 35 (1971): 275, 285.

65. Nancy E. McGlen and Karen O'Connor, *Women's Rights* (New York: Praeger, 1983), 217.

66. Mason, Czajka, and Arber, "Change in U.S. Women's Sex Role Attitudes," 594.

67. Although the Supreme Court's 1996 decision in *Romer v. Evans* removed a recently enacted obstacle to homosexuals' political participation, it did no more than return to the status quo. Unlike its actions in the other areas I have considered in this chapter, the Court did not create a new equality right.

68. 478 U.S. 186 (1986).

69. George H. Gallup, *The Gallup Poll: Public Opinion, 1972–1977*, 2 vols. (Wilmington: Del.: Scholarly Resources, Inc., 1978); *The Gallup Report*, No. 244–245 (January–February 1986): 3; *The Gallup Report*, No. 289 (October 1989): 13; *The Gallup Report*, No. 321 (June 1992): 2.

12

Can Courts Make a Difference?

ERWIN CHEMERINSKY

The 1990s are a time of skepticism about the ability of government to solve serious social problems. The Republican victory at the polls in the 1994 congressional elections is explained, in part, by frustration with government and its efforts at social improvement. Therefore, it is not surprising that doubts are being expressed about the ability of courts to make a difference. Nor is it surprising that academics, those most familiar with the judicial process and its impact, are raising the issue.

Prominent academics such as political scientist Gerald Rosenberg[1] and Professor Cass Sunstein,[2] as well as Supreme Court Justice Ruth Bader Ginsburg,[3] have strongly challenged the ability of constitutional litigation to achieve social change. Some of the chapters in this collection echo this viewpoint. Rosenberg, who has argued elsewhere that litigation "seldom bring[s] reform any closer,"[4] argues here that courts are inherently limited in their ability to influence popular opinion.[5] Political scientist Jeremy Rabkin goes even further and contends that courts are obstructing necessary social change.[6] He suggests, for instance, that Supreme Court decisions limiting aid to parochial schools undermine effective inner-city education and that criminal procedure protections prevent effective neighborhood policing.[7]

There is, of course, a tension between these positions. Scholars such as Rosenberg argue that courts make little difference; scholars such as Rabkin believe that courts make a difference but that it is a negative one. Put together, the conclusion is frightening and profound: courts can have little positive effect but can do serious damage.

The conclusion has potentially significant implications. At the very least, the conclusion means that liberals have no reason to be upset at their recent losses in the Supreme Court because victories would have meant little. More generally, such scholarship suggests that groups seeking social change should not invest their resources in the courts and litigation but should look elsewhere for reform.[8] It also encourages great judicial restraint by judges.

I strongly disagree with the conclusions of these scholars. I believe that courts can make a difference and change the law and that reforming the law can alter society. In part, the problem with such scholarship is that it fails to clearly and consistently articulate criteria for evaluating whether court decisions are successful. Also, the scholarship generalizes from a few areas to broad conclusions about the role of courts. It is a logical fallacy to say that because in some areas the judiciary has had limited impact, the courts usually fail to make much difference. Moreover, the failure in specific areas might be a result of the limitations of particular decisions and not an indication of the inherent limits of the judicial process.

My goal here, however, is not to fully explore the ability of courts to affect social change. Rather, I want to explore how the impact of courts might be assessed. How can scholars systematically assess the effects of judicial decisions? The conclusion that emerges is a relatively narrow one: courts can sometimes make an enormous difference. Analysis must be contextual, not categorical; in some circumstances, courts can have profound effects, but in other circumstances, court decisions will have little effect. It is worth considering what variables determine the effectiveness of judicial actions.

The first section of this chapter explores how the effectiveness or ineffectiveness of courts might be evaluated. The second section responds to the claim that the judiciary ultimately undermines effective social reforms.

How Can the Work of Courts Be Appraised?

Analyzing the Question

The analytical enterprise must begin by clarifying the question. Gerald Rosenberg's *Hollow Hope*, in its subtitle, asks, ''Can courts bring about social change?'' Several things about the question need to be noted. First, it focuses just on courts. The question could be asked even more broadly whether laws can bring about social change. For example, Professor Rabkin laments that despite all of the court decisions concerning equal protection, economic conditions for blacks are relatively unchanged.[9] Over the past thirty-five years, major civil rights statutes have been adopted. The failure to improve economic circumstances for African Americans obviously reflects inadequacies not just of the courts but also, and perhaps even more significantly, of legislatures.[10]

The point is to ask whether it makes sense to evaluate the ability of courts to make a difference apart from the general ability of the law to make a difference. Scholars and policymakers who assert that it is better to direct efforts at social reform at legislatures rather than at courts incorrectly assume that legislatures would be successful in areas in which they perceive court failure.

Second, to ask whether courts can bring about social change is to assume that it is possible to measure causation. Causation obviously is often enormously complex. Change is often a long-term process. The more profound the social change, the longer it is likely to take and the more variables that are likely to be involved. Great care needs to be taken in articulating how causation and change will be observed and measured. If changes are noted, how can we determine whether they result from the courts, from other legal changes, or from other social phenomenan?

Third, the question assumes that litigation and decisions are to be evaluated in terms of the social change that results. At the very least, this evaluation requires deciding what social changes are relevant as a measure of success. Professor Rabkin argues that antidiscrimination laws have not succeeded because of the continuing wealth disparities based on race. The assumption is that the success of these laws in terms of social change is to be measured by the gap between the income of whites and that of blacks. But why assume that income is the only measure of success? Antidiscrimination laws surely succeed if they mean less discrimination and more jobs being available for minorities, even if the black-white wealth gap continues.

Also, for many reasons, focusing on whether court decisions cause social change is an incomplete inquiry. Even if court decisions brought about no social change, they still might serve enormously important ends. Perhaps, most important, court decisions can provide redress to injured individuals. Even if laws forbidding employment discrimination are shown to have had little net effect in eradicating workplace inequalities, the statutes still serve a crucial purpose if they provide compensation to the victims of discrimination. Similarly, even if tort law does not succeed in deterring dangerous products and practices, it can be successful in compensating innocent victims.

Moreover, the redress might be noneconomic. Court decisions can provide vindication to those who have suffered from unconstitutional or illegal practices. *Brown v. Board of Education* was an enormously important statement of equality even if little school desegregation resulted. Richard Kluger eloquently described this impact of *Brown*:

> Every colored American knew that *Brown* did not mean that he would be invited to lunch with the Rotary the following week. It meant something more basic and more important. It meant that black rights had suddenly been redefined; black bodies had been reborn under a new law. Blacks' value as human beings had been changed overnight by declaration of the nation's highest court. At a stroke, the Justices had severed the remaining cords of *de facto* slavery. The Negro could no longer be fastened with the status of official pariah. No longer could the white man look right through him as if he were, in the title words of Ralph Ellison's stunning 1952 novel, *Invisible Man*. No more would he be a grinning supplicant for the benefactions of the master class; no more would he be a party to his own degradation. He was both thrilled that the signal for demise of his caste status had come from on high and angry that it had taken so long and first exacted so steep a price in suffering.[11]

Finally, and most important, court decisions upholding the Constitution can protect key values and thus have great social importance, even if no social change can be linked to the rulings. For instance, court decisions safeguarding freedom of speech protect the rights of individuals to express themselves and lead to a better-informed citizenry, even if no better policies can be linked to the decisions. Allowing the Pentagon Papers to be published did not bring about social change, but it was a crucial vindication for an important constitutional value.[12] Stopping governmental aid to parochial schools does not change society, but it enforces the establishment clause and the separation of church and state.

The point is that the question posed by Professor Rosenberg assumes that courts should be evaluated in terms of their success in bringing about social change. Evaluating the success and importance of courts requires a much broader inquiry than just their ability to effect social change.

Furthermore, it is important to note that courts can play a hugely important role in preventing social change. During the first third of this century, a conservative Supreme Court invalidated progressive legislation protecting workers and consumers, such as laws prohibiting child labor and requiring a minimum wage.[13] Is there any doubt that these decisions prevented significant social change? Likewise, in the current era, Supreme Court decisions invalidating voluntary affirmative action programs and efforts prevent a form of social change.[14] In fact, Professor Rabkin's essay suggests that current constitutional doctrines are now frustrating necessary social change in many areas.[15]

If the impact of courts is to be assessed, the evaluation must account for how courts facilitate and how they impede social change. And it is essential to separate the descriptive and the normative questions. Whether the Supreme Court's decisions limit affirmative action is descriptive; whether that is good or bad is a distinct issue requiring separate consideration.

False Starts

None of the above is meant to imply, however, that it is irrelevant to consider whether courts can bring about social change. Certainly, litigation is often initiated for that purpose, and courts sometimes act with that as a goal. The question then becomes how "social change" is to be defined and measured.

Two measures that often are used seem particularly unhelpful. One is whether courts bring about changes in popular attitudes. For instance, Professor Rosenberg's chapter in this book focuses on whether the Supreme Court's decisions influence popular beliefs about equality. Indeed, assuming that this is a crucial factor in assessing the institutional significance of the Supreme Court, he titles his chapter "The Irrelevant Court: The Supreme Court's Inability to Influence Popular Beliefs about Equality (or Anything Else)." The title suggests that if the Court does not influence popular beliefs, the Court is irrelevant.

This notion seems clearly wrong. If the Court successfully changes the law and if the reform alters society, it should make little difference whether popular beliefs are affected. It is not at all clear why court decisions should be appraised in terms of their effect on public opinion.

Perhaps the argument is that social change is impossible without changing social attitudes. But this is a claim that needs to be supported and not simply asserted. Although sometimes court reform is unlikely to succeed without changes in popular beliefs, there is no reason to believe that it is always the case. Consider the impact of the Court's decisions invalidating Jim Crow laws—the statutes in the South that mandated segregation of restaurants, hotels, parks, and almost everything else. The decisions, by any measure, were successful in desegregating public facilities. Ultimately, the "whites only" signs were taken off restrooms and water fountains and parks and beaches. If this occurred without a change in attitudes, it still was valuable and important. Perhaps, too, it caused a change in attitudes over time. Either way, there was an effect, and few would deny that it was positive.

Public opinion seems an especially inappropriate criterion to use in evaluating the judiciary. Federal judges are not elected and do not face review at the polls. Their insulation from the political process is based on the hope that it will enhance the enforcement of the Constitution. The Constitution is an inherently antimajoritarian document; it limits the ability of contemporary social majorities to act. Therefore, it is inappropriate to evaluate a politically insulated judiciary that is charged with enforcing an antimajoritarian instrument based on how much it pleases and persuades the public.

Also, evaluating the Court based on public opinion seems inherently problematic. Changes in social attitudes likely occur over a long period. Measurement is difficult and depends on the instrument.[16] Also, public opinion—whether measured by opinion polls, press coverage, or textbook content—is a product of countless factors. Methodologically, will it ever be possible to assess the role of the courts in this mix?

A second false start in evaluating courts focuses on whether social changes would have occurred anyway even without judicial decisions. In other words, the analyst concedes that social change happened and that it followed a Supreme Court decision but then argues that the reform would have occurred even without the Court's ruling. For example, Justice Ginsburg attacked *Roe v. Wade* for short-circuiting pro-choice initiatives in several state legislatures.[17]

The difficulty with such arguments is that they are projections of a world that never existed. There certainly are possible scenarios in which legislatures might have done what courts accomplished. Although it is conceivable that state legislatures would have loosened restrictions on access to abortion if *Roe* had not invalidated such laws, it also is conceivable that as pro-choice forces gained political strength, antiabortion groups would have mobilized, just as they did after *Roe*. All sorts of scenarios can be imagined supported by analysis of trends. It is questionable what is gained by the exercise or how much it can ever demonstrate that court action is unnecessary.

Also, a key problem with such projections is that they often fail to account for time or geography. *Roe v. Wade* made abortion legal in 1973 for the entire country. How long would it have been before abortion was legal everywhere in the nation without this decision?

The point is that little is to be gained by guessing how the political process might have come to the same result without judicial action. There never is any way to know.

Courts and Legal Change

In evaluating the ability of the judiciary to change society, two interrelated questions must be addressed. One is whether the Supreme Court's constitutional decisions succeed in changing the government's conduct.[18] The other is whether changing the government's actions makes a difference in society. Although generally these questions are merged, analytically they are distinct. Sometimes the complaint of scholars such as Professor Rosenberg is that Supreme Court decisions are not implemented by governmental officials or are circumvented by them. Sometimes the argument is that other social forces undermine any effect of the decisions.

Consider the example of reapportionment. In *Reynolds v. Sims*, the Supreme Court articulated the rule of one person, one vote.[19] All election districts for any elected body must be approximately equal in population size. This was a dramatic change in the law. The first question is whether this Court decision changed government. The answer is unequivocally "yes"; reapportionment of state legislatures occurred throughout the country. The second question, then, is whether changing the composition of legislatures made a difference in society. This is a much harder question because causation is so difficult to know and measure.[20] Can particular laws be traced to the reapportioned legislatures, and which laws should be regarded as significant enough to be deemed "social change"?

Assessing the ability of Court decisions to bring about change thus requires analysis of when the judiciary is likely to be successful in altering governmental conduct and also analysis of when that is likely to make a difference in society.

WHEN CAN COURTS CHANGE GOVERNMENTAL ACTIONS?

In evaluating the ability of Court decisions to change governmental conduct, several different types of situations exist. First, there are those instances when a court's decision is essentially self-executing; no further action of any governmental official or even of the courts is necessary. The most obvious example is when a court refuses to issue a ruling. For instance, in the Pentagon Papers case, the Supreme Court refused to enjoin the publication of a study of U.S. involvement in the Vietnam War.[21] No further action of any governmental official was necessary, and yet governmental policy was changed.

Second, there are those instances when a court's decision can be fully enforced by the judiciary through its power to dismiss future cases. For example, if the Supreme Court declares unconstitutional a criminal statute, the judiciary can enforce that decision simply by dismissing any future prosecutions brought under the law. The Court, by definition, has changed governance by altering the law and by ending a set of criminal prosecutions. A simple illustration is the Supreme Court's 1995 decision in *United States v. Lopez* invalidating the federal law that made it a crime to have a firearm within 1,000 feet of a school.[22] No longer will the federal government use that statute. If the government tried, the case would be dismissed by the courts.

The Supreme Court's decisions invalidating laws prohibiting the use of contraceptives[23] and forbidding abortion[24] could be enforced by the judiciary. The courts simply could dismiss any future prosecutions brought under these laws.

Third, some Supreme Court decisions upholding the constitutionality of laws or governmental practices encourage governmental action. For instance, a Supreme Court decision upholding a local ordinance might encourage other cities to adopt similar laws. In that way, the Court's ruling will change government. If the Court had upheld the affirmative action program in Richmond, Virginia, the Court might have encouraged other cities to adopt similar set-aside programs.[25] If the Supreme Court had upheld Colorado's Amendment 2, which forbade state or local legal protections for gays and lesbians, other cities and states might have adopted similar laws.[26] I would regard this as a terrible change in government, but it undoubtedly would be a change as a result of the Court's decision.

Fourth, there are Court decisions that require compliance by others in government but that the judiciary can enforce through its contempt power, typified by the classic negative injunction. The court issues an injunction, and violations are punished by contempt. Usually, the threat of contempt is sufficient to gain compliance by the government. If an employer is sued for using a racially discriminatory test in hiring, the court, upon finding a violation of the law, can enjoin future use of the test. If the employer is recalcitrant and continues to use the test, the court can hold the employer in contempt of court.

Fifth, Court decisions enforced through the award of money damages are likely to change governmental conduct. An obvious example is the law of the takings clause. If the Supreme Court were to hold that a taking occurs whenever a governmental regulation decreases the value of a person's property, the judiciary could enforce this ruling by awarding money damages in the future. There is no doubt that such a holding would profoundly alter government because it would have to pay compensation for a wide array of laws, from zoning statutes to environmental regulations.

More generally, damages can deter wrongful governmental conduct. Section 1983 litigation has as part of its purpose to deter government from violating constitutional rights. For instance, the possibility of money damages for sexual harassment provides strong encouragement for governmental employers to refrain from such behavior.

Sixth, some Court decisions require substantial actions by government in compliance and implementation and, therefore, continuing judicial monitoring and enforcement. The most obvious example is the school desegregation litigation. Changing governmental laws that segregated parks or water fountains simply required taking down the "whites only" sign. If the government failed to do this, contempt could be imposed. But desegregating schools was a far more daunting challenge because it required affirmative steps ranging from changing pupil assignments to redrawing attendance zones to busing.

The above six categories are not exhaustive, but they are instructive of the many ways in which courts can change government. In some of the categories, there is a very high likelihood that judicial action will succeed in altering governmental conduct. Denying the government an injunction or invalidating a criminal statute virtually always will succeed in changing governmental behavior. In some of the categories, governmental compliance is less certain. When the Court awards money damages against the government, particularly against the federal government, there is relatively little that the judiciary can do except hope for voluntary compliance. When the Court issues an affirmative injunction, such as for school desegregation, compliance might be a more lengthy and uncertain process.

Those who criticize the impact of Court decisions tend to pick their examples from the most problematic categories. Recognizing the range of situations in which the judiciary can change government helps in properly assessing the ability of courts to make a difference.

WHEN DOES CHANGING GOVERNMENT ACTIONS CHANGE SOCIETY?: LESSONS FROM SCHOOL DESEGREGATION

A distinct, although certainly related, question concerns whether changing governmental conduct really has any effect on society. This inquiry is much more difficult to assess because there are not clear criteria for assessing or measuring social change. "Social change" connotes an overall noticeable effect on society. Yet, few Court decisions possibly could have such an effect. For example, Supreme Court decisions concerning prisoners' rights might be enormously important for those imprisoned, but they are unlikely to cause "social change." Likewise, Court decisions preventing discrimination against nonmarital children might be very significant in the lives of those individuals, but the rulings cannot be assessed in terms of social change.[27]

Therefore, care has to be taken in assessing which cases should be evaluated in terms of their ability to achieve social change. Assuming that such cases are properly identified, then care must be taken to construct a meaningful measure of social change to use in evaluating the impact of the decisions.

There also is another pitfall in this analysis: seeing the ineffectiveness of a particular decision or judicial strategy as proving an inherent weakness of the courts. It certainly is possible to try to assess whether a specific decision or set of rulings brought about certain results. A conclusion that the decisions failed may reflect a general weakness of courts or it may reveal only a misguided approach in those cases.

Those who argue that judicial action can have little impact on society especially point to school desegregation and the legacy of *Brown v. Board of Education*.[28] For instance, Alexander Bickel characterized court-ordered busing as sheer folly, arguing that "no policy that a court can order, and a school board, a city or even a state has the capacity to put into effect, will in fact result in the foreseeable future in racially balanced schools. Only a reordering of the environment . . . might have an appreciable impact."[29]

Yet the story of school desegregation and whether it succeeded is a complicated one and not one that lends itself to a yes or no answer. Some school desegregation was achieved, although much of the promise of *Brown* remains unfulfilled. Some of the failure may have been inherent to judicial actions, but a great deal of it may be because the Court did not implement the proper remedies. Examining the topic of school desegregation is instructive in evaluating claims about the inherent limits of courts in bringing about social change.

It certainly is true that in the years immediately following *Brown*, little desegregation was achieved. In the South, just 1.2 percent of black schoolchildren were attending school with whites a decade after *Brown*.[30] In South Carolina, Alabama, and Mississippi, not one black child attended a public school with a white child in the 1962–63 school year.[31] In North Carolina, only 0.026 percent of black students attended desegregated schools in 1961, and the figure did not rise above 1 percent until 1965.[32] Similarly, in Virginia, in 1964, only 1.63 percent of blacks were attending desegregated schools.[33]

Yet the persistent efforts at desegregation ultimately had an impact. One by one the obstructionist techniques were defeated. Finally, by the mid-1960s, desegregation began to proceed. By 1968, the integration rate in the South rose to 32 percent, and by 1972–73, 91.3 percent of southern schools were desegregated.[34] To point to one example of success, the federal court's desegregation order in Oklahoma City effectively eliminated one-race schools and meant that few blacks or whites were attending schools that were more than 90 percent of one race. Indeed, it was demonstrated that eliminating the court's desegregation order would cause the resegregation of the Oklahoma City schools.[35]

Yet there is no doubt that despite forty years of judicial action, school segregation continues. Indeed, racial segregation in American schools has been increasing over the past decade. A study by the National School Boards Association found "a pattern in which impressive progress toward school integration among blacks and whites in the 1970s petered out in the 1980s."[36] The report predicted that in the 1990s, "large-scale resegregation could be the order of the day in much of the country."[37]

In virtually every area of the country, racial separation in schooling is increasing. In the Northeast, for example, half of the black students in the region attend schools with fewer than 10 percent whites, and a third go to schools that are 99 percent or more minority.[38] At the opposite end of the country, in Los Angeles, the percentage of white students in the public schools has fallen from 40 to 13 percent since the mid-1970s.[39] In Philadelphia, the percentage of white students has dropped from 32 to 23 percent.[40] In St. Paul, Minnesota, the percentage of white students in public schools has gone from 85 to 55 percent.[41]

In 1980, 63 percent of black students and 66 percent of Hispanics were in segregated schools, that is, schools with more than half minority enrollment.[42] Today, nationally, two-thirds of all black children attend schools that are more than 50 percent black.[43] The reality is that most children in the United States are educated with only children of their race, and the separation is increasing.

The key question is why. It is easy to say that the judiciary failed to achieve school desegregation, but is that because courts inherently were impotent in this area or is it because the Supreme Court failed to craft needed remedies? I strongly believe the latter.[44] Two Supreme Court decisions dramatically limited the ability of the judiciary to formulate effective remedies for segregated schools.

First, in *Milliken v. Bradley*, the Court, by a 5–4 margin, dramatically limited the ability of courts to impose interdistrict remedies in school desegregation cases.[45] In *Milliken*, the federal district court ordered fifty-three suburban school districts to participate in the desegregation of the Detroit public schools.[46] On appeal, the Sixth Circuit recognized that "any less comprehensive a solution than a metropolitan plan would result in an all-black system immediately surrounded by practically all-white suburban school systems."[47] The court of appeals held that since "school district lines are simply matters of political convenience . . . they may not be used to deny constitutional rights."[48]

The Supreme Court reversed the imposition of a metropolitan-wide remedy. The Court reasoned that suburban school districts could not be included in the deseg-regation plan absent proof that they committed a constitutional violation. The Court, in an opinion by Chief Justice Warren E. Burger, held that the metropolitan-wide remedy violated the equitable principle that "the scope of the remedy is determined by the nature and the extent of the constitutional violation."[49] The Court declared that "[t]o approve the remedy ordered would . . . impose on the outlying districts, not shown to have committed any constitutional violation, a wholly impermissible remedy."[50]

Although the Court did not completely rule out the possibility of a judicially created metropolitan relief in all cases, the Court made it clear that such a remedy was to be allowed only in extraordinary circumstances in which there was proof of interdistrict violations. The reality, however, is that effective desegregation often requires an interdistrict remedy. The sad fact of American metropolitan areas is that cities are predominately black and that surrounding suburban areas are pre-dominately white. Desegregation obviously requires the ability to combine these students in integrated schools. *Milliken* generally precludes this.

If *Milliken* had been decided differently—not a fanciful possibility since it was a 5–4 decision—there could be much more desegregation of American public ed-ucation. Therefore, the dismal statistics about current segregation are less an in-dication of the inherent failure of the judiciary and more a reflection of the Court's choices.

The second decision that limited effective desegregation, especially in northern cities, was *Keyes v. Denver*.[51] There the Court held that proof of segregation was not sufficient to establish a constitutional violation; rather, there must be proof that segregation resulted from intentionally discriminatory policies.

Segregation is often the product of a multitude of factors. Establishing govern-mental culpability often is difficult, if not impossible. If *Keyes* had been decided differently, then courts could have fashioned desegregation remedies if there was proof of a discriminatory impact. Requiring a showing of discriminatory intent dramatically limited the ability of the federal courts to order desegregation of de facto segregated northern city school systems.

The point is that great care has to be taken in assessing why a judicial policy failed. Scholars such as Professor Rosenberg see the failure to achieve social change as reflecting inherent limitations of courts. But equally or more plausible is the possibility that the Court might have been more successful if it had made different choices. In the area of school desegregation, the reality is that the Burger Court, dominated by four justices appointed by President Richard Nixon, made crucial decisions limiting remedies. It certainly is plausible to imagine different decisions and different results if only the Warren Court had continued for a few more years.

In conclusion, the ability of courts to bring about social change is undoubtedly a product of many factors. What is the nature of public opinion on the subject? *Roe v. Wade* was not overruled by constitutional amendment, and abortion remains legal, in part, because most people favor legalized abortions. To what extent can the Court implement its rulings regardless of public opinion? Redistricting as a result of reapportionment could be mandated and enforced by the courts on their own if necessary. To what extent can governmental officials circumvent Court decisions? School prayers were largely eliminated by the Supreme Court, but they probably continued to exist in some places because teachers ignored the decisions and no parents complained. To what extent can people circumvent or undermine Court rulings? Desegregation was frustrated, in part, by white flight to private schools and to suburban areas.

These are just some of the factors that influence whether Court decisions will have social impact. My ultimate conclusion is that analysis must always be contextual. In some areas, courts can dramatically change government and society. In other areas, courts are likely to have very limited success. Categorical statements about the ability, or lack of ability, of courts to bring about social change are misguided because so much depends on the particular area of law and the social circumstances surrounding the decisions.

Do Court Decisions Preclude Needed Social Change?

The new wave of court bashing goes further than just arguing that the judiciary is largely useless in bringing about social reforms. Scholars such as Professor Rabkin argue that the courts are preventing needed and desirable social changes.[52] Professor Rabkin contends, for example, that parochial schools "tend to do a much better job in imparting the discipline and self-respect needed for orderly learning" but laments that the Supreme Court's decisions prevent governmental subsidies of parochial education, "which might make it more widely available."[53] Similarly, he suggests that criminal procedure protections and procedural due process rights limit the ability of the government to combat drug abuse.[54]

It is tempting to debate each of these examples with Professor Rabkin, but he simply mentions them in passing, and a detailed discussion is beyond the scope of his or my chapter. The issue here is how to evaluate claims, by those such as Professor Rabkin, that courts are obstructing desirable reforms. Although I disagree with each of Professor Rabkin's examples, I certainly agree that courts have the capacity to frustrate needed social changes.

Therefore, I suggest that analysis focus on three questions in assessing whether Court decisions are, in fact, preventing desirable reforms by government. First, would a particular policy, on balance, be desirable? In other words, before ever considering the institutional question about the judicial role, the policy must be evaluated on its own merits. As an example, Professor Rabkin suggests that governmental subsidies of parochial schools would be desirable. Before criticizing the courts for preventing these subsidies, there needs to be consideration of whether they really would be desirable. I certainly think not. They would divert resources from the public schools. They would probably intensify segregation. Most of all, they would mean substantial governmental subsidies for religious institutions, which would breach the wall that should separate church and state. In a debate over the issue, each of these points would need to be developed. The point here is simply that criticizing the courts for preventing subsidies assumes their desirability.

Second, if it is established that the Court is preventing needed social change, the next question must be why. Is it that the Court has weighed the competing policies and simply has made the wrong choice? For example, the current Court is dramatically limiting governmental affirmative action efforts because of its value choices about race and equal protection. In the first third of this century, the Court prevented needed legislation to protect workers and consumers because of its commitment to a laissez-faire economy. The criticism of the Court, therefore, must focus on its value choices.

There are other reasons why the Court might frustrate needed social reforms. Is it that the Court is not sufficiently aware of the problem or the needed solution? Even the most basic constitutional rights are not absolute, and the government can prevail if it meets strict scrutiny, proving that a particular law is necessary to achieve a compelling interest. It may be that the Court does not recognize the importance of the interest or the need for the particular means. Is it that the Court is following outdated precedents?

The third and final question is whether it is possible that the Court will change its approach or whether there are ways to achieve the result regardless of the judiciary's approach. Sometimes the Court will shift course because of apparent social needs or changes in its membership. The dramatic shift in constitutional jurisprudence in the late 1930s probably reflected both the recognition of a need to defer to governmental economic regulations and ultimately the ability of President Franklin D. Roosevelt to change the composition of the Court. Sometimes there are ways of circumventing Court decisions and achieving change despite the judicial impediments.

Court decisions can bring about changes, and those changes might be good or bad. Court decisions can frustrate changes, and those changes, too, might be good or bad. There is no inherent reason why courts, or any other institution, are more likely to succeed or fail. Therefore, discussion about whether courts are preventing needed social change must also be contextual and focus on particular areas of law. Generalizations are worthless.

Conclusion

I have primarily discussed the writings of Professors Rosenberg and Rabkin because they have written chapters in this volume. My goal has not been to write a detailed reply to their chapters but, instead, to regard their writing as representative of a current wave of scholarship that questions whether courts can do good for society.

I must confess that I always have been perplexed by the point of this scholarship. Do any scholars really believe that *Brown v. Board of Education* was a mistake and that the Court should have affirmed the policy of separate but equal?

If the scholarship is making the limited point that courts sometimes fail in their efforts, I agree. It is certainly worthwhile to assess the performance of courts and try to figure out when they are most likely to succeed.

But my sense is that scholarship of this sort often seems to be making a more sweeping point about the role of courts and the futility of litigation. It is here that I strongly disagree. There are times when only courts are likely to succeed, and there are times when only legislative action is likely to be effective. There are times when the actions of both together are essential and times when neither, alone or together, can make a difference. My hope is that the writings of scholars like Professors Rosenberg and Rabkin will be understood as an invitation for such contextual analysis and not as the basis for categorical statements about the role or ability of the courts.

NOTES

I am grateful to Melanie Petross and Cheryl Watkins for their research assistance.

1. Gerald N. Rosenberg, *The Hollow Hope: Can Courts Bring About Social Change?* (Chicago: University of Chicago Press, 1991). For an excellent review of this book, see Neal Devins, "Judicial Matters," *California Law Review* 80 (July 1992): 1027.

2. Cass Sunstein, *The Partial Constitution* (Cambridge: Harvard University Press, 1993).

3. Ruth Bader Ginsburg, "Some Thoughts on Autonomy and Equality in Relation to *Roe v. Wade*," North Carolina Law Review 63 (January 1985): 375.

4. Rosenberg, *Hollow Hope*, 343.

5. See Rosenburg, chapter 11, in this volume.

6. Jeremy Rabkin, "Racial Progress and Constitutional Roadblocks," *William and Mary Law Review* 34 (Fall 1992): 75; see also Rabkin, chapter 6, in this volume.

7. Rabkin, "Racial Progress and Constitutional Roadblocks," 81, 85.

8. Rosenberg makes this point expressly in *Hollow Hope*, 342.

9. See chapter 6.

10. See, e.g., Richard Epstein, *Forbidden Grounds: The Case against Employment Discrimination Laws* (Cambridge: Harvard University Press, 1992). I have criticized Epstein's thesis in a debate with him that is published in "Forum: Should Title VII of the Civil Rights Act of 1964 Be Repealed?" *Southern California Interdisciplinary Law Journal* 2 (Fall 1994): 349, 445.

11. Richard Kluger, *Simple Justice* (New York: Knopf, 1975), 749.

12. *New York Times v. United States*, 403 U.S. 713 (1971).

13. See, e.g., *Lochner v. New York*, 198 U.S. 45 (1905) (invalidating a state law limiting hours that bakers could work); *Hammer v. Dagenhart*, 247 U.S. 251 (1918) (invalidating a federal law prohibiting the shipment in interstate commerce of goods made by child labor); *Adkins v. Children's Hospital*, 261 U.S. 525 (1923) (invalidating a state law that required a minimum wage for women).

14. See, e.g., *Miller v. Johnson*, 115 S. Ct. 2475 (1995) (limiting affirmative action in drawing election districts); *City of Richmond v. J. A. Croson Co.*, 488 U.S. 469 (1989) (invalidating a city's set-aside of public works contracts for minority-owned businesses).

15. Rabkin, "Racial Progress and Constitutional Roadblocks," 80–81.

16. Professor Rosenberg, for example, focuses on the number of press stories about civil rights and the content of textbooks. But these factors seem imprecise, at best, in measuring popular beliefs.

17. Ginsburg, "Some Thoughts on Autonomy and Equality in Relation to *Roe v. Wade*."

18. My focus here is on constitutional litigation, and, therefore, because of the state action requirement—prohibiting the filing of constitutional claims against private actors—the de-

fendant usually will be the government. A similar set of questions, of course, can be asked about the ability of the courts to change private conduct when private actors are named as defendants.

19. 377 U.S. 533 (1964).

20. Rosenberg questions whether significant laws were passed as a result of reapportionment in *Hollow Hope*, 296.

21. *New York Times*, 403 U.S. 713.

22. 115 S. Ct. 1624 (1995). The law was invalidated as exceeding the scope of Congress's commerce-clause authority.

23. See, e.g., *Griswold v. Connecticut*, 381 U.S. 479 (1965).

24. *Roe v. Wade*, 410 U.S. 113 (1973).

25. See *City of Richmond*, 488 U.S. 469.

26. *Romer v. Evans*, 116 S. Ct. 1620 (1996).

27. See, e.g., *Jiminez v. Weinberger*, 417 U.S. 628 (1974) (invalidating a section of the Social Security Act that disadvantaged nonmarital children).

28. 347 U.S. 483 (1954).

29. Alexander M. Bickel, *The Supreme Court and the Idea of Progress* (New Haven: Yale University Press, 1978), 132.

30. Michael Klarman, "*Brown*, Racial Change, and the Civil Rights Movement," *Virginia Law Review* 80 (January 1994): 7, 9.

31. Ibid., 9.

32. Ibid.

33. Ibid.

34. Klarman, "*Brown*, Racial Change, and the Civil Rights Movement," 10.

35. See *Board of Education v. Dowell*, 111 S. Ct. 630 (1991) (the Court held that once unitary status has been achieved in a school system, the desegregation order should be lifted, even if it will result in the resegregation of the public schools).

36. Larry Tye, "Social Racial Gaps Found Nationwide," *Boston Globe*, 8 January 1992, 3.

37. Ibid.

38. Larry Tye, "U.S. Sounds Retreat in School Integration," *Boston Globe*, 5 January 1992, 1.

39. Ibid., 45.

40. Ibid.

41. Ibid.

42. "Illinois Schools Most Segregated," *Chicago Sun Times*, 5 September 1982, 6.

43. Tye, "Social Racial Gaps Found Nationwide," 45.

44. I have developed this argument more fully in "Lost Opportunity: The Burger Court and the Failure to Achieve Equal Educational Opportunity," *Mercer Law Review* 45 (Spring 1994): 999.

45. 418 U.S. 717 (1974).

46. *Bradley v. Milliken*, 338 F. Supp. 582 (E.D. Mich. 1971), *aff'd*, 484 F.2d 215 (6th Cir. 1973), *rev'd*, 418 U.S. 717 (1974).

47. *Milliken v. Bradley*, 484 F.2d 215, 245 (6th Cir. 1973), *rev'd*, 418 U.S. 717 (1974).

48. 484 F.2d at 244.

49. 418 U.S. at 744.

50. Ibid. at 745.

51. 413 U.S. 189 (1973).

52. Rabkin, "Racial Progress and Constitutional Roadblocks," 80–82.

53. Ibid., 80.

54. Ibid., 83–84.

13

The Supreme Court's Pursuit of Equality and Liberty and the Burdens of History

DAVID J. GARROW

The Supreme Court's decision in *Brown v. Board of Education*[1] is commonly regarded as the signal event in the modern quest for racial equality. Confronted with widespread racial segregation of schoolchildren by reason of state law, the Court in *Brown* held that such segregation violated the equal protection clause of the Fourteenth Amendment.

The Court's *Brown* decision, however, did far more than simply declare school segregation unconstitutional. The decision also transformed the Court's role in the modern quest for equality. In its unyielding search for the morally correct result in *Brown*, the Court interpreted the Fourteenth Amendment in a manner that demonstrated that the Court would not be tethered by the burdens of history. In effect, the Court determined that the moral imperative of racial desegregation trumped fidelity to the uncertain intentions of the framers of the Fourteenth Amendment.[2] In so doing, the Court, with the *Brown* decision, unleashed a new era in constitutional jurisprudence.

In the wake of *Brown*, the Court issued a number of other decisions dealing with both equality and personal liberty that reflect the Court's willingness to fashion a Fourteenth Amendment jurisprudence that is not tightly moored to that amendment's demonstrable historical intentions.[3] In the process, the Court has helped transform the modern quest for both equality and personal liberty in ways that have served well the pursuit of justice in America.

Many people have grown up believing that while *Marbury v. Madison*[4] is of course *the* formative U.S. Supreme Court decision of all time, that the Supreme Court's decisions of 1937[5]—perhaps in conjunction with Chief Justice Harlan F. Stone's (or Louis Lusky's) famous 1938 footnote in *Carolene Products*[6]—signal the beginning of the judicial modern age.

But that belief, which was inculcated among at least two successive generations of American judicial scholars, is now all but indisputably out-of-date, for *Brown*, rather than the "constitutional revolution" of 1937, not only demarcates our modern era but, just as important, also paved the way for the Warren Court's two other landmark *antihistorical* rulings—*Baker v. Carr*[7] and *Griswold v. Connecticut*[8] (and for their even better-known progeny, *Reynolds v. Sims*[9] and *Roe v. Wade*[10])—which dramatically expanded the constitutional scope of the Fourteenth Amendment. Absent *Brown*, decisions with *Baker*'s and *Reynolds*'s muscularity are difficult to imagine; absent the most important of *Brown*'s own immediate progeny—namely, *Cooper v. Aaron*,[11] the Warren Court's *Marbury*—much of the post-1954 Court's understanding of its own role, which at present has culminated in *Planned Parenthood of Southeastern Pennsylvania v. Casey*,[12] would have evolved in a decidedly different fashion. In short, *Brown I*, in tandem with *Cooper*, not only marks the beginning of modern America's official condemnation of racial discrimination but also marks the beginning of a wide-ranging transformation of modern American life brought about by a host of high Court decisions that have relied on the justices' dramatically expansive—and aggressively antihistorical—reading and application of the Fourteenth Amendment's equal protection and due process clauses. From schooling to electoral districting to abortion, modern America is to a significant degree the product of muscular judicial utilization of the Fourteenth Amendment; it is also the product of constitutional analysis that has jettisoned the constraints of history. From *Brown* to *Baker* and *Reynolds*, and to *Griswold, Roe*, and *Casey*, I believe we can persuasively argue that it is a *better* America precisely because of how the Court *has ignored* the Constitution's historical limitations in fashioning a Fourteenth Amendment jurisprudence that is responsive to the present-day rather than to the institutional burdens of history.[13]

Careful students of *Brown* can, of course, easily recall that the Supreme Court initially hoped—and sought—to find clear Fourteenth Amendment historical support for resolving the fundamental question that *Brown* and its companion cases[14] presented. Following the first oral arguments in the *Brown* cases, the Court formally propounded five questions to the parties' attorneys. The first two questions asked for historical evidence regarding whether the framers of the Fourteenth Amendment intended or did not intend for it either to prohibit or to allow for the future prohibition of racially segregated public schooling. The third question, however, voicing a presumption that the answers to the first two would "not dispose of the issue," posed the core issue bluntly: "[I]s it within the judicial power, in construing the [Fourteenth] Amendment, to abolish segregation in the public schools?"[15] Eleven months later, on 17 May 1954, the Court baldly, but compellingly, declared that indeed it was.

As we now know, the National Association for the Advancement of Colored People (NAACP) Legal Defense and Educational Fund litigators and their many scholarly collaborators were at first deeply (and justifiably) concerned by the Court's preliminary focus on historical queries whose answers would not hasten, and might well hinder, judicial acceptance of the NAACP's basic contention.[16] But by the time of *Brown* et al.'s rearguments in December 1953, the justices themselves privately no longer regarded the answers to those two historical queries as being potentially determinative. Justice Felix Frankfurter had had one of his out-going law clerks, Alexander M. Bickel, prepare an exhaustive historical research memorandum, and Frankfurter had distributed the impressive product to his colleagues. Although counsel at the time were quite unaware that Bickel's handiwork had firmly directed the justices away from any potential history-based solution to their American dilemma, we nowadays—thanks in part to Mark Tushnet's careful analysis—can fully appreciate that by December the historical questions "were no longer that important" to the Court itself.[17]

Even though there was—thanks to Robert Jackson and particularly Stanley Reed—no internal consensus on *how* to decide *Brown* when the justices met for their decisive conference on 12 December 1953, there nonetheless *was* an unspoken consensus that the fundamental question before them was last June's "question three": "[I]s it within the judicial power . . . to abolish segregation in the public schools?"[18] And when Chief Justice Earl Warren delivered the Court's impressively unanimous opinion in *Brown* five months later, there again, and now for the whole country to see, was an explicit consensus that the core of this question, like others yet to come, concerned not evidence or documentation of "historical intent" but, instead, the nature and reach of "the judicial power."

Warren's opinion, in two early paragraphs that understandably are not among *Brown*'s best-remembered passages but that latter-day scholars should not overlook, deftly but decisively dismissed the decisional relevance of the Fourteenth Amendment's own history. Warren noted how *Brown*'s reargument "was largely devoted to the circumstances surrounding" the Fourteenth Amendment's 1868 adoption. "It covered exhaustively consideration of the Amendment in Congress, ratification by the states, then existing practices in racial segregation, and the views of proponents and opponents of the Amendment. This discussion and our own investigation convince us that, although these sources cast some light, it is not enough to resolve the problem with which we are faced. At best, they are inconclusive."[19] "An additional reason for the inconclusive nature of the Amendment's history" vis-à-vis school segregation, Warren added, was the relatively undeveloped state of public education, especially in the South but also in the North, in 1868. "As a consequence, it is not surprising that there should be so little in the history of the Fourteenth Amendment relating to its intended effect on public education."[20]

So ended the *Brown* Court's analysis—and dismissal—of whether its constitutional adjudication of governmentally imposed racial segregation in public schools was or should in any way be bound by the constraints of history. Most readers pass over these two paragraphs without attributing any special import to them, and such an evaluation, within the four actual corners of the *Brown* opinion, is perfectly appropriate. In a more long-range frame of reference, however—one that encompasses particularly the years from 1962 (*Baker*) through 1973 (*Roe*)—the *Brown* Court's affirmative jettisoning of the Fourteenth Amendment's historical tielines marked the onset of a period of judicial freedom and, some correctly would say, judicial *sovereignty* that dramatically transformed American life for the better.[21]

In 1954 itself, nothing highlighted the Court's Farragut-like approach to mandating constitutional rights[22] more than its companion ruling in the fifth of the *Brown* family of cases, *Bolling v. Sharpe* from Washington, D.C. Since the Fourteenth

Amendment applied its equal protection clause only to the states and not to the federal government, the *Brown* Court found itself having to identify some non–Fourteenth Amendment constitutional grounds for avoiding the utterly incongruous paradox of striking down *state*-mandated school segregation while not being able to void identical governmental policy imposed by *federal* authorities. With a doctrinal dexterity that again may be more significant in historical retrospect than it appeared to be in 1954, the Court—lacking any federally applicable equal protection language—unanimously turned to the Fifth Amendment's due process clause. "[T]he concepts of equal protection and due process, both stemming from our American ideal of fairness, are not mutually exclusive," Chief Justice Warren wrote. While " 'equal protection of the laws' is a more explicit safeguard of prohibited unfairness than 'due process of law' . . . discrimination may be so unjustifiable as to be violative of due process."[23]

Without expressly acknowledging that the due process clause's key word was of course "liberty," the *Bolling* opinion, while conceding that the Court to date had not defined " 'liberty' with any great precision," nonetheless went on to emphasize that the concept was "not confined to mere freedom from bodily restraint. Liberty under law extends to the full range of conduct which the individual is free to pursue, and it cannot be restricted except for a proper governmental objective. Segregation in public education is not reasonably related to any proper governmental objective, and thus it imposes on Negro children in the District of Columbia a burden that constitutes an arbitrary deprivation of their liberty in violation of the Due Process Clause."[24] Any commentators inclined to allege that the new era— or "Second Reconstruction"—of substantive due process first began to rear its assertedly ugly head only in *Griswold v. Connecticut*[25] had best be reminded that as early as May 1954, *Bolling*'s quite uncontroversial language signaled that a highly expansive approach to due process–based constitutional liberty could well go forward hand in hand with *Brown*'s heralding of a new era of equal protection.[26]

Even more so than anything in *Brown* itself, the almost explicit point of *Bolling* is that the traditions and niceties of doctrine *do not matter*—or, at the very most, matter for relatively little—when and where the Court becomes convinced that a fundamental, moral holding needs to be made. But *Brown* and *Bolling* historically should not be weighed or evaluated apart from their most immediate and important progeny, namely the unprecedented "joint" opinion in the 1958 Little Rock school case of *Cooper v. Aaron*.[27] But just as we ought to remind each other today that 1992's *Planned Parenthood of Southeastern Pennsylvania v. Casey*[28] was not *just*, or perhaps even *principally*, about abortion, likewise we need to remember that *Cooper* was not just, or primarily, about school desegregation. Instead, *Cooper*, like *Casey*—and, I think one can argue, also like *Brown*—was fundamentally about the constitutional authority *and* the political role of the Supreme Court itself.

Cooper's most important paragraph spoke to what the Court called "some basic constitutional propositions which are settled doctrine."[29]

Article VI of the Constitution makes the Constitution the "supreme Law of the Land." In 1803, Chief Justice Marshall, speaking for a unanimous Court, referring to the Constitution as "the fundamental and paramount law of the nation," declared in the notable case of *Marbury v. Madison*, 1 Cranch 137, 177, that "It is emphatically the province and duty of the judicial department to say what the law is." This decision declared the basic principle that the federal judiciary is supreme in the exposition of the law of the Constitution, and that principle has ever since been respected by this Court and the Country as a permanent and indispensable feature of our constitutional system. It follows that the interpretation of the Fourteenth Amendment enunciated by this Court in the *Brown* case is the supreme law of the land, and Art. VI of the Constitution makes it of binding effect on the States "any Thing in the Constitution or Laws of any State to the Contrary notwithstanding."[30]

Cooper is arguably the Court's most important declaration of its own authority and role since *Marbury*, but, among at least a small fringe of critical commentators, even some who cannot bring themselves to publicly attack *Brown* or *Bolling* nonetheless feel able to denounce *Cooper*—and particularly that crucial passage in *Cooper*—as one of the Warren Court's "most troubling opinions" because of how it posited "a radical new notion of the status of judicial decisions."[31] *Cooper*, these critics allege, "was not the fulfillment of *Marbury* but rather its perversion,"[32] but the contrarian novelty of such a facially fallacious contention may best be understood as having more to do with *Cooper*'s own most important progeny—namely the 1992 "trio" opinion of Justices Sandra Day O'Connor, Anthony M. Kennedy, and David H. Souter in *Casey*[33]—than perhaps with *Cooper* itself.

But the substantive expansiveness of *Brown*'s application of equal protection was merely the first installment in a new, multipart constitutional scenario. *Colegrove v. Green*[34] should perhaps not be spoken of in the same sentence as *Plessy v. Ferguson*,[35] but if any decision since 1954 can be seen as equal to *Brown* in long-term historical significance, then—as Chief Justice Warren himself repeatedly said[36]—*Baker v. Carr*[37] is certainly *the* case. Justice William J. Brennan, Jr.'s, opinion for the *Baker* Court undeniably took far greater care in clearing away the preexisting judicial underbrush than had Warren's in *Brown*, but the full flowering of equal protection application to the principle of "one person, one vote"—and the Court's explicit citation of *Brown* as helpful precedent for that holding[38]—only came two years later in Warren's opinion for the Court in *Reynolds v. Sims*.[39] The equal protection clause, Warren and five of his colleagues held in *Reynolds*, "guarantees the opportunity for equal participation by all voters in the election of state legislators. Diluting the weight of votes because of place of residence impairs basic constitutional rights under the Fourteenth Amendment just as much as invidious discriminations based upon factors such as race, *Brown v. Board of Education*, 347 U.S. 483 . . ."[40]

Baker, Reynolds, and *Reynolds*'s companion cases[41] all strive far more assiduously than *Brown* and *Bolling* to comport themselves in seeming accommodation with existing precedents. But both textually and historically, *Baker* and *Reynolds*—and perhaps *Reynolds* all the more so, in light of its unwillingness to accept or apply a "federal analogy" whereby only the lower chamber of a bicameral legislature would have to be apportioned into equally populated districts[42]—stand in even more undeniable tension with any intent-based reading of the Fourteenth Amendment's equal protection clause than does *Brown*.[43]

But if critical acceptance of *Brown* is now universal and approval of *Baker* and

Reynolds is widespread but not unanimous,[44] dissent with regard to *Bolling*'s best-known (but rarely if ever acknowledged) descendant, *Griswold v. Connecticut*, is still treated with professional respect, if only because of the undeniable line of derivation that then leads from *Griswold* to *Roe v. Wade*. *Griswold*, like *Brown* and *Baker*, is accepted as *morally* correct even by those who reject its doctrinal grounding, but *Griswold*'s mottled reputation is largely the result not of Justice William O. Douglas's widely recognized compositional shortcomings[45] but of a far more significant jurisprudential legacy—namely the ignominious heritage of *Lochner v. New York*[46]—that until recently only *Bolling*, of all the new, noneconomic substantive due process liberty decisions of the past forty years, has escaped from unscathed.

This issue may well be *the* most important and indeed defining constitutional question of the present age, the question that ought to, and, it is hoped, will, separate this present generation of commentators—namely people who have come to academic maturity in the years since 1973—from the two generations (both children of 1937) that have preceded them.

Perhaps the rudest way in which to pose the question is also the most revealing: Why for more than a half century has *Lochner v. New York* been almost universally viewed as a far more infamous constitutional precedent than, say, *Korematsu v. United States?*[47] *Lochner*, as almost everyone well knows, is widely accepted as *the* symbolic ruling of the "old" conservative Court that prevailed from at least as early as 1895[48] through 1936[49] until being vanquished in the early months of 1937.[50] *Lochner* and its many progeny were resoundingly routed by the constitutional revolution of 1937 (or, more correctly, by the constitutional revolution that began in 1937 and culminated in 1941–42),[51] but the universally acknowledged *ghost* of *Lochner* survived in buoyant health well into the 1960s.[52] Only perhaps in 1973, and then far more certainly in 1992, did clear and convincing evidence finally appear that *Lochner*'s ghost was no longer badly frightening the occupants of America's most exalted judicial corridors.

In *Griswold*, of course, the Court in form, if not in substance, shied away from any prospect of encountering *Lochner*'s ghost in language that epitomizes how powerful and long lasting the jurisprudential overreaction of the 1937 revolution proved to be. "Coming to the merits," Justice Douglas warned, "we are met with a wide range of questions that implicate the Due Process Clause of the Fourteenth Amendment. Overtones of some arguments suggest that *Lochner v. New York* ... should be our guide. But we decline that invitation as we did in *West Coast Hotel Co.* ... We do not sit as a super-legislature to determine the wisdom, need, and propriety of laws that touch economic problems, business affairs, or social conditions."[53]

In *Griswold*, however, Connecticut's anticontraception statute "operate[d] directly on an intimate relation of husband and wife and their physician's role in one aspect of that relation,"[54] and hence Douglas, along with six of his eight colleagues, fled from *Lochner*'s ghost only in form rather than in substance. But even eight years later, in *Roe v. Wade*, only one member of *Roe*'s seven-justice majority, Potter Stewart (a *Griswold* dissenter), was willing to explicitly concede the self-obvious point that *Griswold*, of course, was and always had been a substantive due process liberty decision.[55] While Justice Douglas, a true child of 1937 if ever there was one, still sought to deny what was self-obviously undeniable,[56] the *Roe* majority simply chose to elude the point.[57]

Hence only two decades later, in 1992's *Planned Parenthood of Southeastern Pennsylvania v. Casey*,[58] did a Supreme Court majority directly and explicitly confront the fundamental doctrinal issue that had been sidestepped in both *Griswold* and *Roe*. The *Casey* "trio" opinion of Justices O'Connor, Kennedy, and Souter— joined also in its major parts by Justices Harry A. Blackmun and John Paul Stevens—indicated no hesitation whatsoever and no lingering fear of *Lochner*'s ghost in straightforwardly announcing that "Constitutional protection of the woman's decision to terminate her pregnancy derives from the Due Process Clause of the Fourteenth Amendment." Stressing that "[t]he controlling word in the cases before us is 'liberty,' " the *Casey* majority noted that "[a]lthough a literal reading of the Clause might suggest that it governs only the procedures by which a State may deprive persons of liberty, for at least 105 years, since *Mugler v. Kansas*, 123 U.S. 623, 660–61 (1887), the Clause has been understood to contain a substantive component as well, one 'barring certain government actions regardless of the fairness of the procedures used to implement them.' *Daniels v. Williams*, 474 U.S. 327, 331 (1986)."[59]

Quoting both Justice Louis Brandeis's 1927 concurrence in *Whitney v. California*[60] and Justice John M. Harlan's now-famous 1961 dissent in *Poe v. Ullman*[61] in further support of that point, the *Casey* majority went on to explain that "[i]t is a promise of the Constitution that there is a realm of personal liberty which the government may not enter. We have vindicated this principle before. Marriage is mentioned nowhere in the Bill of Rights and interracial marriage was illegal in most States in the 19th century, but the Court was no doubt correct in finding it to be an aspect of liberty protected against state interference by the substantive component of the Due Process Clause in *Loving* v. *Virginia*, 388 U.S. 1, 12 (1967)."[62]

Most centrally of all, the *Casey* majority forthrightly held that "[n]either the Bill of Rights nor the specific practices of States at the time of the adoption of the Fourteenth Amendment marks the outer limits of the substantive sphere of liberty which the Fourteenth Amendment protects,"[63] a holding that of course spoke not only to the elusions of *Roe* and *Griswold* but also to the substantive essences of *Brown* and *Bolling*. Quoting again twice at some length from the Harlan dissent in *Poe*, the *Casey* majority willingly acknowledged that "[t]he inescapable fact is that adjudication of substantive due process claims may call upon the Court in interpreting the Constitution to exercise that same capacity which by tradition courts always have exercised: reasoned judgment. Its boundaries are not susceptible of expression as a simple rule. That does not mean we are free to invalidate state policy choices with which we disagree; yet neither does it permit us to shrink from the duties of our office," as some of the century's best-known jurists, such as Learned Hand and Felix Frankfurter, no doubt would have advised.[64]

Led by Justice Souter, the *Casey* majority presented perhaps the Court's most extended discussion of the concept of precedent in this century, reviewing not only how *West Coast Hotel Co.*, by overruling *Adkins v. Children's Hospital*,[65] had "signaled the demise of *Lochner*"[66] but also the manner in which *Brown* had vanquished *Plessy*. The heart of Souter's analysis, and the heart of *Casey* itself, however, focused on the institutional and historical grounds as to why *Roe v. Wade* should not and *could not* be overruled. Any such reversal, Souter warned, "would seriously weaken the Court's capacity to exercise the judicial power and to function as the Supreme Court of a Nation dedicated to the rule of law. To understand why this would be so it is necessary to understand the source of this Court's authority, the conditions necessary for its preservation, and its relationship to the country's understanding of itself as a constitutional Republic."[67]

Alluding to the old saw that the judiciary commands neither the purse nor the sword, the *Casey* majority reiterated that the Court's actual power lies largely "in its legitimacy, a product of substance and perception that shows itself in the people's acceptance of the Judiciary as fit to determine what the Nation's law means and to declare what it demands."

> The Court must take care to speak and act in ways that allow people to accept its decisions on the terms the Court claims for them, as grounded truly in principle, not as compromises with social and political pressures having, as such, no bearing on the principled choices that the Court is obliged to make. Thus, the Court's legitimacy depends on making legally principled decisions under circumstances in which their principled character is sufficiently plausible to be accepted by the Nation.[68]

Then, in a core section that actually spoke more about *Brown* than *Roe*, Souter and his *Casey* colleagues put forward in five paragraphs the most institutionally important statement by the Court since *Cooper* and the most substantively significant declaration about the role and function of the U.S. Supreme Court since the time of John Marshall.

> Where, in the performance of its judicial duties, the Court decides a case in such a way as to resolve the sort of intensely divisive controversy reflected in *Roe* and those rare, comparable cases, its decision has a dimension that the resolution of the normal case does not carry. It is the dimension present whenever the Court's interpretation of the Constitution calls the contending sides of a national controversy to end their national division by accepting a common mandate rooted in the Constitution.
>
> The Court is not asked to do this very often, having thus addressed the Nation only twice in our lifetime, in the decisions of *Brown* and *Roe*. But when the Court does act in this way, its decision requires an equally rare precedential force to counter the inevitable efforts to overturn it and to thwart its implementation. Some of those efforts may be mere unprincipled emotional reactions; others may proceed from principles worthy of profound respect. But whatever the premises of opposition may be, only the most convincing justification under accepted standards of precedent could suffice to demonstrate that a later decision overruling the first was anything but a surrender to political pressure, and an unjustified repudiation of the principle on which the Court staked its authority in the first instance. So to overrule under fire in the absence of the most compelling reason to reexamine a watershed decision would subvert the Court's legitimacy beyond any serious question. Cf. *Brown v. Board of Education*, 349 U.S. 294, 300 (1955) (*Brown II*) . . . [69]

The *Casey* majority took note of the costs imposed upon those who were closely identified with controversial watershed decisions.

> The price may be criticism or ostracism, or it may be violence. An extra price will be paid by those who themselves disapprove of the decision's results when viewed outside of constitutional terms, but who nevertheless struggle to accept it, because they respect the rule of law. To all those who will be so tested by following, the Court implicitly undertakes to remain steadfast, lest in the end a price be paid for nothing. The promise of constancy, once given, binds its maker for as long as the power to stand by the decision survives and the understanding of the issue has not changed so fundamentally as to render the commitment obsolete. From the obligation of this promise the Court cannot and should not assume any exemption when duty requires it to decide a case in conformance with the Constitution. A willing breach of it would be nothing less than a breach of faith, and no Court that broke its faith with the people could sensibly expect credit for principle in the decision by which it did that.[70]

"Like the character of an individual," the *Casey* majority warned,

> the legitimacy of the Court must be earned over time. So, indeed, must be the character of a Nation of people who aspire to live according to the rule of law. Their belief in themselves as such a people is not readily separable from their understanding of the Court invested with the authority to decide their constitutional cases and speak before all others for their constitutional ideals. If the Court's legitimacy should be undermined, then, so would the country be in its very ability to see itself through its constitutional ideals. The Court's concern with legitimacy is not for the sake of the Court but for the sake of the Nation to which it is responsible.

"The Court's duty in the present case is clear," they concluded.

In 1973, it confronted the already divisive issue of governmental power to limit personal choice to undergo abortion, for which it provided a new resolution based on the due process guaranteed by the Fourteenth Amendment. Whether or not a new social consensus is developing on that issue, its divisiveness is no less today than in 1973, and pressure to overrule the decision, like pressure to retain it, has grown only more intense. A decision to overrule *Roe*'s essential holding under the existing circumstances would address error, if error there was, at the cost of both profound and unnecessary damage to the Court's legitimacy, and to the Nation's commitment to the rule of law. It is therefore imperative to adhere to the essence of *Roe*'s original decision, and we do so today.[71]

Casey, of course, vindicated *Roe v. Wade*, committing the Court to constitutional protection for abortion in a manner unlikely ever to be undone. *Casey* also offered an extended and significantly intensified reprise of *Cooper* and the powerful historic legacy of *Marbury* and went at least a very long way toward fully elevating *Roe* to the tiny pantheon of American constitutional precedents that perhaps otherwise is peopled only by *Marbury, Brown*, and, possibly, *Baker*.

But in elevating *Roe* to *Brown*-like stature, *Casey* also did, or ratified, something even far more significant as well, something that so far—now more than five years after the event—has received stunningly little attention or discussion. The *Casey*

Court formally and explicitly buried *Lochner*'s ghost. Substantive due process *is*, as it *should be*, a fundamental and fully accepted aspect of present-day American constitutional doctrine.

Casey may well represent the culmination (and conclusion) of a constitutional era that began so dramatically with *Brown* and *Bolling*. Although some conservative scholars now seek to make *Brown* into a badly miscast constitutional poster child for their jurisprudence of "original intent,"[72] such efforts to rebut the interpretive (and doctrinal) radicalism of *Brown* (and *Bolling*) are unlikely to win many followers outside certain narrow precincts. *Brown* heralded not only the Court's explicit freeing of itself from the constraints of historically bounded constitutional "originalism" but also a newly expansive application of the Fourteenth Amendment that energetically encompassed both equal protection and due process. *Brown* opened the institutional door for *Baker*'s and *Reynold*'s revolutionary expansiveness involving equal protection, and *Bolling v. Sharpe* represented the first salvo in a reconstruction of fundamental due process liberty that quietly prepared the doctrinal ground for *Griswold* and for the eventual burial of *Lochner*'s ghost in *Roe* and *Casey*.

Brown and *Casey* are hence bookends to the double-barreled rereading that the Court has accorded the Fourteenth Amendment—both in *Brown* (and in *Baker*) with regard to the equal protection clause and in *Casey* (as in *Griswold* and *Roe* before) with regard to a new rebirth of the due process clause—over these past forty years. If we justifiably celebrate the political revolution(s) heralded by *Brown* (and *Baker*) and if we further celebrate or at least accede to the way in which the *Brown* Court reached above and beyond the Fourteenth Amendment's historical fetters to blot the stain of *Plessy*, so too does *Casey* call on us to acknowledge if not applaud the manner in which the modern Court has similarly expanded due process—like equal protection before it—to hasten another revolution as well. As *Brown* and *Casey* both signify, the modern-day meanings of American constitutional protections should not be, and happily are not, fettered by the burdens and limitations of history.

NOTES

A somewhat different version of this essay, entitled "From *Brown* to *Casey*: The U.S. Supreme Court and the Burdens of History," appears in Austin Sarat, ed., *Race, Law, and Culture: Reflections on* Brown v. Board of Education (New York: Oxford University Press, 1997), 74–88.

1. 347 U.S. 483 (1954).

2. For a survey of conceptual distinctions and specifications concerning "intent," see John G. Wofford, "The Blinding Light: The Uses of History in Constitutional Interpretation," *University of Chicago Law Review* 31 (Spring 1964): 502–3; and Charles A. Miller, *The Supreme Court and the Uses of History* (Cambridge: Harvard University Press, 1969), 20–28, 153–55, 165–66.

3. See *Baker v. Carr*, 369 U.S. 186 (1962); *Reynolds v. Sims*, 377 U.S. 533 (1964); *Griswold v. Connecticut*, 381 U.S. 479 (1965); *Roe v. Wade*, 410 U.S. 113 (1973).

4. 5 U.S. 137 (1803).

5. *West Coast Hotel Co. v. Parrish*, 300 U.S. 379 (1937); *National Labor Relations Board v. Jones & Laughlin Steel Corp.*, 301 U.S. 1 (1937).

6. *United States v. Carolene Products Co.*, 304 U.S. 144, 152 n.4 (1938); see also Alpheus T. Mason, *Harlan Fiske Stone: Pillar of the Law* (New York: Viking Press, 1956), 513–14; Louis Lusky, *By What Right?* (Charlottesville, Va.: Michie Co., 1975), 108–12; Louis Lusky, *Our Nine Tribunes* (Westport, Conn.: Praeger, 1993), 119–32, 177–90.

7. 369 U.S. 186 (1962).

8. 381 U.S. 479 (1965).

9. 377 U.S. 533 (1964).

10. 410 U.S. 113 (1973).

11. 358 U.S. 1 (1958).

12. 505 U.S. 833 (1992).

13. See also generally William E. Nelson, *The Fourteenth Amendment: From Political Principle to Judicial Doctrine* (Cambridge: Harvard University Press, 1988), 4–11; Judith A. Baer, "The Fruitless Search for Original Intent," in *Judging the Constitution*, ed. Michael W. McCann and Gerald L. Houseman (Glenview, Ill.: Scott, Foresman, 1989), 49–71; Mark V. Tushnet, "The Warren Court as History: An Interpretation," in *The Warren Court in Historical and Political Perspective*, ed. Mark V. Tushnet (Charlottesville: University Press of Virginia, 1994), 17–18.

14. See *Brown v. Board of Education*, 98 F. Supp. 797 (D. Kan. 1951); *Briggs v. Elliott*, 103 F. Supp. 920 (E.D. S.C. 1952); *Davis v. County School Board*, 103 F. Supp. 337 (E.D. Va. 1952); *Gebhart v. Belton*, 91 A.2d 137 (Del. Sup. Ct. 1952); cf. *Bolling v. Sharpe*, 347 U.S. 497 (1954).

15. *Brown v. Board of Education*, 345 U.S. 972 (1953); see also Richard Kluger, *Simple Justice* (New York: Knopf, 1976), 614–16.

16. See Kluger, *Simple Justice*, 618–41; Mark V. Tushnet, *Making Civil Rights Law* (New York: Oxford University Press, 1994), 196–99; Jack Greenberg, *Crusaders in the Courts* (New York: Basic Books, 1994), 177–88. As Kluger comments, "[T]he historical evidence seemed to demonstrate persuasively that neither the Congress which framed the Fourteenth Amendment nor the state legislatures which adopted it understood that its pledge of equal protection would require the end of segregation in the nation's public schools." *Simple Justice*, 634. See also Alexander M. Bickel, "The Original Understanding and the Segregation Decision," *Harvard Law Review* 69 (November 1955): 1–65; Alfred H. Kelly, "The Fourteenth Amendment Reconsidered: The Segregation Question," *Michigan Law Review* 59 (June 1956): 1049–86; Alfred H. Kelly, "The Congressional Controversy over School Segregation, 1867–1875," *American Historical Review* 64 (April 1959): 537–63. Cf. Nelson, *The Fourteenth Amendment*, 6–7. Also note Michael W. McConnell's iconoclastic (and generally unpersuasive) argument in "Originalism and the Desegregation Decisions," *Virginia Law Review* 81 (May 1995): 947–1140.

17. Tushnet, *Making Civil Rights Law*, 203–4; see also Alfred H. Kelly, "Clio and the Court: An Illicit Love Affair," *Supreme Court Review* (1965): 142–45; Kluger, *Simple Justice*, 653–55, 668–76.

18 See Kluger, *Simple Justice*, 678–83; Tushnet, *Making Civil Rights Law*, 209–11.

19. 347 U.S. at 489.

20. Ibid. at 489, 490.

21. Cf. Robert H. Bork, *The Tempting of America* (New York: Free Press, 1990), 76–77, 81.

22. After David Glasgow ("Damn the torpedoes! Full speed ahead!") Farragut (1801–

70). See Alfred T. Mahan, *Admiral Farragut* (1897); Charles L. Lewis, *David Glasgow Farragut*, vols. 1, 2 (Annapolis: U.S. Naval Academy, 1941, 1943).

23. *Bolling v. Sharpe*, 347 U.S. 497, 499 (1954).

24. Ibid. at 499–500. "In view of our decision that the Constitution prohibits the states from maintaining racially segregated public schools," the *Bolling* opinion added, "it would be unthinkable that the same Constitution would impose a lesser duty on the Federal Government." Ibid. at 500.

25. 381 U.S. 479 (1965).

26. Cf. Bork, *The Tempting of America*, 83–84.

27. 358 U.S. 1 (1958); see also Daniel A. Farber, "The Supreme Court and the Rule of Law: *Cooper v. Aaron* Revisited," *University of Illinois Law Review* no. 2 (1982): 387–412; Tony Freyer, *The Little Rock Crisis* (Westport, Conn.: Greenwood Press, 1984).

28. 505 U.S. 833 (1992).

29. 358 U.S. at 17.

30. Ibid. at 18.

31. Eugene W. Hickok and Gary L. McDowell, *Justice vs. Law* (New York: Free Press, 1993), 76–77, 81.

32. Ibid., 168.

33. 505 U.S. 833 (1992).

34. 328 U.S. 549 (1946).

35. 163 U.S. 537 (1896).

36. See William J. Brennan, "Chief Justice Warren," *Harvard Law Review* 88 (November 1974): 3; Earl Warren, *The Memoirs of Earl Warren* (Garden City: Doubleday & Co., 1977), 306; G. Edward White, *Earl Warren* (New York: Oxford University Press, 1982); Bernard Schwartz, *Super Chief* (New York: New York University Press, 1983), 410; see also John Hart Ely, "The Chief," *Harvard Law Review* 88 (November 1974): 12.

37. 369 U.S. 186 (1962).

38. See *Reynolds v. Sims*, 377 U.S. 533, 566 (1964).

39. 377 U.S. 533 (1964); see also *Gray v. Sanders*, 372 U.S. 368 (1963); *Wesberry v. Sanders*, 376 U.S. 1 (1964). On *Baker* and *Reynolds*, see especially Richard C. Cortner, *The Apportionment Cases* (New York: Norton, 1970). On *Baker*, see also Gene Graham, *One Man, One Vote*: Baker v. Carr *and the American Levellers* (Boston: Little, Brown & Co., 1972). More generally, see also Robert B. McKay, *Reapportionment: The Law and Politics of Equal Representation* (New York: Twentieth Century Fund, 1965); Robert G. Dixon, Jr., *Democratic Representation: Reapportionment in Law and Politics* (New York: Oxford University Press, 1968).

40. 377 U.S. at 566.

41. *WMCA, Inc. v. Lomenzo*, 377 U.S. 633 (1964); *Maryland Committee for Fair Representation v. Tawes*, 377 U.S. 656 (1964); *Davis v. Mann*, 377 U.S. 678 (1964); *Roman v. Sincock*, 377 U.S. 695 (1964); *Lucas v. Forty-Fourth General Assembly of Colorado*, 377 U.S. 713 (1964).

42. See *Reynolds*, 377 U.S. at 572–73.

43. See Kelly, "Clio and the Court," 135–37; Miller, *The Supreme Court and the Uses of History*, 128–38; Robert H. Bork, "Neutral Principles and Some First Amendment Problems," *Indiana Law Journal* 47 (Fall 1971): 18: "The principle of one man, one vote . . . runs counter to the text of the fourteenth amendment, the history surrounding its adoption and ratification and the political practice of Americans from colonial times up to the day the Court invented the new formula." See also Bork, *The Tempting of America*, 84–87.

44. See Miller's accurate observation that "the apportionment decisions . . . have been accepted as law in a way that other momentous exercises of judicial review have not been."

The Supreme Court and the Uses of History, 119. But see Alex Kozinski, "Spook of Earl: The Spirit and Specter of the Warren Court," in *The Warren Court: A Retrospective*, ed. Bernard Schwartz (New York: Oxford University Press, 1996), 378–81.

45. See David J. Garrow, *Liberty and Sexuality* (New York: Macmillan, 1994), 245–46.

46. 198 U.S. 45 (1905); see also Paul Kens, *Judicial Power and Reform Politics: The Anatomy of* Lochner v. New York (Lawrence: University Press of Kansas, 1990), 159–65.

47. 323 U.S. 214 (1944).

48. See *United States v. E. C. Knight Co.*, 156 U.S. 1 (1895); *Pollock v. Farmers' Loan & Trust Co.*, 157 U.S. 429 (1895).

49. See *Carter v. Carter Coal Co.*, 298 U.S. 238 (1936); *Morehead v. New York ex rel. Tipaldo*, 298 U.S. 587 (1936).

50. See *West Coast Hotel*, 300 U.S. 379 (1937); *National Labor Relations Board*, 301 U.S. 1 (1937).

51. See, e.g., *United States v. Darby*, 312 U.S. 100 (1941); *Wickard v. Filburn*, 317 U.S. 111 (1942).

52. See Helen Garfield, "Privacy, Abortion, and Judicial Review: Haunted By the Ghost of *Lochner*," *Washington Law Review* 61 (April 1986): 293–365.

53. 381 U.S. 479, 481–82 (1965).

54. Ibid. at 482.

55. 410 U.S. 113, 167–69 (1973).

56. *Doe v. Bolton*, 410 U.S. 179, 212 n.4 (1973) (Douglas, J., concurring).

57. 410 U.S. at 153.

58. 505 U.S. 833 (1992).

59. Ibid. at 846.

60. 274 U.S. 357, 373 (1927).

61. 367 U.S. 497, 541 (1961).

62. 505 U.S. at 847–48.

63. Ibid. at 848.

64. Ibid. at 849; see also Gerald Gunther, *Learned Hand* (New York: Knopf, 1994); David J. Garrow, "Doing Justice," *Nation*, 27 February 1995, 278–81.

65. 261 U.S. 525 (1923).

66. 505 U.S. at 861.

67. Ibid. at 865.

68. Ibid. at 865–66; see also Tom R. Tyler and Gregory Mitchell, "Legitimacy and the Empowerment of Discretionary Legal Authority: The United States Supreme Court and Abortion Rights," *Duke Law Journal* 43 (February 1994): 796–98; James Boyd White, *Acts of Hope: Creating Authority in Literature, Law, and Politics* (Chicago: University of Chicago Press, 1994), 168–83.

69. 505 U.S. at 866–67.

70. Ibid. at at 867–68.

71. Ibid. at at 868–69.

72. See McConnell, "Originalism and the Desegregation Decisions."

14

The Judicial Role in
Equality Decisionmaking

NEAL DEVINS

More than forty years after *Brown v. Board of Education*, the quest for equality remains elusive. Conservatives and liberals both complain bitterly about court-imposed solutions to racial isolation. For conservatives, judicial intervention in the name of equality is counterproductive. Jeremy Rabkin, for example, speaks of courts "working with the whimsical imagery of the 1960s," making it "impossible for [inner-city] neighborhoods to cope with the daily assault on their basic security."[1] In sharp contrast, the battle cry from the left attacks the courts for being too weak-kneed. Gary Orfield, for example, laments "the development of case law permitting both the abandonment of desegregation plans and return to segregated neighborhoods schools."[2] The consequence of this supposed judicial abdication, according to Erwin Chemerinsky, is that "American schools are socially segregated and grossly unequal."[3]

Complicating this debate over the judicial role, starting with President Ronald Reagan's 1986 elevation of William Rehnquist to chief justice, the potency of judicial decisionmaking has been called into question. Flying in the face of long-standing attacks against an "imperial judiciary" by conservative critics of the Court, Gerald Rosenberg and other left-leaning political scientists and constitutional lawyers began depicting court-ordered reform as a "hollow hope." For this new wave of Court critics, meaningful reform is accomplished through social movements and elected-branch initiatives. Under this view, *Brown*—although "virtually universally credited with having brought civil rights to national attention"—is pooh-poohed for "contribut[ing] virtually *nothing* to ending segregation . . . in the Southern states."[4]

Having persisted for more than forty years and with no end in sight, the fight over the propriety and force of court-centered solutions to social problems will continue. Indeed, as the first section of this chapter will show, the Court is incapable of pleasing either progressives who plead for an activist judiciary or social conservatives who deplore such judicial interventions. Judicial decisionmaking typically involves the balancing of competing interests and values, a process that is anathema to absolutist solutions. For example, the judiciary, including the exalted Warren Court, has always engaged in interest balancing in sorting out both the violation and the remedy components of school desegregation litigation. For this reason, the failure of southern states to desegregate in the decade after *Brown* reveals as much about the Warren Court's purposeful refusal to issue a meaningful remedy as it does about the limits of judicial authority.

This point is made in some detail in the second section of this chapter. Highlighting the constitutional dialogue between courts and elected officials over school desegregation, employment discrimination, and abortion, the second section uncovers the potency (as well as the limits) of the judicial role in constitutional decisionmaking.

The question of whether courts should attempt to influence social and political norms still remains. By comparing the Supreme Court's failure to play a leadership role in the affirmative action wars with its constructive participation in the battle over abortion rights, the third section suggests that courts should be players, shaping public discourse through decisions with a nationwide impact.

Interest Balancing and Equal Educational Opportunity

The Warren Court

Today, it seems inconceivable that *Brown*'s basic declaration of racial equality tested the limits of judicial authority. When *Brown* was decided, however, segregation was so ingrained in the South that the outlawing of dual school systems promised social turmoil and massive resistance. These deep feelings were not lost either on the Court or on the Department of Justice. In an effort to temper southern hostility, Chief Justice Earl Warren sought to craft a unanimous opinion of limited reach and the Justice Department recommended that the Court *not* specify a remedy in the case. Accordingly, the Court did not issue a remedy when it ruled on *Brown* that "[s]eparate educational facilities are inherently unequal."[5] After another year, in which the public had time to contemplate a desegregated country, the Court issued *Brown II*, declaring that desegregation must proceed with "all deliberate speed."[6]

The Court's bifurcation of its merits and remedies holdings, as well as the absence of judgmental rhetoric in its segregation decision, reveals that the justices sought to improve the acceptability of their decision in *Brown I* by speaking in a single moderate voice. *Brown*, therefore, is a testament not just to the reaches but also to the limits of judicial action. By taking into account potential resistance to its decision, *Brown* also exemplifies the Court's engaging in the type of interest balancing that has set political parameters on judicial intervention in equal educational opportunity. Recognizing that "some achievable remedial effectiveness may be sacrificed *because* of other social interests" and that "a limited remedy [may be chosen] when a more effective one is too costly to other interests,"[7] the Court recognized that victims' rights must be balanced against a broad spectrum of competing policy concerns. Specifically, aside from victims' rights, the *Brown* Court valued local control of public school systems and judicial restraint. Consequently, in addition to taking southern resistance into account as a factor in crafting a remedy that would best serve plaintiffs' interests, the Warren Court slowed down the pace of school desegregation for other reasons.

This conclusion is subject to criticism, for *Brown I*'s failure to specify a remedy or condemn segregation as immoral is easily explainable as the desire to avoid "the costs that a remedy imposes . . . when such costs actually interfere with the remedy's effectiveness."[8] *Brown II*, however, does not lend itself to such an interpretation. Rather than require southern systems to take concrete steps to dismantle dual systems, the Court recognized in *Brown II* that "varied local school problems" were best solved by "[s]chool authorities," that district court judges were best suited to examine "local conditions," and that delays associated with "problems related to administration" were to be expected.[9] The inevitable result of this "remedial" order was inaction. As J. Harvie Wilkinson put it, "[T]he South was audibly relieved by *Brown II*, a victory of sorts snatched from the defeat of only a year ago [in *Brown*]."[10] Indeed, southern newspapers heralded the remedial order, especially since the Court entrusted the implementation of its decision to "[o]ur local judges [who] know the local situation."[11]

Brown II's failure cannot be excused as the best possible remedy in the face of southern resistance. The Court's emphasis on local conditions invited tokenism and delay, and southern school officials and judges acted in kind. The Supreme Court, then, did not seek to provide the type of leadership against which one can measure changes in black-white student contact. In the decade following *Brown*, the Court's only foray into school desegregation is best understood as the Warren Court's defending its institutional self-interest. Pressed—in the Little Rock case—by Arkansas governor Orval Faubus's efforts to block school desegregation, the Court aggressively defended its turf, proclaiming itself "supreme in the exposition of the law of the Constitution."[12] Although a more vigorous role in school cases may have immersed the Court in a thicket that may have otherwise jeopardized its social reform objectives in criminal law and elsewhere, it is indisputable that the Warren Court ducked the school desegregation issue for a decade. In 1968 it finally demanded that school boards "come forward with a plan that promises realistically to work, and promises realistically to work *now*."[13]

The Warren Court's intransigence on school desegregation spanned most of its sixteen-year life. Remarkably, one decade after *Brown*, only 2 percent of black children attended biracial schools in the eleven southern states. In the 1965–66 school year, however, the percentage of black children in biracial schools rose to 6 percent. The turning point here was not hyped-up judicial enforcement; instead, the principal impetus to meaningful school desegregation was rooted in elected-branch action.

Most significant, the implementation of the Elementary and Secondary Education Act of 1965, coupled with the issuance and enforcement of guidelines for Title VI of the Civil Rights Act of 1964, marked a significant expansion in federal power over state education systems. With Title VI's demand that federal grant recipients be nondiscriminatory, Congress became willing to supply billions of dollars of aid for the compensatory education of educationally deprived children. This aid was sufficient incentive for many school systems to comply with the Office for Civil Rights' nondiscrimination standards. Furthermore, by authorizing Department of Justice participation in school desegregation litigation through its 1964 Civil Rights Act, Congress encouraged judicial intervention.

It was against this backdrop of increasing federal involvement in school desegregation that the Warren Court stepped up its own involvement. This parallelism should come as no surprise. With Congress and the White House both making equal educational opportunity a national priority and envisioning an increasing judicial role, concerns of local control and judicial restraint no longer impeded judicial action. Court intervention, instead, was consistent with judicial respect for the priorities set by coequal branches of the federal government.

The Burger and Rehnquist Courts

The Warren Court's school desegregation legacy, then, is one of visionary leadership and a good dose of caution. Against this backdrop, Erwin Chemerinsky goes too far in attacking the Burger Court for deviating from Warren Court decisionmaking. This, of course, is not to say that proponents of a vigorous judicial role in equal educational opportunity should not be critical of the Burger Court. *Milliken I*'s refusal to include suburban counties in Detroit's school desegregation plan, despite the Court's recognition that the state of Michigan was partly responsible for illegal segregation in Detroit schools, explicitly placed the interests of local control and judicial restraint ahead of equal educational opportunity.[14] Likewise, local control triumphed when the Court ruled that a school system may favor neighborhood schools irrespective of ethnically segregated residential patterns, which makes racial isolation "the foreseeable and inevitable result of such an assignment policy."[15]

The Burger Court's recognition of values outside equal educational opportunity, as the Warren Court experience suggests, is inevitable, especially since four members of the Burger Court (William Rehnquist, Lewis Powell, Harry Blackmun, and Warren Burger himself) were appointed by a president, Richard Nixon, who campaigned against judicial activism and for states' rights as part of his "southern strategy." Correspondingly, by 1969, unlike the final stages of the Warren Court, when "the President, congressional leadership, and the public all recognized that protection of the rights of black Americans was the fundamental [social and educational] issue,"[16] both the executive and legislative branches were increasingly found opposing the federal courts in school desegregation questions. Mounting concern over the extension of desegregation to districts outside the South and heightened opposition to the use of mandatory reassignments ("busing") led to increased efforts by both branches to curb federal action in school desegregation. Without the support of the coequal branches of government, judicial intervention was likely to face increasing local resistance. Concerns of the judiciary's self-interest in having its orders enforced, as well as respect owed a coequal branch, warranted a diminished judicial role and, with it, increasing attention to judicial restraint concerns.

What then seems remarkable about the Burger Court is its willingness to enter the school desegregation fray at all. In several instances, the Burger Court did just that, approving fairly broad constructs for defining both the scope of the violation and the sweep of the remedy. In 1971, *Swann v. Charlotte-Mecklenburg Board of Education* recognized the use of black-white pupil ratios and mandatory student reassignments as "starting point[s] in the process of shaping a remedy."[17] For the Burger Court, to eliminate all vestiges of an unconstitutional dual school system, desegregation remedies might have to be "administratively awkward, inconvenient, and even bizarre."[18]

Interest balancing played only a minor role in *Swann*. While not rejecting concerns of the health of children from overly long bus trips, the Court emphasized that the competing value of desegregation will almost always win out. More significant, *Swann* eschewed local control, judicial restraint, institutional self-interest in crafting a clearly workable remedy, and respect for legislative and executive branch preferences in favor of massive far-reaching judicial intervention.

Another measure of the Burger Court's acquiescence to significant judicial involvement can be seen in its refusal to resolve early 1980s challenges by school systems (and the Reagan Justice Department) to continuing judicial supervision of school systems subject to long-standing desegregation orders. Specifically, rather than consider alternatives to mandatory assignments and other intrusive remedies or specify standards defining the termination of judicial authority in this area, the Burger Court put those decisions off for another day.

With the Rehnquist Court, that day arrived. In *Board of Education v. Dowell* and *Freeman v. Pitts*, the Rehnquist Court made clear that federal courts should be willing to terminate desegregation orders, placing increasing emphasis on local control and judicial restraint and, correspondingly, deemphasizing victims' rights concerns. In *Dowell*, pointing to "[c]onsiderations based on the allocation of powers within our federal system" and extolling local control's virtues in "allow[ing] citizens to participate in decisionmaking, and allow[ing] innovation so that school programs can fit local needs,"[19] the Supreme Court approved Oklahoma City's decision to abandon mandatory transportation for students in grades K–4. *Freeman* likewise emphasized limits in the courts' remedial authority: "Returning schools to the control of local authorities at the earliest practicable date is essential to restore their true accountability in our governmental system."[20] Upholding district court authority to relinquish jurisdiction over student assignments, *Freeman* relieved Dekalb County, Georgia, of any obligation to address racial isolation caused by changing demographics.

Dowell and *Freeman*, although welcoming a diminished judicial role, neither require nor encourage district court judges to terminate school desegregation injunctions.[21] Instead, like *Brown II*, these Rehnquist Court rulings empower district court judges to take local circumstances into account in sorting out whether a school system has satisfied its desegregation obligations. *Dowell* and *Freeman* also appear less draconian when placed in their social and political contexts. With the 1980 election of Ronald Reagan, the White House proposed and Congress endorsed "new federalism" in education programs that eliminated targeted funds for minority schoolchildren subject to school desegregation remedies and put in their stead block grant programs that allowed local school systems to purchase computers and the like.

Combusting with "new federalism" initiatives, legislative riders as well as Reagan and Bush Justice Department arguments emphasized local autonomy and attacked mandatory reassignments. In addition to congressional and White House opposition to intrusive judicial remedies, opinion polls suggest that busing is disfavored by the minority community. Rather than expansive judicial intervention, minority interests typically favor magnet school programs and other education-related expenditures.[22] Given the absence of support for mandatory assignments and other intrusive remedies, it is little wonder that the courts themselves would tire of continuing judicial supervision of school systems.

That the Rehnquist Court was influenced by these concerns is as inevitable as the Warren and Burger Courts' recognition of social and political factors in their equal educational opportunity jurisprudence. The election of President Bill Clinton, moreover, has done little to change these tides. As of June 1997, the Clinton administration has left school desegregation alone.[23] Congress, too, remains disinterested in these matters. Without any push for a greater federal judicial presence, the Court is likely to do little in this area. For Erwin Chemerinsky, that is ducking the issue by declaring victory. I, however, would place a less-sinister spin on the evolution of the Court's role in this area. The Court sought to advance equal educational opportunity in fits and starts, sometimes—as in *Brown I* and *Swann*—moving aggressively, and other times—as in *Brown II, Milliken*, and *Freeman*—eschewing an activist role. In the end, the Court settled on a doctrine that roughly matched social and political conditions. Without question, the Court would have played a more aggressive role had voters placed other individuals in Congress, in the White House, and—through the appointments and confirmation process—on the bench. But to expect the Court to rise above its surroundings is unrealistic. Justice Benjamin N. Cardozo reminded us that the "great tides and currents which engulf the rest of men do not turn aside in their course and pass the judges by."[24]

Do Courts Matter?

That judicial action is shaped by social and political forces, however, does not mean that courts do not play a leadership role in affecting public policy and discourse. While it is true, as Gerald Rosenberg aptly notes, that *Brown* neither prompted meaningful school desegregation nor affected public attitudes and beliefs (in part because most Americans were unaware of the decision), it is also true that *Brown*—while limited—was consequential. Furthermore, in assessing *Brown*'s impact, it is critical to take into account what the Court set out to accomplish through its decision.

To begin with, as the first part of this chapter details, *Brown* is a testament to how interest balancing affects Supreme Court decisionmaking. By purposefully limiting the scope and sweep of *Brown*, the Court did not seek to provide the type of leadership against which we can measure changes in black-white student contact. With that said, *Brown* influenced legislative deliberations over the 1964 Civil Rights Act. On the issue of Title VI funding prohibitions, bill sponsor Senator Thomas Kuchel argued that Title VI prevented "unconstitutional" expenditures of federal funds, thereby "furthering a policy of nondiscrimination, and thus eliminating defiance of the law of the land [i.e., *Brown*]."[25] For Kuchel and others, southern resistance to *Brown* made Title VI a moral imperative; otherwise, Congress would knowingly fund blatantly unconstitutional state action. More striking, Title IV of the 1964 Act, authorizing the Justice Department to file desegregation lawsuits, seems a direct response to *Brown*. Act sponsors spoke of "expediting the decade old mandate of the Supreme Court" and noted that civil rights groups lacked the funds needed to launch separate lawsuits in each of 2,000 segregationist southern school districts.[26]

The judicial role in school desegregation, of course, extends well beyond mid-1960s reforms. Indeed, the Supreme Court's approval of busing in its 1971 *Swann* decision was the judiciary's most significant, most controversial, and most debated foray into court-ordered institutional reform. Battle lines had been drawn here, with critics and proponents spinning different tales of white flight and other forms of resegregation, educational achievement, judicial fact-finding and management, and school board compliance. Three things are not in debate, all of which speak to a significant—if not dominant—judicial role.

First, courts affect behavior. When court orders result in new budgeting processes (Boston), the imposition of a statewide tax levy (Kansas City), the building of state-subsidized housing (Yonkers), and the freezing of U.S. Department of Education accounts (Chicago), there is change.[27] More significant, in response to a school desegregation order, some parents do send their children to private schools or move to another school system, although there is typically some increase in minority-nonminority contact in the public schools.

Second, court decisions prompt legislative action. Following *Swann*, President Richard Nixon delivered a national address on the evils of busing and proposed legislation making busing a remedy of "last resort" for school segregation and then "only under strict limitations."[28] Although Congress refused to limit court remedial authority, numerous restrictions on federal financial support of mandatory busing and federal advocacy of busing have been enacted since 1972.[29]

Third, court action or the threat of court action is essential to meaningful school desegregation. In most instances, the threat of legal action prompts "voluntary" reform. Fear of overreaching court orders and the costs of litigation prod such voluntary compliance. In rare instances, school boards look to courts to impose remedies that they support but lack the political courage to endorse. In such cases, courts are far from incidental; they are a necessary conduit to legitimate socially desirable but politically costly behavior. Finally (and most visibly), in some instances, courts impose remedies on reluctant districts. The results here vary dramatically. Sometimes judges or court-appointed special masters can work with community leaders to forge a successful desegregation plan. In those cases, courts play an affirmative instrumental role. On other occasions, court orders are little more than a Pyrrhic victory for civil rights litigants. When a school system prefers resistance to compliance, court action is not likely to succeed. Whether successful compromises outnumber political debacles is an open question. What is clear is that courts can facilitate success stories but only when school systems are willing players.

On the issue of busing, it may be that "[o]nly a reordering of the environment" will result in racially balanced public schools.[30] That courts cannot accomplish that task comes as no surprise. The story of school desegregation reveals that the judiciary is only a piece in a much larger puzzle. Support or resistance from the federal government and local school authorities are also pieces of this puzzle (and perhaps larger ones at that). The Supreme Court often recognizes these limits; its decisions in *Brown* are testament to this sensitivity. That the judiciary is constrained, however, does not mean that the courts are without significant influence here.

Without question, when it comes to race and schooling, "[p]olitics and law . . . each reshape the other."[31] For this reason, just as Rosenberg overstates his case, proponents of judicial activism, too, infrequently take into account inherent limits on judicial authority. Their principal complaint, instead, is that the Court is not sufficiently progressive. Erwin Chemerinsky, for example, waxes poetic about different decisions and different results if only the Warren Court had continued for a few more years.[32]

Nonjudicial forces, whether political or social, are infrequently studied and grossly underestimated. Combined with inherent limits on the judiciary's power to manage reform, these nonjudicial forces suggest that social reform through litigation is a gamble. Along these lines, it cannot be denied that there are instances when court opinions do not bind elected government. Supreme Court decisions limiting religious observance in the public schools and prohibiting the legislative veto, for example, have been disregarded. The public school cases demand that objecting students bear the fiscal and emotional toll of challenging school systems that would prefer to heed religious beliefs ahead of Supreme Court decisions. This price is quite high, and consequently many religious practices remain unchallenged. The legislative veto is a more dramatic, more surprising case, for the affected parties are Congress and the White House rather than "backwater" school systems. Nonetheless, following the Supreme Court's 1983 repudiation of this device in *Immigration and Naturalization Service v. Chandha*, more than 300 new legislative vetoes have been enacted and countless informal arrangements have been made between oversight committees and governmental agencies. The explanation for this widespread disobedience is that neither Congress nor the White House "wants the static model of separated powers offered by the Court."[33] That the Court repudiated the legislative veto hardly matters. With both sides benefiting from legislative veto arrangements, market forces have simply driven them underground.

The legislative veto and religion cases share a common feature. Neither decision creates incentives for compliance. Compliance, instead, is a by-product of the implementing community. Consequently, when the implementing community resists, the judicial impact is muted. In other instances, however, elected government acts affirmatively in the face of a decision that is not self-implementing. When a federal appeals court directed the Federal Communications Commission to take race into account in broadcast-licensing decisions, for example, the commission not only complied with that decision but embraced other policy initiatives to increase the number of minority broadcasters.[34]

Judicial influences are more pronounced when incentives for enforcement are a natural outgrowth of the opinion. Employers now incorporate Title VII employment discrimination rulings into their hiring and promotion practices in order to avoid litigation costs. Likewise, health care providers responded to the extraordinary demand for nonhospital abortions in the wake of *Roe* by opening abortion clinics. Elected government may strengthen these self-implementing decisions. For example, employment discrimination litigation pursued by the Equal Employment Opportunity Commission and Department of Justice quickened the pace of Title VII compliance. Elected government may also oppose self-implementing decisions, which occurred when antiabortion funding restrictions prevented some poor women from seeking an abortion. Yet unlike non-self-implementing decisions, in which governmental resistance is extremely significant, self-implementing decisions can withstand governmental attack. Witness the abortion decision: despite the Supreme Court's approval of the abortion-funding ban in *Harris v. McRae*, abortion rates have remained stable.

Court decisions may also overcome the inertia that sometimes stalls legislative reform efforts. For example, when *Roe* was decided, a vigorous right-to-life movement successfully blocked pro-choice legislative reform efforts in Michigan, North Dakota, and elsewhere. Although 64 percent of Americans supported abortion rights at that time, pro-life forces proved that "[a] small but intense minority can exercise political influence disproportionate to its numbers when a diffuse and silent majority does not organize to fight back."[35] *Roe*'s recognition of abortion rights therefore validated majority preferences while it invalidated the laws of forty-six states.

Roe did more than place public opinion polls ahead of legislative majorities. *Roe* also changed the political culture of abortion. States that had been willing to validate minority preferences by enacting abortion restrictions at the behest of pro-life interest groups reversed course after the Supreme Court signaled its willingness to approve such restrictions in *Planned Parenthood of Southeastern Pennsylvania v. Casey*.

This phenomenon—of elected government's acclimating to and embracing restrictive judicial norms—is not limited to abortion. The 1991 Civil Rights Act approved disparate racial impact proofs of employment discrimination, a measure that would not have been adopted by the 1964 Congress.[36] Congress's change of heart was a direct result of a 1971 Supreme Court decision, *Griggs v. Duke Power Co.*, which recognized disparate impact proofs. In 1991, however, *Griggs* was a nullity—effectively overruled by a 1989 Supreme Court decision.[37] Although *Griggs* was a judicial creation, it was also—by 1991—a cornerstone of employment discrimination litigation. The 1991 Civil Rights Act, by formally embracing disparate proofs, validated judicially created norms.[38]

The 1993 Religious Freedom Restoration Act follows a similar pattern. After the Supreme Court's 1990 *Employment Division v. Smith* decision reversed the longstanding judicial practice of subjecting *all* governmental conduct that burdens religious exercise to exacting judicial review, Congress stepped in to statutorily mandate the Court's preexisting practice.[39] For Congress, *Smith* ran headlong into legislative expectations of vigorous protections for religious exercise, expectations created by long-standing judicial practices.

Courts matter. They matter a lot. Sometimes their orders set in motion market mechanisms that guarantee their effectiveness. Sometimes the threat of judicial action prompts either settlement or legislative initiative. Their opinions influence legislative deliberations and change the status quo. Occasionally, they trump agencies and interpose their normative views into the law. It may be that these influences sometimes exceed the proper judicial role in our system of separated powers, but they *are* judicial influences nonetheless.

Should Courts Matter?

The question of whether courts should play a positive role in shaping these social and political forces remains. For very different reasons, some progressives and many conservatives oppose judicial intervention, arguing that court-ordered " 'civil rights' remedies have not touched the problem of the black underclass, which is at the heart of our current racial discord."[40] While there is an element of truth to claims that "the predictable bias of federal courts—towards legalistic, procedural, and uniform national standards"[41]—is a partial roadblock to single-sex schools and other creative efforts to improve our ever-worsening inner cities, it is also true that the judiciary must make its voice heard on abortion, affirmative action, and other controversial topics.

Courts, especially the Supreme Court, should matter. In our three-branch scheme, the Supreme Court is expected to shape constitutional values and, in so doing, preserve the judiciary's integrity as a coequal branch of government. Along these lines, *The Federalist* papers, in supporting the Court's authority to strike down governmental conduct, spoke of the judicial branch serving as "an intermediate body between the People and the Legislature, in order, among other things, to keep the latter within the limits assigned to their authority."[42] More significant, ongoing dialogues between the courts and elected government play a constructive role in shaping constitutional values.

School desegregation and abortion are particularly vivid examples of this phenomenon. The story of school desegregation is one in which, after the Court's monumental decision in *Brown*, Congress and the executive branch have framed the debate. First, the elected branches, by giving meaning to the *Brown* mandate through mid-1960s reforms, helped to propel increasing judicial scrutiny in *Swann*. Second, after two decades of attacking mandatory reassignments (and appointing Supreme Court justices), the Court has ceded to elected-branch desires and returned much of school desegregation to the control of state and local government. This give-and-take process reveals the ways in which the courts and elected government influence each other. Specifically, while elected government's resistance to busing has tempered Supreme Court doctrine, the federal government's willingness to combat purposeful discrimination is largely rooted in the *Brown* decision.

The saga of abortion rights likewise underscores the appropriately interactive nature of constitutional decisionmaking. Like *Brown, Roe* served as a critical trigger to the recognition of abortion rights. *Roe*, too, prompted elected government into action. As with court-ordered busing, two decades of elected government's resistance (and the appointment of Supreme Court justices) resulted in the Court's returning much of this divisive issue to the states. By reaffirming "the central holding of *Roe*" and repudiating *Roe*'s stringent trimester test in favor of a more deferential "undue burden" standard,[43] 1992's *Planned Parenthood v. Casey* signaled the Court's willingness to uphold state regulation—if not prohibition—of abortion.

Casey, however, did not trigger an antiabortion revolution. Most striking, according to Allan Guttmacher Institute studies, "antiabortion legislators [have] heeded . . . [*Casey*] and curtailed their attempts to make abortion illegal."[44] In 1994, for example, no legislation was introduced to outlaw abortion. Furthermore, in the two years following *Casey*, one-third of abortion-related legislative initiatives would have guaranteed the right to abortion. Finally, of the handful of abortion regulation measures adopted since *Casey*, all involve restrictions approved by the Court: waiting periods, informed consent, and parental notification.

Casey appears to have stabilized, if not resolved, the abortion dispute. While the Supreme Court eviscerated *Roe*'s trimester standard, the post-*Casey* calm reveals that, like *Brown, Roe* shaped elected government's attitudes. Contrary to the pre-*Roe* period (when forty-six states either prohibited or severely limited abortion access), abortion rights—for better or worse—are now a secure feature of our constitutional landscape.

Attaining an equilibrium with regard to school desegregation and abortion required all three branches and all levels of government to do battle with one another. This dynamic process yielded a very nuanced, very delicate (if not very deliberate) compromise. The story of affirmative action, in contrast, reveals the pitfalls of the Court's not staking out a position and thereby limiting its role in the shaping of constitutional values.

More than two decades ago, in *DeFunis v. Odegarrd*,[45] the Supreme Court issued its first nondecision in an affirmative action case. Rather than play a leadership role and define the parameters of governmental authority over race preferences, the Court ducked the issue altogether by ruling the *DeFunis* lawsuit moot. When the Court finally spoke, in *Regents of University of California v. Bakke*,[46] it issued a decision so fractured that no member of the Court joined Justice Lewis Powell's decisive lead opinion. This pattern persists. Supreme Court affirmative action decisions are fact-specific, plurality decisions far outnumber majority decisions, and the values that underlie the Court's rulings are, at best, difficult to decipher.

Witness *Adarand Constructors, Inc. v. Pena*, a 1995 decision in which the Court—by a 5–4 vote—refused for the first time to uphold a congressionally approved affirmative action plan.[47] *Adarand* promised to be a landmark, presenting the Court with an opportunity to resolve a long-standing controversy about whether all race preferences are inherently suspect. The Court settled, instead, on a middle-ground position. Specifically, by insisting that federal, as well as state, affirmative action programs be "narrowly tailored" to serve a "compelling governmental interest," *Adarand* embraced the heretofore rigid strict scrutiny standard of review. However, rather than apply strict scrutiny review to Adarand Constructors' challenge to the government's setting aside of highway construction funds to minority businesses, the Court sent the dispute back to the district court where it had originated. More significant, *Adarand* sought to "dispel the notion that strict scrutiny is 'strict in theory,' but fatal in fact."[48] Referring to the "unhappy persistence of both the practice and lingering effects of racial discrimination," *Adarand* emphasized that "government is not disqualified from acting in response to it."[49]

Adarand's mixed message makes it a rather slippery precedent. Moreover, because the Court remanded the case rather than resolve the dispute, *Adarand* offers little guidance about the application of strict scrutiny review. By refusing to stake out a hard-line position, the Court positioned itself to ratchet up, ratchet down, or maintain its ambiguous application of strict scrutiny review. Furthermore, because the Supreme Court did not fill in the outlines of its decision before the 1996 elections, *Adarand* effectively made the 1996 presidential election a referendum on affirmative action. Specifically, since the next Supreme Court appointee could either tighten or eviscerate the strict scrutiny standard adopted by *Adarand*'s five-member majority, *Adarand*'s future was necessarily hinged to the choice of Bill Clinton (who strongly supported preferences) or Bob Dole (who was lined up against affirmative action). As such, *Adarand* reinforces the purely political nature of affirmative action decisionmaking, thereby undermining the Court's authority and the Constitution's relevance.

Although social and political forces typically play a part in defining the reaches of Supreme Court decisionmaking, Court decisions often play a large role in shaping constitutional and other dialogues that take place among the branches. *Adarand*, in contrast, places few meaningful checks on elected government's action.

Admittedly, the Court's failure to use its bully pulpit to speak about the rightness or wrongness of preferences reflects the public's division and lack of consensus on the affirmative action issue. Nonetheless, by not staking out a position, the Court has played next to no role in shaping public discourse on affirmative action. This is unfortunate—it reduces the level of respect for the Court among the other branches and weighs down the public discourse on affirmative action with meaningless legalisms. In contrast, on issues like abortion and school desegregation, the Court has proved itself a player, shaping policy through decisions that have had a nationwide impact.

Conclusion

"The genius of [our] system lies in the very tension itself, and in our ability to combine active democracy, constitutional principles, and judicial judgment."[50] For this reason, vigorous interchange between the Court, elected government, and the public results in more vibrant and enduring constitutional interpretation. School desegregation and abortion illustrate this phenomenon. In both instances, constitutional dialogues between the Court and elected government have—given both the volatility of the issue and the difficulty of finding a middle-ground solution— resulted in a workable and durable balancing of competing interests.

When it comes to affirmative action, however, the Court has failed to speak in a way that alters the political forces. It has neither defined the terms of the affirmative action debate particularly well nor used its bully pulpit to explain what values are at stake. As a result, although it is often true that "speaking no more broadly than is absolutely required avoids throwing settled law into confusion[,] doing so [on affirmative action] preserves a chaos that is evident to anyone who can read and count."[51]

Constitutional decisionmaking is a never-ending process. It requires the participation of all branches and levels of government. It requires the Court to balance competing values and interests in crafting decisions; it requires elected officials to incorporate judicial norms into their decisionmaking. Consequently, although there may be "a magnetic attraction to the notion of an ultimate constitutional interpreter," complex social policy issues are better resolved through "the sweaty intimacy of creatures locked in combat."[52]

NOTES

1. Jeremy Rabkin, "Racial Progress and Constitutional Road Blocks," *William and Mary Law Review* 34 (Fall 1992): 75, 86. See Rabkin, chapter 6, in this volume.

2. Gary Orfield, "The Growth of Segregation in American Public Schools: Changing Patterns of Separation and Poverty since 1968: A Report of the Harvard Project in School Desegregation to the National School Board Association" (paper presented December 1993), 7.

3. Erwin Chemerinsky, "Lost Opportunity: The Burger Court and the Failure to Achieve Equal Educational Opportunity," *Mercer Law Review* 45 (Spring 1994): 999. See also Chemerinsky, chapter 12, in this volume.

4. Gerald Rosenberg, *The Hollow Hope: Can Courts Bring About Social Change?* (Chicago: University of Chicago Press, 1991), 52. See also Rosenberg, chapter 11, and Delgado and Stefancic, chapter 10, in this volume.

5. 347 U.S. 483, 495 (1956).

6. 349 U.S. 294, 301 (1955).

7. Paul Gewirtz, "Remedies and Resistance," *Yale Law Journal* 92 (March 1983): 585, 589 (emphasis added).

8. Ibid., 599.

9. 349 U.S. at 299–300.

10. Harvie Wilkinson III, "The Supreme Court and Southern School Desegregation, 1955–1970: A History and Analysis," *Virginia Law Review* 64 (May 1978): 485, 490.

11. Reed Sarratt, *The Ordeal of Desegregation* (New York: Harper & Row, 1966), 200 (quoting a southern attorney).

12. *Cooper v. Aaron*, 358 U.S. 1, 18 (1958). See Garrow, chapter 13, in this volume.

13. *Green v. County School Board of New Kent*, 391 U.S. 430, 439 (1968) (emphasis added).

14. *Milliken v. Bradley*, 418 U.S. 717, 741 (1974); see Chemerinsky, "Lost Opportunity," 99.

15. *United States v. Texas Education Agency*, 532 F.2d 380, 392 (5th Cir. 1976), *rev'd, Austin Indep. School District v. United States*, 429 U.S. 990 (1976) (mem.).

16. Gary Orfield, *The Reconstruction of Southern Education* (New York: Wiley-Interscience, 1969), 339.

17. 402 U.S. 1, 25 (1971).

18. Ibid. at 28.

19. 498 U.S. 237, 248 (1991).

20. 503 U.S. 467, 490 (1992).

21. In *Missouri v. Jenkins*, 115 S. Ct. 2038 (1995), however, the Rehnquist Court concluded that educational achievement was not an appropriate goal of a desegregation order. Pointing to the values of local control and judicial restraint enunciated in both *Dowell* and *Freeman*, the Court concluded that educational achievement was too amorphous and, as such, boundless.

22. See Christine Rossell, chapter 8, and Drew S. Days III, chapter 9, in this volume.

23. In one case, *Missouri v. Jenkins*, the Clinton administration did file an amicus brief, unsuccessfully arguing that educational achievement can and should be linked to prior unlawful racial segregation.

24. Benjamin Cardozo, *The Nature of the Judicial Process* (New Haven: Yale University Press, 1921), 168.

25. *Cong. Rec.*, 88th Cong., 2d sess., 1964, 110, pt. 5:6562 (statement of Senator Kuchel).

26. Bernard Schwartz, *Statutory History of the United States: Civil Rights* (New York: Chelsea House Publishers, 1970), 1245 (statement of Senator Kuchel), 1205–6 (statement of Senator Humphrey).

27. The cases are *Morgan v. McDonough*, 540 F.2d 527 (1st Cir. 1976), *cert. denied*, 429 U.S. 1042 (1977) (Boston); *Missouri v. Jenkins*, 495 U.S. 33 (1990) (Kansas City); *United States v. Yonkers Board of Education*, 837 F.2d 1181 (2d Cir. 1987), *cert. denied*, 486 U.S. 1055 (1988) (Yonkers); *United States v. Board of Education of City of Chicago*, 567 F. Supp. 272 (N.D. Ill.), *aff'd*, 717 F.2d 378 (7th Cir. 1983) (Chicago).

28. Equal Educational Opportunities Act, H.R. 13915, 92d Cong., 2d Sess. (1972); see also *Public Papers of the Presidents of the United States: Richard Nixon, 1972* (Washington, D.C.: Government Printing office, 1972), 425–28.

29. See Louis Fisher and Neal Devins, *Political Dynamics of Constitutional Law*, 2d ed. (St. Paul: West Publishing Co., 1996), 246–49.

30. Alexander M. Bickel, *The Supreme Court and the Idea of Progress* (New Haven: Yale University Press, 1972), 132.

31. David Kirp, *Just Schools* (Berkeley: University of California Press, 1983), 70.

32. Chemerinsky, "Lost Opportunity," 1011. See also Abrams, chapter 2, in this volume.

33. Fisher, *Constitutional Dialogues* (Princeton: Princeton University Press, 1988), 228.

34. This episode is discussed in Neal Devins, "*Metro Broadcasting v FCC*: Requiem for a Heavyweight," *Texas Law Review* 69 (November 1990): 125.

35. Kathleen M. Sullivan, "Law's Labor," *New Republic*, 23 March 1994, 42, 44.

36. See Graham, chapter 7, in this volume.

37. *Wards Cove Packing Co. v. Atonio*, 490 U.S. 642 (1989).

38. See Neal Devins, "Reagan Redux: Civil Rights under Bush," *Notre Dame Law Review*, no. 5 (1993): 955.

39. The Religious Freedom Restoration Act, Pub. L. No. 103–141 (1993).

40. Rabkin, "Racial Progress and Constitutional Road Blocks."

41. *Ibid.*

42. Alexander Hamilton, *The Federalist, No. 78*, ed. H. B. Dawson (New York: Charles Scribner's Sons, 1983), 54.

43. 505 U.S. 833, 878 (1992).

44. Alan Guttmacher Institute, *State Reproductive Health Monitor* 5, no. 2 (May 1994): ii.

45. 416 U.S. 312 (1974).

46. 438 U.S. 265 (1978).

47. 115 S. Ct. 2097 (1995).

48. Ibid. at 2117.

49. Ibid.

50. John Agresto, *The Supreme Court and Constitutional Democracy* (Ithaca, N.Y.: Cornell University Press, 1984), 167.

51. *Webster v. Reproductive Health Services*, 492 U.S. 490, 535 (1989) (Scalia, J., concurring).

52. Walter F. Murphy, "Who Shall Interpret?" *Review of Politics* 48 (Summer 1981): 401, 417; Bickel, *The Supreme Court and the Idea of Progress*, 99.

Index

233